Why You Need This New Edition

Johnson/Rhodes, *Human Behavior and the Larger Social Environment: A New Synthesis,* Second Edition

This text enhances students' understanding of human behavior by examining how individuals and families are affected by, and affect, larger social systems. The authors endorse the idea that one must go beyond the individual and family levels to understand human problems within relevant national and global contexts. The text addresses 2008 CSWE standards by introducing conceptual frameworks (perspectives and theories) that are useful in understanding social institutions, social structure, and social settings. It also explores how these social systems promote or deter the health and well-being of individuals and families.

Content new to the second edition reflects current issues and concerns that have an impact on social workers and service consumers.

1. Given the number of active-duty military and returning veterans, and repeated deployments of National Guard troops, the authors have added a **section on the military as a social institution**. This new content addresses the relationship between the economy and the military, as well as examining the role of women, minorities, and gays in the military.

2. The current **recession and its implications** for individual and family well-being are discussed within the context of the American consumer economy.

3. Given the historic nature of the 2008 presidential election, the authors discuss **increasing political divisiveness** and **changing patterns in voting**.

4. The authors have expanded the section on mass media to include all **communication technology**, including its impact on news consumption and the electoral process.

5. Data from U.S. government agencies and national research centers, and information from international sources, was used to **update all topics** with material that was current as of spring 2009. Examples include poverty rates, occupational patterns, incarceration rates, and health-related statistics.

PEARSON

Second Edition

HUMAN BEHAVIOR
AND THE LARGER
SOCIAL ENVIRONMENT
A NEW SYNTHESIS

Miriam McNown Johnson
University of South Carolina

Rita Rhodes
University of South Carolina

Allyn & Bacon

Boston   Columbus   Indianapolis   New York   San Francisco   Upper Saddle River
Amsterdam   Cape Town   Dubai   London   Madrid   Milan   Munich
Paris   Montreal   Toronto   Delhi   Mexico City   Sao Paulo   Sydney
Hong Kong   Seoul   Singapore   Taipei   Tokyo

This book is dedicated to the women who have shaped our lives:
Helen McNown, Mildred Morrison, Marcia Rayho
Mary Ellen Rhodes, Eileen Garvey, Anna Mae Garvey

Executive Editor: Ashley Dodge
Editorial Assistant: Carly Czech
Senior Marketing Manager: Wendy Albert
Marketing Assistant: Kyle VanNatter
Production Editor: Claudine Bellanton
Manufacturing Buyer: Renata Butera
Production Manager: Renata Butera
Cover Photo Credit: Photononstop/Superstock
Creative Art Director: Jayne Conte

Cover Designer: Bruce Kenselaar
Image Interior Permission
  Coordinator: Kathy Gavilanes
Image Cover Permission Coordinator:
  Karen Sanatar
Editorial Production and Composition
  Service: Integra Software Services
Photo Research: Carly Czech
Printer/Binder: Courier, Stoughton

Library of Congress Cataloging-in-Publication Data

Johnson, Miriam McNown, 1946–
    Human behavior and the larger social environment : a new synthesis / Miriam McNown Johnson, Rita Rhodes.—2nd ed.
       p. cm.
    Includes bibliographical references and index.
    ISBN-13: 978-0-205-76366-5 (alk. paper)
    ISBN-10: 0-205-76366-9 (alk. paper)
    1. Social ecology. 2. Social psychology. 3. Social institutions—United States. 4. Social structure—United States. 5. Social service—United States. 6. United States—Social conditions—21st century. I. Rhodes, Rita M.   II. Title.
    HM861.J64 2010
    302—dc22

                                                                        2009042121

10 9 8 7 6 5 4 3 2 1   13 12 11 10 09

Allyn & Bacon
is an imprint of

ISBN-10:   0-205-76366-9
ISBN-13: 978-0-205-76366-5

www.pearsonhighered.com

CONTENTS

PREFACE

The purpose of this text is to help students understand the broader social context within which human behavior occurs. It is the authors' opinion that an appreciation of how large systems deter or promote the health and well-being and development of individuals and families is an essential foundation for social work practice.

In writing this text, one of our goals was to make the material useful to beginning social work students without overwhelming them. We made decisions based on our belief that it is not important for students to learn and memorize specific definitions or lists so much as it is imperative that they be able to reflect critically on new ideas and apply abstract concepts to different situations. With this in mind, we have applied the following strategies. First, we have used a limited number of perspectives and theories that students can learn thoroughly and well. Second, although we have explored many sources, we usually offer a single, simple definition of a term. Our definitions may not agree entirely with what other authors have written, but they work well for material presented in this book. Third, we have reduced some concepts, perspectives, or theories to their most essential elements in an effort to make them more understandable. In doing so, we have sacrificed some complexity that might be appropriately incorporated at more advanced levels of study. Finally, we have arranged concepts in ways that are arguably arbitrary; some social work authors and sociologists have organized them differently. We found this arrangement works best for us and for the students who use this text in their HBSE classes.

This book was written with consideration given to the Educational Policy and Accreditation Standards of the Council on Social Work Education (2008). After studying this book, students should be able to:

- List the assumptions of various perspectives and theories and critically apply them to different situations as they prepare to assess and intervene on behalf of client systems.
- Describe the forms and mechanisms of oppression and discrimination.
- Recognize how a society's social institutions and settings may promote or deter people in maintaining or achieving health and well-being.
- Discuss the importance of difference in shaping human experience.
- Critique and apply knowledge to understand person and environment, with an emphasis on the range of social system in which people live.

Organization of the text

The text is composed of four parts and 10 chapters. The authors recommend that it be used in the first semester of a two-semester foundation HBSE curriculum, with the second semester devoted to understanding family and individual development from a variety of alternative as well as traditional perspectives. It could also follow a course on human development.

Part I is an introduction to the basic theoretical perspectives that social scientists use. In addition, we include preferred social work perspectives. Chapter 1 explains the major perspectives that systematically reappear in the chapters that follow.

Part II presents eight social institutions, beginning in Chapter 2 with politics and the economy. Chapter 3 addresses those social institutions that are, for the most part, government-related: education, criminal justice, and the military. Chapter 4 covers three social institutions that are not government-supported: health care, religion, and the mass media and communications technology.

Part III discusses social structure in American society. Chapter 5 examines social stratification, giving particular attention to the issue of social class in American society. Chapter 6 considers the role of cultural diversity in influencing individuals and families, while Chapter 7 presents information on gender, sexual orientation, and disability.

Acknowledging that human behavior is dependent on context, Part IV gives attention to the social settings that individuals and families inhabit. Chapter 8 covers locational communities. Chapter 9 discusses organizations. Chapter 10 presents residential institutions, which are a likely major source of employment for social workers in the twenty-first century.

In summary, this text represents our effort to reinforce the unique social work outlook that human behavior is shaped by systems beyond the intra-psychic and familial domains. It is essential that students recognize the power of large systems to harm the most vulnerable among us. We believe that such an understanding will well-serve the next generation of social workers.

As we were writing the first edition of this book, the horrors of September 11 were still echoing across the country. As we complete the final editing of this second edition, the country is reeling from an economic crisis and facing uncertainty about the directions that a new administration will take us. We are reminded that the societal context of human behavior is always changing and that social workers need to stay abreast of emerging issues and trends.

Acknowledgments

We would like to express our deep appreciation to the following people: Graduate Assistants Fiona McDevitt, Kimberly Marshall, Anne Wiggins, and especially Carrie Draper for their diligence and resourcefulness; the staff at Thomas Cooper Library for their endless patience; Pat Quinlin, former Editor at Allyn and Bacon, Ashley Dodge, Executive Editor and Carly Czech, Editorial Assistant, for accommodating our schedules and idiosyncrasies. We would also like to express our appreciation to our many colleagues around the country who have provided feedback and encouragement.

Miriam would like to thank Steve Johnson, Matthew Johnson, Elizabeth Johnson Boecher, and Roger Boecher for their understanding and support, and to Lucy and Sophie Boecher for providing a window to the future for their "Nana." Rita would like to thank David Mathisen and Katherine Mathisen-Glisson and Scotty Glisson for continually instructing her about human behavior. She also offers a special thanks to Mary Diane Miller for her support and accommodations to her writing schedule. And to her animal companions, Mingus, Reeces, and Oreo, thanks for reminding her of what's important in life.

Part I

BUILDING ON AN INTEGRATED FOUNDATION

Chapter 1

Introduction to Perspectives and Theories

Where We Begin

Abigail Garvey was seeing her last client for the day. Abby guessed that Jennifer Floyd, like many of her recent clients, would be asking for information about the resources that were available for newly unemployed workers in Oak Grove. Abby was already aware of how precarious Jennifer's economic situation was, having made a referral for her to Consumer Credit Counseling for help in managing her family's credit cards a few months previously.

    Jennifer had been a longtime client of Abby's. Jennifer had met with Abby seven years ago, when she graduated from high school, for career planning. Jennifer was undecided on whether to enroll in classes at the local tech college or take a job at the local car parts manufacturing plant. Jennifer decided to take the plant job because, as she pointed out, she could begin earning money immediately and marry her high school sweetheart, Zachary Floyd. Jennifer was drawn to Zach as someone who had a strong work ethic and the potential to be a loving, involved father. In addition, she was impressed by his strong commitment to his community and country, as demonstrated by his joining the National Guard when he graduated from high school. Zach was already employed at the local plant and had a promising future there.

    Jennifer was determined to join Zach and her older siblings in the community's typical employment pattern—going straight from high school to working in the local plant. Abby remembered thinking at the time that she wished that Jennifer, who was bright and seemed ambitious, had the ability to consider a wider range of options. Six months later, Jennifer was married. A year later, she had her first child and ten months after that, twins. The wages at the plant were not bad, and with Jennifer and Zach working different shifts, obtaining child care was not a problem.

    Now the plant was closing. It was the fourth factory to shut down in the county in the course of five years. The plant was moving to Mexico, where local workers would receive $8 per day to do what Jennifer and Zach had done for $11 an hour. And suddenly Zach was facing possible deployment to the Middle East. Jennifer felt overwhelmed—she and Zach had finally made some progress in paying down their *credit card bills, but now the children all had ear infections that required doctor visits and prescription medication, and their older model car was becoming increasingly unreliable. Because her family and friends were also facing hard times, Jennifer didn't feel that she could count on them for support.*

Abby was not much older than Jennifer. She had foregone four years of salary and had postponed marriage and having children in order to obtain her BSW degree. Despite her training, the words "I told you so" came to mind when she considered Jennifer's predicament. Abby had always thought that the most difficult part of counseling was watching her clients make poor choices. On the other hand, how could anyone have predicted that the U.S. economy would falter so badly and the plant would close? Blaming Jennifer, or telling her what she should have done seven years ago, obviously wouldn't help now.

Like Abby, some social workers may believe that some clients' problems originate in their own poor choices. But social workers are trained to use more than common sense, instincts, and good intentions in analyzing situations. They are taught to understand that human society and all of its parts interact in complex ways that are not easily reduced to simple, linear, cause-and-effect explanations. Jennifer's decision to terminate her formal education at age 18 is not necessarily the cause for her family's impending economic crisis. Abby needs to consider that Jennifer is an employee of an organization, a member of a community, and a participant in an economic system that also shaped her financial decisions.

There are discernable patterns in human behavior and in the social systems that humans create. Jennifer's problems are not unique to her, her employer, or even to her community. Social work courses taught Abby that while she must respect Jennifer's individual choices, there are also other descriptions and explanations of circumstances that will help Abby select an appropriate intervention.

In addition, there are multiple ways of understanding the same events. In counseling sessions, Jennifer will present her view of what is happening and why. Her immediate supervisor, and the executives at company headquarters, might see things quite differently, not to mention the company's stockholders, the town council, her fellow employees, and other stakeholders. Abby will review her own perspectives.

Abby will conclude that all of these points of view have elements of truth, but that one or two of them are more useful in understanding Jennifer's situation, in selecting a practice model, and then in formulating a course of action.

Shifting Perspectives in Social Work

A *perspective* is a particular point of view that reflects "taken-for-granted" assumptions or a system of beliefs. Perspectives provide a broad conceptual and value framework within which theory development or selection takes place (Chess & Norlin, 1991). Most people would agree that a perspective is not intended as a guide for practice. Perspectives have strong explanatory power and are thus useful for assessments, but do not prescribe specific forms of intervention. Instead they allow the thoughtful selection of one or more practice theories.

As a profession, social work has borrowed extensively from other disciplines, including the social sciences (e.g., sociology, psychology), the life sciences (e.g., biology, genetics), and the humanities (e.g., religion, philosophy, history). There is no perspective or body of theories that is totally unique to social work, although some perspectives and theories are used more often than others.

Historically, social workers and social work educators have shifted from one perspective to another. During the 1960s and 1970s, the social work profession moved from an emphasis on intrapsychic phenomena to an orientation that also paid attention to social environments and larger social systems (Leighninger, 1978). The systems perspective served as a theoretical bridge to address person *in* environment as a unitary focus rather than the false dichotomy of person *and* environment that had characterized earlier stages (Hearn, 1979).

The systems theory perspective also views behavior patterns as interactional and reciprocal rather than linear. In other words, rather than an explanation that says, in effect, a particular action on the part of A results in a predicable response from B, systems theorists would say that B is influenced by A, but A is at the same time also influenced by B. A and B could be individuals, families, or groups, or an individual in a family, or a group in an organization, and so forth. The limitations of a linear model seemed to be corrected by an emphasis on thinking systemically.

By the 1980s, the social system approach which emphasized system stability was beginning to be challenged. Although social workers continued to pay attention to person-in-environment concepts, some believed that a clearer understanding of how and why systems change was needed. The ecosystems perspective, which has strong roots in systems theory, replaced the systems perspective with greater attention to process and what happens across encounters, reflecting the reciprocal relationships between organisms and their environments. Both perspectives are described in greater detail next.

Perspectives Used in This Text

Because this text is concerned primarily with the broader contexts of human behavior, it draws heavily on sociological perspectives. In their analyses of macro (large) systems, sociologists predominantly rely on two perspectives: the functionalist perspective and the conflict perspective. Two other perspectives, the social constructionist perspective and the rational/social exchange perspective, are often used in the analysis of smaller systems and individual interactions. We (the authors) believe, however, that the social constructionist perspective and the rational/social exchange perspective offer useful insights in examining some social institutions and social settings. We include the ecosystems perspective because it is especially relevant for social work practice in that it views human behavior as part of reciprocal relationships with and within a context of many levels of systems that are interconnected. Finally, we include both a diversity perspective and a strengths perspective because they are central to the profession's value system.

Two of the perspectives used in this text, the ecosystems perspective and the functionalist perspective, are partially derived from and closely related to the systems perspective. *Systems* are defined as organized wholes comprising component parts that interact in a distinct way and endure over time (Anderson, Carter, & Lowe, 1999, p. 294). The *systems perspective*, also often called *general systems theory* (see von Bertalanffy, 1968), is an interdisciplinary construct developed to identify common principles of organization that can be applied to all phenomena. In other words, this perspective assumes there is a similar underlying order to everything in the universe. Other basic assumptions of the systems perspective include the following:

- Each system has a structure; the parts have a relationship to each other.
- The whole is more than the sum of its parts.
- Everything is connected; a change in any one part affects the system as a whole.

- All systems are, at the same time, made up of smaller (sub)systems and are parts of larger systems.
- Each system has a boundary that separates it from other systems and helps to give it its identity.
- As systems evolve, they become more complex (i.e., the parts become differentiated and more specialized).

While physical scientists use a systems theory perspective to analyze everything from atoms to galaxies, social scientists use it to analyze social systems and their interactions. A *social system* is a social unit, such as a family, group, organization, or community, comprised of elements that are functionally related and interdependent. The parts of social systems do not need to be in close physical proximity to each other. They may have psychological rather than physical boundaries because they exist in social reality rather than in physical reality. The structure of a social system is determined by social roles and shared expectations; often members share common goals.

The assumptions of the systems and social systems perspectives can be illustrated with a school of social work. The school is more than a collection of individuals and spaces, more than faculty, staff, and students, offices and classrooms. It is part of a larger system, a department, college, or university. It contains subsystems, such as student associations and faculty committees. Professors relate to students as instructors, advisors, and mentors; they relate to the administration as employees. In a large school, some staff may have specialized functions (e.g., accounting, clerical support, or supervision of other staff). The obvious boundaries of the school not only include building and classroom walls, but also might include psychosocial boundaries such as ID cards, registration rolls, professional jargon, or a value system that is unique to the profession. It is easy to see how everything is connected and how one part affects the others. For example, if a professor in a foundation course fails to properly prepare students, instructors in subsequent courses will have to change their lessons to accommodate the students' deficiencies.

The Ecosystems Perspective

One of the common criticisms of the systems perspective stems from the abstract way it conceptualizes phenomena. Because systems concepts literally apply to all phenomena, they do not tell us much about any particular element or interaction. "Ecology, the biological science that studies organism-environment relations, offered concepts of these relations that were less abstract than those offered by systems theories and closer to common human experience" (Germain & Gitterman, 1995, p. 816). The *ecosystems perspective* (also called the *ecological perspective*) was introduced to social work by Carel Germain in 1973. It conceptualized the environment as "more than a static setting" for people's lives (Germain & Gitterman, 1995, p. 816). Concepts from ecology were used to supplement the systems perspective. This was consistent with the person-in-environment worldview of

FIGURE 1.1   *Critical Thinking About Social Systems*

See if you can apply systems concepts to your family as a social system. What are the parts and how are they interrelated? What larger systems are they a part of? What are the physical and psychosocial boundaries that set them apart from their larger environment? How has your enrollment in school affected other family members? In what ways has your family become more complex since you were born?

social workers (which Germain and Gitterman write as *person:environment* to signify how closely the two are intertwined).

> The ecological perspective makes clear the need to view people and environments as a unitary system within a particular cultural and historic context. Both person and environment can be fully understood only in terms of their relationship, in which each continually influences the other within a particular context. Hence, all concepts derived from the ecological metaphor refer not to environment alone, or person alone; rather, each concept expresses a particular person:environment relationship, whether it is positive, negative, or neutral. (Germain & Gitterman, 1995, p. 816)

Another construct of the ecosystems perspective is *adaptation*, or the various processes people use to achieve a better level of fit between themselves and the settings in which they find themselves. Social systems, as well as individuals, are involved in a process of continuous adaptation within and with their larger environments. In our school of social work example, adaptation would occur if the university lost funding for work-study positions and school developed paid internships in various social service agencies to fill the gap for financially needy students.

Goodness-of-fit is the extent to which there is a match between an individual's or a group's needs, rights, goals, and capacities and the qualities of their physical and social environments (Germain & Gitterman, 1995, p. 817; Greene, 1999). In our prior example, goodness-of-fit would be achieved if the school recognized that its student body was comprised primarily of full-time workers and changed its course schedule to offer mostly evening and weekend classes.

Other important ecosystems constructs include niche and habitat. Germain and Gitterman (1995, p. 818) define *niche* as the "status occupied by an individual or family in the social structure . . . [often related to] color, ethnicity, gender, age, poverty, sexual orientation, or physical or mental states." *Habitat* is defined as places or settings where individuals can be found. Whereas it is impossible to analyze the natural social and physical environments of humans as distinctly separate from each other, in this text we find it useful to concentrate on niches in Part III and discuss places where people live and work—locational communities, organizations, and residential institutions—in Part IV.

The Functionalist Perspective

The *functionalist perspective* (often called *structural functionalism*) also is closely related to the systems perspective. It is used by sociologists, who are less interested in individual adjustment or smaller social systems than in how society works. They use functionalism to understand larger social systems and the functioning of society as a whole. According to this perspective, "a society is composed of interrelated parts, each of which serves a function and (ideally) contributes to the overall stability of the society" (Kendall, 2008, p. 23). Drawing upon systems perspective and social systems theory, one assumption is that large societal systems reflect a general orderliness and that they maintain a balance or stable state. If one part changes, all the other parts are affected and the system may no longer function smoothly. A recent example is the financial crisis that began in 2008, when a history of risky investments led to the financial collapse of some important Wall Street firms and the need for government bailouts to keep others operating, so that the entire U.S. economy did not collapse.

Systems, ecosystems, and functionalist perspectives assume that systems are constantly changing, but that these change processes are incremental (slow and in small steps) and are self-correcting when the system gets out of balance. Functionalists believe that all social phenomena serve the purpose of maintaining the social system. Functionalists see a useful function in everything in society, including elements, characteristics, or processes that most people would view as negative, such as poverty or racial inequality (Davis & Moore, 1945). Because maintaining the *status quo* supports the interests of those who already hold power and wealth, functionalism is often criticized by those who believe the existing system is unfair.

Theorists who espouse a systems-related perspective (ecosystems or structural functionalism) approve small, incremental, and self-righting changes. There is little expectation that the environment will be markedly changed. This point of view differs substantially from the position of conflict theorists (discussed next) who routinely call for fundamental structural change.

The Conflict Perspective

The *conflict perspective* is another perspective commonly used by sociologists. It is most often linked with Karl Marx, who wrote about inter-class struggle. Unlike the functionalist perspective, conflict theorists argue that social systems are not united or harmonious, but are divided by class, gender, race, or other characteristics that reflect differences in social power as much as anything else. According to this perspective, "groups in society are engaged in a continuous power struggle for scarce resources" (Kendall, 2008, p. 25). In the conflict perspective, problems are defined as social and structural rather than individual, meaning that they can be solved only by social change, not by individual adaptation. Conflict theorists would agree that "it's not the fact that there are rich and poor that generates egalitarian struggle, but the fact that the rich grind the faces of the poor. It's always what one group with power does to another group—whether in the name of health, safety, or security—it makes no difference. The aim, ultimately, of the fight for equality, is always the elimination of subordination . . . no more toadying, scraping and bowing, fearful trembling" (Walzer, 1983, p. 13).

Early social workers recognized structural inequality and oppression, but as a profession they have not until recently drawn upon the conflict perspective as a way to conceptualize human behavior in the social environment. The development of empowerment theories (Lee, 2001; Solomon, 1976, 1987), which have their roots in the conflict perspective, has led to a renewed interest in utilizing this perspective as a way to explain social injustice and privilege. *Empowerment* is a proactive response to assist people who experience systematic forms of harassment and oppression through consciousness-raising and enhancing self-efficacy.

Critics of the conflict perspective note that, particularly without adoption of an empowerment approach, social workers using this perspective may overemphasize polarization and antagonism, viewing clients simply as victims and their opponents as oppressors (Robbins, Chatterjee, & Canda, 1998, p. 85). On the other hand, in contrast to other helping professions, social work has a specific commitment to empowerment at both the personal and group levels.

The Rational/Social Exchange Perspective

The *rational/social exchange perspective* is based on the assumptions that human beings have the capacity to reason, make choices based on consideration of available alternatives and anticipated consequences, and act in their own best interest. Human behavior is believed to be purposeful and goal directed. At the individual level, rational decision-making theories (e.g., rational choice theory, social exchange theory, fair-exchange theory, reciprocity) suggest that people make decisions based on a cost-benefit analysis.

The rational/social exchange perspective has also been applied to larger social systems (groups, organizations, communities, societies) based on the "doctrine of *utilitarianism*—a belief that the purpose of all action should be to bring about the greatest happiness to the greatest number of people" (Kendall, 2008, p. 188). Nevertheless, beyond the individual level, rational decision making by a collective body encounters many barriers, including lack of agreement on political, social, economic, and cultural values and goals; inability to compare competing costs and benefits; and the fragmented nature of policy making in large bureaucracies (Dye, 1998, pp. 25–27). Often benefits can be identified only for specific groups, and many of those are conflicting. Another barrier is that individual actors may look out for their own interests rather than that of the collective body or constituency. The reality is that, at the level of larger systems and social institutions (organizations, communities, government), policies that generate the maximum social gain—the most benefits for the most people—are difficult to develop. In fact, Dye argues that rational decision making "rarely takes place at all in government" (1998, p. 25).

The Social Constructionist Perspective

The *social constructionist perspective* emphasizes the role of the human mind and the shared subjective understanding of localized experiences in defining the social world. ("Localized experience" refers to the notion that all people live in a specific cultural and historical setting that shapes their perceptions.) The constructionist perspective is based on the assumption that there is no objective reality; rather reality is defined by perceptions and is, in fact, a social construction (see Schutz, 1967). From a constructionist perspective, sociological phenomena, such as society and social institutions, considered by most people to be elements of objective reality, are no more than creations of human thought processes. Although constructionists do not deny the reality of such social phenomena, they suggest that it is important to study the subjective interpretations of such phenomena made by individuals and groups. In sum, this perspective suggests that reality is socially constructed through social interaction and people act in accordance with their constructed reality. An important concept in this perspective is that of *standpoints*.

> *Standpoints* are truths or knowledge created through awareness of reality gleaned from particular social locations. The concept of standpoint assumes that all people see the world from the place where they are situated socioculturally. What is considered to be real depends on one's standpoint and is grounded in experiences related to one's position within the sociocultural topography. (Van Den Bergh, 1995, p. xxvii)

The social constructionist perspective is useful in reminding social work practitioners that members of minority groups or other marginalized people may experience a social reality that is quite different from the one experienced by members of the Euro-American middle class.

One criticism of social constructionism is that, if everything is subjective and therefore relative, there is no basis for judging situations or determining preferred outcomes (Robbins, Chatterjee, & Canda, 1998, p. 317). Critics of the social constructionist perspective also worry that if social problems are understood as merely the perceptions and claims of particular groups, then there is no basis for taking action (Best, 1989).

The Diversity Perspective

In the past, the idea that America was a "melting pot" held prominence. Today, most social workers do not accept this as a productive point of view, but rather embrace the notion that celebrating different cultures, as well as other kinds of diversity, is healthy for individuals, families, groups, organizations, and communities. Acknowledging and valuing human diversity is central to the profession's value base and essential for culturally competent practice. "Social workers understand how diversity characterizes and shapes the human experience and is critical to the formation of identity" (Council on Social Work Education, 2008, p. 4). Still, it is important to distinguish between strengths-affirming segmentation of identities and divisions that rest on inequality and serve not to validate differences but to facilitate discrimination (Cohen, 2003, p. 408). Social workers must celebrate diversity while also negotiating resolutions to conflicts in a way that promotes social justice and economic fairness for everyone.

FIGURE 1.2 *Applying the Perspectives*

Imagine you have seven friends who have quite different ideas about the community you live in. Read the description of each friend and decide which perspective guides his or her view of the community.

1. Anthony points to the construction of a new shopping mall that the community attracted through the offer of tax breaks for the developer. He notes that although some citizens objected to the project initially, they were persuaded to support it based on a careful evaluation of the potential long-term benefits compared to the short-term costs. Anthony takes pleasure in the observation that the community can usually reach consensus because citizens are willing to take a logical approach to problems.

2. Although some critics of the community point out the absence of cultural events, Yvonne is quick to respond that there is a thriving amateur theater group and community art programs. The community has recently used tax dollars to buy and renovate an old downtown movie theater to host films that are not available to the general commercial market.

3. Michelle takes pride in the community's response to the special needs of both children and older adults. She notes that in developing new neighborhoods, community leaders and members pay attention to the need for adequate greenspace, sidewalks, and access to public transportation. The community also takes care to screen noise and limit air pollution.

4. James is a big hometown fan. He enjoys the community traditions, such as the annual Fourth of July parade and the community-sponsored Halloween activities for the children. He minimizes any problems the community might have, noting that the city council, the Chamber of Commerce, the schools, and religious bodies all contribute to the smooth operation of the community as a whole.

5. Marquita experiences the community in a totally different way. It makes her upset to see how children in some neighborhoods attend new schools with computers in every classroom, while those in other neighborhoods have rundown buildings and outdated texts. She notes that some neighborhoods have lots of greenspace and recreation facilities, while others are strewn with litter and children play in the streets. Marquita believes that the upper-class people who are the leaders in the community government make decisions that ignore the needs of those with limited resources and power.

6. Kim is not surprised to learn that her friends have such different points of view. She is intrigued by how people can view the same community and develop such different evaluations but is comfortable with the idea that even after extensive conversation her friends may leave with different ideas, all of which have validity.

7. Tom is excited by all of the opportunities in the community to interact with people from different backgrounds, not just in special ethnic celebrations, but in daily encounters. He believes that one of the great assets of the community is the variety of cultures and lifestyles that are found there.

The Strengths Perspective

Another point of view that reflects social work values is the *strengths perspective* (Saleebey, 2002). "While recognizing the fallibilities of people, the strengths perspective brings some balance to the understanding of the human condition" (Saleebey, 2002, p. 265). The strengths perspective views all individuals and groups, regardless of their histories, as having value and capabilities, with resources, skills, motivations, and dreams that must be considered when working with them such that they gain more control over their lives. This perspective offers a basis from which helpers become agents of the client system, which is regarded as having special expertise. Critics of the strengths perspective say that it ignores problems or simply reframes them in a more positive light.

How Theory Informs Practice

A *theory* is narrower than a perspective. It is a proposition that explains or predicts something. In other words, it is an educated guess, based on both previous knowledge and observations. Most scientists treat theories as hypotheses to be tested, not as statements of absolute truth. In other words, a theory is *provisional*; that is, it is used until it is contradicted by objective data supported by a better explanation. A theory may *describe* (how things happen as they do) or *explain* (why they happen as they do). *Prediction* is based on recognizing a recurring pattern so that future events can be anticipated. Prediction may occur without a full understanding or explanation of cause and effect. Usually predictive power alone is not sufficient to develop effective interventions.

Explanatory theories provide a basis for the development or adoption of models of intervention. *Models* provide guidance on how to intervene in a range of situations. They focus on what to do by describing patterns of activities and highlighting certain principles that give professional practice consistency (Payne, 1997, p. 35).

In this text, we concentrate on several perspectives and a limited number of related theories that help to describe and explain human behavior. A good understanding of these provides the foundation for selecting appropriate models for intervention. Social work students will spend more time exploring theories of change and models of practice in other courses.

In general, we would like to think that models flow neatly from theories and that theories are grounded in coherent perspectives. The reality, however, is that the relationship between these three elements is messy. For example, sometimes an innovative practice intervention precedes the development of a theory that explains why it works, and there are some theories that offer no applications that can be translated directly into interventions. Payne (1997) suggests that when all three elements—perspective, theory, and model—are fully developed and in place, the effective practice of social work is more likely to occur.

Part II

INTRODUCTION TO SOCIAL INSTITUTIONS

Social institutions are among the more abstract notions we present in this book. *Social institutions* are defined as patterns of human interaction that meet the basic social needs of a society. These needs include reproduction, and socialization of the young; establishing a hierarchy of power; producing and distributing goods and services; dealing with questions about meaning, such as the purpose of life, the reason for suffering, and what happens after death; transmitting knowledge and skills across generations; treating the sick and injured; providing for dependent members of society; maintaining social order and defending national interests; and disseminating information. Sociologists recognize several basic social institutions that exist in all societies in addition to the family; among these are government/polity, economy, religion, education, and health care. Some recognize or acknowledge additional social institutions. In this book, we will discuss three additional social institutions: criminal justice, the military, and the mass media. These eight social institutions have been selected because they are particularly relevant to social work students. Although social welfare is a social institution that is clearly relevant to social workers and their clients, we are not including it in this book because social work students take complete courses on this topic.

Even though the idea of a social institution might be difficult to grasp, everyone has had experience with the cumulative effects of each of the social institutions discussed in this section. They have as much influence on social work clients as any smaller social system because they provide the context within which families, organizations, and communities operate. The collectivity of social institutions is what constitutes a society.

We restrict ourselves to three or four major perspectives in our discussion of social institutions. These four perspectives are those used by most social scientists/sociologists to explain social institutions: the *functionalist perspective*, the *conflict perspective*, the *rational/social exchange perspective*, and the *constructionist perspective*. These perspectives were defined and described in Chapter 1.

It makes sense that a rational perspective would apply (at least in principle) to the economy and to government-supported social institutions. The reader should not be surprised, however, to learn that the rational perspective is not easily applied to the health care system, mass media, or religion. Although specific organizations within these systems have centralized administrative and decision-making bodies, and there may be alliances and coalitions that act in concert to meet social needs or to promote particular agendas, there are no central coordinating or planning bodies that are charged with (or have the authority for) setting priorities or making policies regarding those systems as a whole.

We believe that social institutions have the capacity to oppress. They also have the capacity to promote well-being, although for many social work clients, that is not what they experience. Thus, we will explore the effects of each social institution as a context for individuals and families, looking in particular at how they deter or promote well-being.

In Part II, we begin with what we believe are the most significant social institutions, that is, economics and politics, in Chapter 2. In Chapter 3, government-related social institutions—education, criminal justice, and the military—are examined. In Chapter 4, non-government-related social institutions—health care, religion, and mass media and communication technology—are addressed. These last six social institutions are examined each in its own right and also in relation to the political economy.

The Political Economy

W e have devoted an entire chapter to the two most important social institutions in America, that is, the economic system and the political system. We will introduce the two separately, but at the end of the chapter, we will discuss how closely they interact. This interaction is so complete that we will label it the *political economy* and thereafter treat it as a single institution.

The Economic System

The *economic system* organizes and regulates a society's production, distribution, and consumption of goods and services. The American economic system is based on *capitalism*. In an American context, capitalism is usually understood as being synonymous with the business world. The three basic characteristics of capitalism typically cited by economists are private ownership, unfettered market competition, and pursuit of profit. These present a clear contrast to the characteristics of *socialism*, which are public ownership, central planning, and collective goals. These pure ideological models seldom exist in reality; instead, many countries have mixed economic models. Even the United States does not have a "pure" form of capitalism, as the government is actively involved in several aspects of economic control.

Issues and Trends in the Economic System

Corporate Capitalism

A *corporation* is "an organization with a legal existence including rights and liabilities, separate from that of its members" (Macionis, 2007, p. 433). As one outspoken Native American environmentalist notes,

> Corporations exist beyond time and space . . . . They do not die a natural death; they outlive their own creators. And they have no commitment to locale, employees, or neighbors. This makes the modern corporation entirely different from the baker or grocer of previous years . . . . Having no morality, no commitment to place, and no physical nature . . . a corporation can relocate all of its operations to another place at the first sign of inconvenience: demanding employees, too high taxes, restrictive environmental laws. The traditional ideal of community engagement is antithetical to corporate behavior. (Mander, 1991, pp. 133–134)

The "profit imperative" and the "growth imperative" are fundamental corporate drives.

Originally chartered by the monarchy and created as extensions of the government, to "promote the general welfare," over time corporations "changed from temporary creations beholden to the state to permanent businesses with a vested interest in serving private capital" (Palmer, 2003). In 1886, the Supreme Court ruled that corporations have many rights similar to individuals, and corporations have since assumed that they can exercise rights to free speech, privacy, equal protection, and against self-incrimination (Hartman, 2002). While small businesses and individual entrepreneurs are often glorified by politicians, the reality is that contemporary American capitalism is about large corporations; *corporate capitalism* dominates the economic system. There are millions of corporations, but only a small number—fewer than a couple of hundred companies—control the vast majority of economic activity (Peterson, 1991).

Sociologists often differentiate between *work establishments*, the actual place where someone works, and *firms*, the parent company or organization (Stockard, 2000). An example of a work establishment would be a local Kentucky Fried Chicken restaurant. An example of a firm would be its "parent company," Pepsico. A majority of workers, especially those in the service sector, go to work in establishments with fewer than 100 employees. A third of all workers, however, are employed by very large firms. Corporations such as automobile manufacturers (e.g., General Motors) and gigantic retailers may employ hundreds of thousands of workers. Walmart is the largest private employer in the world, with 7,800 Walmart and Sam's Clubs stores and revenues larger than the gross domestic product (GDP) of many countries (Saporito, 2007).

Conglomerates are giant corporations that result from mergers and takeovers of smaller corporations. Beginning in the later 1960s, conglomerates began to appear as a result of the mergers of firms with diverse products and services. For example, the enormous profits of the petroleum industry in the 1970s allowed Gulf Oil to buy the Ringling Brothers and Barnum & Bailey Circus (Hodson & Sullivan, 1990).

Noticing that the government had shown little interest in restricting mergers and monopolies, during the 1980s, corporations changed strategies, divested themselves of unrelated firms, and began to acquire firms in the same or similar industries. By the late 1990s, this trend involved mergers of more than 5,000 firms a year and transactions of more than $1 trillion, over five times the level of a decade earlier (Stockard, 2000, p. 378). Many of the acquisitions involved "hostile takeovers," that is, the purchase of a company against the wishes of its owners.

At the beginning of the twenty-first century, these patterns continued. In the financial arena, for example, many investment banking operations were absorbed into large commercial banking companies. For example, Bear Sterns became a part of JP Morgan Chase in 2008, A.G. Edwards became a part of Wachovia in 2007, and later Wachovia became a part of Wells Fargo. None of this could have happened under the Glass-Steagall Act of 1933, which created the Federal Deposit Insurance Corporation (FDIC) and much of the banking regulation that we rely on today. The Leach-Blailey Financial Services Modernization Act of 1999 repealed the language of the Glass-Steagall Act and allowed deregulation in the financial services industry. The following year, passage of the Commodity Futures Modernization Act made it impossible to regulate credit swaps. The mergers and acquisitions continued even during the federal bailout period of late 2008–2009 (e.g., Merrill Lynch was acquired by Bank of America in late 2008), when some corporations were already deemed "too big to fail" (i.e., with so much influence over the national economy that Congress was compelled to use tax dollars to save them from bankruptcy) (Goodman, 2008).

There is probably no entity other than possibly national governments that are big enough to stand up to the power of giant conglomerates. Corporations that are designed to generate profits and that owe allegiance only to their stockholders have little interest in the welfare of employees, consumers, or the environment. Corporate power is felt not only within this country, but internationally as well. They may manufacture component parts in one or several countries, assemble the parts in another, have their corporate headquarters in yet another, and sell their products throughout the world. Multinational corporations profess loyalty to no single nation. In fact, many are larger and more powerful than nation-states.

Changing Patterns of Employment

Today, the production economy of the United States has shifted from industrial manufacturing to one that is predominantly service-oriented and information-based. The new economy provides few openings for unskilled laborers in well-paying manufacturing jobs. Employment in the *service sector* is split between positions requiring technical skills (such as computer programmers) and poorly paid jobs requiring minimal skills. For example, in the fast-food industry, cashiers no longer have to enter prices and make change; they simply hit keys with pictures on them and the customer's change is automatically calculated and discharged. Even the interaction with customers is scripted ("Do you want to supersize that?"). Employment in this part of the service sector does not pay enough to support a family and is unlikely to provide benefits such as health care insurance, career advancement, and retirement plans.

In search of greater profits, many companies moved manufacturing jobs first to the anti-union South and then overseas to reduce labor costs. Employees have little bargaining power in such situations, either individually or collectively. By 2008, only 12.4 percent of workers were union members. Government workers are almost five times more likely to belong to a union as are private sector employees (U.S. Bureau of Labor Statistics [BLS], 2009). Men, black workers, and older workers (aged 55–64) are more likely to be union members than their counterparts (BLS, 2009). The highest level of union membership is in New York State (24.9 percent); the lowest level of union membership is found in Southern states, with North Carolina being the lowest at 3.5 percent (BLS, 2009).

Downsizing refers to large-scale worker layoffs. (Downsizing may also be called "reduction in force" or RIF.) *Outsourcing* means contracting to have tasks normally done within the company performed under a contract with another company. Commonly outsourced jobs include custodial work or payroll functions. *Offshoring* is the term used when the jobs are still controlled by the company itself but moved overseas. Most of the lost jobs are in manufacturing or in telephone call centers (Uchitelle, 2003). An example of this trend is the transfer of customer service and tech support jobs to India where English-speaking, college-educated, entry-level recruits earn $3,650 a year—good wages in India but only a fifth of what an American would be paid for similar work (Carmichael, 2003; Waldman, 2003). Even such traditionally American products as Levi's blue jeans are now being manufactured overseas (Mayhew, 2003). Recently, more highly skilled jobs are being offshored, including aeronautical engineers, software designers, and stock analysts (Uchitelle, 2003). Whereas factory layoffs used to be temporary and related to economic downturns, with employers calling workers back once a recovery began, outsourcing and offshoring practices reflect structural, and permanent, changes in the broader economy.

Since 1979, when manufacturing employment peaked in this country, one in four factory jobs has disappeared (Vieth, 2003). Although other kinds of jobs have been created, the new jobs tend to pay significantly less—as much as 80 percent less (LaLonde, 2007; Uchitelle, 2006). Uchitelle (2006) notes the reality is that there are not enough good jobs available to meet the demands of college-educated and well-trained workers in the United States, which is why so many are working in jobs for which they are overqualified. Recent studies show that long-term unemployment is growing most rapidly among middle-class white-collar and college-educated workers with long work experience (Fletcher, 2008).

Beyond the effects on individuals and their families, which includes depression, domestic strife, and divorce (Uchitelle, 2006), unemployment also has larger consequences including community breakdown and a rise in social conflict. Unemployed persons tend to withdraw from social and civic activities and direct their anger at a variety of targets, including immigrants, minorities, welfare recipients, and the very rich (Thio, 1998, p. 405).

Beginning in the 1980s, American companies learned that by using "temps" they could hold down wages, reduce the costs of employee benefits, and lay off surplus staff at any time. Although many people (such as students, homemakers, and older adults) work part-time by choice, a significant number do so only because they cannot find full-time employment or need to supplement the income from their full-time jobs. *Contingent work* is becoming a characteristic of the American workforce (Larson, 1996). The contingent workforce is made up of part-time and temporary employees. Temporary workers are the fastest-growing segment of the contingent workforce (Kendall, 2008, p. 439). Many contingent workers can be classified as *underemployed*, that is, they are overqualified for the positions they fill. For these workers, job security and employment benefits are an illusion.

Consumerism

Some sociologists have argued that the real focus of the American economy has shifted from one of production to one of consumption (Barber, 2007; Vyse, 2008). This trend has been fostered by the development, since World War II (in order of their appearance), of franchises, shopping malls, "superstores," discounters, home shopping television networks, "cybermalls," and "mega malls" (Ritzer, 1999). In 1983, American household debt equaled 55 percent of income; now it is above 114 percent (Fox, 2007). Household consumption has come to comprise more than 70 percent of our economy (Lewis, 2008; Meyerson, 2008).

The average American is consuming more than twice as much as he or she did a half-century ago. Since 1950, Americans have used up as many of the earth's resources as were used in all the rest of human history. Environmentalists are alarmed that Americans are both extracting resources at rates the planet cannot sustain and producing waste at levels that the planet cannot absorb (Korten, 1995, 1999, 2006). Using an instrument created by the National Geographic Society and GlobeScan to compare individual consumer behaviors, 14,000 individuals in 14 countries were asked to respond to questions that measured their consumption related to housing, transportation, food, and other goods (National Geographic Society, 2008). People in the United States ranked lowest, indicating the worst performance on indicators of sustainability. Other low scoring countries included Canada and France. Individuals in Brazil and India tied for the highest score. People in developing countries tend to live in small houses, own relatively few appliances, and walk, cycle, or use public transportation.

The shift in consumption patterns probably began in the 1920s when producers started marketing directly to consumers, rather than to retailers. From the start, advertising was more about creating consumers than selling individual products (Croteau & Hoynes, 2003). Although the marketing industry claims that it simply provides information so that buyers can make informed choices, many would say that through massive advertising campaigns corporations actually create "needs" (or more accurately, "wants") as much as they provide goods and services in response to consumer demands. (A further discussion of how the mass media encourage consumerism is presented in Chapter 4.) In addition to advertising, another development that has fostered a consumer society is buying on credit. The results are predictable. According to data collected by the administrative offices of the U.S. Courts (2008), more than 1 million Americans filed for bankruptcy in fiscal year 2008. (Rates are down since 2006, when a new federal law, the Bankruptcy Abuse Prevention and Consumer Protection Act of 2005, was implemented. The Act actually did more to protect banks than consumers; it made it more difficult for individuals to file for bankruptcy.)

Globalization

Another profound change in the economy is the globalization of capitalism. According to some sociologists, its impact is comparable to the industrial revolution (Henslin, 2008). As with the industrial revolution, there may be both positive and negative outcomes. One positive consequence for low-income Americans is that their purchasing power may be increased by the availability of inexpensive products made in other countries. An economist suggests that the impact of imports from China alone increases the "real incomes" of such consumers by as much as 5 to 10 percent (Overholt, 2006). Another benefit is the growth in the market for American goods sold overseas. Perhaps the most significant benefit is the improvement in living conditions in countries that are industrializing; for instance, life expectancy in China has increased by over 30 years in the last half-century (Overholt, 2006). On the other side of the globalization trend are concerns about the status of workers, both in the United States and abroad. American workers, especially in the manufacturing sector, are not seeing an increase in their wages and may also face job cutbacks. At the same time, workers in developing countries are paid barely subsistence wages.

The Economic Crisis

The immediate causes of the economic crisis that began in late 2008 are complex and difficult to grasp, even by economists. Most agree, however, that one major factor was excessive risk-taking at many levels—from individual home buyers who overextended themselves based on assumptions of ever-increasing home values, to mortgage companies that took on customers with marginal credit ratings, to regulators "asleep at the wheel," to large financial institutions that bought and bundled risky loans relying heavily on borrowed money to do so (Fox, J., 2008; Gross, 2009; Johnson, 2009; Samuelson, 2008, 2009; Von Drehle, 2009). The results of the crisis are yet to be totally manifested, but preliminary analyses suggest that immediate effects include failing consumer confidence, slowed economic growth, rising rates of unemployment, and significant loss of investment values, with repercussions felt around the world. Government responses will greatly expand the national debt and restrict other important initiatives for years to come.

Understanding the Economic System

Functionalist Perspective

Functionalists believe that large systems are self-correcting, for the most part, if change occurs incrementally. Thus they support a "free market economy" that is allowed to respond to fluctuating supply and demand, expecting to see a cyclical pattern of peaks and troughs. When matters get too far out of balance, as in periods of recession or inflation, the government steps in to make minor adaptations by changing interest rates, adjusting trade agreements, and other activities.

Functionalists also believe that the opportunity for everyone to be a stockholder, as well as a consumer, is a major positive feature of the American economic system. In effect, everyone including workers can also be "capitalists" and share in the profits and the prosperity of a growing company and a strong economy.

Conflict Perspective

The laws of supply and demand and the push for profits are not necessarily consistent with the well-being of workers or consumers. Conflict theorists (including Karl Marx) suggest that those who own the means of production will always exploit the laboring classes. These theorists stress that in order to keep labor costs low and profits high, capitalists view workers as expendable commodities who can be exploited to meet the needs of the company.

One indicator of the exploitation of workers is the enormous disparity between the salaries of workers and those who employ them. (See Chapter 5 for a comparison of CEO salaries and a typical worker's pay.) Salaries of company executives grew as downsizing became a management strategy. Despite all of the heated rhetoric about executive compensation and extravagant bonuses that occurred at the beginning of the financial crisis of 2008, conflict theorists would argue that the focus should not be on the distribution of money, but on the concentration of power—both financial and political—in the hands of a few (Johnson, 2009; Taibbi, 2009).

Rational/Social Exchange Perspective

If the explanation of any social institution can be said to be firmly rooted in a social theory, it is capitalism and social exchange. Adam Smith (1937/1776), one of the earliest economic theorists, suggested that it is self-interest that makes capitalism—and industrial society—function. In business, managers, workers, and customers make decisions based on their own interests. There is no room for sentimentality or idealism. The "market," acting without interference, will find the correct balance so that consumers get the best value for their money and workers are paid what they are worth. Companies that offer shoddily made products or sloppy service are put out of business as consumers seek better deals elsewhere. Workers who do not contribute a value comparable to their wage are laid off. Efficiency—payback on investments—is the key.

Proponents of capitalism assume that the principal of self-interest operates not just among individuals but also among larger systems. For example, a community or even a state, competing with other localities, might offer tax breaks to entice a corporation to build a new plant within its boundaries, thus creating jobs for its citizens.

Constructionist Perspective

Even something that sounds as rational and objective as economics can be partly explained in terms of how members of a society interpret the meaning of work, wealth, and economic exchange. One well-known theorist, Max Weber (1922/1978), suggested that the development of capitalism as an economic system was based on the belief system of early Protestants. The followers of John Calvin believed that worldly success was a sign of one's being in God's favor. According to Weber, Calvinists' religious convictions led them to reinvest their wealth, thus laying the foundations of capitalism.

Later generations of Calvinists retained their personal discipline and their belief system became a work ethic, wherein hard labor and thriftiness were closely associated with morality. The *Protestant work ethic* is firmly established in the American psyche. It suggests that people should work even under conditions that are unfair and/or harmful. The injunction that welfare recipients accept jobs that will not cover their child-care costs is an example of the power of the belief that working is not simply a means of self-support, it is a moral imperative.

Another point of view that has facilitated the growth of American capitalism is the meaning of thrift and of credit and how it is used (Calder, 1999; Hine, 2002; Ritzer, 2001). Those who study the topic have described this trend as a "profound cultural change" (Yip, 2007). At the beginning of the twentieth century, borrowing was frowned upon (Gibbs, 2008; Lewis, 2008; Yip, 2007). Nevertheless, by the 1950s, there was a definite change in attitudes toward money, and households took on debt in the pursuit of consumer goods. This shift away from saving for a rainy day to spending money one doesn't have is clearly illustrated in the titles of a number of recent books on the topic: *Credit Card Nation: The Consequences of America's Addiction to Credit* (Manning, 2000), *Consumed: How Markets Corrupt Children, Infantalize Adults, and Swallow Citizens Whole* (Barber, 2007), and *Going Broke: Why Americans Can't Hold Onto Their Money* (Vyse, 2008). The quality of acquisitiveness used to be discouraged, if not condemned; now Americans are told that consumption is equivalent to patriotism (Gibbs, 2008; Lewis, 2008; Yip, 2007).

Thus, in terms of the socially constructed meanings of work and wealth, we see both continuity and change. Work is still viewed as having inherent value. Wealth, while no longer seen as a sign of salvation, is highly regarded as an indicator of personal worth.

The meaning of consumption may—or may not—change with the 2008 financial crisis: "In hard times, people often rediscover the peace that prudence brings, when you try to spend a little less than you have because tomorrow might be worse. But that feels almost un-American; we're optimists by nature, and we've been living large for so long that solvency feels like a sacrifice" (Gibbs, 2008, p. 96).

The Impact of the Economic System on Individuals and Families

How the Economic System Deters Well-Being

The job of corporate executives is clear; it is to put the corporation's interests, and those of its stockholders, first (Bakan, 2004). Even the greatest advocates of capitalism acknowledge that it is an unfair system, rewarding some very well and leaving others behind. For those at the bottom of the economic hierarchy, the inequity is especially notable. According to the 2000 census, in the midst of the best economic conditions in decades, 9.2 percent of families residing in the "richest country in the world" were still living in "abject poverty" (Economic Policy Institute, 2002). (See Table 5.2 for an illustration of Federal Poverty Guidelines).

Social scientists divide the labor market into two categories. The *primary labor market* provides jobs that carry with them many benefits, including career advancement opportunities. Examples of occupations in the primary labor market are management positions and the professions. Jobs in the *secondary labor market* require few skills, provide minimal benefits, often involve dirty and/or dangerous conditions, and may offer only part-time or seasonal employment; examples include store clerks, fast-food cooks, and farmworkers. People of color and women make up the majority of workers in the secondary labor market. An example of the secondary labor market is the meat-and-poultry packing plants that draw Latinos—some of them undocumented Mexicans—to the Southeast (Herbert, 2006). There they do much of the unpleasant work of transforming hogs into hams and sausages and chickens into breasts and drumsticks—work that Americans prefer not to do. (See Chapter 9 for more discussion of the meatpacking industry.)

Capitalism depends on having a large reservoir of unemployed workers who are willing to work for minimum wage whenever such work is available. The "acceptable"—that is, desired—level of unemployment advocated by the federal government has changed from a goal of zero (full employment) after the Great Depression to 2 to 3 percent during the 1960s and then to 5 to 6 percent as of the mid-1980s (Heilbroner, 1993). Reflecting the recent economic crisis, as of mid-spring 2009, national unemployment rates stood at 8.5 percent, with rates in some states registering in the double digits.

How the Economic System Promotes Well-Being

While it is easy to identify oppressive elements in the modern American capitalist economy, it is important to note ways in which the economy also enhances the well-being of many citizens. The high standard of living in this country, especially in terms of consumer goods (e.g., wall-to-wall carpeting, household appliances, electronics, automobiles), is undeniable. Even the rapid growth of the service sector and its accompanying low wages and job insecurity presents an opportunity for many of the least skilled workers in American society, including high school dropouts, non-English-speaking immigrants, and people with disabilities.

The Political System

The *political system* is the social institution that establishes a hierarchy of power and leadership. It is where decisions are made and carried out, either directly or indirectly. The *government* is the formal organization that has the legal authority to maintain social order by resolving conflicts among members of the society, protect citizens from threats that come from outside its borders, and provide for the common good.

The United States is a representative democracy. This means that political decisions are made by bodies of representatives elected by the people (e.g., city or county councils, state legislatures, and, of course, Congress) rather than directly by the people themselves. Usually decisions are made based not only on what constituents want, but also on a complex process of negotiation and trade-offs, as well as the direct and indirect influence of "special interest" groups.

There is considerable concordance between political ideology (liberal and conservative) and the major political parties (Democrats and Republicans). The Cooperative Congressional Election Study (CCES) survey (cited in Abramowitz & Bishop, 2007) of 24,000 Americans who voted in 2006 showed that 86 percent of Democratic voters were liberals and 80 percent of Republican voters were conservative. Only 10 percent were in the middle.

Historically, conservatives have been considered to be moderate and cautious, and politically linked to fiscal restraint, low taxes, free-market forces, "personal responsibility," and military strength. It may be helpful to think of fiscal (economic) conservatives and social (cultural) conservatives in two categories that only sometimes overlap. In the past several decades, social conservative ideology has also embraced so-called "traditional" viewpoints on many cultural issues, including nationalism, abortion, sexual orientation, gun rights, and the exercise of religion. Historically, liberals have been linked with support for an active role for government, labor unions, economic security, worker safety, civil rights, and reproductive freedoms. More recently, a liberal point of view has included consumer protection, environmental issues, and access to health care. Since the 1980s, the word *liberal* has been used pejoratively in many political contexts, with a subtext that suggests that liberals are wed to high-taxing, big-spending, big government, and socialist ways. On the other hand, most liberals would describe themselves as "favoring proposals for reform, open to new ideas for progress, and tolerant of the ideas and behavior of others," a definition found in the third edition of the *American Heritage College Dictionary*. Many liberal ideas that seemed controversial at the time they were introduced—such as Social Security and racial integration—are now so taken for granted that they have "simply been absorbed into the national self-portrait" (Quindlen, 2004).

Issues and Trends in the Political System

Increasing Divisiveness

Two factors contribute to this pattern of increasing political divisiveness over the last 30 years in the United States: (1) geographic separation and (2) political messages. Bishop (2008) argues that prosperity allows Americans the freedom to live where they want and this has given them the impetus to segregate themselves into "lifestyle ghettos"; in such areas, views can become extreme and people can become more suspicious of outsiders. In national election cycles, the media talk about "red" (Republican-leaning) states and "blue" (Democratic-leaning) states, but a review of Bishop's work suggests that it is not states but counties (or even neighborhoods) that create extreme voter profiles.

Politicians have contributed to the trend of increasing divisiveness by focusing on messages that "energize their base." (See the discussion on redistricting later in this chapter.) Politicians win by rallying their most intense supporters and getting them to the polls. For example, Jonathan

Alter, who writes opinion pieces for *Newsweek* magazine, notes that the use of the terms *values* and *values voters* were initially used to describe citizens who were concerned about what's happened to "old fashioned notions of decency" (2006, p. 51). He laments that when the expression is claimed exclusively by one side the political spectrum, it implies that people on the other side not only "do not share our values" but that they are morally inferior. Other phrases like "real Americans," when used by one side, also suggest that others are not simply in disagreement, but that they are unpatriotic. Such dialogue sets up imaginary barriers between voters and precludes an honest debate about the issues.

Political Influence

A *special interest group* is an alliance of people concerned about some political issue. Influencing legislation is called *lobbying*. The term often has a negative connotation but lobbying is used, mostly legitimately, by special interests groups of all types. These include the National Association of Social Workers, the American Public Welfare Association, and the Child Welfare League of America as well as better-known groups such as the National Rifle Association, the American Association of Retired Persons, and tobacco companies. In addition to contributing to campaigns, special interest groups and their lobbyists may affect legislation by testifying before lawmakers' committees, mobilizing support or opposition to a bill by asking members to call or write letters, and even drafting proposed legislation.

Many special interest groups are not allowed to make political contributions directly. They use *political action committees* (PACs) to promote their political agendas. PACs are organizations that solicit and distribute political contributions as their primary purpose. PACs have been organized by labor unions, trade associations, environmental groups, and religious groups. The number of PACs has grown steadily, from 608 in 1974 to 4,234 in January of 2008 (Federal Election Commission, 2008). Contributors give to PACs rather than to a political party when they want to support a specific political cause.

Election campaigns are increasingly commercialized and expensive. The rising cost of political campaigns at all levels means that politicians and political parties are constantly concerned with raising funds. As a result, individuals with money (or more often, groups and organizations with money) exercise a great deal of influence over the political process. Without good financing, potential candidates do not become actual candidates. Some of the resources bought with campaign funds include consultants, pollsters, speechwriters, and media experts. Some suggest that good consultants have become more important than political parties in successful election campaigns.

As of 2008, individuals are limited to a maximum $2,300 contribution to a candidate; the purpose of this policy is to limit the power of rich contributors. But corporations, labor unions, and issue groups can spend hundreds of millions on commercials *about* candidates—just so long as they do not specifically ask the viewer to *vote* for or against the candidate in the ad. Candidates are not allowed to help prepare these ads, coordinate ad buys or schedules, or even know about them before they air. The candidates are left at the mercy of special interest groups—even when the groups are on their side.

The Power of Incumbency

In addition to the benefits associated with simple name recognition, *incumbents* (politicians already holding office) tend to have huge advantages in fund-raising, and in communicating with voters through free mail privileges, regular access to the mass media, and speech-giving opportunities. Long-serving incumbents also have the advantage of the power of being heads of influential committees; this can be a selling point with voters when questions arise about what they can do for their constituents based on their influence in Washington.

Another advantage that comes primarily to members of the House of Representatives occurs as a result of redistricting. Following the 2000 census, in state after state, legislators set aside their differences to redraw district lines to protect the incumbents of both parties. This means that politicians are choosing their voters, rather than the other way around. With computer technology, the ability to design districts that meet legal requirements while guaranteeing a "safe" district for one party or the other has never been easier (Broder, 2008). In the elections of 2000, 2002, and 2004, when national and statewide races were dramatically close, only 21 House incumbents (less than 5 percent) were defeated, reflecting the effects of redistricting.

The way that district lines are drawn to create "safe" seats for one party or the other means that it is in the primary elections, not the general elections, that House members are selected—effectively denying participation to a large number of voters. The creation of "safe" districts makes these lawmakers less responsive to a broad base of constituents and less willing to compromise with members of the other party when they are serving in Congress (Broder, 2008).

PACs give most of their money to incumbents. The political watchdog group Common Cause (2000) reported that House incumbents had a four-to-one financial advantage over challengers and for Senate incumbents the ratio was six-to-one. Scott Harshbarger, president of Common Cause, noted, "this system is a gravy train for members of Congress—and a meal ticket for special interests, many of whom want something in return." The implication is that political outsiders have little power, and the status quo is supported.

Voter Turnout

Given the situation described above, one is not surprised to find high rates of voter apathy in America. Voter turnout is higher when there is real competition and real choice. In addition, voting conditions can affect turnout. Many other countries allow Sunday voting, multiday voting, and voting by mail. (Some states have made voting easier for their residents by allowing same-day registration and permitting absentee balloting by any voter, not just those who can show they are unable to participate on Election Day.) Compared to participation rates hovering just above 50 percent in the United States, participation rates in other countries tend to be much higher. In Australia, for example, more than 95 percent of eligible voters turn out. Participation rates are higher than 80 percent in Austria, Belgium, Brazil, Bulgaria, Costa Rica, Denmark, Germany, Greece, Israel, Sweden, and Venezuela (International Institute for Democracy and Electoral Assistance (IDEA), 2009). Only 58.3 percent of U.S. citizens reported that they participated in the November 2004 presidential election (U.S. Census Bureau, current population survey, 2005). In the 2008 general election, 61.7 percent of eligible voters turned out (United States Elections Project, 2009).

The election systems in most other democracies involve *proportional representation*, rather than "winner-take-all" systems such as the ones in the United States and Canada. In a proportional representation election, there are multiple candidates representing a district. Winning candidates are determined by the proportion of votes a party receives. If, for example, the "Purple Party" wins 50 percent of the votes in a ten-member district, five of the elected officials would be from the Purple Party. The single-member district system, such as we have in the United States, "routinely denies representation to large numbers of voters, produces legislatures that fail to accurately reflect the views of the public, discriminates against third parties, and discourages voter turnout" (Amy, 2005). As noted already, when redistricting is applied to this model, creating "safe" districts for one party or the other, it is clear how some voters might feel that their votes are "wasted" if they are not supporters of the majority party.

Verba, Schlozman, and Brady (1995) note that American politics is prone to "participatory distortion." Citizens with more income, education, and age are overrepresented in almost every political activity, from contacting lawmakers to contributing funds; voting is the political activity that is least distorted by income, education, and age of participant. Populations that have a higher-than-average voter participation rates include non-Hispanic whites, those 65 and older, women, veterans, married individuals, those with higher household income and more education, and Midwesterners (U.S. Bureau of the Census, 2005). People who hold intense opinions on issues such as gun control and abortion are also more likely to vote. Voter enthusiasm is clearly correlated to perceptions of having a stake in the political system and the outcome of the election. Those who believe they have nothing to gain feel alienated and are unlikely to vote.

Given the historic nature of the 2008 presidential election, with the first African American major party candidate and the first female Republican vice presidential candidate, interest from nontraditional voters increased. Continuing a trend that began in 1992, youth voter turnout rose significantly in 2008 to 52 percent of the eligible youth voting population (Nonprofit Voter Engagement Network, 2008). As a proportion of the overall voting population, the Latino share nearly doubled between 1996 (5 percent) and 2008 (9 percent) and the African American share increased from 11 percent to 13 percent over the same time period (Nonprofit Voter Engagement Network, 2008).

Turnout in Minnesota was the highest in the nation, with 78 percent participation of eligible voters. Minnesota, along with several other high-ranking states, adopted Election-Day registration that permits voters to either update their registration or register to vote for the first time at their polling place (Nonprofitvote.org, 2009). North Carolina, which combined same-day registration and early voting, had the biggest increase (10.8 percent) in turnout in the country (Nonprofitvote.org, 2009; Wang, 2008).

Officeholders

Elective offices in the United States are filled predominantly by white men. Women and people of color are significantly underrepresented in elective office at all levels in proportion to their numbers in the general population.

In other countries, women make up a substantial number of officeholders. For instance, if one were to compare national legislatures, 71 nations have a greater percentage of females (Wallechinsky, 2007). "Women candidates are more likely to emerge and succeed in proportional party-list electoral systems. The candidate-centered system in the United States therefore hampers women's entrance into public office" (Lawless & Fox, 2005, p. 12). Lawless and Fox (2005, p. 127) also suggest that there are fewer women than men in office in this country because women do not *run* for office. This is less a result of discrimination than a lack of political ambition. Women are less likely than men to be recruited to run for office and they are less likely than men to think they are qualified for office. They have more difficulty than men in reconciling family needs with the demands of a political career.

TABLE 2.1   *Women in Congress*

	108th 2003–2004	109th 2005–2006	110th 2007–2008	111th 2009–2010
Senate	14	14	16	17
House	68	71	71	78
Percent of total*	15.3	15.9	16.3	17.7

*100 Members of U.S. Senate, 435 Members of the House of Representatives
Source: Amer, M., & Manning, J. E. (2008, December 31). *Membership of the 111th Congress: A profile.*
Washington, DC: Congressional Research Service.

Women in Congress can be expected to bring up "women's issues"—gender equity, day care, flextime, reproductive freedom, minimum wage increases, and the extension of food stamp programs (Burrell, 1996) and women generally run well as agents of change because they are viewed as outsiders (Romano, 2006). Both Democratic and moderate Republican women in Congress are more likely than men to use their bill sponsorship and co-sponsorship activity to focus on women's issue (Swers, 2002). The longest-serving woman in the U.S. Senate is Barbara Mikulski, a social worker from Maryland. Another social worker serving in the 111th Congress is Debbie Stabenow of Michigan.

In 2008, nearly a quarter (23.7 percent) of state legislators were female; since 1971, the number of women in state legislatures has more than quintupled (Center for American Women and Politics, 2009). As of January 2008, among the 100 largest cities in the United States, 11 had women mayors, 4 of whom were women of color (three African Americans and one Latina).

Minorities may be gaining political influence in Washington, even as their numerical count remains relatively flat, when long-serving minority members of Congress are appointed to powerful committee chairmanships. In 2008, Americans elected their first African American president.

TABLE 2.2   *Minorities in Congress*

	108th 2003–2004	109th 2005–2006	110th 2007–2008	111th 2009–2010
African Americans	39	43	43	39
Hispanics	25	28	27	30
Asians	3	3	8	9
Other*	3	2	1	1
Percent of total for all minorities**	13.1	14.2	14.8	14.8

*Asian Indians and Native Americans
**100 Members of US Senate, 435 Members of the House of Representatives
Source: Amer, M., & Manning, J. E. (2008, December 31). *Membership of the 111th Congress: A profile.*
Washington, DC: Congressional Research Service.

Understanding the Political System

Functionalist Perspective

Modern governments perform the necessary societal functions that private enterprise will not or cannot because there is no profit to be made. Examples include providing safety and protection (e.g., police services, national defense), building and maintaining infrastructure (e.g., roads, sewage treatment plants) and running public facilities (e.g., schools, courts, prisons, parks, and so forth).

Functionalists espouse the *pluralist model* of politics. They argue that there are many competing interest groups making the political process necessarily one of negotiation and compromise. Although few groups are powerful enough to force their agenda on others, many groups are able to thwart the plans of their opposition. Thus, power is widely dispersed and change is slow.

Conflict Perspective

Some conflict theorists, notably C. Wright Mills (1956), have argued that most important political decisions are made not by elected officials but by a *power elite*, or ruling class, made up of extremely wealthy individuals who enjoy easy access to the centers of U.S. politics. Elites come from the upper classes—the wealthy and educated—and are usually white. In the 111th Congress, 204 out of 535 members listed law as their occupation, and 201 listed business; 16 were medical doctors, 13 were former governors, and 3 were former Cabinet secretaries (Amer & Manning, 2008). The vast majority (95 percent) of members of Congress hold university degrees (Amer & Manning, 2008).

Conflict theorists note that the power elite are not participants in some grand conspiracy, but simply are people of similar backgrounds who share mutual interests and agendas, often involving "the welfare of big business." Nevertheless, those who espouse the *power elite model* say that the concentration of wealth and power in a few hands is so great that the people at the top face little opposition. At the same time, the voices of many of the people in the middle and most of those at the bottom have little chance of being heard (Piven & Cloward, 1997).

Rational/Social Exchange Perspective

Modern Western democracies were conceived in the "Age of Enlightenment," an eighteenth-century movement that celebrated the essential rationality of humankind. Philosophers of the time proposed that the "rule of law" should replace the rule of monarchy. Inherent in this concept was the idea that citizens are capable of making logical choices in governing themselves through processes of deliberation and negotiation.

This nation's founders did not trust the general populace to make decisions directly. For example, they established the Electoral College to select the president. Most Americans believe that, especially if they have access to accurate and unbiased information, they can and should make many political choices for themselves. Sometimes politicians allow this process of *direct democracy* through the use of *referendums* on the election ballot. Typically, this happens at the state or local level.

Constructionist Perspective

The constructed meaning of the United States of America has power to influence and shape political directions. Many Americans believe that their country has been especially chosen and blessed by God to lead the world. In the nineteenth century, this idea was expressed in the concept of "manifest destiny"—the idea that God had provided the North American continent to be developed into a utopian society built upon the principles of capitalism, Protestantism, and democracy (Jansson, 2005). (This ignored the fact that indigenous Native Americans had a legitimate claim to the same territory, of course.) Under the George W. Bush administration, this idea of American superiority was expressed or implied as belief in the country's inherent goodness or right in opposing enemies who are invariably described as "evil."

With the exception of Native American and Alaskan and Hawaiian natives, all citizens of the United States, or their ancestors, came from somewhere else. Thus "being an American" in the mind of the general public reflects voluntary allegiance to the United States. Despite support of the idea of freedom of speech, those who challenge mainstream values or criticize national policy run the risk of being labeled unpatriotic if not "un-American" (Alter, 2006). The citizens of other countries derive their sense of themselves from a common history and ancestry; they do not become "un-French" or "un-Korean" by expressing unpopular points of view (Lipset, 1996).

The Impact of the Political System on Individuals and Families

How the Political System Deters Well-Being

As discussed under the conflict perspective, the issues of poor people are not commonly addressed by our political system. The poor are isolated and marked off as deviant by "a predominantly middle-class political culture" (Piven & Cloward, 1997, p. 282). Because they have been left out of the mainstream political process, they have few options to make their voices heard. In the past, these included public demonstrations, sit-ins, boycotts, and rent-strikes. ". . . [D]isruptive and irregular tactics are the only resource, short of violence, available to low-income groups seeking to influence public policy" (Piven & Cloward, p. 284). A recent example of a massive demonstration occurred in March of 2006, when a half-million Latinos marched in the streets of Los Angeles to protest a proposed federal crackdown on illegal immigration ("Immigration issue draws thousands into streets," 2006). Similar demonstrations were held across the country and included staged school walkouts, marches, and work stoppages.

How the Political System Promotes Well-Being

The U.S. Constitution and judicial system stand as examples to the rest of the world in their protection of the civil rights and civil liberties of minorities, women, people with disabilities, and older adults. Americans enjoy individual freedoms unknown in many countries.

Economics and Politics Together: The Political Economy

Political economy is the term used to refer to the pervasive interaction of political and economic institutions. In the United States, politics and the economy are so intertwined that often it is difficult to see them or treat them as separate institutions. Many of this country's laws are based on the ideals of capitalism and much of the "free market" economy is politically supported in one way or another.

The Power of Organizations

Piven and Cloward (1997) suggest that despite political oratory to the contrary, as individuals most Americans have little direct influence on the political process. Instead, political dialogue is carried on between organizations—between government agencies or legislative committees and professional associations, unions, PACs, and business groups—not individuals. Individuals do not have the time, resources, or the interest to regularly monitor and participate in the political process. The complexities of issues and the intricacies of policy making are simply too much for the average citizen to follow. On the other hand, the focus of organizations—to protect the rights, income, occupational roles, property, or other economic interests of their members—makes ongoing interaction with political processes both necessary and potentially profitable.

One of the ways that organizations exercise political power is through lobbying. From 1998 through 2008, the top spenders on lobbying, categorized by industry, included pharmaceuticals/health products ($1.5 billion), insurance ($1.2 billion), and electric utilities ($1.1 billion) (Center for Responsive Politics, 2009b). Among the specific organizations at the top of the list were the American Medical Association ($200 million), American Hospital Association ($163 million), Pharmaceutical Researchers and Manufacturers of America ($147 million), Blue Cross/Blue Shield ($111 million), the National Association of Realtors ($118 million), Exxon Mobile ($111 million), General Motors ($100 million), and Ford Motor Company ($82 million) (Center for Responsive Politics, 2009a). Records from the 2006 election cycle show that nearly all PACs gave the overwhelming portion (89 to 97 percent) of their campaign contributions to incumbents rather than to challengers (Center for Responsive Politics, 2008).

Companies can also pose as generous corporate citizens while gaining political access, but new laws require corporations and their lobbyists to disclose donations they make to the favorite causes of lawmakers. During the first six months of 2008, approximately $13 million was given to charities and nonprofits on behalf of members of Congress (Hernandez & Chen, 2008).

We have already mentioned how giant corporations dominate the American economy and discussed Wright's theory of the power elite. Corporations are the major contributors to both political parties. In response, much of the activity of politicians is aimed at promoting the economic interests of large corporations.

> The . . . claim by corporations that they have the same right as any individual to influence the government in their own interest pits the individual citizen against the vast financial and communications resources of the corporation and mocks the constitutional intent that all citizens have an equal voice in the political debates surrounding important issues. (Korten, 1995, p. 59)

The amazing expansion of the influence of corporations over the federal, state, and local governments in the last 30 years has led to acknowledgment and criticism of *corporate welfare*, the direct subsidies and tax expenditures granted to businesses. Corporate welfare includes programs that offer direct financial compensation to businesses, programs that provide research (R & D) for industries, and programs that provide subsidized loans or insurance. The biggest direct subsidy program is for crop and farm subsidies, which cost taxpayers $21 billion in 2006 (Slivinski, 2007). Some of the biggest companies in America or their subsidiaries—none of which should have trouble funding their own research and development—have received millions of dollars in R & D funds from the federal government through the

Advanced Technology Program (ATP); top beneficiaries include IBM, General Electric, Honeywell, Xerox, Dow Chemical, Motorola, 3M, Ford Motor, General Motors, and Corning (Slivinski, 2007).

Government Spending

Because of its purchasing power alone, the U.S. government has a huge influence over the nation's economy. Total government spending in 2010 is expected to represent 39.9 percent of the gross domestic product (GDP) (Freedman, 2009). The fiscal crisis of 2008–2009 has brought renewed discussion on the proper relationship between government and the private sector. In times of economic crisis, the federal government is unique in its ability to engage in deficit spending to create jobs or stimulate a sagging economy.

Often taxpayer dollars have been directed to less than noble causes. This occurs when law-makers use earmarks to send money to their home states or congressional districts. The terms *pork* and *earmarks* are often used interchangeably, but they are different. *Earmark* refers to any expenditure for a specific purpose that is tucked into a larger bill. Only when the earmark is inappropriately added to the bill is it considered pork. A *pork-barrel project* is a line item in an appropriation or authorization bill that designates funds for a specific purpose in circumvention of the normal procedures for budget review; for example, it is not specifically authorized, not the subject of congressional hearings, and not competitively awarded (Finnigan, 2007). According to Citizens Against Government Waste, there were 546 pork-barrel projects in 1991 and 11,610 in 2008. Probably the best-known recent example of a pork-barrel project was the "Bridge to Nowhere" that became a focus of the presidential campaign of 2008. At a cost of $223 million, the bridge would have connected Ketchikan, Alaska to Gravina Island, which has a population of 50 (Finnigan, 2007).

Inequities in Government Benefits

Links between the government and the economy affect every citizen. Most Americans benefit financially from government programs, but the middle and upper classes benefit more (Abramovitz, 2001; DiNitto, 2000). The rich receive government assistance through various income-tax deductions and government contracts and subsidies to their businesses; individuals in the middle class receive government assistance primarily in the form of home mortgage loans and associated tax deductions, and grants and loans for education. The poor and near-poor receive government assistance in the form of welfare grants, food stamps, Medicaid, and earned income-tax credits.

Regressive taxes are those that tax the poor at a higher rate than the rich. For example, some low-income workers may not pay any income taxes at all, but they do contribute to FICA taxes/Social Security withholding, which is charged against all of their earnings, for benefits they may not live long enough to collect. People with higher incomes do not pay FICA taxes on all of their earnings because there is a built-in maximum ($6,621.60 for 2009). Sales taxes are particularly regressive for low-income people. In states where groceries and medicines are not exempted, the poor pay sales taxes on 100 percent of their income because they must spend it all to meet the expenses of daily living.

Without an awareness of the pervasive influence of the political economy, social workers may be tempted to believe that problems exist solely on the individual or family level. The poor in particular are vulnerable. They lack the resources to use the political system to address their needs. Even skilled social work practitioners cannot counsel their clients out of the difficulties created by the inadequacies and injustice of the larger society.

Looking Ahead

Not only are individuals, families, and communities affected by the political economy, but so are the other social institutions. We will explore these relationships in Chapters 3 and 4.

Chapter 3

Government-Related Social Institutions

Education

 Issues and Trends in Education

  Special Programs and Schools
  Violence, Corporal Punishment, and Sexual Harassment
  Growth in Community Colleges
  Losses in State Funding for Public Colleges, Increasing Tuition
  Resegregation in Public Schools
  College Admissions

 Understanding the Education System

  Functionalist Perspective
  Conflict Perspective
  Rational/Social Exchange Perspective
  Constructionist Perspective

 Relationship of the Education System to the Political Economy

 The Impact of the Education System on Individuals and Families

  How the Education System Deters Well-Being
  How the Education System Promotes Well-Being

Criminal Justice

 Issues and Trends in the Criminal Justice System

  Crime Rates and Violence
  The Incarceration Boom
  Privatization
  The Death Penalty

 Understanding the Criminal Justice System

  Functionalist Perspective
  Conflict Perspective
  Rational/Social Exchange Perspective
  Constructionist Perspective

 Relationship of the Criminal Justice System to the Political Economy

 The Impact of the Criminal Justice System on Individuals and Families

  How the Criminal Justice System Deters Well-Being
  How the Criminal Justice System Promotes Well-Being

The Military

 Issues and Trends in the Military

  Women in the Military
  Gays in the Military
  Subcontracting and Outsourcing

 Understanding the Military

  Functionalist Perspective
  Conflict Perspective
  Rational/Social Exchange Perspective
  Constructionist Perspective

 Relationship of the Military to the Political Economy

 The Impact of the Military on Individuals and Families

  How the Military Deters Well-Being
  How the Military Promotes Well-Being

Looking Ahead

In this chapter, we present three social institutions that are, for the most part, government supported. These social institutions, education, criminal justice, and the military, are particularly important in the lives of many social work clients. We discuss the relationship of each of these social institutions to the political economy and their impact on individuals and families. Because most social work students take entire courses on social welfare, we will not cover this particular social institution.

Education

The function of education is to pass along a society's formal knowledge and skills in a systematic way, with emphasis on learning that will contribute to students' futures as workers and as citizens.

Typically this involves formal instruction by credentialed teachers, within special organizations (schools) designed for the purpose.

Issues and Trends in Education

Special Programs and Schools.   Of particular interest to social workers are those schools and programs that were developed to address perceived deficiencies in the system. These include Head Start, charter schools, magnet schools, and voucher plans.

Numerous studies document the effectiveness of early educational intervention for young children. In the middle 1960s, the federal government began funding *Head Start,* a remedial program for disadvantaged preschoolers designed to give them the skills they need to be ready for kindergarten and first grade. According to the U.S. Department of Health and Human Services, Head Start is based on a "whole child" model; in addition to education, the program provides medical, dental, and nutritional services, and parental guidance. Head Start services are "designed to be responsive to each child's and family's ethnic, cultural, and linguistic heritage" (U.S. Department of Health and Human Services, 2005, p. iii). Whereas initial evaluations seemed to indicate that benefits were short-lived, long-term studies demonstrate better reading scores, a higher rate of high school completion, more college admissions, and higher rates of employment (Barnett, 1995; Svestka, 1996).

Charter schools are supported by public funds but operate more like private schools because they do not answer to a local school board. In 2004, there were about 3,000 charter schools in the United States, serving 761,000 students (Kantrowitz, 2004). *Magnet schools* are public schools that offer special facilities and curricula, focusing on areas such as science or the arts. They were developed in urban areas to hold onto middle-class students who might have otherwise chosen to attend a private school. There are currently 3,000 magnet schools in the country (Macionis, 2007).

Similar to trends in health care provision is an emerging trend in education, the development of Education Management Organizations (EMOs). There are about 40 of these in the United States; the three largest ones are Whittle communications' Edison Project (which operated 133 schools in 2004), Sabis International Education Alternatives Incorporated, and Alternative Public Schools. There are about 300 EMO-operated schools across the country, serving 175,000 students (Gluckman, 2003). The development of EMOs may reflect a desire of local governments to "outsource" education and change its role from "owner-operator" to "general contractor." Given that the education market is larger than defense or auto manufacturing, this is a lucrative area for the development of for-profit companies. Critics are concerned with the privatization of education, which may undermine public school systems (Gluckman, 2003; Kendall, 2008).

About 5 million of the 53 million children enrolled in kindergarten through twelfth grade in the United States attend private schools (Joyce, 2008). More than 4 million (82 percent) of these attend schools with a religious orientation, and more than half of these schools are operated by the Roman Catholic Church (Joyce, 2008). The proportion of children attending private schools in the United States has ranged between 10 and 14 percent since 1930. Under *voucher plans* (also called *school choice*) parents can send their children to a private school and the government pays part or all of their tuition. The idea is to make public schools improve in order to compete for students. Opponents worry that private schools are not accountable to public scrutiny, and that these plans violate the principle of separation of church and state by providing tax-based funding to religious schools. They argue that these plans take much needed monies away from already underfunded public schools, and they encourage racial and ethnic segregation. A quarter of all private schools have minority enrollments under 9 percent (Wright, 2007).

An increasing number of families in the United States are choosing to *homeschool* their children. In the early years of the movement, parents reported religious motives for keeping their children at home. In a 2003 national survey, 85.4 percent of homeschooling parents expressed concerns about the public school environment, including safety, drugs, and peer pressure; 72.3 percent expressed a desire to provide religious or moral instruction; and an additional 68.2 percent expressed dissatisfaction with academic instruction in schools (U.S. Department of Education Survey cited in Joyce, 2008, p. 399). Most homeschooled children are involved in various extracurricular activities with same-age peers, including field trips sponsored by home-schooling organizations, sports, Scouting, 4-H, and church activities.

The *World Almanac* (Joyce, 2008) provides the following information about home schooling. In 2003, 77 percent of homeschooled children were white. Home schooling is spread evenly across economic levels. Almost a quarter of homeschooling parents have not completed education beyond high school; 30 percent have some college and another 25 percent hold bachelor's degrees.

Violence, Corporal Punishment, and Sexual Harassment.   Another contemporary concern in education is the physical safety of students, teachers, and staff. Given the recent history of high-profile school shootings in this country, neither children nor parents believe that schools are safe places. Many school districts have adopted "zero tolerance" policies that require suspension or expulsion for serious misbehavior; such policies are sometimes misapplied to innocent behaviors, such as when a child brings a butter knife from home to cut a piece of fruit packed in her lunchbox. Other schools have resorted to using uniformed guards and metal detectors to prevent possible violence.

On the other hand, statistics show that the level of violence in elementary and high schools is actually holding steady or declining (Henslin, 2008; Macionis, 2007). Most incidents of college campus homicides were the result of interpersonal disputes or drug deals rather than random violence (Fox, J.A., 2008). A student's chance of being victimized is smaller on campus than in any average metropolitan area (Fox, J.A. 2008).

Twenty-one states in America allow corporal punishment in public schools; students can be spanked or paddled for a wide variety of infractions, including chewing gum, being late, talking back to a teacher, sleeping in class, violating the school dress code, or going to the bathroom without permission. According to a 2008 joint report by the Human Rights Watch and the ACLU, 223,190 students in American schools were reported to have received corporal punishment at least once in the 2006–2007 school year; the organizations assume that the real numbers were much higher. In Texas alone, 49,197 students received physical punishment. In Mississippi, 7.5 percent of school children were paddled during this time period, the highest percentage in the nation. Typically, states leave policy decisions on corporal punishment to individual districts; some of the nation's largest school districts have banned the practice.

Psychologists and other experts in child development say that physical punishment is ineffective in shaping behavior, and educational experts argue that such treatment of children by trusted authority figures creates an environment of fear that negatively impacts learning.

Eight in ten students experience some kind of sexual harassment in their schools—incidents include someone spreading sexual rumors about them (75 percent), pulling off or down their clothing

(74 percent), saying they were gay or lesbian (73 percent), or spying on them as they dressed or showered (69 percent) (Axelrod & Markow, 2001).

Growth in Community Colleges.   Since the 1960s, community colleges have provided access to higher education for many students. According to the National Center for Education Statistics (2008), the country's 1,844 two-year colleges enroll 39 percent of all undergraduate college students. Advantages of community colleges include low cost, easier access for minority students, and a focus on teaching rather than research (Macionis, 2007; National Center for Education Statistics, 2007). Average annual community college tuition and fees are less than half of those at public four-year colleges and universities and they have larger percentages of nontraditional, low-income, and minority students (National Center for Education Statistics, 2008).

Losses in State Funding for Public Colleges, Increasing Tuition.   As public colleges and universities lose state funding, they have come to rely more and more heavily on income from increased tuition and fees, research grants, lottery funds, and philanthropists, and cut costs by reducing services, cutting back on scholarships and assistantships, increasing class size, hiring more part-time faculty, and using technology to reach a larger market through distance education and Web-based courses (Brinson, 2003; Burbules, 2000). The costs of attending an institution of higher education have increased faster than the rate of inflation, family income, and student aid funds (Tomsho, 2006). In-state tuition rates at four-year public institutions averaged $2,848 in 1995/1996 (up roughly $1,500 from 1985/1986); in 2005/2006, the cost rose to $5,351 (more than 46 percent in ten years) (National Center for Education Statistics, 2007). Investment of state funds in higher education is at a 25-year low; it fell from about $7,100 per student in 2001 to just over $5,800 per student in 2005 (Kirwan, 2006). Also during the past two decades, there has been a significant shift in the allocation of university-based aid away from students with demonstrated financial need and toward high-ability students who often come from upper-middle-class families (Kirwan, 2006). Many low-income students depend on Pell Grants to finance their college educations. Federal tax credit programs (529 plans) are more likely to help middle- or high-income students than those in the lowest income group (Guerard, 2002; Quinn, 2003). Not surprisingly, fewer children from low-income families can afford to go to college now and if they attend, they must work many hours which jeopardizes their grades and graduation rates.

Resegregation in Public Schools.   Public schools are increasingly filled with students of the same racial and economic background (Cose, 2004; Phillips, 2007). According to a recent report from the Civil Rights Project at the University of California at Los Angeles (Orfield, 2009), the most serious segregation affects Latinos and African Americans; in these groups almost two out of five children attend an "intensely segregated" school (90 to 100 percent minority). White students are more likely to be in schools that are middle class, whereas 40 percent of black and Latino students attend schools where 70 to 100 percent of the children are poor (Orfield, 2009).

According to the UCLA study (Orfield, 2009), patterns vary by locale. In metropolitan areas, with few exceptions, public schools are made up of nonwhite and poor student bodies. Of the nearly 6 million black and Latino suburban students, almost 2 million are in heavily segregated schools; this suggests that in some suburban areas, there is substantial resegregation. The term *de facto segregation* can be used to describe the pattern of racial segregation in schools that results from segregated housing. On the other hand, the typical white child enrolled in a public school today finds himself or herself in a more diverse classroom environment than white children a generation ago. Both the increased exposure to diversity for white children and the growth in isolation for black and Latino children are due to the decline in the number and proportion of white students and the increase in the number of children of color in public schools systems. According to the author of the study, "the U.S. is experiencing the final years of a majority white public school system" and if current trends continue, "segregation will become even more pronounced for black and Latino students" (Orfield, 2009, p. 27).

College Admissions.   Affirmative action policies allow colleges to consider a student's race in making admission decisions. Proponents argue that diversity in a student body is an essential ingredient in a well-rounded education (Bollinger, 2003). They also note that whites have long enjoyed *legacy privilege*—a practice that gives special consideration to the relatives and friends of the rich, powerful, and well-connected. Kinsley (2003) points out, for example, that Harvard accepts 40 percent of applicants who are children of alumni but only 11 percent of applicants generally—a practice that not only confers unfair advantages but makes the student body less diverse.

Opponents of affirmative action say that not only is it a form of "reverse discrimination," but that it benefits primarily middle- and upper-class blacks while reinforcing the idea that minorities are perpetual victims. An alternative that is being tried in some states is called *affirmative access*. Under these plans, public universities admit the top graduates from state high schools, so that students from predominantly minority schools have an equal chance of being accepted (Fineman & Lipper, 2003). Critics say that such programs may result in a larger number of less-qualified students being admitted.

Understanding the Education System

Functionalist Perspective.   In addition to the function of transmitting knowledge and teaching skills, structural functionalists suggest that the education system sorts children and youth and then trains them to fill positions at different levels in society. These theorists believe that schools fill a gate-keeping function by identifying the most qualified individuals, selecting them for advanced education, and channeling them toward leadership positions.

The education system also socializes the young, instilling values of respect, obedience, punctuality, and perseverance. Particularly in the case of mandatory and free public schooling, it serves the purpose of acculturation for the young children of recent immigrants. This is especially important in a country with as much diversity as the United States.

Social institutions have both manifest and latent functions (Henslin, 2008; Macionis, 2007). *Manifest functions* are those that are intended and obvious. *Latent functions* are unintended side effects, and those functions that are often hidden, or at least not acknowledged by participants. Some of these may be positive and some may be negative. Besides the obvious manifest functions of education, this social institution also has latent functions. These include providing free child care and supervision for a significant part of the day—which is particularly helpful for parents who are employed outside the home. Another latent function is keeping adolescents out of the labor market where they might compete for jobs with unskilled adults.

Conflict Perspective.   Social conflict theorists argue that school systems in the United States perpetuate class inequality. This is achieved by *tracking,* or ability grouping, based on standardized tests that magnify small differences (Tobias, 1989). Poor and minority students are assigned to remedial and vocational skills classes where they receive a diluted academic program making it unlikely that they will ever catch up to their white, middle-class peers (Kozol, 2005; Oakes, 1985; Tobias, 1989).

The financial costs of higher education prevent many people with below average incomes from enrolling. When only the affluent can afford to attend prestigious colleges or restrictive programs, social and economic privilege is reinterpreted as personal merit (Macionis, 2007). Our society reserves the most desirable occupational opportunities for those who have four-year or graduate degrees, even if educational attainment is unrelated to the demands and responsibilities of a particular job. In this way, *credentialism* (evaluating a person on the basis of his or her educational background) is used as a strategy to restrict certain careers to a small (and privileged) segment of the population (Collins, 1979).

Gillborn (1992) used the term *hidden curriculum* to describe how schools teach obedience to authority and conformity to cultural norms in addition to the academic curriculum. Learning the student role prepares children for the routines of the work world. Conflict theorists note that middle- and upper-class youth are more likely to be encouraged to think critically and creatively, thus preparing them for leadership roles, while the behaviors of lower-class children are shaped to accommodate the demands of the assembly line and the clerical pool.

Rational/Social Exchange Perspective.   Although some property owners complain that they have to pay high taxes even when they have no children in the public school system, most taxpayers understand the need for educated citizens and workers. (One of the authors has a T-shirt with this slogan on the front: IF YOU THINK EDUCATION IS EXPENSIVE, TRY IGNORANCE.) As a technologically advanced society, the United States relies on a literate worker force and must provide at least a basic education to all members of society to prepare them for their roles as citizens.

Constructionist Perspective.   Social constructionists remind us of the importance of perceptions. Jonathan Kozol, who conducted a study that highlighted the alarming differences in funding levels between affluent suburban schools and inner-city schools, noted the effects of perceptions that "the poorest districts are beyond help" and that resources would thus be "wasted on poor children" (Kozol, 1991, p. 99). He concluded that these "children hear and understand [that] they are poor investments—and behave accordingly. . . . Expectations are a powerful force."

The application of the social constructionist perspective to the education system has focused for the most part on *labeling theory* and *self-fulfilling prophecy* (Merton, 1949). Basically, this suggests two parallel processes. The first affects the students individually. Once labeled "slow" or "a behavior problem," students will come to accept the label and act accordingly. Even when non-pejorative labels are used (e.g., "sharks" or "goldfish"), children know to which level they have been assigned (Tobias, 1989). The second process affects the teachers. Once they believe that a child is "bright" or "struggling," they will respond to the child according to their expectations of how that child will perform—challenging the bright ones and "dumbing down" lessons for the less able children, thus unintentionally creating the results that were predicted. The effects of the labeling process were confirmed in a classic study conducted in the 1960s (Rosenthal & Jacobson, 1968), when elementary teachers were told that certain randomly selected students were "spurters" or "nonspurters," and those in the "spurter" groups subsequently made greater gains.

In another classic study, Ray Rist (1970) observed that after only eight days of class, a kindergarten teacher divided her students into three groups. The "slow learners" were put at a table in the back of the room and the "fast learners" sat at a table next to the teacher's desk. As the year progressed, the fast learners came to think of themselves as smart and the teacher treated them as such. The children in the back of the classroom received little attention. Rist himself concluded that the divisions were based on social class, as there had not been any testing done early in the semester. The same classroom divisions were retained in the first and second grades, thus consigning many students to a long-term negative educational experience based on one teacher's uninformed assessment less than two weeks into their school careers.

Relationship of the Education System to the Political Economy

The education system in the United States reflects the political economy in several ways. Schools foster patriotism by teaching lessons in history, civics, and other social studies. Further, the values of individualism and competition assumed to be crucial to a capitalist economy are promoted in the schools.

Schools also provide captive audiences for advertisers. By accepting corporate donations or sponsorships, brand loyalty is introduced and consumerism is reinforced. Market-driven educational materials are integrated into the school day. For example, Exxon has produced a documentary on the beauty of the Alaskan coastline, McDonald's has created a nutrition chart, and kindergartners are taught to read through a program that uses corporate logos (Kilbourne, 1999, p. 46). While *Channel One* is offered free to school systems as a teaching tool for current events, the reality is that it serves as an unfettered conduit for corporations seeking to reach the youth market (Croteau & Hoynes, 2003). A recent research study (Austin, Chen, Pinkleton, & Johnson, 2006) found that students who watched Channel One were more likely to remember the ads than the news content. Teachers can preview programs and opt not to show them, but they are allowed to reject only 10 percent of the total (Linn, 2005).

Some leading academics (see Bok, 2003 and Gould, 2003) are concerned about the increasing commercialization of institutions of higher education. With rising enrollments exceeding revenues, many schools are becoming more entrepreneurial (Raines & Leathers, 2003). Changes in their missions reflect an increasing emphasis on research, particularly in areas expected to produce commercially profitable intellectual property, and less on educating the future citizens of their state (Zemsky, Wegner, & Massy, 2005). "Hustling for dollars" has become a major focus, with practices ranging from promotion of corporate-academic partnerships, to selling naming rights to buildings or even restricting sales of soft drinks to a single brand (Brinson, 2003). Universities are put in the position of marketing themselves in competition against each other, for students as well as for cash (Brewer, Gates, & Goldman, 2002). For example, in order to make profits from their sports programs, universities reschedule major conference games to meet the broadcast demands of television sports executives, even though fans are inconvenienced, student athletes have to miss classes, and midterm exams are disrupted (Morris, 2003). To attract new students, university campuses have added or updated amenities such as elaborate exercise facilities, high-end coffee shops, wireless Internet computer access, and online courses. A prime example of the entrepreneurial spirit in higher education is the appeal of the University of Phoenix, which offers online degrees in business, criminal justice, education, human services, nursing, psychology, and technology. Profits in distance learning are huge because distance learning requires no classrooms or parking lots; the same courses can be updated/repackaged and sold over and over again (Henslin, 2008).

The Impact of the Education System on Individuals and Families

How the Education System Deters Well-Being. The No Child Left Behind Act was signed into law by President George W. Bush in 2002 and reauthorized in 2007. As of 2005/2006, all public schools must measure students' achievement in reading and math every year for grades 3 through 8 and once in high school (Wallis & Steptoe, 2007). Despite very low levels of federal support—about nine cents out of every dollar—the federal government has set standards for teacher qualifications and how to measuring school success. Although the goal of improvement in public schools was admirable, necessary resources were not included (Dolgoff & Feldstein, 2007; Jennings & Rentner, 2006) Unintended consequences have included "teaching to the test" and reduced class time spent on other subjects, such as science and social studies (Willis & Steptoe, 2007).

Data from a 2005 study indicated that many students were still "left behind." "The knowledge and skills of students of color and those from low-income families are not just low compared with white and more affluent students; they are also low in absolute terms, shutting these students out from meaningful civic engagement and economic opportunity" (Wiener, 2006, p. A13.) Fourth graders cannot distinguish even and odd numbers and eighth grade students cannot convert written numbers into decimals (Wiener, 2006). Even though it is true that low-income districts spend more per pupil than do rich ones, greater resources are needed to address the deficits facing poor children. Schools in low-income neighborhoods have worse facilities and less-experienced teachers. "We reward teachers with higher status and higher pay the farther away they get from the students who need the most help" (Wiener, 2006, p. A13).

Because public schools are largely supported by local property taxes, schools in wealthier communities or neighborhoods have more resources, while schools in poorer communities or neighborhoods have fewer resources. The result is great discrepancies in the quality of education provided to children living in different communities.

As discussed under the Conflict Perspective section, tracking is usually based on the results of standardized tests. Such tests measure not only intelligence and aptitude but also culturally acquired knowledge. Because IQ tests reflect the dominant culture, members of minority cultures will remain at a disadvantage (Macionis, 2007). African American children are overrepresented in special education classes.

On the other hand, when students with emotional or learning problems do not receive the special education services they need, they may act out in frustration and get kicked out—not just out of class, but out of school. On a national level, African American students are suspended or expelled nearly three times as often as white students; in New Jersey, the rate is almost 60 times higher ("New Project," 2007). Rather than receiving the help they need in school, these vulnerable youth are transferred to the juvenile justice system where they are put at increased risk of ending up in adult prisons.

According to one study (Delpit, 1995), rather than embracing diversity in the classroom, many white teachers, out of misdirected goodwill, make a conscious effort to be "color blind." The teachers' failure to acknowledge and celebrate the different heritages and cultures of their minority students makes the students feel invisible. Insensitivity to cultural differences in learning and communication styles hinders minority children, leading to low self-esteem and negative school experiences. For example, Heath (1982) observed that African American children seemed unresponsive to teachers' questions. She discovered that the students thought that questions such as "What is this?" or "What do you call that?" were silly because obviously the teacher already knew the answer. The children came from communities where people asked open-ended questions about whole events: "What did you do today?" or "What did you like best about your field trip?" In their homes, caregivers accepted many different answers, and the answers almost always involved telling a story, describing a situation, or making a comparison.

Children from cultural backgrounds with collectivist rather than individualist traditions may go out of their way to help each other; some teachers perceive this as cheating or not "doing their own work" (Gallimore, Boggs, & Jordan, 1974). Because of their strong cultural value of humility, Asian American children may hesitate to ask questions of the teacher or to take credit for, or show pride in, their work. Teachers need to take this into account when evaluating the classroom interaction of these students.

Children and families with limited English face extra challenges in dealing with school systems. Obstacles include the lack of bilingual teachers, the inability to communicate with school personnel, and the inability to understand school correspondence sent to the child's home (Dale, Andreatta, & Freeman, 2001). According to Fry (2007), almost half (46 percent) of fourth-grade students in the English language learner (ELL) category scored "below basic" in math and nearly three-quarters scored "below basic" in reading. In middle school, two-thirds (71 percent) of eighth-grade ELL students scored "below basic" in math and the same number scored "below basic" in reading. Some migrant worker parents report being intimidated by the educational system even when language assistance is available. The overall result of such factors is that Latino children have a higher drop-out rate than other racial and ethnic groups (Feagin & Feagin, 1999). Not quite 75 percent of all high school freshmen receive a diploma four years later. Graduation rates vary dramatically by state. According to data from the National Center for Education Statistics (Seastrom, Chapman, & Stillwell, 2006) for the class of 2003–2004, the average freshman graduation rate (AFGR) ranged from 57.4 percent in Nevada to 87.6 percent in Nebraska. Fifteen states had rates of 80.0 percent or higher—Connecticut, Idaho, Illinois, Iowa, Minnesota, Missouri, Montana, Nebraska, New Jersey, North Dakota, Ohio, Pennsylvania, South Dakota, Utah, and Vermont. Eleven states and the District of Columbia had rates below 70.0 percent—Alabama, Alaska, Arizona, Florida, Georgia, Louisiana, Mississippi, New Mexico, Nevada, South Carolina, and Tennessee.

Another way to measure drop-out rates is to examine the number of 16- to 24-year-olds who are not in school and have not earned a high school diploma or GED. According to the National Center for Education Statistics (2007), data for 2005 indicate that 9.5 percent of the 36.8 million young people in this age-group fell into this category. This represents a decline from 14.6 percent in 1972, although there has been no significant improvement between 1990 and 2005. Males in this age-group are more likely than females to be high school dropouts (10.8 percent versus 8.0 percent). At 2.9 percent, Asians/Pacific Islanders had the lowest drop-out rate. This was followed by whites at 6.0 percent, and blacks at 10.4 percent. Hispanics had the highest drop-out rate at 22.4 percent. (Data for Native Americans were not included in the report.)

Drop-out rates are also related to socioeconomic status. The drop-out rate (10 percent) for students in the lowest income quintile [fifth] of the population is six times greater than the drop-out rate (1.6 percent) for students in the highest quintile (National Center for Education Statistics, 2007). In other words, students who drop out are more likely to come from families where parents also are likely to have had little schooling. This pattern perpetuates intergenerational cycles of disadvantage. Data show that there has been little change in drop-out rates by income level since 1990.

Drop-out rates also vary along urban–suburban dimensions. Only about half (52 percent) of students in the country's 50 largest cities complete high school; in the most extreme cases (Baltimore, Cleveland, Detroit, and Indianapolis), fewer than 35 percent of students graduate with a diploma (Swanson, 2008).

How the Education System Promotes Well-Being. This country has led the world in the proportion of young people completing different levels of mass education, first for elementary and high schools, later for colleges and graduate schools (Lipset, 1996, p. 21). In 1940, only 24.5 percent of the U.S. population had completed high school; in 2006, that figure had increased to 85.5 percent (Wright, 2007). In 1940, fewer than one in 20 Americans had completed four or more years of college; in 2006, it was more than one in four (Wright, 2007).

Within the past generation, federal laws have enhanced the opportunities for children with disabilities and for female athletes in school settings. The Equal Education for All Handicapped Children Act (PL 94-142) was passed in 1975. Renamed the Individuals with Disabilities Education Act (IDEA) in 1990, it mandates that students with disabilities receive a free and appropriate education. Many schools have *mainstreamed* children with disabilities so that they can attend classes with their nondisabled peers, as well as have access to special education teachers and classrooms, speech therapists, occupational therapists, and physical therapists. Historically, most women had little opportunity for involvement in high school and college sports. Title IX of the Educational Amendments of 1972 prohibited sex discrimination in educational institutions receiving federal funds. This law has led to more funding for women's athletics.

Schools also go beyond instruction to meet some of the more basic daily needs of poor children. They provide screening for visual and hearing problems, some provide dental and mental health services, and most have school nurses. In 2008, more than 30 million children participated in the national school lunch program (U.S. Department of Agriculture, 2008). The program was established under the National School Lunch Act, signed by President Harry Truman in 1946. Under the Seamless Summer Option, schools can continue to feed children from low-income areas during traditional summer vacation periods.

The No Child Left Behind Act has directed greater attention to low-achieving students and increased efforts to improve low-performing schools. In addition to these general benefits, the Act has also led educators to rely more on research to make informed decisions and a small but significant number of eligible students have moved from schools not making "adequate yearly progress" to better performing schools while other students have been able to take advantage of tutoring services that the Act calls for (Jennings & Rentner, 2006).

Criminal Justice

The social institution of criminal justice is America's formal system of social control. It includes a loose confederation of more than 55,000 agencies at the local, state, and federal levels that often operate independently of each other (Kendall, 2005). The *criminal justice system* represents the parts of government that have the political mandate to protect members of society, but abuses of power can also unfairly strip citizens of their freedoms. The system includes a variety of law enforcement organizations (e.g., local police, county sheriffs, federal marshals, Alcohol, Tobacco, and Firearms [ATF] agents, Immigration and Customs Enforcement [ICE] agents, and the courts) and facilities for the incarceration of offenders (e.g., detention centers, reform schools, jails, and prisons).

There are many outspoken critics of the American criminal justice system. Currie (1998, p. 8) for example, states,

If we look squarely at the present state of crime and punishment in America . . . it is difficult to avoid the recognition that something is terribly wrong; that a society that incarcerates such a vast and rapidly growing part of its population—but still suffers the worst violent crime in the industrial world—is a society in trouble, one that, in a profound sense, has lost its bearings.

Issues and Trends in the Criminal Justice System

Crime Rates and Violence. There are three major sources of crime statistics in the United States (the FBI's Uniform Crime Reports, the National Incident-Based Reporting System [NIBRS], and the National Crime Victimization Survey), and each uses a different method of collecting and reporting data. Based on these reports, it appears that crime rates have declined in this country since the early 1990s.

Crime rates are affected by a number of factors, including how crimes are reported and tracked, or whether they are reported at all. For example, since 1975 the number of reported rapes increased by 70 percent (Wright, 2007). A significant part of this increase may have been due to increased levels of awareness and reporting. Changing population demographics, especially the proportion of people between the ages of 18 and 24, may account for some changes in crime rates (Cole & Smith, 2007). Adults over the age of 45 make up a third of the population but account for only 7 percent of arrests for serious crime (Siegel, 2010). Criminologists attribute lower rates of crime (especially robbery, burglary, and auto theft) in the 1990s to a strong economy and job market. The economic woes that began with the financial crisis of 2008 may well lead to an increase in such crimes.

According to Bureau of Justice statistics summarized by Wright (2007, p. 316), victims of most crimes are poor, urban, young people of color. Except for rape and domestic violence, most victims are male. Youths are almost twenty times as likely to be the victims of violent crime as are people over the age of 65. Poor people (i.e., those with household incomes of less than $7,500) are the most likely to be victimized by crime, especially violent crime (Reiman, 2007).

The number of violent crimes in the United States peaked at 1.93 million in 1992 and steadily declined over the next ten years (Wright, 2007). While other crimes continue to decline, the number of violent crimes has been increasing since 2004.

The violent crime rate in the United States is several times higher than countries in Europe and even worse when compared to Asian countries, where rates of violent crime are among the lowest in the world (Macionis, 2007). In 2004, firearms were used to murder 184 people in Canada, 56 people in Australia, 73 people in England and Wales, 5 people in New Zealand, and 11,344 in the United States. (*Brady Campaign Fact Sheets,* n.d.) (see Figure 3.1). A major contributing factor is the extensive private ownership of guns in the United States. According to an article in the *New York Times* (Zernike, 2006), a recent alarming trend in violent crime is the increase in the number of firearm homicides that are apparently the result of minor disputes—or "stupid arguments over stupid things," as the police commissioner of Philadelphia calls them. Suspects tell police they killed someone who "disrespected" them or a family member or gave them a dirty look. Disagreements that in the past would have led to fist fights or perhaps knives, now lead straight to gunfire.

Of particular concern to social workers is the problem of *hate crimes,* a criminal act that is motivated by bias against someone's national origin, race, ethnicity, religion, sexual orientation, or disability (Andersen & Taylor, 2007; Henslin, 2008). Hate crimes were recognized by state governments during the 1980s; by 2005, 46 states and the federal government had enacted hate crimes legislation (Cole & Smith, 2007). The FBI records more than 7,000 hate crime incidents per year (Siegel, 2010) (see Table 3.1). Offenders convicted of hate crimes receive more severe sentences than those who commit the same act but without hatred as the motive. Victims may

FIGURE 3.1   *Gun Violence in the United States*

❏ Currently, an estimated 39 percent of U.S. households have a gun and 24 percent have a handgun.
❏ There are approximately 192 million privately owned firearms in the United States, 65 million of which are handguns.
❏ For every time a gun is used in a home in a legally justified shooting, there are 22 criminal, unintentional, and suicide-related shootings.
❏ In 2004, almost eight young people, aged 19 or younger, were killed every day in gun homicides, suicides, and unintentional shootings.
❏ 75 percent of inner-city seven-year-olds reported having heard gunshots.
❏ The presence of a gun in a home makes it six times more likely that an abused woman will be murdered.
❏ In 2004, firearm homicide was the leading cause of death for black males ages 15 to 34.
❏ Gun violence costs the United States over $100 billion annually.
❏ At least 80% of the economic costs of treating firearm injuries are paid for by taxpayers.

Source: The Brady Campaign to Prevent Gun Violence, 2008.

include businesses, organizations, or institutions, as well as individuals. African Americans, Jews, and gay men are disproportionately the victims of hate crimes. After the terrorist attacks of September 11, 2001, many individuals of Middle Eastern heritage were unfairly targeted because of growing distrust of Muslims and Arabs.

The Incarceration Boom.   In a shift from earlier approaches that emphasized rehabilitation and deterrence, a new philosophy of criminal justice focusing on incarceration of large numbers of criminal offenders, including drug users and pushers, appeared at the end of the twentieth century. Rather than being a response to an increase in crime or a surge in the population, the increased rate of incarceration reflects policy choices.

TABLE 3.1   *Incidents of Hate Crimes in the United States in 2006*

Bias category	*Number of incidents reported*
Race	4,000
Religion	1,462
Sexual orientation	1,195
Ethnicity/national origin	984
Disability	79
Total	7,722

Most common victims	*Number of incidents reported*
Blacks	2,640
Jews	967
Gay men	747
Latinos	576

Source: Adapted from U.S. Department of Justice-Federal Bureau of Investigation (November 2007).

The adult prison incarceration rate was stable from the 1930s until the mid-1970s; between 1980 and 1994, the prison incarceration rate rose by more than 150 percent (Bohm & Haley, 1997, p. 325). This occurred during a period when crime rates were stable or declining, and when the proportion of young adults in the population (those most likely to commit crimes) was also steady or declining. The American penal system held 2,319,258 adults at the start of 2008, reflecting an incarceration rate of more than one in 100, the highest level in the world (Pew Center on the States, 2008). On the other hand, according to Bureau of Justice statistics (Sabol, 2007), the 2006 growth rate was less than the annual growth rate that occurred during the 1990s, suggesting a gradual leveling off.

The Violent Crime Control and Law Enforcement Act passed by Congress in 1994 introduced *three-strikes penalties* for repeat offenders. Many states had "habitual offender laws" on the books before the three-strikes terminology became popular. These laws, including the three-strikes versions, required enhanced prison terms for repeat felony offenders (Secrest, 1999). The strongest criticism of three-strikes laws is that they are not targeting serious offenders. In California, 8.5 percent of the prison population (or more than 13,000 people) are serving prison sentences for simple possession of drugs (Moore, 2004). A man who stole nine videotapes from a K-Mart store was sentenced to 50 years in prison without parole (Greenhouse, cited in Henslin, 2008) and a 27-year-old man was sentenced to 25 years in prison for stealing a pizza (Cloud, cited in Henslin, 2008).

During the last two decades of the last century, drug offenders were the fastest growing segment of the prison population. According to the Office of National Drug Control Policy (1998), three-quarters of the growth in the federal prison population during that time period can be accounted for by the incarceration of drug offenders, and the number of inmates in state prisons for drug-law violations increased by more than 400 percent over the same period. In 1984, Congress passed a law that allowed local law enforcement not only to confiscate but to keep most of the assets that were seized in drug raids. This gave police agencies a financial stake in the war on drugs and contributed to increased drug arrests.

When Congress passed the Anti-Drug Abuse Act of 1986, harsh sentences were mandated. These guidelines differentiated between crack (which is used by poor and minority people) and powdered cocaine (which is used predominantly by middle class and wealthy people). A subject caught with 50 grams of crack faced the same penalty as one with 5000 grams of powder (Rawe, 2007). In two Supreme Court decisions handed down in late 2007, federal judges were empowered to reject these unfair sentencing guidelines. The U.S. Sentencing Commission voted on December 11, 2007, to allow some 19,500 federal prison inmates to seek reductions in their crack-cocaine sentences (Hajela, 2007).

According to a 2008 report by the Pew Center on the States, some states are trying new approaches to reduce the growth of the prison population. Among these efforts are reducing first-time prison admissions through *diversion programs* that steer selected low-risk offenders to community corrections programs or a continuum of treatment services, reducing recidivism by using short-term residential facilities for persistent parole and probation violators, and reducing the risk of reentry by offering specially designed treatment and education programs to inmates.

Privatization. Another trend in the criminal justice system is the construction and operation of prisons by private companies. The private sector has a long tradition of contracting to provide services to inmates, such as provision of meals, medical or psychiatric care, and education; the private sector also has operated detention facilities for juveniles for many years (Bohm & Haley, 1997). In response to the incarceration boom noted above, many states asked private organizations to build and operate new prisons. It appears that not only can private firms open new facilities more quickly than government agencies, but they claim they can save up to 20 percent in construction costs and 5 to 15 percent in operating costs, at least for minimum security facilities (National Center for Policy Analysis, 1995; Reiman, 2007).

In the ten years between 1985 and 1995, the number of prisoners housed in private facilities increased from 935 to 63,595, an increase of almost 7,000 percent (Reiman, 2007). As of 2004, 98,901 inmates were housed in private prisons (Reiman, 2007).

The Corrections Corporation of America (CCA), a private company founded in 1983, dominates the private prison business. According to the third-quarter 2008 financial report found on their Web site (Correctionscorp.com, 2008), CCA is the nation's largest owner and operator of privatized correctional and detention facilities and one of the largest prison operators in the United States, behind only the federal government and three states. The CCA operates 64 facilities, including 42 company-owned facilities, with a total design capacity of approximately 82,000 beds in 19 states and the District of Columbia. It also provides transportation, health care (including medical, dental, and psychiatric services), food services, and work and recreational programs. It has more than 17,000 employees.

Criminal justice and policy analysts disagree about whether privatization has been a success (Shichor, 1999; Territo, Halsted, & Bromley, 2004; Torres, 1999). Those who argue against it worry that companies in the "prison business" are interested in keeping their facilities full, and use their lobbyists to encourage legislation that will result in even higher levels of incarceration (Shichor, 1999). Groups such as the American Civil Liberties Union have criticized conditions in private prisons and the lack of public oversight. Academics who study and teach about the criminal justice system argue that

> [T]here is no evidence that private corrections can solve a correctional institution's fiscal or managerial problems, and this is reason enough not to jump "governmental ship." But it's not the only reason. When people say that they support the privatization of jails, they also say and/or acknowledge a great deal more. They affirm that one of the most important jobs in this country—restricting the freedoms of American citizens—should be taken away from the government and placed in the hands of a corporation whose sole purpose is to generate profits for shareholders. They affirm that profit is an acceptable motive for incarceration and often accept that more inmates equals more profits. They agree that private, for-profit, and often publicly held corporations should be granted the authority to use force, including deadly force. (Territo, Halsted, & Bromley, 2004, p. 509)

The Death Penalty.   The U.S. Supreme Court reinstated the death penalty in 1976, making the United States the only Western industrialized nation that still allows capital punishment. (Fifteen states and the District of Columbia do not have capital punishment statutes [Death Penalty Information Center, 2009]). Between 1977 and 2005, 1,007 individuals were put to death by the criminal justice system in the United States; of these, 651 (62.4 percent) were white, 341 (32.7 percent) were African American, and 15 (1.4 percent) were "other" (Wright, 2007).

Amnesty International (www.amnesty.org, 2008) has been monitoring developments around the use of the death penalty and campaigning for its abolition for more than three decades. In 1977, only 16 countries had abolished the death penalty for all crimes. As of October 2008, more than two-thirds of the countries in the world have abolished the death penalty in law or in practice. Eighty-eight percent of all known executions took place in five countries: China, Iran, Pakistan, Saudi Arabia, and the United States.

In 2006, there were 3,228 prisoners on death row in America (Death Penalty Information Center, 2009). Since its modern peak in 1999, the number of executions in the United States actually has declined dramatically; the 37 individuals killed in 2008 reflected the smallest number since 1994, when there were 31 (Death Penalty Information Center, 2009). Public support for the death penalty has fallen from a high of about 80 percent in the 1980s to between 50 and 66 percent, depending on the poll (Drehle, 2008).

In addition to the basic question of whether it is morally acceptable for a government to kill its citizens for any reason, critics of the death penalty argue that it is inherently unfair because poor, uneducated, and minority men are much more likely to suffer this penalty than are more affluent, well-educated, white offenders. One researcher has identified three other factors that contribute to the inequity of capital punishment. According to Haney (2005), the jury selection process screens out opponents of capital punishment; members of juries do not understand the instructions that might lead them to choose an option other than the death penalty; and jurors are overinfluenced by media portrayals of violent criminals, leading them to disregard mitigating factors such as poverty and childhood neglect.

Dozens of scientific studies have demonstrated that the death penalty continues to be administered in a fashion that discriminates against African Americans and killers of whites (Bohm & Haley, 1997). One reason for this is that many poor defendants who end up on death row are assigned inexperienced, unskilled, or unprepared attorneys. In 1987, the U.S. Supreme Court ruled that state death penalty statutes are constitutional even when statistics indicate that they have been applied in racially biased ways (Bohm & Haley, 1997).

The death penalty is also administered unevenly across various regions of the country. Five states (Florida, Missouri, Oklahoma, Texas, and Virginia) accounted for 66 percent of all executions since the death penalty was reinstated in 1976 ("An end to the death penalty," 2009).

The most powerful rationale for discontinuing the death penalty is that there cannot be certainty that judgment is without error (Siegel, 2010). For instance, between 1973 and 2005, 124 prisoners were released from death row in 25 different states because they were either improperly convicted or because documentation of their innocence was presented after sentencing (Wright, 2007).

FIGURE 3.2 *Critical Thinking About the Death Penalty*

Is capital punishment always wrong?

Many people are opposed to capital punishment on moral grounds. Some people think, however, that perpetrators of particularly heinous crimes deserve the death penalty. One example of this is child rape.

Can you frame arguments on both sides of this issue?

You might want to consider the following questions.

- ❏ If you are against capital punishment, should you be consistent and be against it in all cases?
- ❏ Are some criminals beyond rehabilitation?
- ❏ Should some criminals be removed permanently from society?
- ❏ Should we consider the costs of lengthy appeals or lengthy prison sentences?
- ❏ What is the potential effect on crime victims of different kinds of sentencing?

Ask your instructor to tell you about NASW's position on this topic.

Reversing its 1989 ruling, in June 2002 the U.S. Supreme Court held that the Eighth Amendment ban on cruel and unusual punishment does indeed prohibit the execution of a capital offender who is mentally retarded. During the intervening time between rulings, 16 states had enacted laws prohibiting the execution of mentally retarded persons. Many other states are currently developing procedures to implement the court's decision.

On March 1, 2005, the U.S. Supreme Court ruled (5–4) that it is unconstitutional to sentence to death an individual who committed the crime while under the age of 18. This decision was based in part on information provided in a brief submitted by National Association of Social Workers and six other organizations (Stoesen, 2005).

Understanding the Criminal Justice System

Functionalist Perspective.   Functionalism is based on the assumption that members of society subscribe to the same values and presumes that the laws of a society reflect that consensus. Punishing deviance reinforces agreement about societal norms. The sociologist Emile Durkeim (1964/1895) argued that instead of disrupting society, deviance serves to produce social solidarity.

Consistent with a functionalist perspective, one response to deviance is to *rehabilitate* (i.e., "correct") offenders. This approach emphasizes constructive improvement not only through external control (i.e., probation or parole, or incarceration) but also by offering skills training, counseling, and treatment for drug and/or alcohol abuse. The goal is for the offender to conform to societal expectations and become a functioning member of society.

Another option is to remove deviants by deporting, incarcerating, or executing them. Currie (1998, p. 30) reports that incarceration is modestly effective with "high-rate" offenses, such as robbery and burglary. It is much less so for violent crimes, such as homicide, because for some offenses, especially murder, the first serious crime may be the only one the offender commits. Both approaches, rehabilitation and removal, have the ultimate goal of keeping society in balance.

Conflict Perspective.   Conflict theorists would say that the criminal justice system erroneously defines problems as occurring at the individual, rather than at the societal level, and therefore efforts to address social conditions are rejected (Macionis, 2007). "To look only at individual criminality is to close one's eyes to social injustice and to close one's ears to the question of whether our social institutions have exploited or violated the individual. . . . " (Reiman, 2007, p. 176).

Conflict theory looks to differences in socioeconomic class to understand and explain both deviant behavior and societal responses to it. Individuals from all class levels break the law, but they commit different kinds of crimes. People from low socioeconomic backgrounds are more likely to commit property crimes. Property crime includes robbery, burglary, larceny, and motor vehicle theft. Conflict theorists believe that chronic unemployment inherent in the capitalist system leads poor people to commit property crimes in order to survive (Thio, 2000).

Rational/Social Exchange Perspective.   Gordon (1973, p. 174) notes that "nearly all crimes in capitalist societies represent perfectly *rational* [italics in original] responses to the structure of institutions upon which capitalist societies are based." This is because most crimes are motivated by a desire for money or goods and thus are an understandable way of coping with inequity (Reiman, 2007). But even individuals who already have much more than they need may engage in illegal activities if they think they can get away with it. *Deterrence theory* suggests that people who are rational will refrain from committing crimes if they believe that the "costs" of the punishment will outweigh the "benefits" of the crime (Siegel, 2010). Given current rates of recidivism, some criminologists doubt the value of incarceration as a deterrent.

Constructionist Perspective.   The definition of "deviance" varies according to cultural norms. No act is criminal or delinquent in and of itself, only the response of the criminal justice system, determined by political processes, makes it so. For example, prostitution is legal in Nevada but not in any other state. Gambling is still illegal in many places, but most states now promote government-sponsored lotteries as a preferred alternative to raising property or income taxes. Even on a much smaller scale, the definition of deviance and/or labeling of deviants may vary according to circumstance. In a classic study of high school behaviors, Chambliss (2007/1973) found that when two different groups were engaged in the same behaviors (truancy, drinking, vandalism, wild parties, and petty theft), one group was generally viewed positively, while the other was not. Boys from upper-income families were not only never arrested, but described as "most likely to succeed." The boys in the other group were from lower income families and were labeled "troublemakers."

Relationship of the Criminal Justice System to the Political Economy

All Americans are constantly bombarded by commercial messages that promote materialism. Sociologist Robert Merton (1949) identified the problem of imbalance between a society's cultural goals and the means that people have to achieve those goals. Cloward and Ohlin (1960) extended Merton's thinking and argued that crime results not only from limited opportunities, but also from the existence of *illegitimate opportunities*. For example, residents of inner-city slums have the same aspirations for "success" as do middle- and upper-class people. "At the very least overwhelming numbers of the poor give allegiance to the values and principles of the dominant American culture" (Ryan, 1976, p. 134). The problem is that because they lack access to good education, training, and legitimate employment opportunities, they are attracted to alternate opportunities for making money: robbery, burglary, drug dealing, prostitution, pimping, gambling, and other "hustles."

Dyer (2000) reports that prison labor benefits the American economy. In 2002, 3.5 percent of prisoners in the United States produced goods and services worth $1.5 billion (Cole & Smith, 2007). In the federal prison system, the minimum wage is 23 cents an hour and the maximum is $1.15 (Siegel, 2010). Goods produced include clothing and textiles, electronics, and office furniture (Siegel, 2010).

As noted already in the Issues and Trends section, the construction and operation of prisons have become a big business. This "has created a large and politically potent constituency of those whose jobs and status depend on yet further expansion [of the inmate population]" (Currie, 1998, p. 7). In fact, Dyer (2000, p. 2) suggests that the most plausible explanation for the unprecedented growth in the U.S. prison population is the money that ends up in the bank accounts of the shareholders of some of America's best-known corporations; underwriting prison construction by selling tax-exempt bonds is now estimated to be a $2.3 billion annual industry itself.

Eric Schlosser, in an article in the Atlantic Monthly, wrote

> The prison-industrial complex is not a conspiracy . . . it is a confluence of interests that has given prison construction in the United States a seemingly unstoppable momentum. It is composed of politicians . . . who have used the fear of crime to gain votes; impoverished rural areas where prisons have become a cornerstone of economic development; [and] private companies that regard the roughly 35 billion spent each year on corrections not as a burden on American taxpayers but as a lucrative marker. (Schlosser, 1998, p. 54)

In addition, unions of prison workers have supported the growth of prisons. For example, unions in California make large contributions to political campaigns and have supported tough sentencing laws, such as Proposition 184 (three-strikes penalties) that enhance the length of sentences (Segal, 2008).

The Impact of the Criminal Justice System on Individuals and Families

How the Criminal Justice System Deters Well-Being.   As noted previously, the United States has the highest incarceration rate of any nation in the world, at 750 per 100,000 residents (Pew Center on the States, 2008). This rate is nearly five times as high as the worldwide average of 158 (Webb, 2009). More than one in 53 adult men in the United States is behind bars (Reiman, 2007).

The Criminal Justice System and Minorities.   Given the opportunities for discretionary decision making at various stages of the criminal justice process, there is ample opportunity for discrimination. According to a number of studies cited by Andersen and Taylor (2007), African Americans and Latinos are more likely to be arrested, convicted, and incarcerated for offenses than are whites. Other factors being equal, minorities receive harsher sentences and are less likely to be released on probation. They also are more likely to be victims of excessive use of force by police. A study by Bridges and Steen (1998) documents that probation officers consistently portray African American youths differently than white youths in their written court reports, more frequently attributing blacks' delinquency to negative attitudes and personality traits. The number of blacks behind bars jumped 62 percent between 1990 and 2005 (Wright, 2007); nearly one in nine African American males between the ages of 25 and 34 is in prison (Pew Center on the States, 2008).

Historically, police officers have been white although equal opportunity and affirmative action programs are changing that. Still, most judges are white, male, and middle, if not upper, class (Kendall, 2008). Using Alabama as an example, Jesse Jackson (2003) noted that the prison population increased by 600 percent in the past 30 years, while the population grew by only 30 percent. Over two-thirds of the prisoners were black. Only 16 of Alabama's 220 judges were black. None of its appellate judges were black. None of the district attorneys were black, and only 8 of 67 county sheriffs were black. "The back of the cell has replaced the back of the bus," Jackson argued.

Racial profiling is the term used to describe disproportionate law enforcement activities that target people of color. Several research studies have found that police officers regularly stop and/or search African American and Latino drivers at a higher rate than white drivers (Cole & Smith, 2007; Siegel, 2010). In June of 2003, the federal government admitted that racial profiling was an issue with its directive to federal law enforcement officers that forbids targeting religious, ethnic, or racial minorities (CBSNEWS.com, 2003). Nevertheless, the directive makes a distinction between routine law enforcement and threats to national security or border security. Although it is broadly forbidden, the policy permits consideration of ethnicity or race if there exists "trustworthy information" that certain groups of people are engaged in specific criminal or terrorist activities. Some states are enacting their own bans on racial profiling.

Sometimes members of society see crimes as less socially significant if the victim is viewed as less worthy. This practice is called *victim discounting* (Schaefer, 2008, p. 246). Although close to half of all homicide victims are African Americans, nearly four out of five of those executed had murdered a white person (Wright, 2007).

The Criminal Justice System and Social Class.   The FBI does not collect or report data on the socioeconomic class of arrested and convicted persons. Although violent crime is a serious problem among the poor, especially in inner-city neighborhoods, the majority of people who live there have no criminal records. Individuals with family incomes of less than $7,500 are more likely to be the victims of crime, especially violent crime; in general, the poorer a person is the more likely he or she is to be a victim of crime (Wright, 2007).

People from middle- or upper-class backgrounds commit white-collar crimes—income tax evasion, bribery of public officials, embezzlement, fraud, or other crimes committed by people in the course of their employment or financial affairs (Sutherland, 1940). These crimes do not involve violence, but in their efforts to enrich themselves, white-collar criminals may cause significant harm to consumers, investors, or employees (Macionis, 2007). Recent examples would be the scandals at the Enron, WorldCom, and Tyco corporations that were uncovered early in 2002. Victims of these crimes included both employees and stockholders; thousands of jobs and billions of dollars were lost. In response, the U.S. Justice Department embarked on a five-year battle to hold top executives responsible for a flood of accounting fraud and corporate failures, and Congress overwhelmingly passed legislation to force companies to set up stronger internal controls (Masters, 2006).

The important point is that the laws against white-collar crimes are relatively lenient and seldom enforced (Macionis, 2007). The probability of getting arrested, convicted, and sent to prison is strongly associated with social class. Geis (1999) asks, "Is it fair that a person who steals a television set should do prison time while a person who bilks the government out of millions walks away with a fine or a community service sentence?" (p. 154). On the other hand, lawmakers are beginning to respond to public pressure to exact stiffer penalties for white-collar criminals (Masters, 2006).

The Criminal Justice System and Gender.   For both men and women, the most common types of arrests are for driving under the influence (DUI), larceny, and minor criminal offenses; these account for almost half of the arrests for both sexes. Men are much more likely than women to be arrested for major property crimes and violent crimes; when women are arrested for these types of crimes it is typically as accomplices to men (Steffensmeier & Allan, 2000). Women are more frequently arrested for nonviolent property crimes, such as shoplifting, passing bad checks, credit card fraud, and employee theft (Steffensmeier & Allan, 2000).

In the two decades between 1980 and 1999, the number of women in prisons increased sixfold (Chesney-Lind, 2002). Between 2000 and 2006, the average growth rate for all state and federal prisoners was 1.9 percent; for women, it was 2.9 percent (Sabol, Minton, & Harrison, 2007). On the other hand, men continue to be incarcerated at a rate almost nine times greater than women (Wright, 2007).

Female prisoners' past lives have put them at particular risk for certain health problems. According to the Center for Disease Control and Prevention [CDC] (2003), women often enter prison with sexually transmitted diseases and somewhere between 22 percent and 58 percent have Hepatitis C. Many women also suffer from depression and PTSD associated with histories of abuse. While 5.6 percent of male state prison inmates report having a mental impairment, 11 percent of females report having one (Maruschak, 2008).

Female inmates are more likely than male inmates to have children and to have been living with those children immediately prior to incarceration. Forty-six percent of female prisoners are single parents compared to 15 percent of male prisoners (Mumola, 2000). Women are likely to have their parental rights terminated as they are often the sole guardians of their children (Chesney-Lind, 2002). At the time of their arrest, 6 to 10 percent of women are pregnant (CDC, 2003). It is common practice to shackle pregnant female inmates, even during labor (Siegel, 2010). In 1998, more than 1,400 women had a baby while incarcerated (CDC, 2003). Of pregnant state prisoners in 2004, only 53.9 percent received some type of prenatal care (Maruschak, 2008). The provision of residential programs for inmate mothers and their infants is very limited.

The Criminal Justice System and Children and Youth.   Most states establish a maximum age under 18 years, the age of legal majority, for juvenile court jurisdiction. In some states, minors who are charged with certain offenses may or must be prosecuted as adults. In 49 states, juvenile court judges can transfer cases to adult court; in 26 states, certain types of violent crime such as murder, rape, and armed robbery must be tried in adult court (Cole & Smith, 2007).

Diversion of Resources.   In 2007, total state spending on corrections topped $49 billion (Pew Center on the States, 2008). One in every 15 dollars in state discretionary money goes to corrections (Pew Center on the States, 2008). In 2006, corrections budgets exceeded education and Medicaid. Four states, including Michigan, spend more on corrections than on higher education (Heinlein & Cain, 2008). For example, as of fall 2008, an amount less than $11,000 covered tuition and fees for an academic year for a full-time undergraduate student at the University of Michigan. To house an inmate in a Michigan state prison for a year, the cost is $31,325 (see Figure 3.3).

Even a portion of the dollars spent on the criminal justice system could make a big difference in the education, housing, and medical treatment of the poor, especially poor children who

---

FIGURE 3.3   *An Example of Prison Costs*

Prison costs in Michigan

- ❑ There was a fourfold increase in the number of prisoners over the past 25 years; the state's prison population is expected to grow by another 12 percent within five years.
- ❑ It costs an average of $200 a year for each Michigan resident to support the state prison system.
- ❑ The cost to house each inmate is $31,325 per year.
- ❑ One of every three state employees works for the corrections department (compared to one in ten 25 years ago).

Source: Heinlein & Cain, *The Detroit News* (2008).

are otherwise at risk for becoming the criminals of the future. "We know that poverty is source of crime, and yet we do virtually nothing to improve the life chances of the vast majority of the inner-city poor" (Reimann, 2007, pp. 29–30).

An indirect, often unreported cost of incarceration is that prisoners are unlikely to pay child support, victim restitution, or taxes. For example, in 2001 three-quarters of the Massachusetts prison population had paid no mandated child support; in contrast, two-thirds of parolees made at least partial child-support payments (Pew Center on the States, 2008).

How the Criminal Justice System Promotes Well-Being.   In a society that is unable or unwilling to invest in prevention or rehabilitation, incarceration provides short-term security and protection by keeping offenders locked up. Many people believe that as a growing "industry," the building of new prisons offers economic opportunities in rural communities that have no other alternatives for generating new jobs. Prisons offer appealing opportunities because "they don't pollute, they don't go out of business, [and] they don't get downsized" (Lamb, cited in Dyer, 2000, p. 16). (See Chapter 10 for further discussion on this topic.)

The authors found it difficult to identify other benefits of the criminal justice system. Perhaps the better strategy to ensure security in this country would be the promotion of fair and equal treatment of all individuals, regardless of their race, class, gender, or age. The rights of the accused are not protected by our current criminal justice system, and it does a poor job of keeping the members of society safe from harm. Van Wormer (2001, p. 227) suggests that "today we face not a crime crisis . . . but a criminal justice crisis. The solution to the problem has become the problem: the war on crime has become a war on people, Black people, poor people, drug addicts, and the mentally ill."

The Military

The military is a social institution that dates from at least the beginning of recorded history. It is designed to protect a nation from internal and external threats. Traditionally, the United States has reserved the use of military force to protect its borders and citizens and to support its friends and allies elsewhere. The military (National Guard) also is used in times of internal danger, such as when armed forces are needed to protect a community during or after a devastating natural disaster. In the past, military troops were used to put down widespread riots (such as the race riots that occurred in major cities after the assassination of Martin Luther King, Jr., in 1968), or to protect vulnerable citizens in extreme circumstances (such as when National Guard troops were called upon to protect African American children as Federal court orders for school integration were being carried out in parts of the South in the 1960s).

A rigid hierarchy is an important characteristic of the military. People serving in the military are categorized according to a number of formal levels, or ranks, with those in higher levels enjoying extensive privileges and those in lower levels expected to exhibit strict obedience and conformity. An important distinction between the United States and many other countries is that the head of the military (the Secretary of Defense) and the Commander in Chief (the President) are both civilians.

According to the Office of Undersecretary of Defense, Personnel and Readiness (2008), at the end of 2006, there were slightly less than 1.15 million enlisted troops and just under 208,000 officers serving in the U.S. military. In addition, there were nearly 703,000 in the reserves, with approximately 113,000 officers. The active duty military workforce is younger than its civilian counterpart. African Americans were equitably represented in the military overall. Proportions of most other minorities also were representative of the civilian population. Women comprise between 14 and 17 percent of active duty and reserve troops. Military women are more likely to be members of a racial minority group than are military men. In addition to the growing presence of women in the military, the proportion of married members has also increased, hovering around 50 percent for enlisted personnel and at higher levels for officers. In general, male service members are more likely to be married than are women members. Military personnel are more likely to be high school graduates than their civilian counterparts and a vast majority of officers hold college degrees. The South is slightly overrepresented in terms of regional origin of military members.

In 1973, military conscription (the draft) ended and the United States changed to an all voluntary force (AVF). Many people join the military based on a sense of calling, captured in words like "duty, honor, and country," setting aside individual self-interest in favor of a presumed higher good (Moskos, 2000, p. 27). Nevertheless, with the end of conscription, marketplace factors began to play an increasing role. As employment prospects in the civilian job sector diminish, young people, especially members of less affluent classes, find opportunities for specialized training, job security, housing, health care, and travel offered by the military more enticing. In 2008, as stock values dropped and the housing market collapsed, more members of the military decided to re-enlist (Crumbo, 2003).

Issues and Trends in the Military

Women in the Military.   Women have served in the country's armed services dating as far back as the Revolutionary War, when they nursed the ill, laundered clothing, and cooked for the troops (Women in the Army, 2008). Many of the jobs performed by the women of that time are now known as military occupational specialties. Although they were not allowed to enlist in the Continental Army, women played a vital role by joining their husbands during campaigns. The most famous example of early military service by a woman was Mary Hays McCauley ("Molly Pitcher"), who replaced her fallen husband at his cannon during the Battle of Monmouth in 1778. Beginning in 1942, separate military units were established for women: the Women's Army Corps (WAC) and Women Accepted for Voluntary Emergency Services (WAVES). The military services were integrated by gender in 1948 when President Truman signed the Women Armed Services Integration Act. Women were admitted to the military academies in 1976. Beginning in the 1990s, basic-training was integrated in all of the armed forces, except the Marines (Moskos, 2000). On October 1, 1994, a new Department of Defense policy stated that dangerous jobs would not be closed to women but it failed to open ground combat assignment jobs to females (Willens, 1996). Since that time women have served aboard warships (except submarines) and as combat pilots (Moskos, 2000). Operation Desert Storm, popularly known as the first Gulf War (1990–1991), represented another major turning point for women in the military, in that the lines between combat and noncombat zones were blurred (Willens, 1996). Currently, women serve in 91 percent of all Army occupations (Women in the Army, 2008).

Gays in the Military.   In 1994, after much negotiation among the members of the administration, Congress, and service chiefs, a new policy was developed (Moskos, Williams, & Segal, 2000). The Defense Authorization Act, known colloquially as "don't ask, don't tell," forbade the military to inquire about a service member's sexual orientation, but if the individual publicly self-disclosed, he or she was to be discharged. (For information on policies in other countries on gays serving in the military, see Chapter 7.) Between 1994 and 2007, more than 9,500 military personnel were discharged under the "don't ask, don't tell" policy. The Government Accountability Office estimated that the cost to replace them exceeded $190 million (Hendren, 2005). A year later, a new estimate increased that amount by 90 percent (White, 2006).

Subcontracting and Outsourcing.   An increasing number of tasks in the military are being performed by civilians; these include both menial jobs and highly skilled technical jobs (Moskos, Williams, & Segal, 2000). Private contractors were used on an unprecedented scale in the Iraq war and comprised the second largest deployed "force," outnumbering all non-U.S. forces combined ("Private warriors," 2005). Important concerns that arise from military functions being assigned to nonmilitary personnel are accountability and chain of command. The Department of Defense and Department of State have been criticized for awarding huge contracts to private companies without sufficient competition or oversight. The chain of command is threatened when private contractors have tactical responsibilities but are not getting the same information or direction that military forces receive ("Private warriors," 2005).

Understanding the Military

Functionalist Perspective.   The manifest function of the military is to provide security for the members of a society. Historically, on the other hand, the military also was used to expand a country's resources at the expense of other nations. The military also supports latent functions; these include providing training and employment to young adults and promoting values such as nationalism, patriotism, and obedience to authority.

Conflict Perspective.   Conflict theorists would argue that the burden of defending the country falls disproportionately on poor and minority members of society. For example, during the Vietnam War, young men who were enrolled in college were given deferments while their working-class peers were subject to the draft. Although recent data do not reflect a great disparity across race and class in military service, it is reasonable to believe that youth who have limited educational and employment options are more likely to enlist.

Rational/Social Exchange Perspective.   At a macro level, federal lawmakers argue for the value of a strong military in terms of readiness in case of attack, but also as a deterrent to possible aggression on the part of other nations. At the same time, such support translates into income for their districts for defense-related industries and military bases. At the global level, a rationalist perspective suggests that military intervention in other countries is based, at least in part, on a rational assessment not only of potential threats, but also of potential and real benefits, such as control over oil reserves.

Constructionist Perspective.   As with other social institutions, the military has created its own language to shape perceptions of its role and mission. In 1947, the Department of War became the Department of Defense. Wars are no longer called "wars," but operations: for example, "Operation Urgent Fury" (Grenada, 1983), "Operation Just Cause" (Panama, 1989), "Operation Desert Storm" (Iraq, 1990–1991), "Operation Enduring Freedom" (Afghanistan, 2001–present), and "Operation

Iraqi Freedom" (Iraq, 2003–present). Whereas the term "war" suggests a massive and long-lasting undertaking, "operation" implies a strategic and short-term enterprise. The military also creates euphemisms to describe the more disturbing facets of war, such as "collateral damage" for unintended civilian casualties.

Relationship of the Military to the Political Economy

According to Kendall (2008), during World War II, the industry of the country expanded in order to produce military goods, such as airplanes, ships, tanks, and guns. After the war ended, the country had to decide what to do with this large military capacity and determined that if it were to remain a world leader, then national defense needed to be a continuing priority.

President Dwight Eisenhower, in his farewell address to the nation in 1961, both supported and warned the country about what he called the "military-industrial complex":

> We recognize the imperative need for this development. . . . [but] in the councils of government, we must guard against the acquisition of unwarranted influence, whether sought or unsought, by the military-industrial complex. The potential for the disastrous rise of misplaced power exists and will persist. We must never let the weight of this combination endanger our liberties or democratic processes. We should take nothing for granted. Only an alert and knowledgeable citizenry can compel the proper meshing of the huge industrial and military machinery of defense with our peaceful methods and goals, so that security and liberty may prosper together. (Public Papers of the Presidents, 1961)

Despite Eisenhower's concerns, the military budget continued to be a significant part of the country's economy. The United States spends almost as much on its military as all other nations combined and it leads the world in the value of arms sold to other nations (Wallechinsky, 2007). According to the Lockheed Martin corporate Web site (2008), in the 1990s, a series of mergers ended in the "Big Three" weapons manufacturers—Lockheed Martin, Boeing, and Raytheon. A large proportion of Lockheed Martin's business is with the Department of Defense; the corporation employs 140,000 people in 1,000 facilities, in 500 cities and 46 states and 75 nations worldwide.

The Impact of the Military on Individuals and Families

How the Military Deters Well-Being.   Even though other wars have resulted in more deaths (about 115,000 in the Civil War and more than 290,000 in World War II ["America's Wars: U.S. Casualties and Veterans," 2008]), recent improvements in battlefield care, including better body armor, forward-deployed surgical teams, and swift medical evacuations mean that significant numbers of troops who would have died have survived. In Iraq, the survival rate for wounded troops exceeds 90 percent (Philpott, 2005). On the other hand, survivors often return home with significant impairments: burns, loss of limbs, and traumatic brain injury (TBI). As of March 2008, more than 65,000 troops in the Iraq and Afghanistan operations have been wounded or injured or have contracted a serious disease (Stiglitz & Bilmes, 2008). This large number was unanticipated and the military health care system has been stretched beyond capacity. In early 2007, *Washington Post* reporters (Priest & Hull, 2007) secretly investigated conditions at the Walter Reed Army Medical Center outpatient unit over a period of four months and brought to light serious shortcomings, including decaying facilities, pest infestation, lost paperwork, and lack of case management services. In response to public outcry and Congressional hearings, the commander in charge of the Center was fired and the Army initiated the development of a plan designed to help the Army become more patient-focused (United States Government Accountability Office [GAO], 2007).

In addition to physical wounds, significant numbers of soldiers have returned home with mental health diagnoses. The number of Iraq and Afghanistan war vets diagnosed with post-traumatic stress disorder (PTSD) in 2006 was more than 29,000 and in 2007, it rose to more than 48,000, with few of these counted in the official casualty reports (Isikoff & Reno, 2007). Based on a study of previously deployed individuals, the Rand Corporation estimates that, as of October 2007, there were 300,000 individuals suffering from PTSD or major depression and that a further 320,000 vets experienced a probable TBI (Tanielian & Jaycox, 2008).

Individuals diagnosed with PTSD, major depressive disorder, and TBI are likely to have problems with substance abuse and are at increased risk for attempting suicide; these conditions are also associated with impaired relationships, difficulties with parenting, and domestic violence (Tanielian & Jaycox, 2008). Male veterans are twice as likely to die by suicide as compared to their civilian peers in the general population (Kaplan, Huguet, McFarland, & Newson, 2007). A Pentagon task force concluded that the number of mental health professional available to vets is "woefully inadequate" (Isikoff & Reno, 2007, p. 10).

The Veterans' Administration estimates that about one-third of the adult homeless population is veterans. On any given night, 195,000 vets are homeless in America and as many as twice that number are homeless over the course of a year ("Overview of Homeless-ness," 2007). The three primary causes of homelessness among veterans are mental illness, financial troubles, and the lack of affordable housing (McClam, 2008). Since many Vietnam veterans did not begin showing manifestations of stress disorders until ten years after return-ing home, it is difficult to estimate the long-term impact and social cost of war experiences for Iraq and Afghanistan vets.

Unlike the draftees of the Vietnam War era when most soldiers were young, single men, half of today's all-volunteer military personnel are older reservists and guardsmen who are married with children, so the burdens of deployment are shared by families (Skipp & Ephron, 2006). Deployment length and frequency are risk factors for both individual mental health and family functioning. Previously, overseas deployments averaged less than 12 months. Tours of duty in Iraq and Afghanistan can last as long as 15 months, and repeated redeployment is not uncommon.

In 2007, about 700,000 American children had at least one parent stationed overseas in mili-tary service; having a parent in a war zone is one of the most stressful events a child can experience (American Psychological Association, 2007) and more than 1,200 children have lost a parent to the operations in Iraq or Afghanistan (Brant, 2006).

In addition to parental separation, another stressor for military families is repeated geo-graphic relocation, which may occur as often as every two to three years (Herzog, 2008). Due to frequent moves, the children experience change in school, loss of friends, and separation from extended family members.

How the Military Promotes Well-Being.   Historically, tens of millions of U.S. veterans have received service-related benefits such as training, tuition benefits, housing aid, medical care, employment preferences, and retirement pensions (Campbell, 2004). Following World War II,

8 million returned veterans received a college education or vocational training under the G.I. Bill (the Servicemen's Readjustment Act, signed into law by Franklin D. Roosevelt) (Ephron, 2007). Congress passed an updated version of the G.I. Bill in 1985. It was designed more as a peace-time recruiting tool than a war-time benefit; it covers average in-state tuition costs at public universities, but does not include housing and other educational expenses (Ephron, 2007).

According to Pentagon officials, bad news for the economy is good news for the military, as retention and recruitment numbers jump (Milburn & Manning, 2008). Military service guarantees a pay check and benefits, even in bleak economic times. For a new high school graduate with little or no work experience, it would be difficult to find a better starting wage—almost $30,000 after the first four months, including the value of free housing, free food, and income-tax advantages (Powers, n.d.). The person who comes into the military as a commissioned officer makes an average starting salary of about $46,000 and after ten years of experience will earn more than $94,000 a year (Powers, n.d.). Everyone in the active military gets free (or almost free) housing and medical care and an annual clothing allowance.

African Americans have benefited from a military that was among the first U.S. institutions to become racially integrated after President Truman signed Executive Order 9981 on July 26, 1948 (Borlik, 1998). Compared with an oppressive civilian society at mid-century, the military offered more opportunities for job security and advancement. This more positive feature of the military environment continues to the present day. African Americans report that race relations are better in the military than in civilian life (Moskos & Butler, 1996). The military is the only social institution in the country where white men routinely take orders from black men.

Looking Ahead

In the next chapter, we will examine social institutions that are not closely associated with government. These social institutions, health care, religion, and mass media, are also an important part of the context of the lives of social workers and those they serve.

Chapter 4

Non-Government-Related Social Institutions

Health Care

Issues and Trends in Health Care

Paying for Health Care
U.S. Health Care in a Global Perspective
Health and Weight
Mental Health and Mental Illness
Alternative Medicine and Holistic Health Care
Cure Versus Care

Understanding the Health Care System

Functionalist Perspective
Conflict Perspective
Constructionist Perspective

Relationship of the Health Care System to the Political Economy

The Impact of the Health Care System on Individuals and Families

How the Health Care System Deters Well-Being
How the Health Care System Promotes Well-Being

Religion

Issues and Trends in Religion

Civil Religion
Religion and Political Office
Fundamentalism
Religion-Related Controversies in Social Work

Understanding Religion

Functionalist Perspective
Conflict Perspective
Constructionist Perspective

Relationship of Religion to the Political Economy

The Impact of Religion on Individuals and Families

How Religion Deters Well-Being
How Religion Promotes Well-Being

Mass Media and Communications Technology

Issues and Trends in Mass Media and Communications Technology

Violence in the Media
Mass Media, Communications Technology, and Children
Diversity and the Media
The Internet
Trends in News Consumption
Technology and U.S. Elections
Changing Patterns of Ownership: Media Mergers

Understanding the Mass Media and Communications Technology

Functionalist Perspective
Conflict Perspective
Constructionist Perspective

Relationship of Mass Media and Communications Technology to the Political Economy

The Impact of Mass Media and Communications Technology on Individuals and Families

How Mass Media and Communications Technology Deter Well-Being
How Mass Media and Communications Technology Promote Well-Being

Looking Ahead

In this chapter, we discuss three non-government-related social institutions, their interaction with the political economy, and their impact on individuals and families. Like the social institutions discussed so far, they are also important in the lives of social work clients.

Health Care

Health care is the social institution whose purpose is dealing with disease and injury and improving health, on both an individual and community level. Typically, in the United States, public health officials are concerned with issues of prevention, while medical practitioners are more focused on treatment and/or cure after the fact, even though they might offer advice on healthy living.

Not long ago, patients in the United States used a *fee-for-service* system to access medical care. They themselves, or more commonly their health insurance company, paid whatever the health care provider charged. Within the last 30 years, managed care, a new system of health care, has grown substantially. *Managed care* is a health care delivery system that sends patients to preselected care providers with prearranged agreements on what costs will be covered. *Health maintenance organizations* (HMOs), *preferred provider organizations* (PPOs), and other kinds of managed care programs also challenge the fee-for-service system by strict review of recommended treatments. These programs can require that patients receive prior approval before receiving treatment and can refuse to pay physicians or hospitals if they deem that the treatment was unnecessary. This helps to hold down health care costs. Another way of holding down costs is the use of diagnosis-related groups (DRGs) as defined by the federal government. The government has established a set amount that it will pay for a patient within a DRG category. Hospitals can profit if a patient is discharged earlier than the allowed time, but they lose money if the patient stays longer. The result of this is that some patients are discharged before they are truly ready to go home.

Issues and Trends in Health Care

Paying for Health Care. Individuals can subscribe to group health care plans on their own, but more typically they are covered by their employers' plans (or under the family plan of a working spouse or parent). According to the Department of Health and Human Services, Assistant Secretary for Planning and Evaluation (ASPE) Issue Brief (2005), employer-sponsored insurance covers about 60 percent of the population. Medicare covers 14 percent of the population (mostly individuals age 65 and older) and Medicaid, including State Children's Health Insurance Programs (SCHIP), covers another 13 percent of the population (primarily children, pregnant women, and elderly and disabled people who qualify due to low income and/or other circumstances). Only about 6 percent of the population directly purchases private coverage.

The uninsured population is not one unchanging group of individuals, but rather a constantly changing cohort that reflects the changing nature of employment in the economy (ASPE, 2005). According to ASPE data, about half of the insured are without coverage for a full-year or longer. Due to lack of money and insurance coverage, many Americans forego preventive care, putting their health at serious risk. In 2007, more than 45,657,000 Americans (15.3 percent of the population) had no medical insurance coverage (U.S. Census Bureau, 2007 and 2008 Annual Social and Economic Supplements). The vast majority of the uninsured are working individuals or the children of those who work; in 2004, almost half of the uninsured (46 percent) worked full time, while another 28 percent worked part-time or for part of the year (ASPE, 2005).

The United States is one of the few industrialized nations where illness or injury can lead directly to financial catastrophe. In America, one in six working-age adults carries medical debt, and medical expenses are believed to cause at least 425,000 bankruptcies annually ("Inequality and health care," 2006). In an extensive study of bankruptcies filed in 2001, a group of Harvard University researchers (Himmelstein, Warren, Thorne, & Woolhandler, 2005) found that about half of the personal bankruptcy filers cited medical causes, although more than 75 percent of them had insurance at the onset of illness. Financial problems included both direct and indirect medical-related costs: medical bills, drugs, and curtailed employment due to personal illness and/or to care for someone else who was seriously ill.

U.S. Health Care in a Global Perspective.   The leading causes of death in the United States and other developed countries are heart disease, cancer, and stroke. Contributing factors are obesity and tobacco use. In many low-income nations, poor people do not live long enough to develop these chronic diseases; instead, they die from malnutrition, dehydration, internal parasites, and diseases such as malaria, tuberculosis, influenza, and pneumonia. Risk factors in these countries include deficiencies in micronutrients like iron and zinc, unsafe sex practices, unsafe water, poor sanitation, and indoor smoke from solid fuels (The World Health Organization, 2002). In contrast to low-income countries, the United States ranks first in terms of access to clean water and sanitation facilities.

The number of women in poor countries who die in childbirth is almost the same as it was 20 years ago. Women in Afghanistan and in Sierra Leone in West Africa have a one in eight chance of dying in childbirth during their lifetime (Walt, 2008). This rate compares to one in 4,800 in the United States, one in 8,200 in Britain, and one in 17,400 in Sweden.

The United States spends far more money per person on health care than any other country. In 2008, the amount averaged $7,026 for every man, woman, and child in the nation (Park, 2008), which is more than twice the average of the 30 wealthy nations in the Organization for Economic Cooperation and Development (Begley, 2008). Health care costs are rising much faster than the cost of living; they now account for 16 percent of the gross domestic product (Park, 2008; Satullo, 2008). The United States is an early adapter of technology, but has a relatively low supply of CT scanners and MRI devices compared to other countries (Reinhardt, Hussey, & Anderson, 2004). It falls behind other nations on a variety of measures: 43 countries have more doctors per capita, 49 have more hospital beds per capita, 33 have a lower infant death rate, and 28 have a lower maternal death rate; the United States ranks 30th in life expectancy for women and 28th for men (Wallechinsky, 2008). Health outcome disparities across racial and ethnic groups in the United States are notable. For example, black women are twice as likely as non-Hispanic white women to suffer the loss of a baby; this is largely due to a lack of insurance which leaves them without access to regular checkups (Park, 2008).

Why are health care costs so high in America? The price of care, and not the amount of care delivered, is the primary difference (Anderson, Reinhardt, Hussey, & Petrosyan, 2003; Anderson, Hussey, Frogner, & Waters, 2005). Medical malpractice insurance accounts for less than 1 percent of spending and defensive medicine (when doctors order unnecessary tests) makes up no more than 9 percent of total spending on health care in the United States (Anderson et al., 2005). Americans pay twice as much for prescription drugs as do patients in other industrialized countries (Anderson et al., 2005). Other factors that contribute to high costs include high salaries paid to American health professionals (Anderson et al., 2003; Gerencher, 2005; Krugman, 2005) and a high level of administrative costs due to the complex multitude of public and private reimbursement systems (Krugman, 2005; Reinhardt, Hussey, & Anderson, 2004).

Health and Weight.   In sharp contrast to the malnutrition suffered by citizens in low-income countries discussed above, the United States has a significant public health problem with overeating. Two-thirds of American adults are overweight or obese (Brink, 2005), and according to the National Health and Nutrition Examination Survey (NHANES, 2003–2006), 33.3 percent of men and 35.3 percent of women are obese. (See Table 4.1 for data on the increasing rates of obesity in children.) Overweight is defined as having a *body mass index* (BMI) between 25 and 29.9; obesity is defined as having a BMI of 30 or greater. (BMI = weight in pounds divided by height in inches, multiplied by 703.) Overweight and obese individuals are at increased risk of high blood pressure, osteoarthritis, type 2 diabetes, coronary heart disease, stroke, gallbladder disease, sleep

TABLE 4.1   *Increasing Prevalence of Obesity Among American Children*

Age	1976–1980 (%)	2003–2006 (%)
2–5	5	12.4
6–11	6.5	17.0
12–19	5	17.6

Sources: Centers for Disease Control and Prevention, 2008; Data from the National Health and Nutrition Examination Survey (NHANES), 1976–1980 and 2003–2006.

apnea, and some cancers (endometrial, breast, and colon) (Center for Disease Control, Obesity and Overweight Health Consequences, 2008). One study suggests that obesity reduces life expectancy by four to nine months (Brink, 2005).

Social causes of obesity include sedentary lifestyles (low levels of physical activity, both at work and at home); eating large quantities of food; and consuming salty, fatty, and sugary foods. Poor people are at increased risk because stores in low-income neighborhoods offer fewer fresh fruits and vegetables and more processed snack foods.

Dieting with a goal of being very thin, rather than being healthy, is a type of eating disorder. *Anorexia nervosa* is characterized by dieting to the point of starvation; people with anorexia are obsessed with food and their body image. *Bulimia* involves binge eating followed by induced vomiting (purging) and/or laxative use to avoid weight gain. The stereotypical victim of eating disorders is a young white, middle-class heterosexual woman, but research suggests that the problem also exists among women of color, working-class women, lesbians, and some men (Thompson, 1994). Many women develop eating disorders at least in part in response to a desire to conform to societal norms of feminine beauty as portrayed in the mass media (Kilbourne, 1999).

Mental Health and Mental Illness.   According to the National Alliance on Mental Illness [NAMI], *mental illnesses*

> are medical conditions that disrupt a person's thinking, feeling, mood, ability to relate to others, and daily functioning. . . . Mental illnesses can affect persons of any age, race, religion, or income. Mental illnesses are not the result of personal weakness, lack of character, or poor upbringing. Mental illnesses are treatable. Most people diagnosed with a serious mental illness can experience relief from their symptoms by actively participating in an individual treatment plan. (NAMI, 2008b)

According to NAMI (2007), one in four adults—approximately 57.7 million Americans—experiences a mental health disorder in a given year. One in 17 lives with a serious mental illness, such as schizophrenia, major depression, or bipolar disorder, and about one in ten children has a serious mental or emotional disorder. Major depressive disorder is the leading cause of disability in the United States and Canada for those between the ages of 15 and 44. There are about 5.2 million adults in America who have a co-occurring mental health and addiction disorder. The *Diagnostic and Statistical Manual of Mental Disorders* of the American Psychiatric Association classifies various addictions (e.g., drugs, gambling, sex) as mental illnesses.

Mental illnesses usually strike individuals in the prime of their lives, often in adolescence and young adulthood (NAMI, 2008b). Half of all lifetime cases of mental illness begin by age 14, three-quarters by age 24 (NAMI, 2007).

Medical research continues to document organic causes for many forms of mental illness—genetic predispositions or chemical imbalances, for example. Environmental factors also play a role. Certain stigmatized statuses, such as being poor or a member of a minority group, can add to a person's stress level.

Again according to NAMI (2007), fewer than one-third of adults and half of children with a diagnosable mental disorder receive any mental health services in a given year. Twenty-four percent of state prisoners and 21 percent of local jail prisoners have a recent history of a mental health disorder (NAMI, 2007). Of those high school students age 14 and older who have a mental disorder, over 50 percent drop out. (NAMI, 2007).

In October of 2008, Congress passed and the President signed the Paul Wellstone-Pete Domenici Mental Health Parity and Addiction Equity Act. This culminated a nearly 20-year effort to require group health plans to cover treatment for mental illness on the same terms and conditions as all other illnesses. This means that group health plans will no longer be able to impose limits on inpatient days or outpatient visits or require higher deductibles or cost sharing for mental illness or addiction treatment that are not also applied to all other medical-surgical coverage (NAMI, 2008a). Such practices had long been commonplace.

Alternative Medicine and Holistic Health Care.   *Alternative medicine* refers to nontraditional practices, such as those used by Native American healers and some imported from Asian cultures, that are not included in the traditional medical curricula taught in the United States and Great Britain. These include acupuncture, yoga, meditation, tai chi, and qigong (Tyre, 2004). In response to patient demands, the U.S. medical establishment has begun to make accommodations to these alternative treatments (Henslin, 2008). Experimental drugs or nondrug treatments not currently accepted by the medical establishment are also sometimes classified as alternative medicine (Canadian Holistic Medical Association, 2008). What once was "alternative" may become "conventional," suggesting that the use of the term *holistic* may be preferable in some cases. *Holistic medicine* is "a system of health care which fosters a cooperative relationship among all those involved, leading toward optimal attainment of the physical, mental, emotional, social and spiritual aspects of health. It emphasizes the need to look at the whole person, including analysis of physical, nutritional, environmental, emotional, social, spiritual, and lifestyle values . . . holistic medicine focuses on education and responsibility for personal efforts to achieve balance and well-being" (Canadian Holistic Medical Association, 2008).

Cure Versus Care.   Many health care providers are uncomfortable dealing with terminal illnesses. They feel that they have failed if a patient dies. Statistics show that 90 percent of health care dollars are spent for treatment in the last two or three years of life (U.S. Census Bureau, 2000). The *hospice* movement, on the other hand, provides *palliative care* (i.e., comfort, pain relief) and "death with dignity." It focuses on quality of life for terminally ill people rather than triumph over disease. Social workers are likely to play a more significant role in hospice care than in hospital care.

Adults can express their preferences about various types of life-extending medical interventions, but also need to take legal steps to protect themselves from unnecessary medical intervention. By writing a *living will* and giving *durable power of attorney for health care* to a trusted friend or relative, they have the opportunity to exercise control over potentially painful and invasive but ineffective medical treatment at a time in the future when they are unable to speak for themselves. A living will allows them to make the decision of whether life-prolonging medical or surgical procedures are to be continued, withheld, or withdrawn, as well as when artificial feeding and fluids are to be provided or withheld. Physicians and health care providers are directed by the living will to follow the patient's instructions. To be valid, the proper form must be used for each state and it must be executed in compliance with the laws of the state. The living will generally becomes operative when it is provided to the physician or other health care provider *and* the patient is incapable of making health care decisions for himself or herself, such as when he or she is permanently unconscious and unable to communicate.

Understanding the Health Care System

Functionalist Perspective. Structural functionalists view illness as dysfunctional because it prevents individuals from performing their assigned roles. This point of view was articulated by James Buchanan Duke, the founder of the Duke Endowment. He explained his support for the expansion of health care facilities in the Carolinas in a newspaper interview in the 1920s, saying, "People ought to be healthy. If they ain't healthy they can't work, and if they don't work they ain't healthy. And if they can't work there ain't no profit in them" (Goulden, 1971).

A primary function of U.S. health care system is to maintain a healthy workforce. The fact that the vast majority of those individuals who have health insurance coverage receive that benefit through their employer makes clear the link between financial support for health care and the needs of the political economy. Tax-supported insurance (e.g., Medicaid) for nonworkers tends to be stingy and often stigmatizing.

Conflict Perspective. The *medical establishment* includes health care providers, laboratories, clinics, pharmaceutical companies, hospitals, medical supply manufacturers, and insurance companies. Through its political and financial clout, the medical establishment has become the most lucrative business in the country. In theory, the supply-and-demand of a capitalist system should keep health care prices competitive, but in reality, the members of the medical establishment, not health care consumers, determine the demand by deciding what kinds of medical services and supplies are needed and then providing them at the prices they set. Often there are inherent conflicts of interest, as when doctors have financial investments in laboratories, pharmacies, hospitals, and medical supply companies. It is difficult to know if a doctor has made a choice based on the needs of the patient or the needs of his or her pocketbook.

One recent study (Cosgrove, Krimsky, & Vijayaraghavan, 2006) examined the degree and type of financial ties to the pharmaceutical industry of panel members responsible for revisions of the *Diagnostic and Statistical Manual of Mental Disorders* (*DSM-IV-TR*) (American Psychiatric Association, 2000). Of the 170 DSM panel members, 95 (56 percent) had one or more financial associations with companies in the pharmaceutical industry and 100 percent of the members of the panels on "Mood Disorders" and "Schizophrenia and Other Psychotic Disorders" had financial ties to drug companies. Of note here is that the connections are especially strong in those diagnostic areas where drugs are the first line of treatment for mental disorders. The leading categories of financial interest held by panel members were research funding (42 percent), consultancies (22 percent), and speakers bureau (16 percent).

As the gatekeeper of the profession, the American Medical Association controls who can provide medical services by controlling who is licensed to diagnose and treat patients, and prescribe drugs, effectively eliminating some competitors (such as homeopathic healers) and controlling those who remain (e.g., nurses, social workers, and physical therapists). Early in the twentieth century, physicians expanded their practice opportunities by campaigning against midwifery. Using the power of the AMA, they persuaded many states to make it illegal for anyone but a physician to deliver babies.

In a more recent example of attempted control by the medical establishment, the South Carolina State Board of Dentistry repeatedly challenged the right of dental hygienists to provide teeth cleaning services in schools by demanding that each child first be examined by a dentist (Werner, 2007). The Federal Trade Commission had to step in to enforce state laws supporting access to these services by children, alleging unfair trade practices.

Constructionist Perspective.   Both "illness" and "health" are culturally defined. An example is our understanding of pregnancy and childbirth. Pregnancy was once thought of as a normal part of a woman's life. Even though childbirth was often dangerous or even fatal, women delivered their babies at home with the help of female relatives or nurse-midwives. As noted above, physicians redefined pregnancy as a medical condition and delivery as a medical emergency that required the assistance of a specially educated person, usually meaning a male obstetrician. Both the patient and the physician socially reconstructed even routine births as medical crises requiring inpatient hospitalization. Other routine problems and processes that have been medicalized include short stature, menopause, hair loss, and trouble sleeping.

Other examples of the social construction of illness are addictions and behavior problems such as overeating, phobias, and adolescent rebelliousness. These were once identified as personal weaknesses or eccentricities, but came to be defined as diseases or mental disorders. Once these problems were medicalized, physicians became the primary supervisors of treatment as well as gatekeepers to those applying for medical benefits. Contextual factors, such as family patterns, poverty, violence, trauma, and oppression, were seldom viewed as relevant in explaining or contributing to the disorders.

Relationship of the Health Care System to the Political Economy

Like other American social institutions, health care is highly integrated with the political economy. In contrast to most other countries, in the United States health care is not a right of citizenship, but a commodity that is delivered to consumers through the private market system. The United States is the only industrialized nation that offers neither national health insurance nor guaranteed health services. Conservative politicians and the medical establishment have always campaigned against proposals for the development of government health care programs and also oppose government intervention in the delivery of health care services.

Sociologists (see Thio, 2000, pp. 388–389, for example) argue that although medical care appears to be organized like any other business in the free market, it is quite different. Consumers do not have much input into purchasing choices because they cannot determine what they need. Sick or injured people are not in a good position to question their doctors' choices. They rely on the medical establishment to tell them what to get and how much they must pay. Most have few incentives to "comparison shop" because they pay only a share (about one-third) of the costs directly.

Health care consumers would like to believe that physicians have their patients' interest as their primary concern. However, as discussed above, the profit motive may influence their decisions about the course of treatment. Likewise, patients would like to believe that their HMO has their best interests at heart, but most people have learned otherwise. Like more traditional insurance programs, the goal of the health maintenance programs is (1) to make a profit for their stockholders and (2) to make sure the hospitals and doctors are paid if patients are too sick to work or if fees are more than they can afford. In other words, the ultimate concern is for the financial well-being of the insurance company and the care providers rather than the health of the consumers. This is reflected in exclusions for "preexisting conditions" or excessively high insurance rates for individuals who have serious or chronic illnesses.

An interesting example of the potential conflict between making a profit and offering good health care is the sharp rise in the rate of Caesarean births. In 2006, C-sections represented 31.1 percent of births, a 50 percent increase over the previous ten years (Yabroff, 2008). Advocates for natural childbirth say that hospitals that are driven by profits and concerned about malpractice charges guide expectant mothers to choose surgery.

Another example of the close ties between the health care establishment and the political economy is the change in legal restrictions that now allow pharmaceutical companies to directly market prescription drugs to the public. Between 1995 and 2000, the number of drug industry staff employed in doing research dropped slightly (from 49,000 to 48,000); during the same time, sales staff increased from 55,000 to 87,000 (Barry, 2002). In 2004, the pharmaceutical industry spent $57.5 billion on marketing and $31.5 billion on research and development (Gagnon & Lexchin, 2008). The drug industry is already by far the most profitable in America with returns on investments three to eight times higher than the median revenues for other industries (Barry, 2002).

The Impact of the Health Care System on Individuals and Families

How the Health Care System Deters Well-Being. The medical establishment focuses on microorganisms to explain ill health but often does not consider the harmful effects of poverty. From the perspective of the members of the medical establishment, people in the lower economic classes contribute to their own poor health by eating the wrong foods and living in unsanitary conditions. They seldom question the reasons behind these "choices." By not taking context into account, the medical establishment reduces a societal level issue to an individual one.

Scientific medicine has not done a good job of meeting the needs of women, people of color, poor people, and older adults. Women and members of racial and ethnic minorities are less likely than white males to receive aggressive and sophisticated health care and mental health care.

In 1999, Congress directed the Agency for Healthcare Research and Quality (AHRQ) to produce an annual report, starting in 2003, to track "prevailing disparities in health care delivery as it relates to racial factors and socioeconomic factors in priority populations" (U.S. Department of Health and Human Services, 2006). The first National Healthcare Disparities Report (NHDR), released in 2003, was a comprehensive national overview of disparities in health care among racial, ethnic, and socioeconomic groups in the general U.S. population; the 2004 NHDR initiated a second critical goal of the report series—tracking the nation's progress toward the elimination of health care disparities (U.S. Department of Health and Human Services, 2006).

According to the 2006 National Healthcare Disparities Report (U.S. Department of Health and Human Services), for most core quality measures, blacks, Hispanics, and poor people received inferior quality care compared to their reference groups. For most measures for poor people, disparities were *increasing*; for most measures for minorities, significant improvements in disparities were not observed. Increasing disparities were especially prevalent in chronic disease management. Other prominent disparities included colorectal cancer screening, vaccinations, hospital treatment for heart attacks and pneumonia, services for diabetes, treatment of tuberculosis, nursing home care, and children hospitalized for asthma. One study (Pletcher, Kertesz, Kohn, & Gonzales, 2008) found that when white patients experience pain they are significantly more likely to receive a prescription for an opioid than black, Hispanic, or Asian patients. (An opioid is drug that has a morphine-like action in the body.) Another study reported that pharmacies in African American neighborhoods are less likely to carry opioid analgesics than those in white neighborhoods; the researchers concluded that persons living in predominantly minority areas experienced significant barriers to accessing pain medication, with greater disparities in low-income areas regardless of ethnic composition (Green, Ndao-Brumblay, West, & Washington, 2005).

Other problems occur when patients do not speak English or come from a cultural background with a uniquely different understanding of illness and medical treatment. Reliance on young children to interpret complex medical explanations for parents or grandparents, or ignoring important cultural and religious beliefs, may result in unnecessary suffering or even death (Kelly, 2008; Underwood & Adler, 2005).

The American Association of Retired Persons (AARP) reports that older adults are often denied preventive care routinely provided to others, are less likely to be screened for life-threatening diseases, and are "routinely overtreated, undertreated, or even mistreated by health care professionals with little or no training in geriatrics" (Pope, 2003, p. 7). They also are consistently underrepresented or excluded from clinical trials (Pope, 2003, p. 8).

The issue of paying for health care was discussed earlier. The experiences of poor people in the health care system are quite different from those who are affluent or well-insured. The poor may use public health clinics and emergency rooms for primary care. They are unlikely to receive preventive care or adequate follow-up services. National Public Radio (2007) reported on the case of a young African American boy who died from untreated tooth decay when the infection reached his brain. His case caught the attention of the House Oversight and Government Reform Committee, which questioned why one-third of the children on Medicaid fail to be seen by a dentist in any given year. The reason is that Medicaid reimbursement is so low that few dentists will see Medicaid patients.

How the Health Care System Promotes Well-Being.   Obviously, the American health care system has been effective in dealing with many health care problems. Immunizations have resulted in a great reduction or total elimination of some infectious diseases, and other advances in health care technology have produced artificial replacements for limbs and organs, innovative fertility treatments, and life-saving treatments for very low-birth-weight babies. The public health system and occupational safety regulations have done much to reduce health risks from many sources (e.g., lead poisoning, asbestos, on-the-job injuries, and so forth.)

Despite concerns about health care delivery in this country, the National Center for Health Statistics (NCHS) documents a decline in mortality and an increase in life expectancy (National Center for Health Statistics, 2007; Rodu & Cole, 2007). In the early years of the twenty-first century, the NCHS reported declining death rates for all major diseases. During this period, cancer rates dropped 8 percent, heart diseases declined 18 percent, stroke 19 percent, and flu-pneumonia 13 percent.

Religion

Religion is the social institution that organizes a system of beliefs and practices related to aspects of life having to do with the supernatural. It involves the things that are sacred in people's lives—those that inspire awe and reverence—as opposed to everyday experiences. Religion as a social institution is not the same thing as denominational theology or personal spirituality. Social scientists are less interested in specific religious doctrines or beliefs than they are in religious groups and organizations, the behavior of individuals within these groups, and on conflicts between religious groups (Roberts, 1995, p. 28). In this chapter, we explore the influence of religion on American society.

Religions typically include three elements: beliefs, practices (rituals), and a community of believers (Durkeim, 1965/1912). Most formal religions also include norms or rules for how people should behave.

A survey conducted by the Gallup Organization on behalf of the Baylor University Institute for Studies of Religion revealed that only about 10 percent of Americans have no ties to a congregation, denomination, or faith group; other surveys, which ask the question in a different way, suggest that 14 to 16 percent are "unaffiliated" (Pew Forum on Religion and Public Life, 2008; "Survey finds many have religious ties," 2006). The majority of the unaffiliated are people who describe their religion as "nothing in particular," while only about a fourth of the "unaffiliated" self-identified as agnostics (2.4 percent of all those interviewed) or atheists (1.6 percent) (Pew Forum on Religion and Public Life, 2008). Of Americans aged 18 to 29, one in four reports that he or she is not currently affiliated with a religious group suggesting that religion is less salient for younger adults than older adults (Pew Forum on Religion and Public Life, 2008).

Compared to other Western industrialized countries, religion is more important to Americans. According to the Pew Global Attitudes Project (2002), on a global level, faith is negatively correlated with average national income, except in the case of the United States—that is, countries with more wealth tend to be less religious. The religious views of Americans are more closely compatible to those of developing countries. In Africa and Latin America, a majority of citizens see religion as very important.

The Pew Forum on Religion and Public Life (2008) describes religious affiliation in America as "both diverse and extremely fluid" (p. 1). If one includes change in affiliation from one type of Protestantism to another, more than four in ten Americans have either switched religious affiliation, moved from being unaffiliated to being affiliated, or dropped any connection to a specific religious faith.

The United States is home to more than 280 religious denominations (Thio, 2000, p. 320). According to the Pew Forum on Religion and Public Life survey (2008), 78.4 percent of Americans report that they are Christian; Jews, Buddhists, Muslims, and Hindus together make up 4.7 percent. Among the 51.3 percent of respondents who were identified as Protestants, three distinct religious traditions are represented: evangelical Protestants 26.3 percent, mainline Protestants 18.1 percent, and historical black Protestants 6.9 percent. Catholics constitute 23.9 percent of respondents.

Evangelicals are members of Protestant churches who believe in being "born again" or "saved"; members stress the importance of scripture and converting nonbelievers. *Christian fundamentalism* is a conservative type of evangelicalism; believers affirm the inerrancy of the Bible as the literal word of God.

Many of the religious denominations remaining stable or showing growth in America reflect the arrival of refugees from Asia, the Middle East, and Latin America. Membership levels in the Roman Catholic Church, for example, remain stable because while the church is losing some members, it is gaining others, primarily first-generation immigrants from Mexico and other Catholic countries. But the longer they are in the United States, the more Latinos appear to be open to other faiths. Although Latinos remain the fastest-growing ethnic bloc in the Catholic Church, they are also the fastest-growing segment among Mormons and Methodists (Campo-Flores, 2005). The fastest-growing segment of Presbyterian and Methodist faiths are ethnic Korean congregations (Schaefer, 2008, p. 345). Generally the larger "mainline" Protestant churches (e.g., Disciples of Christ, Episcopal, United Church of Christ, United Methodist, Presbyterian, and Congregational churches) have lost members or are struggling to maintain the size of their membership roles. Many members of mainline Protestant faiths have been leaving them for churches that follow strict codes of behavior and rigid interpretations of Biblical teachings (Schaefer, 2008, p. 154). Southern Baptists, Jehovah's Witnesses, the Church of Latter-Day Saints (Mormons), the Church of God, Assemblies of God, the Church of the Nazarene, the Church of God in Christ, Catholic Pentecostals, and Seventh-Day Adventists are among the churches enjoying significant growth (Stockard, 2000, p. 312).

Religion is linked to ethnicity and nationality in all parts of the world. Faith communities in America represent a very high degree of racial and ethnic segregation. This pattern reflects each group's culture, not a history of forced segregation. Latinos are likely to be Catholic, as are people of Irish, Italian, and Polish descent; many people of Greek descent belong to the Greek Orthodox Church, and African Americans are likely to be members of the African Methodist Episcopal (AME) or black Baptist churches. Many Southeast Asian refugees from Vietnam, Cambodia, and Thailand are Buddhist. Recent Arab immigrants are likely to be followers of the Islamic faith (Muslims). Research studies show that the religious involvement of different ethnic groups within the same denomination varies considerably even though the church is a powerful force for assimilation (Schaefer, 2008).

Patterns of religious affiliation are also strongly related to geographic region in the United States. This has implications for who might be considered a member of a "religious minority" in different parts of the country. Southern Baptists dominate in the Southeast, Catholics in the Northeast and Southwest, Lutherans in the upper Midwest and upper Great Plains, and Latter-Day Saints (Mormons) in Utah and Idaho. Jews once comprised fully one-third of the population of New York City. Many Jews have now left the urban centers of the Northeast to settle in the suburbs and in the Sunbelt states of Florida, Arizona, and California (Shapiro, 1999).

Today, many Americans show tolerance and support for religious diversity. Nevertheless, they may have little knowledge about faith traditions outside their own. The authors of this text believe that it is important for social work practitioners to have a basic understanding of major religions. In some types of social work intervention, knowledge of religious culture can facilitate treatment (Rey, 1997). We recommend that students make an effort to expand their knowledge of different religious traditions.

Many theologians divide common world religions into two major groups, "Western" and "Eastern." The three major *Western religions* (Judaism, Christianity, and Islam) actually originated in what Americans call the Middle East. They are monotheistic religions (espousing belief in one god). Their followers form congregations and worship formally in groups at specific times and in specific places (i.e., in synagogues, churches, and mosques). Other characteristics of Western religious beliefs are a sense of conflict between the spiritual and the secular, the importance of sacred texts, a perception of time as linear, and a view of each person as a unique creation. Major *Eastern religions* (Hinduism, Buddhism, and Shintoism), on the other hand, have multiple deities and/or subdeities. There is a belief in the harmonious duality or balance of spiritual and worldly elements, time is viewed as cyclical, and souls are believed to transmigrate between beings (reincarnation). Confucianism and Taoism, widely practiced in the Far East, are usually considered to be philosophies rather than religions.

The importance placed on *proselytizing* (actively seeking converts) varies considerably among religions. Followers of Eastern religions place much less emphasis on proselytizing than do Christians and Muslims. Hinduism, for example, makes no effort to change the beliefs of others but rather finds ways to integrate them under the great umbrella of traditions that comprise the Hindu faith. Judaism is nonproselytizing because to be Jewish typically involves not only a religious commitment but an ethnic heritage as well. (This is discussed further in Chapter 6.) Outreach programs are mostly limited to efforts by Reform Jews aimed at non-Jewish partners and children in mixed marriages.

Issues and Trends in Religion

Civil Religion.   While many countries have an official "state religion" (examples include Belgium, England, Iran, Ireland, Israel, Italy, Saudi Arabia, Spain, and Sweden), the United States, of course, does not. On the other hand, Americans do not practice the strict "separation of church and state" that many believe is constitutionally required. The government at many levels supports religion through tax policies, publicly supported chaplains, and invocation of God's presence at ceremonial occasions. Polls show that most Americans do not object to the inclusion of religion in the public realm as long as no particular denomination is favored (Wolfe, 1998). In fact, it is considered "un-American to be godless, or worse, to attack religion" (Thio, 2000, p. 329).

Sociologists describe the United States as having a form of *civil religion*, a kind of hybrid of religion and politics (Bellah, 1967; McGuire, 1997; Roberts, 1995) that acts like a social glue for a pluralistic society (Will, 2004). American civil religion promotes faith in a supreme being (however individuals choose to understand the deity) and the "American way of life," including individual freedom, patriotism, and the moral authority of elected leaders in times of crisis. Civil religion also has its rituals, including singing the national anthem at sporting events and displaying the flag as a sacred symbol on national holidays and other occasions. American presidents, beginning with Ronald Reagan, have concluded their speeches with "God bless the United States of America," which evokes the civil religion of the nation.

Religion and Political Office.   In the United States, there is no "religious test" for public offices, meaning that no elected official can be required to espouse any particular religion or belief. The basis for this is found in Article VI, Section 3, of the U.S. Constitution, which states

> The Senators and Representatives before mentioned, and the Members of the several State Legislatures, and all executive and judicial Officers, both of the United States and of the several States, shall be bound by Oath or Affirmation, to support this Constitution; but *no religious test shall ever be required as a qualification to any office or public trust under the United States* (italics added).

The use of a "religious test of office" was widely debated in the presidential election of 1960, when John F. Kennedy's Catholic background was a concern to many Protestants who worried that he would be under the control of the Pope. Kennedy addressed these concerns in a speech to a gathering of Southern Baptist ministers in September of 1960, reassuring his audience that "I do not speak for my church on public matters—and the church does not speak for me" and succeeded, for a time, in removing religion from the scope of legitimate campaign topics (Garnett, 2008).

Evangelical Protestants were the base for the creation of the "Moral Majority" movement, led by the Reverend Jerry Falwell in the late 1970s and early 1980s. Falwell persuaded evangelicals to become involved in politics to address what they considered to be pressing moral issues of the day. From 1980 through 2008, the evangelical "values voters" have been an important voting constituency and played a central role in the election of many Republican candidates at all levels, and, at the presidential level, Ronald Reagan, George H. W. Bush, and George W. Bush.

The religious beliefs of presidential candidates came under increasing scrutiny in the 2008 presidential election. Virtually all candidates were challenged during the primary campaigns, and in the presidential debates, to talk about their personal faith. Academic researchers who study religion and politics noted a change in tone, in addition to increasing emphasis on religion, in recent campaigns; "What you see instead [of a ceremonial reference to God] is the use of God as kind of a political weapon that doesn't just celebrate faith, but is used to identify enemies and to try to position ideas against each other" (Kevin Coe, cited by George, 2008). This use of religion to promote divisiveness and engage in political gamesmanship offers the potential to exploit the beliefs of people of faith for political gain.

Fundamentalism.   Some religious scholars (e.g., Hunter, 1991) believe that there is a new realignment of religious difference that is not based on doctrine or denomination; in fact, this realignment sometimes cuts right through the middle of a congregation or denomination. The dividing line is between conservatives/fundamentalists and liberals/interpretationists.

Fundamentalists in Western religious traditions accept the literal meaning of scripture, that is, they believe it is the "inerrant word of God." Their assumption is that a text means whatever it means to somebody who is reading it today (Helminiak, 1994, p. 25). Fundamentalists assert the absolute correctness of their own beliefs and reject religious pluralism. In national surveys, 30 percent of American adults describe their religious upbringing as "fundamentalist" (NORC, 2003).

Interpretationists use a historical-critical approach to reading sacred texts (Helminiak, 1994, pp. 26–27). This approach is called "historical" because it requires that the text be put back into its historical and cultural context before deciding what it means. It is called "critical" because it requires careful thought and detailed analysis. Liberals/interpretationists are likely to be found among United Methodists, Episcopalians, Congregationalists, and Presbyterians, as well as Reform Jews.

Despite expectations that religious fundamentalism and political conservatism go hand in-hand, the reality is often more complex. Davis and Robinson (1996) found that although fundamentalism was correlated with conservative views on nontraditional families, feminist and gay causes, and prayer in school, fundamentalism was not associated with attitudes on economic issues. Instead the researchers found that people with fundamentalist beliefs were more likely than their liberal/interpretationist counterparts to support organized labor and believe that profits should go to workers rather than stockholders. Recently, the evangelical agenda has been expanded to include concerns about poverty and the environment (Dionne, 2007).

Readers should note that when evangelical causes and issues are discussed, the focus is typically on white evangelicals. Black evangelicals have a long history and strong presence in social justice, including the civil rights movement (Dionne, 2008).

Religion-Related Controversies in Social Work.   Social workers often experience two different kinds of value dilemmas related to religion. In some agencies, they may feel pressure to use religious beliefs as a context for the provision of services. In other situations, they may find that their personal religious beliefs are in conflict with those of their clients and/or the profession.

In 2000, presidential candidate George W. Bush proposed the establishment of *faith-based social services* as an alternative to traditional social service programs. Supporters of this initiative believed that faith-based services supply the moral content that is lacking in secular nonprofit or government agencies (Karger & Stoesz, 2010). The social work profession and social work practitioners have a long history of providing services under religious auspices and within religious settings (National Association of Social Workers [NASW], 2006). Nevertheless, when the Faith-Based and Community Initiatives Act was passed, the NASW responded on its Web site with statements of concern about the possibility of (1) government-funded organizations proselytizing to people seeking aid, (2) limiting access to services based on lack of religious affiliation or observation, (3) hindering existing nonprofit social services agencies that are not faith-based, and (4) using employment practices that discriminate on the basis of religion (NASW, 2002). At least one of these concerns was justified in 2005 when a federal judge in New York ruled that a religious service organization can hire and fire employees on the basis of their religious beliefs and practices, even if their salaries come from taxpayer funds (Cooperman, 2005). When government-supported social service programs are imbedded in faith-based organizations, professional ethics dictate that social workers respect clients' religious preferences (or lack of religious affiliation).

Perhaps more commonly, some practitioners experience dissonance between their own religious beliefs and practices and those of their clients and/or the values of the social work profession. Typically these conflicts arise in the context of disagreements over gender roles (i.e., patriarchy), the physical discipline of children, homosexuality, and abortion.

Understanding Religion

Functionalist Perspective.   Functionalists believe that the social order is enhanced by the existence of organized religion(s) (Durkeim, 1965/1912) and civil religion. Religion encourages conformity by providing cultural norms or by *sacralizing* those norms that already exist (i.e., conferring supernatural legitimacy on the norms and laws of society) (Roberts, 1995). Religion unites people through shared symbolism and values. Civil religion expressly encourages patriotism and nationalism.

Conflict Perspective.   Although clearly religion has been used in many times and many places to justify persecution, violence, and even war, conflict theorists focus on how the institution of religion supports the existing social hierarchy and the interests of the ruling class. Historical examples include the Christian teaching of the "divine right of kings" in Europe during the Middle Ages and support of the caste system by the Hindu religion in India. In this country, religion has been used to endorse the status quo by legitimating the destruction of Native Americans, the slavery of Africans, and the oppression of women.

Many religions encourage people to focus on "another world to come" rather than working toward change in this one. The most famous critique of religion from a conflict perspective was offered by Karl Marx. In his statement "religion is the opium of the people," he meant that religion is like a drug that causes people to be complacent and docile even when they are exploited.

Constructionist Perspective.   Most religious people would argue that their beliefs are the result of divine inspiration, provided indirectly through prophets, clerics, and religious texts or perhaps directly to themselves individually. Social construction theorists say that people construct religious beliefs as a means of responding to life's uncertainties, tragedies, triumphs, and other great questions, trying to explain the unexplainable, find reason in the unreasonable, and perhaps gain the favor or assistance of supernatural forces. Organized religion is based on a shared construction of reality. Because they are matters of faith rather than fact, neither social workers nor scientists in any discipline can prove or disprove specific religious doctrines or beliefs.

Relationship of Religion to the Political Economy

As noted in Chapter 2, Max Weber linked the development of capitalism to early Protestant beliefs. The "Protestant work ethic" continues to be touted as the basis of America's prosperity. Because American Catholics and Jews are also prosperous, and because capitalism is flourishing in non-Christian/non-Protestant countries such as Japan, Taiwan, and South Korea, Weber's theory probably is best used to explain the early emergence of capitalism rather than its continuing success.

At the end of the twentieth century, the ideas flowed in the other direction as organized religion began borrowing marketing strategies from the business sector (Kroll, 2003; Lewis, 1996; Staples, 1998). Congregations have become "the religious equivalents of Walmarts" in designing programs to meet the needs of their members and "competing vigorously to offer their flavor of salvation" (Thio, 2000, pp. 330–331). Sociologist James Henslin (2008, p. 553) describes the "online marketing of religion," noting such developments as chat rooms directed by rabbis, priests, ministers, and imams; online donations by credit card and Internet pay providers; online counseling for spiritual problems; and emailed prayers.

In principle, the American people are committed to the "separation of church and state" (meaning a public policy of neutrality toward religion). The Founding Fathers (Thomas Paine, Benjamin Franklin, George Washington, John Adams, Thomas Jefferson, and James Madison), reacting to European state religions, were quite clear in their rejection of a theocratic form of government (Morgan, 2004). Their concern about the misuse and abuse of religion was codified in the First Amendment to the U.S. Constitution, commonly called the "establishment clause": *Congress shall make no law respecting an establishment of religion. . . .* The First Amendment prohibits the creation of a national religion and prohibits the government from preference toward one religion, or for religion over nonreligion. Despite the apparent clarity of the First Amendment, there are individuals and organizations that insist that the United States was founded as a "Christian nation" and furthermore, that the Constitution does not mandate a "wall of separation" between church and state. The phrase "wall of separation" was first used in a letter written by Thomas Jefferson in 1802; the letter was cited in decisions by the U.S. Supreme Court in 1878 and again in widely publicized decisions in 1947 and 1948 (Hutson, 1998).

The government not only tolerates but encourages religion in a variety of ways. These include its tax policies (exemptions for religious organizations and contributions to them), laws (including a 1954 law adding "under God" to the Pledge of Allegiance and a 1955 law requiring that "In God We Trust" appear on all U.S. currency), and practices (such as provision of funding for chaplains in Congress, the armed forces, and prisons; use of the Bible for rituals of "swearing in," and recognition of religious holidays). As noted above, recent administrations support the idea of faith-based social services, which blurs the distinction between secular and religious agencies.

Regardless of the intentions of the Founding Fathers, in practice, Americans today not only permit but insist on public manifestations of religiosity on the part of government officials. The power and grace of God (or "Providence," or "the Supreme Being") are regularly invoked. Political leaders may even use religion to shield their choices from criticism by saying that they prayed for divine guidance before reaching a decision, thus suggesting that questioning them is akin to questioning God.

Many have argued that Americans need to be concerned when those in power use their own religious point of view to interpret and judge the actions of others (Rosenblatt, 2001; Suskind, 2004). The endorsement by public officials of a particular religious view, or even of religion in general, suggests that adherence to a religious creed is a prerequisite or an advantage to those seeking justice and fair treatment. "People who govern in the name of God attribute their own personal preferences to God and therefore recognize no limits in imposing those preferences on other people" ("Center Sues to Remove Monument," 2002). Organizations such as the American Civil Liberties Union, Americans United for the Separation of Church and State, the Interfaith Alliance, and the Southern Poverty Law Center work to protect the interests of religious minorities and atheists from overzealous judges and lawmakers.

The Impact of Religion on Individuals and Families

How Religion Deters Well-Being.   As mentioned earlier, the Bible has been used to justify slavery and racism (Hill & Cheadle, 1996). The Christian faith to which slaves were introduced in America encouraged them to accept their inferior status.

The beliefs, ritual expressions, norms, and organizational structures of organized religions routinely subordinate women (McGuire, 1997). The Bible was written by men, edited by men, translated by men, and interpreted by men; until recently, most Biblical scholars were male. Thus one should not be surprised to see that men receive favorable treatment in Christian religious belief and practice. Traditional religions have placed women in exalted but protected positions. "Protected" often meant protected from becoming leaders (Schaefer, 2008, p. 156). Patriarchal views in sacred texts and many contemporary religious practices continue to reinforce gender inequity (McGuire, 1997; Roesler, 2005). Like other major religions of the world, the three Western religions (Judaism, Christianity, and Islam) are traditionally patriarchal. Orthodox Judaism, Roman Catholicism, and Islam continue to exclude women from the highest spiritual leader roles, although growing numbers of Protestant denominations, as well as Reform and Conservative Jews, allow women to lead congregations (Macionis, 2007; Simpson, 2008). Nevertheless, in many denominations, women are assigned to assistant clergy or co-pastor positions and find it more difficult than men to secure jobs in large, prestigious congregations (Schaefer, 2008). For example, even in the relatively progressive United Methodist Church, where 23 percent of the clergy are female, only 85 women lead the largest congregations, compared to 1,082 men in those positions (French, 2009).

In some other countries, where religion and government are intertwined, the power of the state may be used to impose conservative interpretations of religious restrictions on women. One of the most egregious examples was the Taliban rule in Afghanistan, where women could not leave their homes without male chaperones, were denied the right to education and to employment, and could not be properly examined by health care professionals (Roesler, 2005).

Controversies over "gay rights," "gay marriage," and the ordination of openly gay clergy are putting strains on the unity of many religious denominations. In many American churches, the divide is not geographic (as it was over slavery and abolition) but over a basic understanding of tradition and scripture (Goodstein, 2007). People on both sides of the issue cite Bible verses in support of their respective positions, with conservatives and fundamentalists using a more literal interpretation and liberals arguing that scripture must be understood in context and that one may not choose to believe and follow some verses (e.g., Leviticus, 18:22 and 20:13) and ignore others (e.g., Leviticus 11:10, 15: 19–24, 19:19, 19:27, or 25:44). Some religious leaders preach that we should insist "that all citizens receive—at the least—the respect that their status as human beings created in the image of God demands. To succumb to—or worse, to incite—fear and hatred of brothers and sisters because of their sexual orientation is to deny both God's love for us and ours for God" (Brill, 2005, p. A9).

Some religious denominations in America, especially those that are more conservative, appear to promote homophobia (Helminiak, 1994; Hill & Cheadle, 1996). Although the message may be "hate the sin, love the sinner," their rhetoric supports an atmosphere of intolerance toward gay men and lesbians, which can encourage acts of violence. Recognition of the biological determinants of human sexuality (as supported by numerous research studies) creates a dilemma for religious people who cannot then reconcile their interpretation of the Bible with the idea that people do not choose their sexual orientation (Meyerson, 2007).

Because America is a nation of mostly Christians (although not a "Christian nation" in an official sense), discrimination against members of minority religions and atheists is common (Miller, 2008). This may take the form of the obvious (such as pressure to participate in Christian prayers, or reluctance to make accommodations for non-Christian holy days or rituals) to the simply thoughtless (such as describing any generous or ethical person as an example of "a good Christian," forgetting that other faith traditions also promote moral behavior). Some Christians may ask, "Why can't we have organized prayer in public schools, or the Ten Commandments posted in the courthouse or a nativity scene in the public square? After all, this country was founded on the principle of majority rule," forgetting that in this country religious beliefs and practices are matters of individual discretion and not matters to be decided by majority vote.

Overzealous proselytizing can be interpreted as a threat by members of religious minorities. For example, Raspberry (1999) reported that the Southern Baptist International Mission Board urged its denomination members to pray for the conversion of Jews: "Pray each day for Jewish individuals you know by name . . . Love them as you would an unsaved relative." The president of the Union of American Hebrew Congregations, Rabbi Eric Yoffie, responded, "There's a kind of theological arrogance that pervades all of this, a certain willingness to play God, and an absence of awareness that these sorts of statements throughout history are associated with coercion, hatred and violence. . . . We'd like a little less love and a little more respect."

How Religion Promotes Well-Being.   Organized religion promotes the well-being of individuals, families, and society in many ways. First, religion establishes values of cooperation, altruism, and often social justice. Second, many congregations provide social services and support for individuals and groups. In addition, many religious organizations, and in particular African American churches, have nourished social movements.

Most great cultures, and all the major religions, have obliged their people to help the less fortunate, including widows, orphans, the sick or disabled, and even traveling strangers (Morris, 1986). The history of social work as a profession is closely linked to Christian traditions of helping the poor (e.g., the Charity Organization Societies). The profession also draws heavily on the Jewish principle of *tzedakah,* which can be translated as a combination of charity and justice. The traditions of Judaism emphasize the goal of promoting self-sufficiency among recipients of charity, and in protecting them from embarrassment or stigma.

One of the five pillars of Islam is *zakat*, or almsgiving. *Zakat* "is a Muslim's worship of God by means of his wealth through an obligatory form of giving to those in need" (Haneef, 1993, p. 48). Although Islam does not factor in the history of Western social work, its values are consistent with those of the profession.

People who attend church, or synagogue, or mosque regularly enjoy better mental health, probably because they have more friends as well as a support system to help them with problems in their lives (Mishori, 2008). Many religious congregations provide information and referral to connect members and other community residents to social services, training opportunities, and jobs, and sometimes grants or other funding. Their facilities also provide some social services and limited financial support to people in crisis (often members of the congregation but also to other residents of the local community). Black churches have historically functioned as social service agencies in the African American community. Congregations often provide meeting space free of charge or for a very small fee for other social organizations within their community. Many denominations support hospitals, nursing homes and retirement centers, children's homes and residential treatment centers, adoption and foster-care agencies, family life education programs, day-care centers for young children and older adults, after-school programs and recreation programs for school-aged children and adolescents, and refugee resettlement—if not with funding then with volunteers or gifts in kind (such as meeting space).

Religious organizations can provide continuity for immigrants to this country. The "ethnic church" performs multiple roles for racially and culturally distinct minorities, providing guidance, emotional support, and a broad range of social activities and outlets (Kim, 1999, p. 366). Churches, temples, and mosques help members retain a sense of identity by providing a place for religious and ethnic fellowship. People who are persecuted and discriminated against in other areas of life find interior strength and external social support in a wide variety of religious beliefs and practices. Religious organizations may offer one of the few welcoming "communities" for specific minorities. For example, the Metropolitan Community Church provides a safe haven and worship experience for gay men and lesbians.

African American churches served as a cradle for the civil rights movement and a training ground for the development of civil rights leaders. Religion can be the catalyst to those seeking social justice, inspiring individuals to break out of the limited roles prescribed for them by the society (McGuire, 1997). Black congregations continue this tradition of civic participation, frequently serving as platforms for collective mobilization. Religious congregations are especially successful in organizing local residents for political action in part because they "enjoy relations with other community institutions and congregations, larger religious bodies, and specialized, parallel religious organizations or private and public institutions" (Foley, McCarthy, & Chaves, 2001, p. 221).

Mass Media and Communications Technology

The mass media manage the flow of images and ideas across society; they are a common source of information and a source of socialization. The mass media have the potential to present similar depictions of the world to tremendous numbers of otherwise different and unrelated people (Turow, 1992). The depictions that the media deliver have the power to affect people's attitudes toward social issues, other people, and even themselves. "Media products are unique in one vital respect. They do not manufacture nuts and bolts: they manufacture a social and political world" (Bagdikian, 2004, p. 9). One media expert noted, "everywhere, the media flow defies national boundaries. This is one of its obvious, but at the same time, amazing features. . . . If there is a [global] village, it speaks American, it wears jeans, drinks Coke, eats at the golden arches, walks on swooshed shoes, plays electric guitars, recognizes Mickey Mouse, James Dean, E.T., Bart Simpson, R2-D2, and Pamela Anderson" (Gitlin, 2001, p. 176).

Because it has multiple functions and serves individual needs, it is unclear whether the Internet is a "mass medium"; it does not fit the usual definition as it lacks centralized control that decides what shall be distributed to the general public (Bagdikian, 2004, p. 56). Nevertheless, it appears that the Internet has changed not only the method of delivery, but also the nature of the product that is delivered (Kinsley, 2006). Blogs and podcasts present more immediate, individualized, less objective content. In a world with tens of millions of bloggers, the messages received are not only more much more numerous and varied but also much less verifiable (Parker, 2006). Each blogger holds a "megaphone" of sorts, but only a very few hold a degree in journalism.

The mass media are what some sociologists call an "emerging social institution." They are relatively new in human history, dating from the invention of movable type in 1436. Not until the 1840s, with the invention of the telegraph, was long-distance communication separated from transportation (Croteau & Hoynes, 2003). One might note the contemporary irony that people who are immersed in a crisis that cuts them off from their television sets and computers may know much less about what is going on in their immediate vicinity than do media consumers thousands of miles away.

The development of newspapers, magazines, radio, movies, network television, cable TV, and the Internet, and the ubiquitous presence of electronic devices, have made the media an increasingly powerful and influential social institution. In 1950, only 9 percent of American homes owned a television; by 1955, the percentage had jumped to 64.5 percent and by 1965, it increased to 92.6 percent (Television Information Office, 1985). Now virtually all American households have at least one television set. In 1997, 16.6 percent of American households had cable TV service; in 2006, 86.2 percent had cable or satellite service (Rust & Yoder, 2007).

Based on a national survey, the Nielson Company reports that nearly 75 percent of American households have a computer (Nielsen Media Research, 2006). Homes with incomes over $60,000 are 50 percent more likely to own a home computer than homes with a lower income. Of those with Internet access, 95 percent go online at least once a week and 37 percent go online more than once a day. Nonusers of the Internet are more likely to be minority, rural, and low-income families (Bagdikian, 2004).

In 2003, 91 percent of American children aged three and over (nursery school through grade 12) used computers and about 59 percent used the Internet (National Center for Education Statistics, 2006). Many disadvantaged children used the Internet only at school (National Center for Education Statistics, 2006).

According to comScore Inc. (2008), a global Internet information provider, as of March 2006, 14 percent of the world's population aged 15 and over used the Internet. The United States ranks first in the number of users, but is not even among the top 15 in average hours spent online by individuals; Israel, Finland, South Korea, the Netherlands, and Taiwan are the top five. The top online properties worldwide are MSN-Microsoft, Google, Yahoo!, eBay, Time Warner, Amazon, and Wikipedia.

Issues and Trends in Mass Media and Communications Technology

Violence in the Media.   Probably the most notable contemporary issue related to the mass media is concern about the graphic portrayal of violence. The American Medical Association, the American Academy of Pediatrics, and the American Psychological Association have gone on record reporting the negative effects of violence in the mass media, especially on television and in films, based on studies that show correlations between viewing patterns and aggressive behavior. (Documenting correlation is not the same as proving cause and effect; there may be other mitigating factors that make some children more vulnerable to effects of violence in the media [see Figure 4.1].) Research studies on violence on television have documented that children become less sensitive to the pain and suffering of others, are more fearful of the world around them, more likely to behave in aggressive and harmful ways toward others, and more accepting of use of violence as a way to solve problems (American Academy of Child and Adolescent

FIGURE 4.1   *Critical Thinking About Violence and the Media*

Research has documented a significant correlation between viewing television violence and aggressive behaviors. Which of these possible explanations of association seems most plausible to you?

❑ Children who are more aggressive are drawn to aggressive programming.

❑ Portrayals of violence in the media lead children to be aggressive (by providing models of aggression).

❑ There is a reciprocal relationship between aggressive behavior and viewing violence (each causes the other to increase).

❑ Both behaviors are caused by another variable, such as inattentive parents.

Source: Adapted from Kundanis (2003).

Psychiatry, 2002; American Psychological Association, 2008). A review of 20 years of research also indicates that violent video games increase aggressive behavior in children and adolescents; children who play more violent video games also have more arguments with authority figures (American Psychological Association, 2005). The American Academy of Child and Adolescent Psychiatry (2004) reports that common themes in music videos include advocating and glamorizing abuse of drugs and alcohol; pictures and explicit lyrics presenting suicide as an "alternative" or "solution" to problems; sex which focuses on control, sadism, masochism, and incest; and violence toward women, in addition to graphic violence in general.

Even local news programs tend to focus on violence. A study analyzing the content of 52 markets on March 11, 1998, found that 46 percent of the news was about crime, disaster, war, or terrorism (LaFayette, 1998). The newspaper axiom "If it bleeds, it leads" influences the electronic media as well. Sensational violent crimes make up less than 1 percent of all crimes, but they constitute a majority of crime coverage, leaving viewers and readers with a badly distorted picture of their world (Dyer, 2000, p. 87).

Mass Media, Communications Technology, and Children.   As one expert noted, "the place of the media in the lives of children is worth special attention—not simply because children are uniquely impressionable but because their experience shapes everyone's future" (Gitlin, 2001, p. 17). Television was the first mode of mass media to prompt legislation to protect children's interests. The 1990 Children's Television Act (CTA), along with the Federal Communication Commission (FCC) sets limits on advertising for children's programs. The Telecommunication Act of 1996 required both television and cable operators to provide the V-chip, a mechanism to give parents and other caregivers control over inappropriate programming.

The American Academy of Pediatrics suggests that no child under age two years should watch screen media (Knell, 2006). Nevertheless, "baby videos designed for one-month-olds, computer games for 9-month-olds, and TV shows for one-year-olds are becoming commonplace," according to a Kaiser Family Foundation study of the media (Rideout, Hamel, & Kaiser Family Foundation, 2006, p. 4). Another study found that 40 percent of children regularly watch television by three months of age, and by age two years, 90 percent watch an average of one and a half hours of TV each day (Jackson, 2007). One in three children, six and younger, has a television set in his or her bedroom (Rideout, Hamel, & Kaiser Family Foundation, 2006, p. 4). Rather than using television as a babysitter, two-thirds of parents are convinced that the medium is a good source of learning and helps children get along with others (Jackson, 2007). The Kaiser Family Foundation study noted that parents use TV or DVDs as a "safe" activity to entertain their children while they get ready for work or do household chores; as a tool to change the mood of grouchy, hyper, or squabbling children; as a reward for good behavior; to facilitate transitions, such as calming down before bedtime; and as an instructional tool for teaching basic reading and counting skills (Rideout, Hamel, & Kaiser Family Foundation, 2006).

One PBS television program, *Teletubbies*, proclaims that it is designed to "introduce young children—ages one to three—to the wonders and magic of high-tech" (PBS Kids, 2004). Aware that children under two were routinely watching *Sesame Street* (a program aimed at children ages two to five), the Sesame Workshop (formerly known as the Children's Television Workshop, a nonprofit organization behind the production of several children's educational programs) developed *Sesame Beginnings* DVDs, providing parents and caregivers of children under two with content specifically designed for babies and toddlers. Products ranked Level 1 are for babies from birth to six months. Other videos designed especially for babies include "Classical Baby" and "Baby Einstein." And there are Internet Web sites that are directed specifically at preschoolers (e.g., *Teletubbies*, *Poisson Rouge*).

Diversity and the Media.   In the United States, the media are extremely powerful simply because they are unavoidable. Either from direct viewing or reading, or from secondhand reports, Americans obtain the vast majority of their knowledge and beliefs about life outside of their direct experience from media sources (Lester, 1996, p. 6). Americans are becoming more comfortable with being a diverse nation, but minority cultures are increasingly defined by advertisers and scriptwriters rather than reflecting genuine ethnic heritage. Unfortunately, portrayals that assume and reinforce negative stereotypes are common (Lester, 1996, p. 7).

Although the proliferation of cable channels has allowed for "niche marketing" and "narrowcasting"—programming directed at specific minorities (e.g., African Americans, Spanish speakers)—studies show that rather than encouraging cultural integration, this pattern may further segregate those populations from the mainstream. In other words, African Americans watch programs with predominantly black casts and whites watch programs with predominantly white casts, and the demand for broadly popular series such as *The Cosby Show,* which appealed to people of all races, no longer exists (Schaefer, 2008). Because ultimately the goal of the media is to generate profits, diversification to include underserved audiences is likely to occur only if they are identified as growing consumer markets (Turow, 1997).

The Internet.   According to a Pew Internet & American Life Project survey (2009), 93 percent of American youth aged 12 to 17 use the Internet. Levels of usage drop off with age, with 45 percent of 70–75-year-olds using it and 27 percent of those 76 or older. Teens and young adults use the Internet for entertainment and communicating with friends and family; older generations use it as a tool for research, shopping, and banking (Pew Internet & American Life Project, 2009). Many older adults find it difficult to use many Internet Web sites, preferring those that have senior-friendly features, such as simpler layouts, larger type fonts, and higher color contrast between words and backgrounds (Joseph & Stone, 2005). Experts expect that by the year 2020, mobile devices will be the primary connection tool to the Internet for most people in the world; intellectual property law and copyright protections will be jeopardized by those who find ways to copy and share content without payment; and the divisions between personal time and work time and between physical and virtual reality will be further erased (Pew Internet & American Life Project, 2008).

A threat of a different kind is found in the expansion of the Internet and its uncensored Web sites that not only dispense inaccurate information but also actively promote discrimination and violence against vulnerable groups. The Southern Poverty Law Center reported that there were 630 active U.S.-based hate sites on the World Wide Web in 2008 ("Hate Websites," 2009). Organizations with Web sites included groups affiliated with the Ku Klux Klan (52 sites), Neo-Nazis (89 sites), White Nationalists (190 sites), Racist Skinheads (25 sites), Christian Identify (37 sites), Neo-Confederate (25 sites), and Black Separatists (40 sites). The Pulitzer Prize winning columnist Thomas Friedman wrote,

> because the Internet has an aura of "technology" surrounding it, the uneducated believe information from it even more. They don't realize that the Internet, at its ugliest, is just an open sewer, an electronic conduit for untreated, unfiltered information. Worse, just when you might have thought you were all alone with your extreme views, the Internet puts you together with a community of people from around the world who hate all the things and people you do. (Friedman, 2002, p. A9)

On a more positive note, more and more people are using the Internet for job-related tasks and to inform themselves on a variety of topics, such as medical conditions, weather reports, current events, and consumer goods. In academic settings, both students and instructors have come to rely on the resources offered online.

A study by the Annenberg Public Policy Center (Stange, 2006) found that almost 60 percent of young people aged 14 to 22 use the Internet as their primary source of news. The study also found that reading newspapers increases political awareness, but utilizing the Internet increases both political awareness and civic engagement.

Trends in News Consumption. According to the Pew Research Center for the People and the Press (2008) since 1993, the proportion of Americans who read a newspaper on a typical day has declined by about 40 percent and the proportion who routinely watch nightly network news has fallen by half. The proportion of young people who get no news on a typical day has increased substantially over the past decade. But 15 percent of Americans have a "smart phone" (e.g., iPhone or Blackberry); more than a third of them report they get news using these devices.

As technology has transformed mass communications, there have been major changes in the print media. Between 1950 and 2005, the number of daily newspapers in the United States declined from 1772 to 1425 (Rust & Yoder, 2007). Within the last 30 years, almost half of the afternoon dailies in large cities have either gone out of business or merged with a morning paper (Bagdikian, 2004). Three respected city daily newspapers, the [Denver] *Rocky Mountain News,* the *Minneapolis Star Tribune,* and the *Seattle Post Intelligencer,* shut down in early 2009. Isaacson (2009) suggests that the problem is not that people are no longer reading newspapers, but that the papers are giving away content for free on their Web sites. He says that newspapers traditionally relied on three revenue sources—newsstand sales, subscriptions, and advertising—and under the new business model, they rely only on the last of these.

In 2007, American newspapers recorded their worst sales decline in modern history (Mutter, 2008). Newspaper stocks fell an average of 83.3 percent in 2008; the Tribune Company, which publishes the *LA Times* and the *Chicago Tribune*, filed for bankruptcy protection in December (National Public Radio, January 12, 2009).

In a January 2009 interview on NPR, Leonard Downie, Jr., who was executive editor of the *Washington Post* for 17 years, discussed the financial crisis of the newspaper industry.

> It's definitely the end of an era, but it's not the end of time for journalism. It's the end of . . . the era of the big, strong newspapers. All their staff expanded, they made lots of money, their circulation reached a peak. It was the golden era of American newspapers. [Despite the decline in circulation] we have acquired this huge audience on the Internet of 10 to 20 million unique visitors a month. So more people are reading *Washington Post* journalism than ever before. The series of articles we did on how soldiers were being treated—wounded soldiers were being treated at Walter Reed Hospital had 5 million page views and an extraordinary response from people across the world over the Internet that forced the government to take immediate action to change things at Walter Reed, fire the Army secretary, et cetera. None of that would have been possible without the Internet. So that's the good news. (National Public Radio, January 12, 2009)

Downie also expressed concern about newsrooms shrinking due to economic pressures and whether or not some cities around the country are going to have sufficiently large staffs to cover their communities. Unlike other media, newspapers are crucial to American civic life. Citizens need vital information about property taxes, the school system, changes in utility rates, and local elections and the only medium that provides detailed information about these matters is the printed newspaper (Bagdikian, 2004).

In contrast to newspapers, magazine consumption has increased, primarily because of niche marketing (Rust & Yoder, 2007). The proliferation of magazines reflects the increasing variety of consumer goods. When a product has sufficient sales, it can generate a new magazine focusing on that area—everything from motorcycles to bridal gowns.

Technology and U.S. Elections.   For the first time in a U.S. presidential election campaign, in 2008, ordinary citizens became active participants by producing their own material on the contenders, putting together countless political ads and mashups of video and audio clips and user comments. "The term is 'user-generated content'—a fancy way of saying that anyone with a computer now can become a player in politics" (Alter, 2008, p. 4).

Major political candidates began using the Internet for effective fund-raising in 2004. Barack Obama used technology to great effect during his presidential bid. In his 21-month campaign, he built a list of 3.1 million contributors and more than 10 million supporters (Fouhy, 2008; Murray & Most, 2008). Using online social networking, he drew crowds of 75,000 to his campaign speeches in the spring of 2008, 150 times the size of the audiences he saw early in the race (Alter, 2008). Those in his email database made up a volunteer corps that registered millions of voters and served as the backbone of his get-out-the-vote operation on Election Day (Murray & Most, 2008). A supporter stated that Obama's use of technology "will reinvent the relationship of the president to the American people in a way we probably haven't seen since FDR's use of radio in the 1930s" (Connolly, 2008). Obama has created the first truly "wired" presidency.

Changing Patterns of Ownership: Media Mergers.   In 1983, there were 50 dominant media corporations. The decade of the 1990s witnessed a concentration of entertainment and news media ownership. Five large conglomerates now own and operate television networks, radio stations, film studios, music studios, book publishing companies, video rental and movie theater chains, and magazine and newspaper outlets. The five are AOL Time Warner, the Walt Disney Company (which owns ABC), News Corporation owned by Rupert Murdoch (which owns Fox News and the

Wall Street Journal), Viacom (which owns CBS), and Bertelsmann (which is the largest publisher of English language books in the world) (Bagdikian, 2004). Rather than competing with each other, these five corporations cooperate with each other in a way that expands their individual power; acting individually, any one of them can control market conditions (Bagdikian, 2004). For example, in Europe AOL Time Warner partners with both Bertelsmann and News Corporation in cable operations.

Understanding the Mass Media and Communications Technology

Functionalist Perspective.   For most Americans, print, film, radio, music, television, and the Internet are central parts of daily life. These media experiences have the social effect of creating a common frame of reference. Functionalists would say that elements of the popular cultural have the effect of strengthening social bonds. Disseminating information and entertainment are clearly the manifest functions of the mass media. Although their function as an agent of socialization is sometimes manifest (as in programs like *Sesame Street*), often people are unaware of how television and other media continue to socialize not only children but also adults. They support mainstream cultural values (e.g., individualism, competition, and patriotism). Another function of the mass media is to promote commerce by marketing goods and services.

Conflict Perspective.   Conflict theorists argue that the mass media are controlled by the wealthy and powerful, who use them to mold public opinion and to help preserve their place of privilege. The messages put forth by the mass media reflect the positions of the owners and managers. "Who gets depicted, what about them gets depicted, why, with what consequences, at what time, and in what situation" is determined in the corporate boardroom (Turow, 1992, p. 164).

Many groups in society are losing access to the public sphere through the media as a result of the mergers discussed under Issues and Trends section. This has limited the ability of sections of the community to voice their interests, their opinions, and their priorities and has prevented other groups from responding to, or even being aware of, these different voices (Curran, 1992, p. 102). There is a "fundamental contradiction between the ideal that public media should operate as a public sphere and the reality of concentrated private ownership" (Golding & Murdock, 1992, p. 23). McChesney (2000, pp. 29–30) argues that such a concentration of economic, cultural, and political power into so few hands—and mostly unaccountable hands at that—threatens the very basis of democracy.

Constructionist Perspective.   The messages that the mass media present play a central role in organizing the images and conversations through which people make sense of the world (Golding & Murdock, 1992, p. 15). A vast body of research has demonstrated that media content does not reflect the realities of the social world.

The late George Gerbner and his colleagues at the Annenburg Public Policy Center at the University of Pennsylvania have studied the mass media for many years. They are concerned about television's role as an "electronic storyteller," replacing traditional cultural sources and monopolizing the socialization process. Most of what we know (or think we know) comes from stories in our culture, not from direct personal experience. With the ever-present effects of the mass media, everyone in America views the same images and listens to the same dialogue, defining what is to be valued and what is to be discounted. There is a homogenization of culture, with much of it being presented for the "lowest common denominator" or, at least, at the level that will bring in viewers and attract sponsors. Gerbner's *cultivation theory* (Gerbner, Gross, Morgan, & Signorielli, 1994) suggests that heavy viewers of television come to develop a common outlook on the world that is consistent with what they see on TV. Because images are similar across television channels, heavier viewers hold more stereotyped views of social groups than do light viewers (Gerbner et al., 1994), they are more sexist (Signorielli, 1993) and racist (Gerbner, Gross, Morgan, & Signorielli, 1982), and more likely to believe that the world is a violent and dangerous place (Gerbner, et al., 1994).

Relationship of Mass Media and Communications Technology to the Political Economy

The media are often referred to as the "Fourth Estate" or the "fourth branch of government." This designation reflects the idea that the media (originally print journalists or "the press") have an important role in overseeing government functioning, and in particular in revealing abuses of state authority (Curran, 1992). This "watchdog" role is supposed to override all other functions in importance. One might argue that now the threat to individual freedom lays not so much with government abuse as with corporate oligopoly. One of the consequences of corporate control of the media is that reporters are less likely to investigate the actions of the conglomerates that pay their salaries (Curran, 1992).

Underwood (1993) reported that as marketing has become the focus of most newspapers, MBAs with a background in the business world began to replace people with journalistic experience in executive positions. The clear goal of media executives is to create steady profits. The easiest approach for audience maximization (and the advertising revenues that follow) is to create a light, entertainment-oriented product, even in news programming. Media analysts Neil Postman and Steve Powers (1992) argued, for example, that television news was primarily "entertainment fodder." Because advertisers, not consumers, are doing the most important buying, the principle product being sold by the media is the *audience* (i.e., consumers), not newspapers, magazines, or programs (Croteau & Hoyes, 2003).

In the 1990s, several sources (e.g., Jacobson & Mazur, 1995; Kerwin, 1992; Masterson, 1993) documented the often successful efforts of advertisers to get editors of magazines and newspapers to censor content that might reflect negatively on their companies or their products. For example, in 1996 Chrysler sent a letter through its ad agency, PentaCom, telling magazines that carried its advertising that they would need to be notified in advance of "any and all editorial content that encompasses sexual, political, social issues, or any editorial that might be construed as provocative or offensive" (Baker, 1997, p. 30). Although automakers "apparently lead the pack," manufacturers of packaged goods and large retail outlets are also touchy about the content of articles and editorials (Baker, 1997, p. 31). Some sponsors claim they fear reactions of activist groups despite evidence that consumer boycotts do little, if any, damage to sales.

Despite the disquieting trends noted above, the United States is one of very few countries where the general perception is that the media should be controlled exclusively by market forces rather than being responsible to the public well-being (Lazar, 1994). In fact, there has been increasing deregulation of American broadcasting, prompted in part by a proliferation of cable channels that supposedly allow the presentation of a wide variety of programming and opposing points of view on all topics.

Politics has become inextricably intertwined with the mass media, and in particular, with television. The medium of television has been accused of having negative effects on the American election process, in particular in relation to the increased cost of political campaigns and a focus on candidates' images rather than campaign issues (Perse, 2001). The soaring costs of modern election campaigns are a direct reflection of the price of airtime. It is now virtually impossible to get elected to national or state office without an effective media campaign.

The media also detract from American politics by treating political life as a "spectator sport." The sports metaphor of "winning" and "losing" dominates media news and discussion (Croteau & Hoynes, 2003). During the 2008 presidential campaign, newspapers and many major TV networks provided almost daily updates on each candidate's standing in a variety of public opinion polls, eliciting images of a slow-motion horse race. Media coverage of campaigns focuses on the comparative electability of the candidates rather than where they stand on issues. In response to media pressure, candidates often are presented as personalities (created through a process called *packaging*). Instead of studying and taking a position on an issue, politicians may say something that simply reflects the results of a recent poll or focus group. With a growing demand for 24/7 political coverage, news programs resort to broadcasting repetitions of short blips and slips. Of course, citizens need more adequate information to make informed decisions in the voting booth.

The Impact of Mass Media and Communications Technology on Individuals and Families

How Mass Media and Communications Technology Deter Well-Being

Images that Hurt and Mislead. A multitude of studies have been conducted to analyze how the media present people of different genders, sexual orientations, ages, social classes, physical (dis)abilities, and racial and ethnic backgrounds. A majority of viewers and readers believe that media messages, even advertisements aimed directly at them, have little impact. Media critic Jean Kilbourne (1999, p. 27) notes, however, that "the most effective kind of propaganda is that which is not recognized as propaganda."

Affluent white men have historically controlled the mainstream media, which helps to explain why some groups are virtually invisible and others are presented in a negative light. In fact, the pervasiveness of a white perspective in the media is one of its most powerful characteristics. The media do not talk about "white culture," or "the white community," as they do "Latino culture" or "the black community," suggesting that whiteness is to be taken for granted and the norm against which all other groups are to be measured (Croteau & Hoyes, 2003).

There are two questions to be addressed in relation to vulnerable populations and the media. First, are they even there? And second, what is the nature of the images presented? A study conducted in 2000 of television and theatrical roles showed that African Americans received almost 15 percent of all roles cast (which is larger than their proportion in the U.S. population). Latinos, however, and Asian Americans were badly underrepresented (4.9 percent and 2.2 percent, respectively) (Screen Actors Guild, 2001). In a two-week sample of the four major networks and the WB Television Network, Mastro and Behm-Morawitz (2005) found that 80 percent of characters were white, 14 percent were black, 4 percent were Latino, and 1.5 percent were Asian. Native Americans are virtually invisible outside of reruns of old Westerns.

Television commercials are a significant source of information for children; children are more likely to pay attention and are more receptive to their messages than adults. Children who do not have direct experience with racial diversity are more likely to draw on televised representations of majority and minority cultures. Children's perceptions of race and ethnicity are shaped by depictions of social power, defined by comparative visibility, status, and roles assigned to characters in TV ads. A study of television commercials in children's programming on all broadcast networks and Nickelodeon found that 74 percent of all primary characters were white, 19.4 percent were African American, 2.2 percent were Latino, and 2 percent were Asian American (Li-Vollmer, 2002). Native Americans were only a fraction of 1 percent of primary characters—"virtually undetectable" in the author's opinion (Li-Vollmer, 2002, p. 220). As other media studies have found, African Americans were slightly over-represented, while other minorities were underrepresented. Minority characters were more visible in public service announcements (PSAs), where they accounted for 65 percent of the primary characters; in product advertisements, only 22 percent of primary characters were minority members. White characters appeared in commercials for every type of product, but the presence of minority characters was dependent on the type of product advertised. About a third of the Asian characters were used to advertise technology-related products, such as computers and video games (one of the smallest categories); less than 5 percent of whites, less than half of 1 percent of blacks, and no Latinos appeared in technology commercials. Almost all (97 percent) of Latino characters were found in ads for restaurants. (This may be a result of the efforts of the advertisers for fast-food chain restaurants to reach broad audiences by being inclusive in their commercials; in fact, they underuse white characters.) African Americans were often cast as athletes or as musicians, singers, and dancers. Whites were shown as professionals, and as problem solvers. When commercials were racially integrated, the solo speaking parts were most likely to be given to white characters. Modest increases in the number of people of color who appear in commercials are insignificant when compared to the biases in the roles depicted. "Few adults, let alone children, are likely to analyze the differences in the distribution of race in various kinds of product commercials or the settings in which various characters appear, or even the occupational roles assigned; as a result, both adults and children would be hard pressed to even consciously recognize the racial biases, no matter how sensitive they are to such issues" (Li-Vollmer, 2002, p. 224).

Network news anchors are overwhelmingly white and male (Poniewozik, 2008), as are the guests on Sunday morning news and talk shows. A two-year study by the National Urban league (Jones, 2006) of broadcasts from January 1, 2004, through December 31, 2005, revealed that 61 percent featured no black guests, and of the black guests that did appear, three individuals (Condoleezza Rice, Colin Powell, and Juan Williams) accounted for 65 percent of all appearances. According to a Media Matters follow-up study ("Sunday Shutout," 2007), two out of every three guests were white men, only 1 percent of the guests were Latino, and men outnumbered women by a four-to-one ratio. Blatantly racist images—the bloodthirsty savage, or the shuffling, slow-witted black servant—now are rarely found in the media, although that was not always the case. Nevertheless, people of color are often restricted to certain types of programming. For example, Mastro and Greenberg (2000) noted that over three-quarters of all roles for Latinos were in crime dramas and the majority of roles for African Americans were in either sitcoms or crime dramas. In a break with the past, Mastro and Behm-Morawitz (2005) found that African Americans were often cast as police officers.

The family and heterosexual relationships central to the plots of many films, music videos, and television programs ensure that women are regularly included in media roles (Croteau & Hoynes, 2003, p. 212); nevertheless, women have never achieved 50 percent parity in network broadcast television (Comstock & Scharrer, 2007). In a study conducted by Aubrey and Harrison (2004) on children's programs, the same uneven gender content was apparent, with only 29 percent of lead characters and 35 percent of the minor characters being female. A study of 47 Nintendo and Playstation games found that 72 percent of the characters were male (Beasley, Collins, & Standley, 2002) and it is rare for a main character to be female (Comstock & Scharrer, 2007). As with other minorities, women and girls in the media are often presented in biased ways. Compared to boys, girls under 20 are disproportionately represented on television and women over 50 almost disappear (Lauzen & Dozier, 2005); findings suggest that an emphasis on youth applies more strongly to females than to males (Comstock & Scharrer, 2007). Females who are below average in weight are clearly overrepresented in programming that is popular with teenage girls, and female characters tend to be critical of themselves regarding weight and body shape (Fouts & Burggraf, 1999). Music videos and television commercials also idealize slimness. The appearance of girls and women in video games is designed to appeal to adolescent boys; they are highly sexualized with large breasts and scanty clothing (Comstock & Scharrer, 2007). A muscular ideal for males has also been advanced in most forms of the mass media.

The literature continues to suggest that stereotypical gender behaviors are also portrayed in music videos and computer games (Comstock & Scharrer, 2007). When females appear on children's television, they are likely to be portrayed as nurturing, passive, subdued, and dependent, in contrast to the active, aggressive, and adventurous male characters (Barner, 1999). In spite of these general patterns in children's programming, there are recent examples of nonstereotypical portrayals to be found, generally on PBS and Nickelodeon channels (Comstock & Scharrer, 2007).

Gender stereotyping is greater in advertising than in programming. In prime-time television commercials, women are assigned to perform household tasks and child care (Scharrer, Kim, Lin, Lu, 2006). When men do perform these tasks, they are likely to be portrayed as incompetent. Print ads feature pencil-thin female models with large breasts (often computer-enhanced) with implicit subtexts that suggest that women are subservient to men, if not obviously sex objects (Kilbourne, 1999). Even images that magazines present of mothers mask the reality of women's lives. "No one tires, no one frets, no one sweats. Motherhood is presented as a series of appealing snapshots" (Schwartz, 1996, p. 78).

Subtle differences in the language that is used signify that a male perspective is the norm in American society. For example, coverage of women's events includes constant *gender marking*: announcers make clear it is the NCAA *Women's* National Championship Game, while the men's version is billed simply as the NCAA National Championship Game.

One study (Signorielli, 2001) of occupations depicted on prime-time television found an increase in the number of professional roles held by women; however, these were unlikely to be combined with family responsibilities.

As with African Americans and women, the number of portrayals of lesbians and gay men in the media has grown, and their portrayal has slowly become less stereotypical (Croteau & Hoynes, 2003).

There were positive representations of gay men on television beginning in the late 1970s and early 1980s. The first lesbian female lead in a situation comedy on prime-time network television was Ellen DeGeneres, in *Ellen*, in 1997. Although her series was cancelled the following year, she is now a successful and popular talk-show host. The first gay male lead of a situation comedy appeared a year later with the introduction of *Will & Grace*. *Will & Grace* was the most successful show with multiple gay characters in lead roles. Throughout its eight-year run, *Will & Grace* earned 16 Emmy Awards. Another prominent gay-themed show, *Queer Eye for the Straight Guy*, premiered in 2003. This Emmy-award-winning reality series was premised on stereotypical skills that gay men are assumed to possess: including interior decorating, grooming, and gourmet cooking and featured five gay men who offered make-over advice. *Queer Eye* ended production in 2006 but continues in syndication. While other programs did not feature gays in leading roles, there were recurring gay characters on several shows, such as *Friends, Mad About You, Dawson's Creek*, and *The Simpsons*.

The Gay and Lesbian Alliance Against Defamation (GLAAD) reported that the 2008–2009 television season had 16 gay and bisexual characters in prime-time series, more than double the seven of the previous year ("Broadcast TV Sees Big Boost on Prime-Time Series," 2008).

Between regular and recurring characters, GLAAD reported the highest number of gay, lesbian, and bisexual characters that had occurred in its 13 years of monitoring network television. Founded in 2002, a GLBT premium channel, *here!TV*, airs on all major U.S. cable systems ("here! Gay television on demand," 2009). Gay characters on American scripted television programs continue to be primarily white males (Comstock & Scharrer, 2007).

People with disabilities are largely absent from the media. When they are presented, their disability is usually the focus of the story. Persons with disabilities very seldom appear as simply another character, either central to the plot or incidental (Makas, 1993; Nelson, 1996). One notable exception is the main character on the Fox network television medical drama, *House*. Due to an infection in his right thigh, Dr. House lost a substantial portion of the muscle in his upper leg and uses a cane to assist with walking. Another exception is PBS, and in particular *Sesame Street*, which routinely includes children and adults with disabilities without portraying them as either victims or heroes.

Although many of the early television sitcoms featured working-class families (*The Honeymooners, Andy Griffith Show, The Waltons, Happy Days*) as well as a few of the more recent ones (*Roseanne, All in the Family, Sanford and Son, The Simpsons, Everybody Loves Raymond, The King of Queens, Family Guy*), overwhelmingly, the society portrayed in American media is middle or upper class. Affluent images are the most obvious in advertising but they also are apparent in television programming (Croteau & Hoynes, 2003). Examples of middle- and upper-class TV families include *Ozzie and Harriet, Father Knows Best, Dick Van Dyke Show, Cosby Show, Family Ties, Dallas, Judging Amy, Mad About You, Frasier, West Wing*, and *Desperate Housewives*.

Prime-time television programming presents a world that is also skewed in the representation of the age of the main characters. Older adults in particular are missing. In a research study that covered a time period from 1993 to 2002, Signorielli (2004) found that less than 3 percent of prime-time characters were 65 years and older. Overrepresentation of characters between the ages of 30 and 50 might be explained by an economic model that suggests that the industry is trying to attract viewers in a prime consumer demographic group, but this model fails to account for the exclusion of those over 60, who have more disposable income (Comstock & Scharrer, 2007; Lauzen & Dozier, 2005). It may be that a larger societal bias against the aged is at play.

Public Health Issues.   The content of television programs and commercials may have a negative impact on viewers' health. Sports programming, for example, is flooded with soda, beer, pizza, fast food, and snack food commercials. Similar products, with the omission of beer and the addition of candy and sweetened breakfast cereals, appear in commercials in children's programs. Too often, children's distorted understanding of nutrition comes from Saturday morning television (Signorielli & Lears, 1992). Today, teens drink twice as much soda as milk; this is the opposite of the pattern that prevailed a generation ago (Kilbourne, 1999, p. 46). According to a Kaiser Family Foundation study (2007), the majority of foods that children see advertised on television are foods that contribute to childhood obesity. The study noted the abundance of advertisements for junk food and also pointed out the lack of public service announcements for healthy eating. In 2006, the nation's largest food and beverage companies spent about $1.6 billion marketing their products to children, according to a Federal Trade Commission Report (Freking, 2008). Spending on ads for soda came to $492 million and fast-food restaurants reported spending $294 million. There is no advertising for fruits and vegetables because there is no "branding" of those products (Comstock & Scharrer, 2007).

In a fascinating study funded by Stanford University and the Robert Wood Johnson Foundation (Tanner, 2007), three- to five-year old children were presented with identical food items in

McDonald's and unmarked wrappers; the children always favored the food in the brand-name packaging. According to the researchers, the children's perception of taste was "physically altered by the branding" (Tanner, 2007, p. B7).

Alcohol and tobacco use are commonly associated with exposure to advertisements and to programs that present drinking and smoking as glamorous activities with no consequences (Perse, 2001). Alcohol is the most frequently advertised beverage in televised sports and the most common type of drink portrayed in programming. More underage youth drink alcohol than smoke tobacco or use illicit drugs. Half of the alcohol advertising on radio is aired during youth-oriented programs (CDC, 2006). Researchers studied 24 G-rated Disney films that contained an animated human character and found 18 had at least one instance of "alcohol exposure," defined as a "continuous display" of an alcoholic product (e.g., beer, wine) on the screen (Ryan & Hoerrner, 2004).

Tobacco ads were banned from the broadcast media in 1971; however, through print ads and clever product placement, tobacco companies are able to effectively target not only adults but also children. Cigarette smoking occurs even in G-rated children's films (Ryan & Hoerrner, 2004) and is frequently portrayed in many popular films (Comstock & Scharrer, 2007).

The mass media are also effective in promoting the idea that casual sexual activity brings no negative consequences (Lowry & Shidler, 1993). A 2002 study found that "two-thirds of all television shows airing between 7 a.m. and 11 p.m. had some sexual content, and roughly one in seven shows now includes a portrayal of sexual intercourse, either depicted or strongly implied" (Brown, 2002, p. A3). A study analyzing 1,154 programs (excluding newscasts, sports events, and children's shows) from the 2004–2005 television season (Kaiser Family Foundation, 2005) found that seven in ten programs on cable and broadcast networks contained sexual content and the most popular shows with teenagers are more likely than other programs to feature sexual inferences or images. A RAND Corporation study on the effects of television on teens' sexual activity (2004) found that watching TV shows with sexual content apparently hastens the initiation of teen sexual activity, but shows with content about contraception and pregnancy can help to educate teens about the risks and consequences of sex—and can also foster beneficial dialogue between teens and parents. Beyond television, research also documents risks associated with popular music. Teens who listen to songs with degrading sexual content are more likely to engage in early sexual behavior (Martino et al., 2006).

Repeal of the Fairness Doctrine.   The Fairness Doctrine was a federal law, enacted by Congress in 1949, that required radio and television stations to provide a minimum amount of time for discussion of civic issues, allowing equal time for opposing viewpoints. In the mid-1980s, the National Association of Broadcasters launched a successful campaign to repeal the Act. In the six months following the repeal in 1987, civic discussion on the air dropped by 31 percent and since then has virtually disappeared in major markets (Bagdikian, 2004). In February 2005, a representative from New York and 23 co-sponsors introduced a bill that would have required that a station cover important issues fairly and hold local public hearings about its coverage twice a year, but the bill never made it out of committee. Opponents of the Fairness Doctrine argue that it is possible for just about any point of view to be heard in today's media (including the Internet). Proponents worry that cable TV programs, bloggers, and talk-show radio hosts tend to target a specific audience that then fails to investigate sources that offer opposing viewpoints.

How Mass Media and Communications Technology Promote Well-being.   Social learning theory suggests that children will imitate behaviors they observe. In addition to the negative effects noted earlier in this section of the chapter, studies have shown that young viewers of programs like *Mr. Rogers' Neighborhood* exhibit pro-social behaviors such as being more cooperative and helpful and talking about their feelings (Friedrich & Stein, 1975). A longitudinal study of the effects of television viewing by preschoolers was associated with a number of positive characteristics in adolescents: getting higher grades, reading more books, being more creative, valuing achievement, and acting less aggressively (Anderson, Huston, Schmitt, Linebarger, & Wright, 2001).

One of the most positive aspects of the mass media is their potential to capture the nation's attention and support in the struggle against injustice or fraud. The civil rights movement of the 1960s was nurtured through media exposure. The investigative journalism of Bob Woodward and Carl Bernstein of the *Washington Post* led to the resignation of Richard Nixon when they exposed illegal activities related to the Watergate scandal. During the Vietnam War, seeing film footage from the frontlines on the evening news was at least in part responsible for a growing antiwar sentiment that shifted perceptions and public support.

Television offers a cheap source of entertainment for people who cannot afford to go out, or are restricted to home for other reasons. It may be the only connection some older adults or other isolated individuals have to the world outside of their homes. TV viewing may be the only activity that some families are able to share.

The importance of the communication function of the media becomes particularly clear during an emergency situation. Residents of communities that experience natural disasters (e.g., blizzards, hurricanes, floods, earthquakes, and tornadoes) rely on the media, especially radio and television, for up-to-the minute information. Now many people across the country also turn to the Internet for breaking news; this was especially apparent on September 11, 2001. Media coverage may facilitate and reinforce societal cohesion, giving listeners and viewers a sense of connection to others who are sharing a common experience (Perse, 2001, p. 62).

Looking Ahead

In these last three chapters, we have examined eight social institutions. Each social institution helps to organize social relations in a particular sector of social life.

A concept that describes the hierarchical relationships among people in different social status groups is social structure. We examine social structure as it relates to class, race and ethnicity, gender, sexual orientation, and disability in the next three chapters.

Part III

INTRODUCTION TO SOCIAL STRUCTURE IN AMERICAN SOCIETY

Society refers to a group of people who occupy a defined territory and share a common culture. *Social structure* is "the framework that surrounds us, consisting of the relationships of people and groups, which give direction to and set limits on behavior" (Henslin, 2008, p. 99). In explaining how sociologists study social structure, Grusky (1994) suggests that they look at several key concepts. One is how much inequality exists, and another is how rigid the system is, that is, how easily individuals move from one level to another. (In this text, we will use the term *inequality* to refer to numeric differences, and *inequity* when inequality appears to be the result of economic or social injustice.) Another concern is how traits present at birth, such as sex, race, and ethnicity, influence subsequent social standing. In this section, we discuss social structure in relation to social class, race and ethnicity, and other social statuses (gender, sexual orientation, and disability). The perspectives that were used to explain social institutions will be used again to contribute to a deeper understanding of social structure.

As noted in Chapter 1, a *niche* is defined as a "status occupied by an individual or family in the social structure"; Germain and Gitterman noted that our society is "studded with marginal, stigmatized, and destructive niches that denigrate human beings" (1995, p. 818). Of particular interest to social workers is the fact that some groups suffer from discrimination and oppression, while others enjoy unearned privilege. Particular statuses, such as being poor, dark-skinned, female, gay or lesbian, or disabled, are characteristics of "populations at risk." Rather than just viewing these people as victims of oppression, we will identify the diverse strengths that they have.

Chapter 5 covers social stratification (social class). The impact of social class on individuals and families is discussed and special attention is given to the experiences of the poor.

In Chapter 6, we discuss racial and ethnic groups and their characteristics, beginning with the American "mainstream" (white, middle class) values and continuing with the cultural characteristics of various racial and ethnic minorities. We have tried to avoid stereotyping these groups, and readers should understand that no brief, general description applies to all individuals in a population. Also, students should not expect to become "culturally competent" practitioners based on reading a few paragraphs in a HBSE text. In particular, students and practitioners need to remain aware of the *diversity within diversity* of many racial and ethnic groups. In other words, there may be as much variability *within groups* as among them. Your instructor can provide a list of recommended readings to help you get started in expanding your insight into the experiences of specific racial and ethnic groups.

In Chapter 7, we discuss other social statuses, beginning with gender and sexual orientation and ending with persons with disabilities. Again, experiences of inequity are presented.

Many beginning social work students feel overwhelmed by the issues of social injustice brought to their attention in Human Behavior courses. Our intention is to make you critical thinkers, not to lead you to despair. As students, as social workers, and as citizens you will have many opportunities to advocate on behalf of vulnerable populations.

Social Stratification

Social Class in America

Sociologists have yet to reach agreement on how many social classes are there in America and what principal "fault lines" should be used to define them (Grusky, 1994, p. 4). Of greater interest to social workers, perhaps, are the issues of how the lifestyles, attitudes, and personalities of individuals are shaped by their class "locations," and what types of social processes and public policies serve to maintain or challenge discrimination (Grusky, 1994, p. 5).

The idea of social class is one way to describe the inequalities that are present in American society. To be a part of a *social class* is to rank with others in terms of wealth, power, and prestige. This ranking separates people into different groups that experience different opportunities in life and different ways of looking at the world. In fact, sociologists argue "no aspect of life goes untouched by social class" (Henslin, 2001, p. 270).

Inequality is most clearly observed in the amount of wealth held by people in different social classes. *Wealth* refers mostly to real estate and stocks and bonds, and unearned income such as capital gains and executive bonuses, while *income* reflects salary and wages. In the United States, inequality in wealth is much greater than inequality in income. Most of the very rich (those whose net worth is in the hundreds of millions) derive their wealth from inheritance; it is very difficult to become rich simply by working hard. There are exceptions, of course. According to the Forbes list of the 400 richest Americans in 2008, among the top 25, there are 6 first-generation billionaire entrepreneurs who made their money in computers and technology (Forbes, 2008). Others, such as members of the Walton family (Walmart) or Mars (candy), clearly inherited their wealth.

Class distinctions are often difficult to describe. The following section will explore the most common criteria: wealth, occupational prestige, and education.

At the very top of the *upper class* are the members of the "upper-upper" class, sometimes called the "blue bloods," "aristocracy," "old money," or "high society." They comprise less than 1 percent of the total U.S. population (Macionis, 2007). The matter of birth and inheritance

TABLE 5.1 *TANF Maximum Benefits for a Family of Three, June 2003*

High Level Status	Monthly Grants ($)	Low Level Status	Monthly Grants ($)
Alaska	923	Mississippi	170
California	679	Tennessee	185
Wisconsin	673	South Carolina	204
Vermont	639	Arkansas	204
Massachusetts	633	Alabama	215

Source: U.S. Department of Health and Human Services, Administration for Children and Families, Office of Family Assistance (2006, December). *Temporary Assistance for Needy Families Program (TANF): Seventh Annual Report to Congress.*

separates the "upper-uppers" from the "lower-upper" class, which is also described as "new rich," the "working rich," or the "corporate class." Most of these families have enormous wealth. The "new rich" (about 3 to 4 percent of the population) may achieve their status through entrepreneurship, or as one of the corporate elite, or as one of the rare star athletes or entertainers who command exorbitant salaries, or as winners of the lottery.

The *middle class*, comprising 40 to 45 percent of the U.S. population (Kendall, 2008; Macionis, 2007), is the one most shaped by education. It also can be broken down into two groups, the "upper middle" and the "average middle." The "upper middle" class is comprised of the "elite" professionals, such as physicians, lawyers, and upper-level managers. The "average middle" class, on the other hand, is composed of members of the "minor" professions, such as social workers, teachers, and nurses, as well as middle managers and small business owners. Members of the middle class are dependent on salary income rather than inherited wealth and their employment is the source of their status.

We have combined the *lower-middle class* and the *working class* because the distinctions between them are often blurred. People in this class may be skilled laborers, firefighters and police officers, and clerical personnel. Lower-middle-class people who may have been well-paid factory workers now find themselves "downsized" and working several part-time service jobs in order to maintain their lifestyle. This group constitutes almost one-third of the population (Kendall, 2008; Macionis, 2007).

The *working poor* make up about 20 percent of the population (Kendall, 2008). These are people whose income falls below the official poverty line even though they have jobs, at least part of the year. Their jobs are unskilled and include work such as house cleaning, seasonal farmwork, and fast-food service. These workers typically receive minimum wage and no employee benefits.

The *underclass/permanent poor* may be found in isolated rural areas or concentrated in urban centers. They have little or no connection with the job market. Those who are employed typically have temporary positions doing menial labor. Public assistance is their main source of support. About 3 to 5 percent of the population falls into this class (Kendall, 2008).

Distribution of Wealth and Income in the United States

An accumulating body of data, reported by the Economic Policy Institute (2002), documents the growth in inequality between economic classes in America. The pattern in the 1980s was for the top wage earners to pull away from the middle and the middle to pull away from the bottom. In the 1990s, the bottom and middle wage earners grew closer together, while the top pulled even further away from the rest.

The top 20 percent of the population receives almost half of all income; in contrast, the poorest 20 percent receive only 4 percent of the country's income (Henslin, 2008, p. 270). Comparisons of chief executive officer (CEO) pay to a typical worker's pay have been tracked over time. A typical worker's pay is calculated as the average hourly compensation of production/nonsupervisory workers—about 80 percent of payroll employment (Mishel, Bernstein, & Shierholz, 2009). In 1965, a CEO made 24 times what the typical worker made. In 2000, the ratio peaked at 298 and it stood at 275 in 2007 (Mishel, Bernstein, & Shierholz, 2009).

The severe recession that began in the fall of 2008, along with the federal bailouts that followed, brought to the public's attention not only the high levels of executive compensation, but also the extent to which well-paid CEOs appeared to be out-of-touch with the economic experience of everyday Americans. One example was when the heads of three Detroit automobile manufacturers, General Motors, Ford, and Chrysler, came to Washington to appear before a Congressional committee, seeking billions of federal dollars to keep their companies running. Each traveled in a private company jet, at a cost of roughly $20,000 for each trip. Recognizing the irony of the situation, one Congressmen asked, "Couldn't you all have downgraded to first class or jet-pooled or something to get here?" (Milbank, 2008).

A usual way to measure inequality is to divide American society into quintiles (fifths) and then make comparisons. For example, those in the fourth (next to top) quintile, while doing quite well, had on average less than half the income of those in the top quintile. While incomes at all levels increased between 1991 and 2005, the average in the lowest quintile increased by only $4,400, while the average increase for the highest quintile was $61,100 (see Table 5.2).

This disparity in income is accounted for, in part, by the low wages paid to those at the bottom of the income scale and has the effect of making the rich, richer and the poor, poorer. The minimum wage for American workers as of mid-2009 is $7.25 per hour. (The minimum wage is applicable to nonsupervisory, nonfarm, private sector employment under federal law.) The period of 1997 to 2007 was the longest time during which the minimum wage was not adjusted. The minimum wage has never been sufficient to support a family if only one member of the family is employed. A worker

TABLE 5.2   *U.S. Income by Quintile*

Changes in Income for Each Fifth of the U.S. Population (adjusted for 2005 dollars)			
	1991	**2000**	**2005**
Highest fifth	114,700	176,300	175,800
Fourth fifth	69,100	83,700	83,900
Third fifth	48,700	59,100	57,200
Second fifth	31,600	39,400	37,500
Lowest fifth	12,400	18,800	16,800

Source: Adapted from the Congressional Budget Office report released in May of 2007, based on the U.S. Census Bureau's Current Population Surveys from 1992 to 2006.

TABLE 5.3 *2009 Federal Poverty Guidelines*

Size of Family Unit	Poverty Guideline ($)	Required Gross Monthly Income ($)	Required Approximate Hourly Income ($)
1	8,860	738	4.26
2	11,940	995	5.74
3	15,020	1,252	7.22
4	18,100	1,508	8.70
5	21,180	1,765	10.18
6	24,260	2,022	11.66
7	27,340	2,278	13.14
8	30,420	2,535	14.63

Source: Federal Register (2009, January 23). *2009 Poverty Guidelines for the 48 Contiguous States and the District of Columbia* (Vol. 74, No. 14).

making $7.25 an hour for 40 hours a week for 52 weeks a year earns $15,080. The federal poverty guidelines list $22,050 as the "poverty line" for a family of four (see Table 5.3).

In most states, companies can pay workers as little as $2.13 per hour if their wage plus tips equals the minimum. Many of these workers are employed in the food service industry and many are women ("Federal minimum wage hike affects relatively few workers," 2008). Some states have minimum wage standards that are higher than the federal minimum. When state wages are different from the federal level, the higher rate prevails.

Class difference is not just about wages and salaries. An accurate measure of wealth includes all assets (savings, stocks, bonds, life-insurance policies, real-estate holdings, paintings, jewelry, antiques, and so forth). Wealth in the United States is highly concentrated. The wealthiest Americans can live on the dividends from their investments without having to touch the principal or work for a salary. The richest 1 percent of U.S. households owns 34.3 percent of the nation's private wealth, more than the combined wealth of the bottom 90 percent. The top 1 percent also owns 36.9 percent of corporate stock (Beeghley, 2008).

According to the U.S. Department of Agriculture (2007), more than one in ten (10.9 percent) of American households were food insecure at least some time during the year. *Food insecurity* is defined as not having access at all times to enough food for an active, healthy life, necessitating recourse to emergency food sources or other extraordinary coping behaviors to meet basic food needs. About one-third of food insecure households (4.6 million U.S. households) had very low food security—meaning that the food intake of one or more adults was reduced and their eating patterns were disrupted at times during the year because the household lacked money and other resources for food.

Poverty as a Special Concern for Social Workers

Social workers are particularly interested in the people at the bottom of the socioeconomic scale—those who suffer from poverty. Because of the profession's commitment to social justice, the needs of the poor are a major focus of change efforts.

Deciding what poverty is, is a problem in itself. Americans think of hunger and homelessness as indicators of the existence of poverty. Clearly most people in the world today, and especially people in the United States and other industrialized countries, do not experience deprivation in the same way that the vast majority of people in the world experienced in past centuries or as some people experience today in a few areas of the world. Nevertheless, there are millions of people in this country who do not have enough to eat or adequate shelter. We call this *poverty as deprivation.*

Another view of poverty is *relative poverty* (called *subjective poverty* by some sociologists). This is the sense of deprivation experienced when people compare themselves to others who have more of a society's resources. In other words, it is the everyday experience of inequality.

There are many misconceptions about who "the poor" are. One of the most common is that the poor are primarily people of color and single mothers and their children. Whereas these groups constitute a disproportionate number of those living in poverty, they are not the majority.

As the heads of poor families, women are overrepresented in poverty. This *feminization of poverty* is related to increases in the rates of divorce, separation, and out-of-wedlock births; fathers not paying child support; and a reduction in government benefits. Even when women are employed, they are more likely to live in poverty than male heads of households because they are more likely to be employed in the secondary labor market (see Chapter 2). On average, women who head families earn only 70 percent of the income of men who head families (Henslin, 2008. p. 290).

Although whites make up the majority of people living in poverty in the United States, people of color are overrepresented among the poor and they are more likely to be among the extremely poor. More than 4 percent of Asians, more than 8 percent of Latinos, and more than 11 percent of African Americans had incomes under 50 percent of the poverty line, compared to 3.4 percent of whites (U.S. Census Bureau, 2007).

As a distinct age-group, children in the United States are more likely to be poor than adults or the elderly. In 2005, 17.6 percent of American children lived in poverty; the rate for children under six was 20.1 percent in 2003 (last available data) (Mishel, Bernstein, & Shierholz, 2009). Poverty rates are higher for African American children (32.8 percent) and Latino children (28.6 percent) compared to white children (10.5 percent), according to the 2005 U.S. Census Bureau statistics (Macionis, 2007). Poor children are more likely to die in infancy, to be malnourished, to have health problems, to drop out of school, to be involved in criminal activities, and to have babies while they are in their teens—thus perpetuating the cycle of poverty (Henslin, 2001, p. 278).

U.S. poverty rates are highest in central cities, but they are higher in rural areas than urban areas as a whole (Henslin, 2008; Macionis, 2007). Counties with the highest poverty rates (more than twice the national average) are found in Appalachia, across the Deep South and parts of the Southwest, along the border with Mexico, and in the Dakotas (Macionis, 2007). Rural populations are likely to be less educated and well-paying jobs are more scarce than in urban areas (Henslin, 2008).

Social Mobility

There is an almost universal belief in America that upward social mobility—change in social status—is possible for anyone (Adler, 2009). In the United States, social mobility is closely linked to educational attainment and economic opportunity.

According to Macionis (2007, p. 290), sociological research suggests that rates of social mobility in the United States over the past century have been high; however, most of the upward movement has been within one social class rather than between classes. A study by the Economic Mobility Project of the Brookings Institution (Isaacs, 2007b) compared incomes of parents in the 1960s and their children's incomes 40 years later. Findings showed that median family income had increased by 29 percent, but as we have noted elsewhere, the biggest gains were at the top of the class structure rather than being evenly distributed. The second generation was more likely to live in smaller families or households and to have a second wage earner, and although their incomes were higher than their parents, only one-third (34 percent) were described as "upwardly mobile" (surpassing their parents economic ranking by one or more quintiles).

Another study (Hertz, 2006) reported that children from low-income families have only a 1 percent chance of reaching the top 5 percent of the income distribution, compared to the children of the rich, who have a 22 percent chance. Children in the middle quintile of parental family income have about an equal chance of moving either up (36.5 percent) or down (39.5 percent) the income ladder. Hertz also reports that the United States has an unusually low level of intergenerational mobility compared to other countries, such as France, Germany, Sweden, Finland, Norway, Denmark, and Canada.

Beginning in the 1960s, when the economy boomed and civil rights legislation lowered racial barriers, many African Americans moved into the middle class (Beeghley, 2008; Cherlin, 2008; Henslin, 2008; Macionis, 2007). There is now a second generation of middle-class African Americans enrolling in colleges across the country (Massey, Charles, Lundy, & Fischer, 2003). Nevertheless, in a period between the 1960s and the late 1990s and early 2000s, almost half (45 percent) of black children whose parents were solidly middle class fell to the bottom of the income distribution (Isaacs, 2007a).

Historically, a woman's social ranking was equated with her husband's. Women also had less opportunity for upward mobility than men because they were limited to occupations that offered little opportunity for career advancement. When marriages end in divorce, women commonly experience downward social mobility. Both sons' and daughters' family incomes in adulthood are similar to that of their own parents; an exception is lower upward mobility rates for the daughters of low-income parents compared to sons (Isaacs, 2007c). This is at least partly due to their becoming single parents.

White women have gained more from equal opportunity laws and affirmative action programs than have people of color. A loss of manufacturing jobs and other unfavorable economic conditions has slowed the social mobility of many minority groups.

Whereas strong kinship networks in minority families act as a buffer against the hardships of poverty, the expectations for reciprocity may hinder upward mobility (Stack, 1997/1974). And although generally one thinks of upward social mobility as a good thing, individuals who change their social class, even through the support and sacrifices of their families, may find themselves painfully alienated from their parents and cut off from their cultural roots (Sennett & Cobb, 1973). For people of color who succeed, there may be additional expectations of "payback" to relatives and communities left behind that make the transition even more difficult (McClain, 1986/1981).

Structural mobility occurs when significant changes in society propel many people up or down the social class ladder at the same time. Generally, the trend since 1900 has been toward upward mobility, due to the expansion of the economy and a dramatic increase in average educational attainment. One recent change has been the downward mobility of many middle class and blue-collar workers as a result of the elimination or exportation of manufacturing jobs (discussed in Chapter 2). The long-term effects of the deep recession that began in late 2008 are yet to be analyzed.

Understanding Social Stratification

Functionalist Perspective

Functionalists believe that an unequal class structure is necessary for a successful society (Davis & Moore, 1945). According to this view, people will work hard only if they receive rewards commensurate with their skills and education. Thus, in order to fill the most important positions in society, the system has to provide exceptional rewards to draw talent away from less important and easier work. The Davis-Moore thesis suggests that social stratification mandates meritocracy, a social hierarchy in which positions are awarded based on ability and credentials. Poverty is also "functional" in this view, because it keeps up the demand for low-wage jobs and ensures that the "dirty" work of society gets done, as well as providing a market for cheap goods.

The "rags to riches" myth—the idea that anyone can make it in America—is functional for society because it encourages people to strive for success. It also places blame for failure on the individual. Functionalists are comfortable with the conviction that poor choices, such as dropping out of school or having babies outside of marriage, lead to a life of poverty.

Conflict Perspective

Critics say that the Davis-Moore thesis ignores inequalities based on inherited wealth and other forms of unearned privilege. Conflict theorists argue that inequality is the result of oppression. Social class involves prestige and power, as well as economic inequality. Typically, those with the most prestige, power, and wealth want to protect their privileges, while those without try to get more.

Karl Marx, who developed conflict theory, believed that social class was the most important factor in understanding human behavior. He said that capitalist societies were composed of two classes: the *bourgeoisie*, who owned the means of production and the *proletariat*, who sold their labor to the owners. Marx saw great inequality in wealth and power arising from the exploitation of the proletariat, which, he argued, made *class conflict* inevitable. Marx predicted that inequality would result in revolution. Contemporary Marxists believe that a lack of class consciousness precludes this revolution.

Sociologists who subscribe to the conflict theory perspective argue that the structure of society itself keeps some people from moving up in the social hierarchy by limiting access to education or training. These researchers and academics suggest that race, age, and gender discrimination, as well as changes in the job market, restrict the life experiences of many individuals in a capitalist society. Most sociologists and social workers reject individualistic explanations such as laziness and lack of intelligence, and other stereotypes that appear to blame the victims of class oppression.

Constructionist Perspective

Constructionism is about subjective understanding. Americans have a different understanding of social class than do Europeans (Adler, 2009; Page & Jacobs, 2009). One does not see a strong class consciousness in the United States, particularly among laborers. Workers think of themselves as middle class (or aspire to being middle class) and hence lack a sense of shared interests with other low-income people. Vanneman and Cannon, in their 1987 book, *The American Perception of Class*, suggested the problem is that the United States has no leftist political party to organize the lower classes and express their interests.

In contrast to Euro-Americans, who see social status as rooted in wealth and prestige, some minorities may have a different understanding of social class. For example, African Americans view class as detached from income and instead based upon identified middle-class behaviors. These behaviors would include maintaining good family relationships, participating in the community, and dressing appropriately (Vanneman & Cannon, 1987, p. 227). Some occupational roles, such as teacher or clergyperson, also contribute to a valued class position. These are examples of how a vulnerable group can set internal community standards for evaluating worth, separate from those of the larger society.

The Impact of Social Stratification on Individuals and Families

Human needs can be divided into several categories. The effects of social class are experienced in all these.

Addressing the Concerns of Daily Life

Finances.   No matter what kinds of problems people have, access to money makes it easier to cope. Many problems "go away" if funds are available to fix them—paying for auto or plumbing repairs, for example, or retaining an attorney, hiring a housekeeper, or scheduling a "mental health getaway." People who have disposable income can focus on other things.

Most people in the middle class have some money in savings. Some have enough equity in their homes to be able to borrow against it in case of emergencies. Middle-class parents expect their children to attend college and provide them with "enriching" experiences, such as music lessons or summer camp, and family trips to museums, historic sites, and other educational places.

Most people in the lower-middle class/working class do not have savings accounts. They live paycheck to paycheck. An illness or injury or temporary layoff (or even a car repair or broken major appliance) constitutes a financial crisis. They pay 15 to 20 percent more for most goods and services than do the better off, because instead of paying cash they pay with their credit cards and then are charged interest and late fees. If a family started with a $10,000 credit card balance at

FIGURE 5.1   *Critical Thinking: The Experience of Growing Up in Different Social Classes*

Reflect on your childhood and your family of origin. What were the indicators of social class that were apparent to you as a child, besides your parents'/caretakers' occupation, education, and income? For example, what did you own, where did you live, what experiences did you share, and what were your expectations for your future?

18 percent interest and made only minimum monthly payments, it would take 56 years to pay off the debt and the interest cost alone would total $28,079.

> The working poor may be described as living on an "economy budget" (approximately 155 percent of the poverty level). They can afford basic necessities if purchased at the lowest possible cost, but must forego the simple pleasures that members of the middle class enjoy: cable or satellite TV, babysitters, eating out in a nice restaurant, going to the movies, vacations that involve staying at a motel, professional haircuts, special lessons or camp or even weekly allowances for the kids. (Schwarz & Volgy, 1992)

Typically, members of the underclass/permanent poor have no cash reserves and a negative credit history. They rely on friends and relatives, then title loans and pawn shops, for help with short-term financial needs. They may pay interest rates at high as 300, 400, or even 700 percent to get "immediate" tax refunds or to borrow against anticipated paychecks. Often they must rely on in-kind trade-offs (an hour of babysitting in exchange for a ride to the clinic) to make ends meet. Even if they receive a windfall, they cannot get ahead financially because they feel they must help out those who have helped them in the past (Stack, 1997/1974).

Even on an everyday basis, the poor and working poor give more to others, proportionately, than do wealthier individuals. According to U.S. Bureau of Labor Statistics (Greve, 2009), the poorest quintile of America's households contribute an average of 4.3 percent of their income to charitable organizations. The working poor, who are likely to be recent immigrants, are the most generous group (Brooks, 2006). Those in the richest quintile give at less than half the rate of those at the bottom of the income scale, 2.1 percent (Greve, 2009).

Housing.   Shelter is a basic human need. Home ownership is the bedrock of the "American dream." The good news is that nationally, levels of home ownership have increased among both white and nonwhite populations. Home equity is an important source of financial security for low-income and minority households, but it is difficult for low-income people to pay rent and save for a down payment at the same time.

The lack of affordable housing is a critical issue for the working poor. The United States Conference of Mayors (2008) reported that the high cost of housing was a main cause of hunger. Writing for the Habitat for Humanity newsletter, the Director of Harvard University's Joint Center for Housing Studies summarized America's housing crisis (Retsinas, 2002). Referring to federal guidelines that suggest that housing should not consume more than 30 percent of a family's income, he noted that one in eight American families spends more than 50 percent. He concluded that for those full-time workers who make only the minimum wage, there is no county in the United States where they could afford to rent a two-bedroom apartment. Given these data, it is not surprising to learn that the homeless population in America is growing.

Ascertaining the actual number of homeless in the country is difficult. Most studies limit themselves to counting people in shelters or those receiving services from soup kitchens; this methodology underestimates the number of homeless people. A 2000 U.S. Department of Education study cited by the National Coalition for the Homeless (2008) found that only 35 percent of homeless children lived in shelters; 34 percent lived doubled-up with family or friends and 23 percent lived in motels and other locations. A study of formerly homeless people found that the most common places people who had been homeless stayed were vehicles (59.2 percent) and make-shift shelters, such as tents and boxes (24.6 percent) (National Coalition for the Homeless

(2008). In 2008, 12 cities reported an increase in homelessness because of the home foreclosure crisis; the tenants of rental units in buildings where the landlord faced foreclosure were the most vulnerable to becoming homeless (United States Conference of Mayors, 2008).

Health.   Although white people generally enjoy better health than people of color, the reason appears to be related to socioeconomic status rather than genetic factors. There is a negative correlation between health status and economic class; the lower a person's class, the less likely it is that he or she will enjoy good health, at any age. For the very young, the disparity is particularly notable. In the United States, the children of the rich can look forward to a healthy childhood, while those who are poor are as vulnerable to risk as those in many developing countries. The 2004 infant mortality rate for the United States was 6.9 deaths per 1,000 births (Wright, 2007). This is higher than 33 other countries in the world, including Singapore (2.3), Japan (2.8), and Sweden (2.75) (Wallechinsky, 2007).

Infant mortality rates within the United States vary considerably from one region to another and among racial groups. At 13.6 deaths per 1,000 births, infant mortality rates for African Americans are more than double the 5.7 rate for whites (Centers for Disease Control and Prevention, 2007). There may be many reasons for this discrepancy, but an important factor is the quality of medical care received by people of different socioeconomic groups. Research indicates that the negative effects of childhood poverty on health and well-being continue into adult life (Reynolds & Ross, 1998).

Poor people cannot afford to buy fresh fruits and vegetables and other sources of high grade, low fat nutrition. Diets high in fat and sugars contribute to various health problems, including obesity, high blood pressure, high cholesterol, and diabetes. And it may be more than a matter of having the cash available for groceries. A study published in the *New York Times* (Epstein, 2003) reported that there were four times as many supermarkets in white neighborhoods as black ones, and three times as many bars in poor neighborhoods as rich ones. Fast food and cigarettes are abundant in inner-city areas, and healthy alternatives are limited.

The United States is the only industrialized country that relies upon private health insurance to cover the majority of its population (Rodberg & McCanne, 2007). In the United States in 2007, more than 45,657,000 Americans (15.3 percent of the population) had no medical insurance coverage (see Chapter 4). The nonpoor usually are insured through group policies with their employers. The working poor are an exception: they frequently are not covered by health insurance at work, yet they earn too much to qualify for Medicaid and not nearly enough to be able to afford to buy insurance on their own. The poor are largely covered by the federal/state Medicaid program; unfortunately, Medicaid reimburses providers at such a low rate that many clinics and most dentists will not accept Medicaid patients.

Many uninsured people do not have an ongoing relationship with a personal physician. They delay treatment as long as they can, often until there is a crisis, and then must use the emergency room where there are likely to be long waits and no follow-up.

Mental Health.   As is the case with physical health, the lower classes also suffer more than the wealthy from mental health problems. Anxiety and depression are the two most common illnesses. While these often have a genetic component, they are profoundly influenced by the individual's social class (Mirowsky & Ross, 1989). Clearly stress is related to mental illness. While the well-to-do experience stress, they also have more resources (e.g., money, staff, time, access to professionals) available to deal with it. Access to private mental health practitioners is correlated with economic status. People with Medicaid are seen in public clinics, often by inexperienced staff or student interns. People of lower socioeconomic status not only experience obvious stressors but also must contend with a subjective experience of lack of control over many elements of their lives. A real or perceived sense of control over one's life may be the most important factor in reducing risk for mental illness (Mirowsky & Ross, 1989).

Transportation.   Many Americans are dependent on their automobiles because their communities do not provide adequate alternatives. Lack of transportation seriously limits the poor in their efforts to seek and maintain employment. The working poor generally cannot afford cars; even if they can buy a used vehicle, they cannot afford to keep up with insurance and maintenance expenses. They must rely on public transportation, which is nonexistent in rural areas and offers only limited service in many smaller cities and in suburbs. With many jobs moving from the center city to the suburbs, the urban poor are even more constrained in their efforts to be self-supporting.

Crime.   There is an inverse correlation between income and victimization. The most likely crime victims live in households with incomes under $7,500 (Wright, 2007). Low income women are at higher risk of being physically assaulted by an intimate partner than are women in higher socioeconomic statuses. A shelter worker estimated that 85 percent of her clients returned to battering relationships because of difficulties in finding housing and employment (American Civil Liberties Union, 2001).

A common cliché is that "justice is blind"; the reality, however, is that one's chances of getting arrested, convicted, and sent to prison are significantly shaped by class membership.

> *For the same criminal behavior* [italics in original], the poor are more likely to be arrested; if arrested, they are more likely to be charged; if charged, more likely to be convicted; if convicted, more likely to be sentenced to prison; and if sentenced, more likely to be given longer prison terms than members of the middle and upper classes. (Reiman, 2007, p. 112)

When lower-class status is accompanied by membership in a minority group, the probabilities increase.

Of course, the reality is that the rich and powerful also commit crimes. In comparison to the crimes committed by the poor (those included in the FBI Index), white-collar crime is more costly and probably more widespread (Reiman, 2007, p. 123). As noted in Chapter 3, white-collar crime is defined as crime committed by people of high social position in the course of their employment or financial affairs (Sutherland, 1940). Examples of white-collar crime are bank embezzlement, business fraud, and antitrust violations. A recent high profile example is the fraudulent scheme concocted by Bernard Madoff, which cost thousands of investors more than $50 billion; among the losers were well-known individuals such as Steven Spielberg and Larry King, and nonprofit organizations such as Yeshiva University, New York University, the Elie Wiesel Foundation for Humanity, and many charitable organizations and pension funds ("Madoff's victims," 2009). It is estimated that such crime costs the country $400 billion per year (Henslin, 2008). Reiman (2007) suggests that the criminal justice system often fails to define the unethical and dangerous acts of those who are well off as crimes. He adds that while poverty contributes to crime by creating need, wealth can contribute to crime by unleashing greed.

Access to Technology. Based on a 2006 national survey, the Nielson Company reported that homes with incomes over $60,000 are 50 percent more likely to own a home computer than homes with a lower income. Two-thirds of households with incomes under $25,000 lack Internet access (U.S. Department of Commerce, Economics and Statistics Administration, 2005). The relative disadvantage of children who do not have access to computers and the Internet in a technology-based society will continue to grow.

Belongingness and Connections

Family Life and Child Rearing. People of similar background tend to intermarry. This is most true for the "upper-uppers." The trend in America in the twentieth century was for religion to become a less important criterion for spouse selection and level of education to become more important (Cherlin, 2008).

Several trends in marriage, childbearing, and divorce are strongly correlated with the level of education. College graduates, although they delay marriage, have a higher lifetime probability of marrying than do people without college degrees; college graduates are less likely to have a child out-of-wedlock than noncollege graduates; and the rate of divorce has been declining for college graduates and increasing for those who did not graduate from high school (Cherlin, 2008, pp. 125–126).

There are significant differences in child-rearing patterns across social classes. According to Kohn (1977), lower-class parents expect their children to conform and comply. Middle-class parents, on the other hand, encourage creativity and independence in their children and tolerate more individuality. Lareau (2002, 2003) proposes that working-class and middle-class families hold different views about how children develop. She suggests that working-class parents think of children as developing naturally, while middle-class parents believe that children need to be cultivated. Given this viewpoint, middle-class parents are likely to provide their children many organized activities, such as sports, music lessons, and tutoring, whereas working-class parents are more likely to let their children choose their own activities at home or in the neighborhood. When parents cannot provide child care themselves, upper-class families may hire live-in nannies. Middle-class families use day-care providers. In lower-middle-class and working-class families, parents may seek employment on different shifts to meet child-care needs and/or rely on kin to take care of their children.

Connections to the Community and Beyond. Upper- and middle-class people often socialize with colleagues and coworkers, sometimes using their contacts to advance their careers. Middle-class friendships involve shared interests and leisure pursuits. Working-and lower-class people tend to spend their free time with relatives. Rubin described these extended family contacts as "the heart of working class social life" (1976, p. 191).

Members of the upper class, particularly wealthy women who are not employed may be involved in volunteer work for various nonprofit organizations; in addition to the value of their contribution to the larger community, these activities build important alliances and interpersonal networks (Ostrander, 1980). Many middle-class people are involved in community activities that relate to their children's interests: Scouts, PTA, soccer, neighborhood organizations, and so forth.

Values and Attitudes

There persists a belief that the poor differ from other Americans in the values that they hold. Probably the most notable proponent of this view was Oscar Lewis (1966), who believed that it was the values that the poor embraced that kept them in their lower-class status. According to Lewis, those living in this *culture of poverty* were unable to delay gratification or plan for the future, and these deficiencies were passed from generation to generation. While Lewis blamed the poor for their poverty, other theorists point to structural reasons for their plight. William Julius Wilson (1996), for example, holds that lack of opportunity rather than lack of motivation is the cause of poverty.

Like Lewis, many people believe that poverty is the *result* of negative attitudes and behaviors. Research, however, indicates that poverty may be the *cause* of values and behaviors typically associated with lack of success in American culture. When they have resources available, previously poor people share the same attitudes that other members of society espouse. Even when they are destitute, the poor tend to have the same dreams as the middle class. In his classic 1967 study of "street-corner" men, for example, Elliot Liebow found that his African American male study participants had internalized the values of the majority culture. It was their impoverished environment that prevented their acting on these values.

The Global Impact of Poverty

The distinction between relative and absolute poverty, discussed earlier in this chapter, is critical to understanding global inequality. In many countries of the world, absolute poverty is defined by a lack of resources that is life-threatening; insufficient nutritious food is a leading cause of premature death, especially among children (Wright, 2007). The World Health Organization estimated that worldwide 27 percent of children under age five were underweight, contributing to about 3.4 million child deaths in 2000, including about 1.8 million in Africa and 1.2 million in Asia (Wright, 2007). The United Nations defines as poor those individuals whose earned income is below a dollar per day; using that definition, about 28 percent of the world's population lives in poverty (Kendall, 2008).

Whereas industrialized nations may have pockets of poverty, the *majority* of people living in least industrialized countries have no access to clean water or medical services. Many reside on the streets or even within city dumps (Packer, 2006). Resolving world poverty requires varied approaches; delivering food and clothing provides only short-term relief. What is needed is sustainable economic development.

Looking Ahead

Social class remains a topic that is not easily acknowledged or discussed. By keeping it invisible, the effects of inequality can be attributed to other causes. Americans worry about crime, drug abuse, and family dissolution. It would be a major step toward social justice if the nation's concerns turned to poverty and a host of other problems directly traceable to racism and economic marginality. Racism is addressed in Chapter 6. In Chapter 7, we discuss other populations at risk.

American Society and Cultural Diversity

The United States as a Multicultural Society

Clearly, the United States has a majority, dominant, or mainstream culture, but it supports various minority or subdominant cultures as well. Whereas America has been called a *melting pot*, meaning that different immigrant cultures become blended into a uniquely "American culture," it really is more like a tossed salad, where diverse groups retain and share their distinctive subcultural flavors while living together in a larger society. Another term for this pattern is *cultural pluralism*.

Obvious elements of culture are those we can directly observe, such as language, clothing, body adornment, music, dance, or architecture. Culture includes shared beliefs as well as behaviors; culture promotes a sense of group solidarity. It is more than simply the history, language, and traditions of a people, however. "It involves a form of self-conceptualization that the individual assumes or others assign" (Lukes & Land, 1990, p. 155).

Identifying the *majority* or *dominant culture* in America is not just a matter of counting members of different racial and ethnic groups. The dominant culture is a reflection of the power of its members as well as their numbers. The dominant culture is supported by a society's social institutions (discussed in Chapters 2, 3, and 4). For example, the need to learn and use the dominant language (English) is demanded in public schools and by most employers (acting as agents of the political economy). These are powerful forces of socialization and control.

Cultural patterns set some members of society apart from the mainstream. Typically, when we think of *cultural minorities*, recent immigrant groups with distinct languages and traditions come to mind. Mass migration to the United States in the last decades of the twentieth century, largely from non-European countries, made America far more multiethnic and multicultural than ever before. In fact, census experts estimate that by 2050, the United States will be a "majority-minority" country (i.e., there will be more people of color than whites) (Meacham, 2009). More than three-quarters of the residents of Hawaii and of the District of Columbia are members of a minority group (Texeira, 2005). In California and New Mexico, minorities also outnumber whites, comprising 55.5 percent and 56.5 percent of the populations of those states, respectively. But cultural minorities also include groups that have lived here for hundreds of years, such as the African Americans whose ancestors arrived in the holds of slave ships. Native Americans have been living here for tens of thousands of years, long before any of the "majority" population arrived. Because of their physical characteristics (interacting with the forces of discrimination and oppression), these racial minority groups have not been fully assimilated into the mainstream and have instead retained many unique cultural features.

If culture is about a perception of difference, of separation from the mainstream, of shared language, values, norms, and experiences, then there are gay and lesbian cultures and a disability culture. From this perspective, the notion of homosexuality or disability is one of group belonging-ness and distinction from other groups who do not share that identity (Cruikshank, 1992; Gilson & DePoy, 2002). We explore this topic further in the next chapter.

Many minority cultures have recognized *communities*.[1] The community protects the social identity of its members in the face of stigma. Many minorities, including gay men and lesbians and people with disabilities, as well as racial and ethnic minorities, are enriched by their connections to their *identificational community* and its shared traditions.

The Council on Social Work Education (the body that sets the standards for accreditation of social work programs) requires that content on cultural diversity be included in the curriculum (CSWE, 2008). It is important that social work practitioners not only tolerate or accept differences, but that they celebrate *diversity* as a source of strength for individuals, families, and communities, and for our society as a whole.

In the United States, social workers are likely to be professionally involved with individuals and families not only from a variety of social classes, but also with individuals, families, groups, and communities from different ethnic, racial, and cultural traditions. Knowledge of these differences and skill in applying it (referred to as *cultural competence*) is a prerequisite for professional practice. There are many implications of cultural differences for social work assessment, counseling, intervention, and community organization efforts (Fontes, 2005; Sewell, 2009; Webb, 2001). What is considered normal or even preferred in some cultures may be frowned on or condemned in others. (For example, many Asians find the common dominant American cultural pattern of isolating infants and small children in beds and rooms of their own surprising.)

New Arrivals

According to the U.S. Bureau of the Census, in 2003 America's foreign-born population stood at 33 million, an increase of 69 percent over 1990 (Wright, 2007). The proportion of foreign-born is 11.7 percent, or one in nine. Latin Americans and Asians were more than three-quarters of those newcomers. Demographers estimate that the U.S. population will grow from 296 million in 2005 to 438 million in 2050; of that increase in population, 82 percent will be the result of immigrants arriving after 2005 and their descendents (Meacham, 2009).

In addition to cultural differences brought with them from their country of origin, racial and ethnic minorities also differ in terms of the conditions of their arrival and the length of time they have been in the country. There are three categories of new arrivals: immigrants, refugees, and undocumented aliens. *Immigrants* come more or less voluntarily, responding to both "pull" and "push" factors. Sometimes the "pull" factor—dreams of joining relatives and achieving success in a new country—is stronger. At other times, the "push" factor—escaping from squalor and starvation—is stronger. Examples include the Irish fleeing the potato famine in the nineteenth century, or Haitians or Dominicans escaping the pervasive poverty of their island in the twentieth century. *Refugees*, on the other hand, are forced out of their home countries by war or other extreme political conditions and their lives or liberty would be endangered if they returned. One example is the "boat people" and other refugees who fled Southeast Asia after the end of the Vietnam War in 1975. Other large groups of refugees have included eastern Europeans, Afghans, Ethiopians, Cubans, and Salvadorans. As a result of their experiences, many refugees suffer from posttraumatic stress disorder. *Undocumented aliens* are, typically, unskilled laborers who are in this country illegally trying to find work.

Although the United States makes the largest financial contribution of any country to world-wide refugee assistance programs, many nations much smaller than the United States host many more refugees. The United States ranks sixth in the ratio of resettled refugees to the host country population (behind Australia, Canada, New Zealand, Norway, and Sweden) (U.S. Committee for Refugees and Immigrants, 2008). Some groups are not welcomed. For example, although they claim to be fleeing persecution, most Haitians are classified as economic migrants rather than refugees and thus denied asylum and admission to the United States. On the other hand, since the 1950s, the United States has had a tradition of accepting refugees leaving communist nations, such as Cubans and Southeast Asians, in numbers greater than regulations would ordinarily permit (Schaefer, 2008).

Light-skinned newcomers have the advantage of "blending in" with the majority group in America, at least in terms of appearance, so that they have greater freedom of choice in becoming members of the dominant culture. According to a study conducted using an 11-point scale to describe skin color, immigrants with darker skin received lower wages than those with lighter skin (Hersch, 2006). In an interview with the *Washington Post*, the researcher noted, "I don't think that any explanation other than discrimination is possible—and I am not one to draw such inferences lightly. . . . On average, being one shade lighter has about the same effect as having an additional year of education" (Morin, 2006). Beside physical appearance, other factors that make assimilation easier are youth, education, bilingualism, the degree of similarity of the background culture to the mainstream culture, and the availability of cultural mentors (Queralt, 1996, p. 67). Structural changes in the U.S. labor market (i.e., loss of middle-class industrial jobs that represented an important rung on a ladder leading from unskilled and semiskilled jobs to skilled and supervisory occupations) present significant challenges to the children of contemporary immigrants, as do the drugs and gangs present in many central city neighborhoods where new immigrants are likely to live (Portes & Rumbaut, 2006).

The result of successful efforts to blend is called *cultural assimilation* (also referred to as *acculturation*). Cultural assimilation means being able to function on equal terms with the rest of society by understanding and following cultural norms. Achieving a higher level of integration is called *structural assimilation*, which means being fully accepted into the institutions and social circles of the mainstream group. Some sociologists argue that *marital assimilation* (intermarriage between members of different groups) is the highest level of integration. Nevertheless, there are many instances of intermarriage (such as U.S. servicemen bringing home Korean brides) that do not reflect evidence of full acceptance of a minority group into the majority society.

Under the 1965 Immigration and Naturalization Act, individuals who are at least 18 years of age, and who have lived in the United States continuously for at least five years (three years for spouses of U.S. citizens) are eligible to become *naturalized* U.S. citizens if they can read, write, and speak English, and pass a test on American history and civics.

The price of full assimilation is the disappearance of the ethnic group. Some people instead choose to be *bicultural*, meaning that as individuals they are able to successfully negotiate more than one culture, usually the dominant one as well as their own. Typically, these individuals are first exposed to socialization within their minority cultural group and later to significant experiences with the majority culture. This is common for children and adolescents of first-generation immigrants and refugees. Another example of biculturalism is the way African American parents and other caretakers prepare their children to deal successfully with the negative encounters they will be exposed to in the majority culture (see, for example, Carothers [1990]).

Ethnicity, Color, and Race

Ethnicity differs from race (and class) in that it is characterized by cultural distinctions—language, customs, values, beliefs, holidays, music, food, dress, and so forth. These are characteristics shared by people with a common history, and at one time, a common geographic location. First-generation immigrants often live in *ethnic enclaves*, such as Chinatown, the Barrio, Little Havana, or Little Saigon that help them preserve their ancestral culture (Portes & Rumbaut, 2006).

Religion is often closely tied to ethnicity (see Chapter 4). Membership in a non-Protestant religious group (e.g., Catholic, Eastern Orthodox Christian) has helped to define and preserve the distinctiveness of many white ethnics, such as the Italians, Irish, Poles, and Greeks (Min, 1990; Schaefer, 2008).

Many social workers and sociologists use the term *people of color* to refer to "Americans whose ancestors or who themselves came from non-European areas of the world and who can be identified through the color of their skin" (Stockard, 2000, p. 59). This sounds simple enough, but defining "white," either legally or culturally, has been a lengthy, controversial, and often logically inconsistent process in this country (Rasmussen, Klinenberg, Nexica & Wray, 2001).

The broad categorizations of "white" and "nonwhite" people is a variant on the questionable practice of identifying and designating different races (Close, 2000; Conley, 2001). Even the U.S. Census bureau struggles with the notion of race; its instructions to citizens say that they are to classify themselves by race as it "reflects common usage not an attempt to define biological stock." The 2000 census gave Americans the opportunity, for the first time, to identify themselves as belonging to more than one race. The majority of Americans (97.6 percent) still chose a single category (Wright, 2007). The most common choice for mixed race was white/American Indian or Alaska Native, followed by white/Asian. A total of 410,285 respondents identified themselves as being a member of three races.

It wasn't until European explorers began encountering people who looked quite different from them that the idea of human *races* developed (Begley, 1995; Conley, 2001). Generally, racial categories are based on physical characteristics, such as hair texture, facial features, skin color, and body build. At first glance, the categories appear to be self-evident. Nevertheless, when scientists try to categorize people by various other biological factors, such as blood type or biochemistry, they come up with quite different arrangements. For example, using blood type, Germans would be in the same category as New Guineans, and using lactose tolerance, Norwegians would be lumped together with the Fulani of Nigeria (Begley, 1995). This, and the fact that race is differently defined in different cultures, suggests that racial categories as we use them every day are social constructs rather than biological realities. Many of the nations of Central and South America, for example, including Mexico and Brazil, have complex systems of placing people in a myriad of racial groups using a *color gradient* along a continuum from light to dark (Schaefer, 2008). The majority of anthropologists today agree that using the concept of race to distinguish among different populations of humans is meaningless. In fact, most scientists (and many social work students) would argue that there is but one "human race."

Scientific biological arguments to the contrary do not keep Americans from using race as a kind of mental shorthand to categorize and stereotype large populations. In fact, being perceived as members of particular races has very real consequences for everyone in American society today. Especially for people of color, race shapes their daily experiences in ways that whites seldom appreciate. The stresses or hassles associated with being a member of a minority group make getting through the day more difficult for many people.

On the other hand, stress is accentuated by poverty. The dual influence of race or ethnicity and socioeconomic class status is called *ethclass* (Queralt, 1996, p. 3). Ethclass suggests that an individual's life chances, lifestyle, and behaviors are influenced by the interaction of class and race/ethnicity. For example, the life experiences of an African American physician differ substantially from those of an African American nursing aide.

Inequity and Privilege

A *minority* is a population group that shares a distinctive identity and is subjected to stigma, prejudice, discrimination, and oppression. Characteristics (e.g., color, language, religion, national origin) that define minority status vary in different societies (Schaefer, 2008). Minority does not necessarily connote small numbers, but rather refers to a subordinate position in society. For example, women make up a slight numerical majority of the population but are in a subordinate position and therefore are considered a minority. Even when, as a whole, they outnumber whites (as is predicted to occur in this century), people of color will continue to be a minority in the United States.

A *stigma* refers to any physical or social attribute that so discredits or devalues a person's social identity that it disqualifies that person from full social acceptance in the minds of others (Goffman, 1963). One might argue that having dark skin, kinky hair, and a broad, flat nose is still a stigma in American society. In the case of gay men and lesbians, stigma results from a violation of the mainstream cultural norm of heterosexism. In the case of persons with disabilities, stigma results from a violation of mainstream cultural norms of appearance and ability. Being disfigured as a result of an accident or war injury or using a wheelchair may be stigmatizing in this society.

Prejudice is a negative *attitude*, often based on an irrational generalization, about an entire group of people. A prejudice biases someone against another person simply because the second person is identified as a member of a particular group. An example of prejudice is the belief that Arabs are likely terrorists. *Discrimination* is an unfavorable *action*, or unfair treatment, directed toward members of a minority group. An example of discrimination is declining to hire someone with a disability even though that disability is unrelated to job requirements. *De jure* discrimination is discrimination that is supported by the law; an example is the practice of segregation that was enforced in Southern states before the civil rights movement brought legislative and judicial changes. *De facto* discrimination is discrimination that continues to exist although it is illegal; an example would be realtors who purposely steer African American buyers away from white neighborhoods. Discrimination can be a reaction to many characteristics, including not only race or ethnicity, but also religion, national origin, immigration status, class, gender, sexual orientation, disability, age, and appearance. *Oppression* is "a form of discrimination that is long term, systematic, and institutionalized (i.e., embedded within key social structures such as the educational system, the health care system, and the criminal justice system)" (Queralt, 1996, p. 171).

Xenophobia is a fear of, or contempt for, anything foreign, which may or may not be related to race or ethnicity *per se*. *Nativism* refers to beliefs and practices that favor native-born citizens over immigrants (Schaefer, 2008, p. 100). Periods of high immigration are typically marked by nativist resistance that characterizes newcomers as a threat to the integrity of national culture (Portes & Rumbaut, 2006, p. 344).

Inequalities of status and opportunity are probably inevitable in most societies. *Privilege* is a special advantage or benefit enjoyed by a group or population. When some people are oppressed, others enjoy privilege, regardless of whether they actively support or take part in acts of oppression either collectively or individually. This is an idea that makes many privileged individuals uncomfortable.

In her classic essay, "White privilege and male privilege," Peggy McIntosh has listed 46 situations and describes how her experience is "privileged" because of her white complexion. For example, "I can swear, or dress in secondhand clothes, or not answer letters, without having people attribute these choices to the bad morals, the poverty, or the illiteracy of my race. . . . Whether I use checks, credit cards, or cash, I can count on my skin color not to work against the appearance that I am financially reliable" (McIntosh, 2001, p. 98).

Insensitivity to privilege is common in the mainstream culture. Tropman (1989) notes "the belief that one earns one's status is an important value within American society" (p. 7). To deny the effects of race, to espouse *color blindness*, works only if one assumes that being white is no different than being any other color (Kincheloe, Steinberg, Rodriguez, & Chennault, 1998). Whiteness is a socially constructed and hence arbitrary category; nevertheless, to be white is to escape the real and entirely nonarbitrary prejudice, discrimination, and oppression experienced every day in this country by people of color. Recently, empirical research studies have highlighted the complexities of white racial identity and how the experience of whiteness can differ (see McDermott & Samson, 2005).

Exploring Mainstream and Minority Cultures

It is difficult to describe the commonalities of large populations without oversimplifying. We caution readers to be aware that any discussion of cultural values and practices does not imply that every individual in that culture fully subscribes to its values or norms. It is important to remember that there is much *within-group variability* and that *between-group differences* are often exaggerated. Particularly for social work practitioners, it is important to explore with the individual client the meaning that culture holds for him or her rather than making assumptions based on group membership.

We will now discuss cultural characteristics, beginning with "mainstream" values. Although a number of mainstream social values were identified and described over 50 years ago (Williams, 1957), discussion of white, middle-class values in American social work texts is a relatively recent development. The earlier omission reflects the arrogance of the white middle class in assuming that while other groups were different, their own ways were already understood and accepted as the norm and the best model for successful life in America, with no further need for elaboration. Many whites don't think of themselves as having race or ethnicity. Because the majority of social work students and instructors were white and middle class, this assumption was not questioned.

We believe that that even white, middle-class students need to be given the opportunity to reflect on the characteristics of mainstream culture. A discussion of minority cultures follows.

Mainstream American Values

The mainstream or dominant culture in the United States is usually associated with the white, middle class. Historically, this group has been further defined as white, Anglo-Saxon Protestants (WASPs)—generally understood to be immigrants from Great Britain. The choice of English as the official language of the country and the predominance of Protestantism as the majority religion, as well as the adoption of a legal system based on English law, reflect the power and influence of early English, Welsh, Scottish, Scots-Irish, and Irish Protestant settlers. The dominance of WASPs in this country is "most evident in the widespread use of the terms 'race' and 'ethnicity' to refer to everyone but them" (Macionis, 2007, p. 377). Gradually, (white) immigrant groups from other parts of Europe have joined the WASP majority. (Some students might be surprised to learn of the historic reluctance of WASPs to accept "undesirable foreigners," such as Germans and Irish Catholics.)

Much of the core of the mainstream American value system has remained intact through its history and continues to receive widespread support (Prigmore & Atherton, 1986) even though some of the values are inconsistent with each other or even contradictory (Tropman, 1989; Williams, 1957). What is thought of as traditional American culture is the legacy of white, middle-class Euro-American descendants of immigrants from Great Britain (England, Northern Ireland, Scotland, and Wales), Germany, and Ireland, with somewhat less influence from immigrants from other countries in Western and Eastern Europe and the Mediterranean coast. Because of their white skin color, similar religious background (Christianity), and frequent intermarriage, members of these immigrant nationalities quickly adopted the mantle of the dominant group (Queralt, 1996), shaping and refining U.S. mainstream culture. Among the values that characterize this culture are (1) work; (2) achievement—especially as it is reflected in economic success and material comfort; (3) self-reliance, independence, freedom, individualism, and competition; (4) equality before the law; (5) science, logic, progress, efficiency, and practicality; (6) geographic mobility; (7) informality and directness in personal relationships; (8) moralism; (9) time awareness; and (10) youthfulness and an orientation to the future. (The descriptions that follow are true for many white, middle- and upper-class Americans, but readers should be aware that there are many variations within this group, just as there are among members of minority/nondominant groups.) There are also urban/rural differences as well as regional differences (see, for example, Escott & Goldfield [1991]).

1. The American **emphasis on work** is derived from a Puritan heritage that valued work for its own sake. The *Protestant work ethic* is recognized as the moral basis for the American capitalistic economic system and policies in social welfare. Work for economic gain is considered the path to success, a sign of personal morality, and a moral obligation (see detailed discussion in Chapter 2). Many Americans, for example, feel uneasy in contemplative or meditative activities and prefer to keep busy and "work hard" even in their leisure pursuits. Only paid employment is considered "real" work. For example, lack of respect for the homemaking and child-care responsibilities of stay-at-home mothers is reflected in welfare reform policies that require poor mothers to leave their young children in day-care centers and seek jobs outside the home.

2. Although education and occupational status are important, **achievement** and success in America are often measured in terms of income and wealth. *Conspicuous consumption*—the purchase of showy automobiles, large houses, fashionable clothing, flashy jewelry, and expensive electronic goods, whose primary purpose is not utilitarian but to impress others—is a modern American characteristic. This trend toward ostentation is a cultural trait promoted even further by a continual stream of media advertising that tells potential customers "you are what you own."

3. Linking the values of work and individualism is the American myth of **self-reliance.** The tendency of Americans to overestimate what they have accomplished on their own and deny how much they owe to others began with the fiction that colonial Europeans built a land of plenty out of nothing. In reality, however, the abundant concentrations of game and edible plants they found were not natural but had been developed by the stewardship of Native Americans (Kehoe, 1999). Recent research demonstrates that as they moved westward across the continent, American pioneers were dependent on a large network of kin, neighbors, religious institutions, and government programs (especially the availability of free or low-cost land).

Belief in the importance of **individual rights** over those of the family, the collective, or community life is a particularly American characteristic, although its roots can be found in the emergence of capitalism in seventeenth-century Europe. Neither contributing to the group's well-being nor placing the group's well-being first are fully appreciated in American mainstream culture; this contrasts markedly with cultures where the extended family or group is more valued than the individual, as is common in many minority communities (Ewalt & Mokuau, 1996).

Closely linked to the values of achievement and individualism is the American value of **competition**. This competition occurs not just between sports teams or business enterprises, but also among individuals in groups and even within families. Americans tend to have a dichotomous point of view: if you are not a winner, you must be a loser. There is little sense that with less competition and more cooperation, everyone could "win."

4. The Constitution of the United States was written by men who deliberately rejected the traditional social stratification of Europe; consequently, Americans have a formal **commitment to equality** before the law (Prigmore & Atherton, 1986). Over time, this concept has been extended to mean an equality of opportunity for social and economic rewards. Nevertheless, for many years, rewards not resulting from achievement, such as those associated with being white or male, were considered the natural order of things. Unfortunately, the continuing prevalence of sexism, heterosexism, institutional racism, nativism, and other group superiority themes mars the American societal ideal of true equality.

5. Perhaps because they live in a relatively young society, Americans tend to value **science, logic, progress, efficiency,** and **practicality**. Technical efficiency tends to be valued for its own sake, rather than for what it serves to accomplish (Prigmore & Atherton, 1986). There is a belief that all problems can be solved by science, eventually if not right away. Aesthetics, sentimentality, spirituality, mysticism, rituals and ceremonies, and reverence for the past are often viewed with skepticism.

6. Americans have always valued geographic **mobility**. Historically, they pressed toward new frontiers. Now individuals and families move far away from home to take advantage of educational or career opportunities, or simply to seek adventure and change. Adults are often separated from their families of origin by thousands of miles. Even married partners sometimes work and live in different communities or even different states.

The profusion of private automobiles reflects a uniquely American obsession with being able to go where and when one wants, without having to rely on or to consider anyone else. In the 1950s and 1960s, public financing in America was gradually redirected from the streetcars and trolleys that served urban and poor families and used instead to provide new roads for suburban commuters and their cars, promoting urban sprawl, traffic congestion, and pollution. (This is discussed further in Chapter 8.)

7. Americans prefer **informality** and **directness** in personal relationships. With its emphasis on equality, American society downplays the use of honorifics and formal titles ("your majesty," "your lordship"). Americans in the mainstream culture often ignore both age and occupational or social status, addressing relatives, close friends, and distant acquaintances, or even strangers by their first names (although this is less common in the South). Direct confrontations about misunderstandings and frank discussion of feelings are not uncommon. There is a sense that "honesty" in relationships is more important than diplomacy.

8. As a group, mainstream Americans have traditionally expressed their **morality** by responding promptly to calls for help and giving generously to victims of disease and natural disasters. Typically, this humanitarianism is expressed in organized and impersonal ways through large charities such as the Red Cross or the United Way. To most Americans, humanitarianism means private, nongovernment support for those who are in trouble "through no fault of their own" (Prigmore & Atherton, 1986).

On the other hand, many members of the American mainstream are quick to blame chronically poor people, minorities, and other client populations for causing their own problems and are reluctant to support them through government programs or direct subsidies, even though the country as a whole possesses enormous wealth (Jansson, 2005; Prigmore & Atherton, 1986; Ryan, 1976). The American cultural obsession with self-reliance and independence may come at a significant cost to others in the family, group, organization, or community. A narrow Puritanism that seeks reasons for disapproval of others leads to viewing the dependent state of the poor and unsuccessful as *immoral* rather than simply unfortunate. The core value of individual responsibility exonerates society and confirms personal failure for those who cannot or do not reach success (Day, 2009, p. 7).

9. The American mainstream group puts a **premium on time**, which they schedule, regulate, and measure exactly (Queralt, 1996, p. 76). In fact, involvement in friendships, and religious or other community activities are often evaluated in terms of the time investments they require. (Minority groups in America tend to be much more flexible in their use of time.)

10. Whereas minority groups in the United States value and respect the aged, mainstream America has had a long-standing **infatuation with youth**. In a quickly changing society, the aged often have not been appreciated for their wisdom and experience.

African Americans

African Americans are the now the second largest minority group in the United States (ranking just below Hispanics/Latinos in the 2000 census). The ancestors of most African Americans came to this country not as immigrants or refugees but as slaves. Scholars disagree about the relative impacts of the cultural practices of their West African homelands, the slave experience, and more recent oppression as victims of institutional racism, on their current condition. Recent black immigrants have come from Haiti, Jamaica, Trinidad and Tobago in the Caribbean and from Nigeria, Ethiopia, Ghana, and Kenya in Africa.

Beginning in 1910 and lasting through the 1920s, there was a *Great Migration* of African Americans from the rural South to Northern industrial cities such as Chicago, New York, Philadelphia, St. Louis, and Detroit (Walker, 1999), where they were employed in meatpacking, automaking, and steel-manufacturing plants. Nevertheless, the majority of African Americans still live in the South.

Clear vestiges of African-based folklore, religion, language, and music remain despite the passage of generations and the historic slave experience of African Americans (Schaefer, 2008). Strong kinship bonds are the most enduring cultural strength that black Americans brought with them from the African continent (Hill, 1999). African Americans are more likely than whites to care for children and older adults in an extended family network (Goldscheider & Bures, 2003;

Schaefer, 2008, p. 240). Data show that grandparent caregivers are most commonly African American grandmothers; 9 percent of African American children are living in a grandparent's household compared to 6 percent of Hispanic children and 4 percent of non-Hispanic white children and 3 percent of Asian American children (Cherlin, 2008; Fuller-Thomson & Minkler, 2000). The African American family remains a resilient and adaptive social institution despite threats of poverty and discrimination (Billingsley, 1992).

William Julius Wilson (1987, 1996), among others, has argued that a decline in the rate of marriage among African Americans is closely linked to the economy, and particularly the loss of semiskilled and skilled blue-collar jobs in urban areas. In an interesting study, Lundquist found that there were no significant differences in marriage patterns for blacks and whites in the military. She explains these findings by noting that the military "provides stable employment and offers opportunities for educational and career mobility, particularly for those with fewer opportunities in civilian society" and an "overall social milieu" devoid of much of the racial discrimination present in civilian society (Lundquist, 2004, p. 752). Such an analysis supports the thesis that racial differences in African American family formation trends in U.S. society result not from cultural norms, but are a response to economic and social limitations and opportunities.

After the family, religion is the most important aspect of the lives of most African Americans (Sudarkasa, 1997). African Americans are more likely than whites to attend church, with most of them affiliated with Protestant churches and half being members of Baptist congregations (Schaefer, 2008). For more than 300 years, African American churches have served as community centers, promoting the rights of black Americans and providing both informal and formal social services (Walker, 1999; Wilson, 1996). A variety of non-Christian groups have also exerted a great influence on African Americans. Between 1.6 and 1.7 million or about 5 percent of all African Americans are Muslims and more than 20 percent of American Muslims are African Americans (Schaefer, 2008).

In addition to the values discussed above, Hill (1999) has also made a strong case for both achievement and work orientation being central to African American culture. He argues that the majority of low-income African Americans prefer work to welfare, and that black parents at all income levels hold high educational aspirations for their children. Schaefer (2008) reports that working-class blacks indicate a greater desire for their children to attend college than do working-class whites and that poor blacks are more likely to be working and have more than one wage earner in a family.

As with all minority groups, one has to consider the effects of class as well as race in understanding African American culture. In his book *The Declining Significance of Race* (1978), sociologist William Julius Wilson stated that while racism remains an important factor, social class is becoming more central to understanding the African American experience. He suggests that there are two quite different African American worlds: one that is located in the inner city where joblessness and violence define everyday life and the other located in the middle-class suburbs where good jobs, good schools, and opportunity prevail (Wilson, 1996). The black middle class in the United States has grown substantially since the 1960s (Cherlin, 2008). On the other hand, according to Oliver and Shapiro (1995), while the income gap was closing (blacks earned 76 cents for each dollar earned by whites), the gap in wealth remained extreme; blacks held just 23 cents worth of assets compared to each dollar of assets owned by whites, and if cars and homes were excluded, that ratio dropped to *one cent* for every dollar. We would add another category of experience: African Americans living in rural areas of the South, where school districts have few resources and jobs are disappearing.

Arab Americans

There have been several waves of Arab immigration to the United States, the first beginning around 1875. Arab Americans trace their ancestry to 22 countries in the Middle East (Arab American Institute, 2009). Most Arab countries are predominantly Muslim, but not all people from the Middle East are Arabs, nor are all Arabs Muslims. An Arab American is a person descended from people whose native tongue was Arabic and who lived by Arab cultural traditions and values; a Muslim is a follower of the Islamic religion and may or may not be Arab (Banks, 1997). The majority of Arab Americans are Christian; 35 percent are Catholic, 24 percent are Muslim, 18 percent are Eastern Orthodox, and 10 percent are Protestant (Arab American Institute, 2009). Recent Arab immigrants are more likely to be Muslim, but only about one-fourth of the Muslims in the United States are Arabs (Banks, 1997).

The U.S. Census doesn't use an Arab American classification. In terms of racial classification, the government has at different times considered Arab immigrants to be Asians, "other Asians," Caucasian, white, black, or "colored" (Suleiman, 1999). Socially, Arabs are treated as "honorary whites" or "white but not quite" (Samhan, 1999). They are not considered a minority for purposes of legal protection against discrimination in employment or housing. Most Arab Americans identify themselves by national origin rather than by ethnicity. Because there is so much diversity among Middle Eastern immigrants, they lack a sense of solidarity (Walbridge, 1999).

There are about 3.5 million Arab Americans in the United States, living in all 50 states and the District of Columbia. Most live in metropolitan areas; the areas with the most Arab Americans are Detroit, Los Angeles, Chicago, New York (Brooklyn), and Washington, D.C. (Arab American Institute, 2009). Arab Americans operate small stores in central cities, following the footsteps of Jewish and Korean entrepreneurs (Schaefer, 2008). On average, Arab Americans are better educated and have higher median incomes than other Americans (Arab American Institute, 2009).

Asian Americans and Pacific Islanders

Asian women married to American servicemen account for some of the Asian immigration after 1950. The Immigration and Naturalization Act of 1965, which came into full effect in 1968, abolished discrimination based on national origin and ended 40 years of Asian exclusion. Min (1995a) reports that the proportion of immigrants from Asia, as a percent of all immigrants, increased from 9 percent in 1960 to 25 percent in 1970, and then to 44 percent in 1980.

A total of 11.9 million people in the United States described themselves as Asian or part Asian in the 2000 census (Wright, 2007). In the 1980 census, 3.4 million Americans identified themselves as Asians and Pacific Islanders. This was a doubling of the 1970 census figures due primarily to the influx of Southeast Asian/Indochinese refugees (Vietnamese, Laotians, and Cambodians) after the Vietnam war ended in 1975. By 1990, the numbers had doubled again. The breakdown of Asian Americans by major nationality groups in 2002 were Chinese (23 percent), Filipino (20 percent), Asian Indian (16 percent), and 10 percent each for Vietnamese, Korean, and Japanese (Cherlin, 2008).

Asian Americans are probably the most internally diverse American minority group, representing immigrants from many different nations and cultural traditions. Unlike Latinos, the majority of whom are Catholic and Spanish-speaking, Asian Americans represent a wide variety of religions and languages. Asian Americans also experience diversity related to generational differences (Min, 1995a). Japanese Americans, for example, distinguish among the *Issei* (first generation), the *Nisei* (second generation), the *Sansei* (third generation), and the *Yonsei* (fourth generation) and

FIGURE 6.1   *Sample Naturalization Test Questions**

1. What is the supreme law of the land?
2. The idea of government is in the first three words of the Constitution. What are these words?
3. What do we call the first ten amendments in the Constitution?
4. What is one right or freedom from the first amendment?
5. How many amendments does the Constitution have?
6. What are two rights in the Declaration of Independence?
7. Name one branch or part of the government.
8. What stops one branch of government from becoming too powerful?
9. We elect a U.S. senator for how many years?
10. The House of Representatives has how many voting members?
11. We elect a U.S. representative for how many years?
12. Who does a U.S. senator represent?
13. Why do some states have more representatives than other states?
14. If the president and the vice president can no longer serve, who becomes president?
15. How many people are on the Supreme Court?

---

*Answers are in Figure 6.2 at the end of this chapter.
Source: U.S. Citizenship and Immigration Services (2008). Civics Flashcards for the new naturalization test. Retrieved from http://www.uscis.gov.

their experiences in this country (Nishi, 1995; Schaefer, 2008). Koreans distinguish the *Ichomose* or "1.5 generation"—the middle-aged, bilingual and bicultural adults who accompanied their parents to the United States when they were young (Schaefer, 2008).

South Asians—people from India, Pakistan, Bangladesh, and other South Asian countries— are culturally similar to one another and distinct from other Asian groups (La Brack, 1999; Min, 1990). South Asians experienced British colonization and thus many of these immigrants grew up speaking English, at least in school. Typically, those who arrived in America since 1995 are educated, wealthy, and urban. Many are professionals in the health care field; more than 25 percent of foreign-born dentists and more than 20 percent of foreign-born doctors in the United States are from India (Sweis & Guay, 2007). Others are employed in service industries as cabdrivers, motel managers, and convenience store clerks (La Brack, 1999; Mogelonsky, 1995). Most South Asian immigrants share a religious identity either as Hindus or as Muslims (Min, 1990). The South Asians are the second largest Asian American population (Schaefer, 2008).

The most recent wave of Asian arrivals—the Southeast Asian/Indochinese refugees who arrived in the late 1970s and early 1980s—included not only Vietnamese, Cambodian, and Laotian nationals, but also many ethnic Chinese from all three countries and various highland tribal peoples such as the Lao Hmong and Yao and the Vietnamese Montagnards. These refugee groups had a wide range of educational and economic backgrounds and a variety of language and cultural traditions. Unlike immigrants who move voluntarily, most of the Indochinese refugees survived a stressful, frightening, and often traumatic escape to freedom. Whether they left their homeland by sea or by land, the casualty rate en route was high; this was followed by months or even years of waiting in overcrowded refugee camps in Thailand or Malaysia. Many of those who had education and high status occupations in their native countries had to accept menial jobs in America due to language difficulties or lack of formal credentials. Those whose background was agrarian also had to struggle to adjust to modern American society.

An additional difficulty for this refugee population resulted from their initial dispersal across every state in the country. They were spread out because they had no previous family ties, there were no established ethnic communities, and per federal policy, they had to be "matched" with congregational sponsors who agreed to take responsibility for them. Refugees later moved on (*secondary migration*) to areas where the climate was more familiar and other members of their nationality had gathered. Thus, many Indochinese are now found in California, where more than half of Vietnamese Americans, Cambodian Americans, and Hmong Americans live (Gold, 1999). There are also settlements of Vietnamese in Texas and Louisiana. On the other hand, many refugees remain closer to their original sponsors; for example, there are large groups of Cambodians in Massachusetts, Rhode Island, and Washington, and Hmong in Minnesota and Wisconsin.

Many of the cultural values of immigrants from East Asia (i.e., people from China, Japan, and Korea) are derived from Confucianism. This philosophy promotes *filial piety* and other strong family-centered values. For example, one value is to bring honor to the family, or at least to avoid bringing it shame—in fact, this is a central tenet of Asian cultures (Ho, 1987). Confucianism also teaches the importance of maintaining social harmony. Harmony in interpersonal relationships is accomplished through tact, delicacy, and politeness. Contributions to unity and harmony are more valued than are competitive success or self-satisfaction. Confucianism emphasizes a hierarchical or vertical ordering of society on the basis of age, gender, and social position, specifically in the relationships between father and son, husband and wife, older brother and younger brother, "ruler" (e.g., teacher, employer) and "subject" (e.g., student, employee). These prescribed roles suggest formal styles of interpersonal interaction and contribute to the smooth interaction of individuals in different social roles.

Although they have many cultural similarities, because of the brutal acts of occupying Japanese forces in Manchuria and Korea before World War II, Chinese and Korean Americans may limit their contact with Japanese American communities (Min, 1995a). Also, because most Korean Americans are Christians, their communities are often united through congregational connections, unlike Chinese Americans who are more likely to follow traditional Asian religious practices.

Many Confucian values are shared by refugees from Vietnam, Laos, and Cambodia. Buddhism has also shaped Asian values across the centuries. Buddhism stresses the values of self-control, humility, generosity, mercy, and of cultivating a correct lifestyle. People from many Asian backgrounds are exceedingly reluctant to brag, or even to claim individual credit for their accomplishments. Westerners may be surprised at this level of humility.

Asian Americans are often called the *model minority* since they seem to have succeeded economically, socially, and educationally without significant confrontations with the white majority. Asian American children are more likely than any other ethnic group to grow up with both parents (Henslin, 2008; Wu, 2002). In 2004, Asian American and Pacific Island families had a higher average household income than non-Hispanic whites. Some sociologists contend that the economic success of Asian Americans can be attributed to cultural values: self-discipline, an emphasis on formal education, and a strong entrepreneurial spirit. Asian Americans are well-represented in professional occupations and in the small business sector (Min, 1995b). Many new Asian immigrants have accepted menial jobs and lived as groups in tight quarters until they saved enough to buy a small business such as a gas station, green grocery, convenience store, laundry, or restaurant where all members of the family helped out. Although family income for Asian Americans is higher than whites, this reflects larger household size and the fact that more family members are employed.

Pacific Islanders were first recognized in the U.S. census in 1980; they were listed separately from Asians in the 2000 census (Wright, 2007). The largest subgroup is the Native Hawaiians, followed by Samoans, Guamanians, and Chamorros (the indigenous people of the Mariana Islands [Wright, 2007]). In 2006, there were more than 1 million people who identified themselves as at least part Native Hawaiian or Pacific Islander, and more than half of those identified themselves as being Native Hawaiian and Other Pacific Islander alone (Wright, 2007). Most Pacific Islanders live in Hawaii or in cities on the west coast of the United States (San Francisco, San Diego, Seattle, and Los Angeles). As with many other minority cultures, there is a common theme of group affiliation, collective effort, and commitment to family (which is broadly defined, and may be as large as a whole village) (Mokuau & Tauili'ili, 1992).

Filipinos are the third largest Asian American group in the United States (Schaefer, 2008). The Philippines is the most Westernized country in Asia (Min, 1995a). A Spanish colony beginning in the middle of the sixteenth century, the Philippines came under the control of the United States in 1898, after the Spanish-American War. The earliest Filipino immigrants arrived as American nationals. In 1934, the islands gained commonwealth status and gained full independence in 1946, when residents lost their unrestricted immigration rights. Filipinos learn English in public schools and immigrants to the United States adjust more easily because of the strong American cultural influence in their homeland. Like many other ethnic groups, there are strong regional, linguistic, and religious differences among Filipino immigrants; these differences tend to hinder the development of intraethnic ties (Schaefer, 2008).

Latinos

According to the Census Bureau, Latinos are the fastest-growing minority group in the United States. Between 1980 and 2005, the number of Latinos nearly tripled from 14.6 million to 42.7 million (Wright, 2007). Latinos accounted for half of the U.S. population growth between 2000 and 2007 (Pew Hispanic Center, 2008a). The fastest rates of Latino population growth occurred in the Southeast, led by South Carolina with an 8.7 percent increase in 12 months, followed by Tennessee, North Carolina, Georgia, Alabama, and Mississippi (Gamboa, 2008). California still has the largest number of Latinos, with 13.2 million, comprising 35.9 percent of the state's population, but they constitute more than 25 percent of the populations of Arizona, New Mexico, and Texas as well (Gamboa, 2008; Wright, 2007). This increase was due to high immigration and high birth rates. Latinos as a group have a fertility rate that is about 40 percent higher than Americans overall; in 2006, they had a fertility rate of 3 children per woman, compared to an average for all groups of 2.1 children per woman (Stobbe, 2008).

As of 2005, Latinos made up more than 14 percent of the population, and African Americans made up 13.3 percent if one includes "black only" and those who identify themselves as black and at least one other race (Wright, 2007). The Census Bureau estimates that by 2100, Latinos will constitute one-third of the U.S. population (Wright, 2007).

Latinos can be divided along lines of class, race, and culture. The dominance of the Spanish language, however, as well as a growing political awareness, is a unifying force among Latinos. Most Latinos in the United States speak Spanish; others speak Portuguese, French, Dutch, English, and Native American languages such as Quechua, Mayan, Aymara, and Guarani, and Creole dialects (Castex, 1994). Although Spanish-language television and periodicals help to promote a *panethnic identity* among Latinos, many still identify primarily with their country of origin (e.g., *Cubano/a*, *Mejicano/a*) (Schaefer, 2008).

Hispanic is the term that has been used by the federal government for this minority group since 1978. The term *Latino/a* is preferred by most academics. It is geographically more accurate because it refers to people from Central and South America rather than to people from Spain. It is more politically correct because it affirms Latinos' native, precolonial identity. Neither Latino nor Hispanic is a racial classification. Latinos may identify themselves racially as white, Native American, black, or a mix of two or more of these. The term *Chicano/a* is commonly used in the West and Southwest for Latinos of Mexican descent who were born in the United States. *La Raza* (which literally means "the people") connotes pride in pluralistic Spanish, Native American, and Mexican heritage (Schaefer, 2008, p. 277).

The majority (64.1 percent) of Latinos in the United States trace their roots to Mexico (Pew Hispanic Center, 2008b). An unknown number of Mexicans have immigrated to the United States illegally; the Census Bureau sets the number at about 5 million (Cherlin, 2008). The next most numerous in terms of national origin are Puerto Ricans (9.0 percent) and Cubans (3.4 percent) (Pew Hispanic Center, 2008b). These proportions are quite different in different parts of the United States; for example, of the more than 3 million Latinos living in South Florida and the Tampa-Orlando area of central Florida, 32.5 percent are Cuban and 18.3 percent are Puerto Rican (Pew Hispanic Center, 2008b).

Latinos had established settlements in Florida and New Mexico before the Pilgrims arrived in New England, but the majority of Latinos now living in this country have come in the last century, with most arriving since World War II. The pattern of immigration for the major Latino groups differs considerably. More immigrants have come to the United States from Mexico than from any other country in the world (Pew Hispanic Center, 2008a). Nowhere else in the world do two countries with such different standards of living share a relatively open border; the proximity of Mexico encourages immigrants to maintain strong cultural and social ties with their homeland (Schaefer, 2008). All Puerto Ricans are U.S. citizens and as such move back and forth freely between their island and cities on the U.S. mainland. More so than other Latinos, they sustain multiple familial, economic, and social relations that span geographic borders (Falicov, 1998, p. 40). Colombians and Dominicans also maintain a high level of contact with their countries of origin (Waldinger, 2007). Some sociologists (Baca Zinn, Wells, & Wells, 2000) are using the term *transnational families* to describe families that maintain high levels of contact with both their country of origin and their country of residence.

Most Cuban Americans came to this country as refugees, either as a result of the Cuban Revolution in 1959, during the program of "freedom flights" between 1965 and 1973, or as part of the Mariel boatlift in 1980. Until recently, due to politically imposed barriers, Cuban Americans had the least contact with their native country of all Hispanic immigrants (Waldinger, 2007).

The church is the most important formal organization in the Latino community (Schaefer, 2008, p. 294). A growing number of Latinos in the United States are joining Protestant churches, especially conservative evangelical or Pentecostal denominations (Pew Hispanic Center, 2007). Many of the churches are small, often with Spanish-speaking leadership, and the majority of Latino congregations offer a strong sense of community (Pew Hispanic Center, 2007; Schaefer, 2008). Nevertheless, the vast majority of Latinos (more than two-thirds) remain committed to Catholicism, and Latinos account for over a third of Roman Catholics in the United States (Pew Hispanic Center, 2007). Traditional Catholic rituals continue to be practiced in Latino homes. A particular focus of devotion is the Virgin of Guadalupe, the patron saint of Mexico. Falicov (1998, p. 146) describes her as "the perfect fusion of indigenous Aztec and Catholic European elements, the only brown-skinned virgin who validates the promise of Catholicism for indigenous persons [throughout Latin America]. In fact the Virgin of Guadalupe has many Indian names."

Most Latinos embrace *familism*, or pride and closeness in their families. Familism is generally seen as a good thing, as extended families provide support throughout an individual's lifetime.

On the other hand, it may have the negative effect of discouraging youths from taking advantage of opportunities that would separate them from their families (Schaefer, 2008, p. 292). Mexican Americans more frequently live in extended families than non-Hispanic whites (Cherlin, 2008). These households are likely to include brothers, sisters, or cousins of the household head, and also members of the generation preceding the household head.

Latino immigrants contribute much to the U.S. economy (Maciel & Herrera-Sobek, 1998). Undocumented workers in particular take jobs that are unattractive to most American citizens (Portes & Rumbaut, 2006). Their work is critical to American agriculture and they also contribute to the construction, meatpacking, restaurant, and textile industries. The American rich probably benefit most from Latino immigration through the services of underpaid gardeners, maids, cooks, and nannies. Undocumented Latino workers pay local (e.g., sales) and federal (e.g., FICA) taxes for which they will never claim any benefits (Maciel & Herrera-Sobek, 1998, p. 6).

Latinos have earned a reputation as employees who are hardworking and less likely to complain about poor working conditions or low wages than native-born workers (Engstrom, 2001). The commitment of Latinos to work differs from that of middle-class Anglos who are likely to be motivated by individual achievement. Latinos are more likely to toil because they firmly believe they have to for the survival and well-being of their children and other loved ones. On behalf of their families, they are willing to work overtime and/or "moonlight," and accept grueling, exploitative working conditions (Falicov, 1998, p. 124).

Latinos in the United States routinely send *remittances* back to family members in their country of origin. According to the Inter-American Development Bank (IDB), immigrants sent approximately $45 billion in 2006; on the other hand, about 90 percent of their earnings are put back into the U.S. economy through the purchase of work-related expenses and living essentials (Sanchez, 2006).

Latino immigrants arriving in 2005 were likely to be better educated and much less likely to be low-wage earners than those arriving in 1995 (Greenstein, 2007). Although the annual average household income of less than $20,000 for Latinos puts them below the official U.S. poverty level, this amount represents more than ten times what they would make in their home country (Sanchez, 2006).

Native Americans

In this text, we will use the term *Native Americans* to refer only to those indigenous peoples who are native to the North American continent. (Thus Native American Indians and Alaskan Natives are included, while Hawaiians, and natives of Guam and Samoa, who also are indigenous peoples, are covered under the Pacific Islander category.) Although some Native Americans prefer the term *American Indian* (Lewis, 1995), because of the many legitimate objections to its use (see Herring, 1999) we will use the former term. Other terms sometimes used for this population include *First Americans* or *Original Americans* (Herring, 1999), and *First Nations* (Kehoe, 1999). The federal Bureau of Indian Affairs defines a Native American as a person whose "blood quantum" (i.e., proportion of native blood) is at least one-fourth (LaFromboise & Graff Low, 1998). Native Americans tend to identify as members of a nation first, and then as members of a tribe (Herring, 1999). The term *tribe* is usually a designation for a kin-based group without political institutions (Smith, 1986). A *nation* has a political organization (Winthrop, 1991). For example, the Cherokee Nation comprises five tribes.

At the time of their arrival in the Americas, European immigrants confronted hundreds of Native American tribes speaking over 700 different languages (Schaefer, 2008). Many of the indigenous cultures were quite advanced, incorporating agricultural practices such as irrigation and crop rotation, ceramic and metallurgical crafts, networks of roads and bridges, and democratic forms of governance. Because of a lack of natural immunity to European diseases, as well as the genocide perpetrated by European invaders, their numbers were reduced to about one twentieth of the original population, yet more than 300 distinct Native American tribes survive in the lower 48 states and more than 200 in Alaska (Lewis, 1995). According to the 2000 U.S. census, there are over 4 million U.S. citizens who identify themselves as at least part Native American or Alaskan Native; this included 2.4 million who reported only Native American or Alaskan Native (Ogunwole, 2006).

A third of Native Americans reside on reservations and designated "American Indian areas" (e.g., trust lands) (Ogunwole, 2006). Almost half of Native Americans and Alaskan Natives live in the West. Alaskan Natives comprise 15.4 percent of the Alaskan population. Native Americans make up about 9.8 percent of New Mexicans, 8.5 percent of South Dakotans, and 8 percent of the population of Oklahoma (Wright, 2007). The state with the largest number of Native Americans is California, with 421,346 individuals, but they make up only 1.2 percent of the population there. According to the 2000 U.S. census, the largest tribes are the Cherokee (281,069 individuals) and the Navajo (269,202 individuals) (Wright, 2007). Outside of Alaska, Native Americans can be considered an "invisible" minority because they are concentrated in so few states and because many live on reservations (Henslin, 2008).

Native Americans are a heterogeneous population. They vary in terms of their language, residence (rural, urban, reservation), level of acculturation, and socioeconomic status (Herring, 1999). Their rate of participation in the labor market is lower than the country as a whole, and they are twice as likely as the U.S. population as a whole to have incomes below the poverty level (Ogunwole, 2006). Native Americans are the most disadvantaged minority in the United States. They rank behind others in income, employment, housing, nutrition, and health, and ahead of others in alcoholism, school drop-out rates, infant mortality, delinquency, and mental illness (Henslin, 2008; Kendall, 2008).

After legal victories in the 1960s, Native Americans gained some control over reservation lands. Beginning in the middle 1970s and into the 1980s, reservation Indians took advantage of their legal status as "domestic dependent nations" to open gaming (gambling) halls and casinos. In 2002, there were 290 Indian casinos run by some 130 tribes in 37 states (Bartlett & Steele, 2002; Fixico, 2002). Especially for those casinos located near other tourist attractions or major population centers, this new economic endeavor provided cash income to support schools, housing, day-care centers, health clinics, community recreation centers, nursing homes, industrial parks, convenience stores, and museums (Bartlett & Steele, 2002; Kehoe, 1999). While the majority of Native Americans continue to live in poverty, profits from casinos are going to many non-Indian investors, including foreigners. Only a quarter of gaming tribes distribute cash directly to their members, and most members receive no more than a few thousand dollars each.

Although tourism and the sale of crafts are important sources of employment on many reservations, they do not improve the tribal economy significantly (Schaefer, 2008). Many Native Americans also work for the government, especially in the Bureau of Indian Affairs, but also in state and local governments and for the military.

Even though there are differences among tribes, including the degree of acculturation to the mainstream, there are some common characteristics of most Native American cultures. For example, Native Americans, like many other minorities, take a more collective view of society than the white middle-class mainstream culture. That includes emphasis on the importance of the family, group primacy, and noncompetitiveness. Individual achievement is not valued. Other important Native American values include sharing, cooperation, noninterference, harmony with nature, a present (and cyclical rather than linear) time orientation, and a deep respect for elders (Herring, 1999, p. 72).

Although many Native Americans have been converted to Christianity, many continue to embrace elements of their traditional religions as well. Native American religious beliefs have been misrepresented and oversimplified as "worship of Mother Earth." In fact, First Nations peoples had many prophets and philosophers and fairly complex cosmologies that generally conceptualized a female reproductive power gifted to women and plants (Kehoe, 1999). Native American groups have tried without success to limit tourist access to numerous sacred sites that are located on public lands, such as Grand Canyon, Zion, and Canyonlands National Parks.

Native Americans, like other minority groups, are reasserting pride in their ancestry. This is reflected in a surge in self-identified membership (almost quadrupling between the 1960 census and the 1990 census) and interest in restoring native languages to daily use (Kehoe, 1999). Although it has meant the loss of better-educated Indians from the reservations, the movement of Native Americans to urban areas has contributed to the development of intertribal networks. *Pan-Indianism* refers to intertribal social movements in which several tribes unite in common identity (Schaefer, 2008, p. 178). *Powwows*, featuring dancing, singing, and competitions, are organized events that celebrate Native American culture and educate the general public (Parfit, 1994). On the other hand, despite the attractiveness of pan-Indianism, many Native Americans resist movement toward a common identity in favor of primary identification with their own tribes (Henslin, 2008; Schaefer, 2008).

White Ethnics and Jews

The term *white ethnics* refers to immigrants from Europe whose language and culture have differed from white Anglo-Saxon Protestants. About half of the U.S. population falls in this category, although many of the earlier arrivals have intermarried and now describe themselves as having a mix of ethnic/national backgrounds—or simply as "white" or "American."

Many early European immigrants (the Dutch, Germans, Scandinavians, and Scots-Irish) spread out across the frontier and became farmers and landowners. Later immigrants were more likely to stay in large cities on the East coast and in the Midwest, where the first generation or two remained in ethnic enclaves with people from similar backgrounds. There are still high concentrations of Poles in the Chicago and the Milwaukee areas, for example (Pacyga, 1999). The country experienced a surge of immigration from Europe between 1880 and 1914. They comprised 40 percent of the population of the 12 largest cities in the country, and another 20 percent were second-generation descendants; 60 percent of the industrial labor force was foreign-born (Brody, 1980). Living conditions were abysmal: wages were below subsistence level, working conditions were hazardous, crowded tenements were firetraps, and food poisoning was common (Jansson, 2005). Even with the movement of white ethnics to the suburbs, full assimilation into the mainstream culture was curtailed by the revival of ethnic pride in the 1970s (Radzilowski & Radzilowski, 1999).

On the other hand, Schaefer (2008) reports that the ethnicity currently embraced by English-speaking whites is typically *symbolic*. Symbolic ethnicity does not influence what people do or say, or whom they befriend or marry. It may, in fact, be more a result of experiences in the United States than practices brought from the home country. Some "ethnic" foods and "ethnic" celebrations actually began in the United States. Participating in boisterous St. Patrick's Day parades and drinking green beer, for example, is not how March 17 is observed in Ireland.

Jews are considered by some sociologists to be another white ethnic minority group. They entered America in several waves, beginning before the Revolution, peaking with the immigration of German Jews between the 1820s and 1870s, and again with Jews from Poland, Russia, Romania, and other parts of Eastern Europe between 1880 and 1924 (Shapiro, 1999). Despite a long history of anti-Semitism in Europe, most Jews who migrated to the United States came voluntarily until the early 1930s when the tyranny of the Third Reich in Germany drove many from Germany, Austria, Poland, and Hungary (Schaefer, 2008). Another wave of immigration, particularly from Eastern Europe, occurred after World War II. In the 1960s and 1970s, many Jews came from Israel, the Soviet Union, and Iran. From the beginning, Jewish immigrants settled in eastern port cities, including Newport, Philadelphia, Charleston, and Savannah. In the early twentieth century, approximately half of America's Jews lived in New York City (Shapiro, 1999). Currently, the United States ranks first among nations in the number of Jewish citizens, accounting for 41 percent of the world's Jewish population (Schaefer, 2008). Jewish organizations report that there are 5.2 million American Jews (United Jewish Communities, 2001).

There are three major divisions of Jews in the United States: Orthodox (the most traditional), Conservative, and Reform (the most liberal). Differences are reflected in how traditional rituals are accepted and practiced. Many Jews tend to identify themselves as a cultural or ethnic minority rather than as a religious one (Lipset & Raab, 1995). They express their identity through a variety of political, cultural, and social activities. For observant Jews, acts of fasting, eating only permitted foods, and the study of the Torah and the Talmud assume more importance.

The acculturation pattern of Jews has been an exception to the general American pattern of success partnering with conservative political values. Although on the whole Jews are prosperous, they are politically liberal rather than conservative (Chanes, 2008; Shapiro, 1999). This political orientation may derive from their own long history of oppression that leads them to empathize with other disadvantaged groups. Another explanation is the Jewish religious principle of *tzedekah*, the obligation of the fortunate to help individuals and communities in difficulty (Chanes, 2008).

The tendency of young Jews to marry outside their faith community (at a rate of 47 percent from 1996 to 2001) and the reluctance of their non-Jewish partners to convert are contributing factors to the numeric decline of this ethnic group; this trend is also hastened by low fertility rates (United Jewish Communities, 2001). Almost all children whose parents are both Jews are being raised Jewish, compared to one-third of the children who have only one Jewish parent.

The Jews' sense of family, community, and heritage remains strong. According to Chanes (2008), Jews connect to their community, traditions, and other Jews in a variety of ways. Most Jews participate in selected holidays and forms of cultural involvement, maintain strong social connections to other Jews, and regard being Jewish as very important. Smaller proportions of Jews—ranging from a quarter to a half—are variously engaged in other aspects of Jewish life as well, such as synagogue affiliation, charitable giving, volunteering, and many ritual observances. Today, a greater proportion of Jewish children attend Jewish day schools than ever before, and a greater proportion of Jewish college and graduate students take Jewish studies courses than in earlier years.

Understanding Racial and Ethnic Inequity

Discrimination against minorities is no longer legal in this country. While overt expressions of blatant racial and ethnic prejudice diminished considerably in the last half of the twentieth century, prejudice has not disappeared. Modern prejudice is more subtle, more diplomatic, less conscious (Myers, 1999). It may be that people are trying to suppress unpopular, unwanted thoughts (Devine, 1995) or that they have learned when and where prejudicial talk is not acceptable (Southern Poverty Law Center, 1995).

Myers (1999) summarizes how social psychologists explain prejudice using *social identity theory*. A number of experiments have supported the basic assumptions of this theory: (1) we find it useful to put people into categories, (2) we associate ourselves with certain groups (*in-groups*), and (3) we compare our group to other groups (*out-groups*) with a built-in bias favoring our own group. When resources are scarce and people feel insecure and frustrated, prejudice and discrimination toward out-groups are more common. Members of out-groups may be *scapegoated* for negative social and economic conditions over which they have no control, because it is safer to blame them than to confront people in power.

Functionalist Perspective

Functionalists believe that society works smoothly when everyone shares the same culture. Particularly in times of scarcity or external threat, a sense of "we-ness" (in-group membership) promotes social solidarity. Functionalists therefore are apt to support strict limits on immigration and encourage minorities to pursue cultural assimilation. That is, they encourage minorities to adopt the dominant group's language, values, and norms and stifle their own.

The functionalist perspective emphasizes how the parts of society are structured to maintain its stability. Schaefer (2008, p. 17) notes that, from a functionalist point of view, racist ideologies provide a moral justification for maintaining a society that routinely deprives certain groups of their rights; racist oppression discourages subordinate people from questioning their lowly status; racist myths encourage support for the existing order; and racist beliefs relieve the dominant group from having to address the economic and educational problems faced by subordinate groups.

Conflict Perspective

The conflict perspective often is used to examine relationships among racial and ethnic groups because it readily accounts for the presence of tensions and competition (Schaefer, 2008, p. 17). Conflict theorists argue that powerful people use prejudice and discrimination to hold onto their status in society by exploiting minorities. This is especially true in economic arenas. Elites benefit when inter-group racial or ethnic prejudices keep nonelites from recognizing the interests they share in common. Capitalists exploit racial and ethnic strife to produce a *split labor market*, that is, workers are divided by race and ethnicity across job statuses (Bonacich, 1972; Roediger, 2002). For example, in some places, higher status (and cleaner) jobs such as driving trucks or other pieces of equipment, are reserved for whites, while people of color pick up the trash, spread the asphalt, or shovel the dirt. There is an implied threat, held over the heads of white workers, that should they strike, minority workers would be called upon to fill their positions. The consequence, according to conflict theorists, is that the working class is divided, and white workers perceive the source of their insecurity in minority workers rather than in the capitalist owners of the company (Henslin, 2008).

Portraying the problems of racial and ethnic minorities as their fault rather than recognizing the role of the dominant majority in developing and/or maintaining the system is sometimes listed as an example of *blaming the victim* (Ryan, 1976). Conflict theorists remind policy makers that the ultimate responsibility for social problems must rest with those who possess the power and authority to change them (Myrdal, 1944; Southern, 1987).

Some conflict theorists also are concerned about the role of the United States in promoting a *brain drain*, or the immigration of skilled technicians and professionals away from their homes in developing nations where their talents are needed. Wu (2002), for example, notes the high proportion of health care professionals among Asian and South Asian immigrants. In addition, when immigrants from other countries are recruited to fill prestigious and financially rewarding positions in America, the United States can continue to ignore native-born members of subordinate groups who could be trained to enter these fields (Schaefer, 2008).

Constructionist Perspective

Our discussion about the difficulty of defining "race" should make clear the role of social construction in race and ethnic relations. Constructionists focus on how labels produce prejudice. Labels lead to *selective perception* or *filtering*; that is, they cause people to pay attention to certain things and ignore others (Henslin, 2008). For instance, if you believe that all Asian American students are good at math, you may fail to take note of one who excels in art.

"Racial and ethnic labels are especially powerful. They are shorthand for emotionally-laden stereotypes. The term *nigger*, for example, is not neutral" (Henslin, 2008, p. 345). Neither is "honky," "chink," "spic," or "kike." (Scornful terms also applied to other minority groups: "femi-nazi," "fag," "dike," "cripple," and "retard" are examples of other hurtful labels). Such words arouse powerful emotions and get in the way of rational discourse.

Constructionists stress that people are not born with prejudices. Instead children are socialized to be prejudiced through interaction with others, particularly those who hold strong prejudices themselves. Americans live in a society where racial and ethnic stereotypes abound.

American Society and Experiences of Racial and Ethnic Inequity

All racial and ethnic minorities have been victims of discrimination and oppression at some time in American history. This continues today, most notably in underrepresentation in elective office, discrimination in housing and employment, lack of access to medical care, overrepresentation in the criminal justice system, and everyday hassles. Historically, the experiences of minority groups may have been different but all suffered tremendously. Social cohesion within these populations, including the development of mutual aid organizations and advocacy groups, has greatly facilitated their advancement in American society. The populations are presented below, roughly in chronological order in relation to when they arrived in North America.

The Experience of Native Americans

Although the United States never had an official policy of deliberate extermination of Native Americans, use of the term *genocide* is not inappropriate in describing the actions of many white settlers (invaders) and their government that decimated the populations of indigenous people on the North American continent. The nature of the violence perpetrated against Native Americans (see Bordewich, 1996) as well as the total disregard for human life might bring one to question which people were more deserving of the label "savage." The U.S. government broke treaty after treaty as it forced Indian nations to move westward to clear land for white settlers. Over half of the Cherokee Nation died on the *Trail of Tears*, the path of their forced removal from the southeastern

United States to Indian Territory (Oklahoma). Native Americans were not granted U.S. citizenship until 1924 and could not vote in Arizona or New Mexico until 1948. Until 1930, Native American children were separated from their families and sent to special Indian boarding schools where they were forced to wear Anglo-style clothing and punished when they used their native languages. Many schools serving Native American children today fail to meet their needs; there are few Native American teachers and the curriculum is presented from a Euro-American perspective. Underenrollment is a problem at all ages, from elementary school through college. *Internal colonialism* is the term used to describe treatment of subordinate groups like colonial subjects by those in power (Schaefer, 2008, p. 172).

A bit more than 2 percent of the landmass of the United States is designated as reservations or trust lands. Reservations range in size from less than 100 acres to the 16 million acres of the Navajo reservation that covers parts of Arizona, Utah, and New Mexico (Snipp, 1999). Historically, reservations have been marked by severe economic distress. Although the federal government has always encouraged Indians to support themselves through agriculture, less than 1 percent of all reservations lands is highly productive farmland (Snipp, 1999). According to the Southwest Indian Foundation (2009), the average per capita income on the Navajo reservation is $6,217; 58 percent of Indian persons on the Navajo Reservation live below the poverty level and 43 percent of the Navajo labor force is unemployed. Native Americans living on reservations experience poor health, unmet medical needs, and high rates of crime; many children never attend school or drop out of elementary school (Schaefer, 2008). Native American men living on reservations have an average life expectancy of less than 45 years and women less than 48 (Churchill, 1994).

The Experience of African Americans

Between 1619 and the 1860s, more than 500,000 Africans were brought to America as slaves (Walker, 1999). At the beginning of the Civil War, only 10 percent of blacks in America were free. Although not all slaves were brutally treated, most lived under barely subsistence conditions, and it was not uncommon to separate slave families at the auction block. The slave family had no standing in law; marriages between slaves were not legally recognized. *Slave codes*, laws developed to restrict the rights of slaves, varied from state to state, but there were common themes (Schaefer, 2008, p. 202). For example, it was against the law to teach slaves to read or to give them books, including the Bible. Slaves could not buy or sell anything except by special arrangement. Slaves could not testify in court except against another slave. Slaves could not leave their owners' property without a pass indicating destination and expected time of return. Violators of slave codes were whipped, mutilated, or killed. Female slaves were routinely raped.

Slavery ended in the South with the Emancipation Proclamation in 1863. The Thirteenth Amendment to the Constitution, ratified in 1865, permanently abolished slavery and the Fourteenth Amendment, ratified in 1868, further protected the rights of former slaves. Nevertheless, African Americans soon lost ground. In 1896, the Supreme Court ruled in *Plessy v. Ferguson* that "separate but equal" treatment was acceptable. *Jim Crow* laws in the South enforced segregation in housing, employment, education, and all public accommodations and severely limited independent African American economic initiatives. *Lynching* (executing someone without a legal trial, usually by hanging) was a mechanism of terror used to keep black citizens from challenging the status quo. There may have been as many as 6,000 lynchings in this country between 1892 and 1921 (Feagin & Feagin, 1999). Another mode of control was arbitrary arrest and imprisonment; often black convicts were used to provide free labor for both public and private enterprises. African Americans were denied the right to vote through a series of quasi-legal obstacles, such as poll taxes and literacy tests.

Although they have always participated in the defense of this country, African Americans have not received equal treatment in the military until relatively recently. The first casualty of the American Revolution was a black man, Crispus Atticus. Five thousand African Americans served continuously during the Revolutionary War; African Americans made up 10 percent of the Union forces and 25 percent of the Union Navy in the Civil War and some 500,000 African Americans served overseas in World War II (Walker, 1999). African Americans in the U.S. military were assigned to segregated units until the middle of the twentieth century.

In 1954 in *Brown v. The Board of Education*, the Supreme Court voted unanimously that "separate but equal" was unconstitutional under the Fourteenth Amendment. The following year, blacks in Montgomery, Alabama, launched a boycott against that city's segregated bus system, led by Dr. Martin Luther King, Jr. Largely in response to the massive demonstrations, marches, sit-ins, and boycotts that followed, Congress passed the Civil Rights Act of 1964, the most far-reaching legislation to protect the rights of African Americans since the abolition of slavery.

Although legally protected from discrimination, African Americans still suffer from the effects of prejudice. Examples of mistreatment include the deliberate burning of African American churches and *racial profiling* (individuals targeted for unfair treatment by law enforcement personnel because of the color of their skin). As noted in Chapter 4, African Americans receive less adequate medical care than do whites. Some argue that stress resulting from racism and suppressed hostility exacerbates hypertension (high blood pressure) among African Americans, a critical factor in higher mortality rates from heart disease, kidney disease, and stroke (Schaefer, 2008).

Federal studies of the home lending industry, and federal lawsuits, have consistently found evidence of racial discrimination; blacks get high-rate loans much more often than do whites with similar or smaller incomes (Appelbaum & Mellnik, 2005). Since 1989, under the Home Mortgage Disclosure Act, the Federal Reserve has been required to report annually on home lending activity in the United States. Data reported in 2006 indicate that 54.7 percent of African Americans and 46.1 percent of Hispanics pay a higher-than-typical interest rate for home mortgages compared to whites (17.2 percent) (Aversa, 2006). While lenders applaud the fact that more minorities are getting home loans, critics say that in a process of "reverse redlining" (see Chapter 8) lenders are now targeting black neighborhoods for the sale of high-rate loans (Appelbaum & Mellnik, 2005).

When elected to office, African Americans serve predominantly black districts and communities; they hold a disproportionately small share of elective and appointive offices in the United States. For many citizens, the election of an African American president in 2008 marked the beginning of a new era in American politics. It remains to be seen how that will affect the interpretation of the role of African American leaders in the United States.

The Experience of Asian Americans

More than 300,000 Chinese migrated to California between 1850 and 1880, where most performed manual labor for the railroads, and for farmers and miners (Yung, 1999). As "aliens" and persons of color, they had no legal rights and could not become citizens. They were often the target of mob violence—beaten, burned, shot, and lynched (Yung, 1999; Wu, 2002). In the worst of the confrontations, 200 armed white mineworkers in Rock Springs, Wyoming, drove out 600 Chinese mineworkers, killing 29 of them; all of the whites were acquitted in subsequent trials (Wu, 2002). Racism, and fears on the part of white laborers that they would lose their jobs to Asian immigrants, led to the passage of the Chinese Exclusion Act in 1882 (Yung, 1999). This legislation was repealed in 1943, probably because the Chinese were American allies in World War II.

The need for cheap laborers was soon filled with Japanese immigrants, who began coming to the west coast somewhat later than the Chinese. As they became more successful, they faced similar legal restrictions on their rights. California passed legislation (the Alien Land Laws) in 1913 and 1920 that prohibited the purchase of land by Japanese residents (Jansson, 2005). In 1922, the U.S. Supreme Court ruled that foreign-born Japanese could not become American citizens because they were not Caucasians.

Early in World War II, Japanese Americans, including many who were born in this country, were rounded up and moved to ten *internment camps* located in remote rural areas in seven states, taking only what they could carry with them (Tamura, 1999). All people on the west coast of at least one-eighth Japanese ancestry were taken to assembly centers for transfer to evacuation camps; two-thirds of the evacuees were U.S. citizens (Schaefer, 2008). This has been described as "one of the most vicious forms of discrimination ever sanctioned by U.S. laws" (Kendall, 2008, p. 337). Italian Americans and German Americans faced no similar persecution, even though the United States was at war with Germany and Italy as well as Japan. After a Japanese American challenged the constitutionality of the process, the U.S. Supreme Court ruled the detainment unconstitutional on December 18, 1944 (Schaefer, 2008). The last Japanese internment camps were closed in 1946. Four decades passed before the American government issued an apology to these Japanese Americans and their descendents and paid $20,000 to each internment camp survivor, beginning in 1990 (Takaki, 1993).

Asian Americans remain underrepresented in politics, far below the level for blacks and Latinos, but their influence is growing as with their overall increase in population numbers and the proportion with citizenship status. Hawaii, where Asian Americans make up the majority of voters, has elected Asian American governors and U.S. senators. Gary Locke, a Chinese American, was governor of Washington from 1997 to 2005 and Piyush "Bobby" Jindal, an Indian American, was elected governor of Louisiana in 2007 after serving in the U.S. House of Representatives.

Although in comparison to other groups, Asian Americans appear to be doing well financially, there are several arguments that this is not an accurate reflection of their true economic status. They are concentrated in large cities such as San Francisco, Los Angeles, New York, and Honolulu, where living expenses are much higher than in the rest of the country on average. Asian Americans live in larger households than do white Americans and a slightly higher proportion of Asian American women work outside the home compared with white women. It is not fair to compare the household family income of an Asian American family which may pool the wages of a husband, wife, grandparent, child, and cousin with a white household with a similar income derived from the work of just one family member (Wu, 2002). Asian Americans are also more likely to be self-employed than white Americans; they put in longer hours and have fewer benefits than employees of large companies (Wu, 2002).

The Experience of Latinos

Mexican immigrants were able to move freely across the U.S. border until 1924 when the Border Patrol was created. Being concentrated in the Southwest, Latinos were isolated politically and therefore fell victim to exploitation by landowners (Jansson, 2005). Employers often played on the fears of undocumented workers that they would be found and deported in order to stifle protests against harsh working and living conditions. Cesar Chavez successfully developed and led the United Farm Workers in the 1960s to demand legislation that would protect agricultural workers from work-related hazards, as well as promoting their right to unionize (Day, 2009). Nevertheless, across the nation, on-the-job deaths of foreign-born workers have been increasing and overall death rates for Latinos are consistently higher than those of white and African American workers (Phillips, 2008). South Carolina led the nation in on-the-job death rates for Latino workers between 2003 and 2006; 88 percent of those injured were foreign-born and 63 percent were in the construction industry (Phillips, 2008). (See Chapter 9 for a discussion of injuries in the meatpacking industry where many Latinos are employed.)

Increasing numbers of Spanish-speaking immigrants and their growing political, social, and cultural visibility has led to a resurgence of anti-Latino sentiment. This has been reflected in welfare reform legislation at both the national and state levels that led to drastic cuts in benefits previously available to immigrants (Gutierrez, 1999). In 1996, Congress passed the Personal Responsibility and Work Opportunity Reconciliation Act (PRWORA), which gave states the option of ending Medicaid coverage for legal immigrants and excluding legal immigrants who had worked for less than ten years in the United States from SSI and Food Stamp eligibility (Jansson, 2005, p. 392). Efforts to make English the "official language" of the country and many states were initiated in the early 1980s. As of 2008, there were 26 states with active "English-only" laws. Ironically, the vast majority of first-generation immigrants (from all countries) who come to the United States as children speak English well and English-only is the predominant pattern by the third generation, with the exception of American communities along the Mexican border and in areas of high ethnic density, such as among Cubans in Miami, where bilingualism is more common (Portes & Rumbaut, 2006, pp. 229–230).

The Experience of White Ethnics and Jews

Although most were fair-skinned, immigrants from Ireland, Italy, Greece, Russia, and Eastern Europe faced discrimination based on their religions (Catholicism, Eastern Orthodoxy, and Judaism). Strong anti-Catholic sentiment had already developed in the mid-1800s when roughly one and one half million Irish peasants immigrated to America to escape the 1845–1848 "potato famine" in their homeland. By the 1850s, nativism, especially in opposition to Roman Catholics, became an open political movement in America. Anglo-Americans believed they were being overrun and anti-Catholic, anti-Irish, and anti-immigrant sentiment often merged (Jansson, 2005).

Both Irish Americans and Italian Americans have been subjected to institutionalized discrimination in employment, with "swarthy" Italians being perceived as "not white" (Gambino, 1975; Sensi-Isolani, 1999). Mob violence directed against Catholic individuals and their property was common across the country between 1834 and 1854 (Schaefer, 2008). More than 30 Italians were lynched in the South between 1890 and 1910 (Sensi-Isolani, 1999). Anti-Catholic suspicion was clearly still an issue in the 1960 presidential election when John F. Kennedy ran for office. Hostility expressed toward white ethnics is often taken less seriously than is racism. For example, "Polish jokes" are less likely to be challenged than are antiblack remarks.

The civil rights of Jews were affected by the "blue laws" enacted by states and cities forbidding a variety of activities on Sunday. (Jews celebrate the Sabbath from sundown Friday to sundown Saturday.) Eastern European Jews who immigrated in the early twentieth century were associated with Marxist politics and hence faced discrimination on that account. Jews were excluded from many premier colleges and universities, as well as clubs, hotels, and some residential neighborhoods (Thio, 2000). They also faced discrimination in employment (Selzer, 1972).

Prejudice and discrimination against Jewish people is called *anti-Semitism*. The most virulent and overt anti-Semitism in the United States occurred in the 1920s and 1930s. Well-known American leaders, such as Henry Ford and Charles Lindbergh, contributed to anti-Jewish sentiment by lending credence to fraudulent conspiracy theories (Schaefer, 2008).

In past centuries, Jews were often used as scapegoats and blamed for all kinds of problems, including plagues; at one time, they were expelled from the nations of Spain, France, and England. For nearly 2000 years, various Christian groups argued that all Jews share in the responsibility of the Jewish elders who condemned Christ to death and used that to justify anti-Semitism. A 2007 survey found that 27 percent of Americans believed that Jews were responsible for the death of Christ, up from 25 percent in 2002 (Anti-Defamation League, 2007). Nevertheless, much anti-Semitism has more to do with negative attitudes related to stereotypes of Jews as being overly clannish and financially shrewd (Wilson, 1996), and feeling more loyalty toward Israel than the United States (Anti-Defamation League, 2007).

The *Holocaust* refers to the state-sponsored systematic persecution and annihilation of Jews by Nazi Germany and its collaborators. Between 1933 and 1945, two-thirds of Europe's total Jewish population was killed, including 90 percent of the Jewish population of Germany, Austria, and Poland (Schaefer, 2008). Despite irrefutable evidence and the testimony of eyewitnesses and survivors, a very small but vocal group of people called *Holocaust revisionists* claim that the events of the Holocaust never happened. Jews have been, and continue to be, targeted by the Ku Klux Klan and neo-Nazi skinheads. The Anti-Defamation League of B'Nai B'rith tracks reported anti-Semitic incidents, which include harassment, threats, assaults, and vandalism. A chilling recent development is the use of the Internet to spread hatred toward Jews. In spite of persistent discrimination, Jews have achieved substantial success in the areas of business, education, law, medicine, and the arts.

The Experience of More Recent Arrivals

Among the problems facing many immigrants and refugees in the United States today are language barriers, lack of employment opportunities and/or labor market exploitation, lack of educational attainment, lack of access to health care, racism, and religious intolerance. Those who lack immigration documents (illegal aliens) are particularly likely to experience problems.

Many Middle Eastern immigrants and American citizens of Middle Eastern descent experience unwarranted prejudice, suspicion, and discrimination (McCarus, 1994). More than a third of Arab Americans report that they or their family members experienced discrimination because of their ethnicity, both before and after the events of September 11, 2001 (Telhami, 2002). Soon after the tragedies, at least five individuals were killed just because they appeared to be Arab or Muslim;[2] and another 1000 physical and verbal attacks on Middle Easterners and South Asians were reported in a period of eight weeks (Ahmad, 2002). This was accompanied by government acts of racial profiling of "Muslim-looking" individuals at airports and detention or deportation of immigrants from Muslim countries.

Negative media portrayals of Arabs and Muslims and omissions or inaccuracies in history and social science texts in North American schools have contributed to perceptions of these peoples as inferior, uncultured, threatening, anti-American, anti-Christian, anti-Semitic, greedy, cruel, and barbaric (Banks, 1997). After 9-11, some Americans felt hostile toward people of Middle Eastern backgrounds; most people now are careful to draw distinctions between members of a whole culture and a small number of extremists.

FIGURE 6.2   *Naturalization Test Answers*

1. The Constitution
2. We the people
3. The Bill of Rights
4. Freedom of speech, religion, press, assembly and petition the government
5. 27
6. Life, liberty, and pursuit of happiness
7. Executive, legislative, and judicial
8. Checks and balances
9. 6
10. 435
11. 2
12. All the people of the state
13. More people
14. The Speaker of the House
15. 9

Source: U.S. Citizenship and Immigration Services (2008). Civics Flashcards for the new naturalization test. Retrieved from http://www.uscis.gov.

Looking Ahead

While members of ethnic and racial minorities often grow up in supportive communities, members of other minority populations do not have that advantage. In Chapter 7, we will examine the experiences of women, sexual minorities, and persons with disabilities. Each of these populations has found ways to cope and succeed despite experiences of discrimination and oppression.

Endnotes

1. There is a confusion that derives from two common uses of the word *community*, one as a town or neighborhood and the other as a "sense of community" or a social network among people who share some interest, personal characteristic, or organizational/associational tie. The latter *identificational communities* are mental constructs. Often, identificational communities develop in response to experiences of discrimination and oppression. The boundaries of identificational communities may or may not be consistent with neighborhood boundaries where minorities live.

2. Two of the victims were Sikh Indians, one was an Indian Hindu, one was Pakistani, and one was an Egyptian Coptic Christian (Ahmad, 2002).

Chapter 7
Other Social Status Groups

In this chapter, we introduce the concept of social statuses and examine how they apply to three disadvantaged groups: women, gay men and lesbians, and people with disabilities. Social workers often join with these populations in advocacy efforts toward social justice.

Social Status

"A *status* is a socially defined position in a group or society characterized by certain expectations, right, and duties" (Kendall, 2008, p. 140). The term *status* is commonly associated with high or prestigious positions in society, but sociologists use the term to describe any specific position. For example, each year college students preparing for professions begin internships with different organizations. They are expected to be prompt, dress appropriately, pay attention to their supervisor or mentor, and bring what they learn back to the classroom for discussion. The status of "student intern" is similar across many disciplines. While "student intern" is a temporary status, many other social statuses are long term or permanent.

Ascribed statuses are social positions that are conferred at birth or assigned later in life, based on characteristics over which an individual has little or no choice or control. Sex and race are good examples of ascribed statuses. Other kinds of statuses are more within the control of the individual; they are assumed voluntarily as a result of personal choice or direct effort. These are called *achieved statuses*. Being a college graduate is a good example of an achieved status. Some statuses in American society carry more power and privilege than others. These include being white, male, heterosexual, and nondisabled. Other valued statuses are afforded to those people who belong to Christian religious denominations, are youthful, attractive, tall and slim, professionally employed, articulate, wealthy, and famous.

The concepts of prejudice, discrimination, oppression, and privilege that were discussed in relation to race and ethnicity in Chapter 6 also apply to the ascribed statuses of gender, sexual orientation, and disability. Nevertheless, the experiences of women; gay men, lesbians, bisexual, transgendered, and questioning (GLBTQ) persons; and people with disabilities may be quite different from those of racial and ethnic minorities. Members of racial and ethnic minorities have the advantage of being part of families and communities that can help them in the process of developing a positive self-identity and in negotiating the demands of the dominant culture (Carothers, 1990; Lukes & Land, 1990). It is highly unlikely, on the other hand, that a gay man or a person with cerebral palsy will grow up in a family and community made up of other gay men or people with cerebral palsy. For these individuals, the first part of the socialization process will come from the dominant culture, complete with negative stereotypes. They are not isolated from society, but they are isolated from each other. Although there are supportive *identificational communities* (see definition in endnotes in Chapter 6) of sexual minorities and people with various types of disabilities, most individuals must seek them out as they become adults. (The Deaf community is an exception, as you will see later in this chapter.) The situation for women, for the most part, is even more complex. They live in a society that is *patriarchal*—meaning that, by and large, men hold the power to make formal decisions and determine policies. Although women may join together for support and advocacy, the majority of them owe at least a part of their social standing to the efforts of their fathers and husbands. Just as homosexuals must interact with heterosexuals, and people with disabilities must interact with the nondisabled, women interact daily with males, both in formal situations and also in intimate relationships as partners and caregivers, as daughters, sisters, wives, and mothers.

Gender

The terms *sex* and *gender* are often used interchangeably. In our discussion, *sex* will refer to biological differences and *gender* will refer to those differences that are culturally constructed and socially transmitted.

Among the real biological differences between the sexes are chromosomal, hormonal, and brain-structure dissimilarities that determine primary and secondary sex characteristics (such as reproductive organs, breast size, and facial hair) and instinctive behaviors. Among biologically supported behavior differences are physical aggression, visual-spatial ability, and sexual behavior (Lippa, 2002).

Although biology determines many aspects of sex-related behaviors, society and culture define gender. The significance of gender is that "it is a device by which society controls its members. Gender sorts us, on the basis of sex, into different life experiences. It opens and closes doors to property, power, and even prestige" (Henslin, 2008, p. 300).

Children are socialized by their families, schools, peers, and the mass media to conform to culturally approved gender expectations (*gender roles*). Even in this age of increasing attention to gender equality, girls are still encouraged to look pretty, nurture others, play cooperative games, and be "nice." Boys are encouraged to be tough, competitive, independent, and achievement-oriented.

It is often difficult to separate out what is biological from what is cultural. No human being has ever been raised without the presence of gender socialization and therefore purely biological influences on behavior cannot be isolated for study. While the possibility for a biological explanation of some behaviors cannot be ignored, these behaviors are always expressed in a social environment. Research on sex and gender differences is still being conducted; what is clear, however, is that the context of women's lives is different from that of men's. As already noted, the United States (like virtually all other societies) is patriarchal. Just as racial and ethnic minorities experience inequities in a society that is dominated by whites, women experience inequity in a society dominated by males.

Understanding Social Stratification and Gender

Functionalist Perspective.   From a functionalist perspective, a division of labor between men and women, particularly in the family, is the natural order of human society. A complementary set of roles, with men providing economic support and making decisions and women providing care and emotional support, ensures that important societal tasks will be fulfilled (Parsons & Bales, 1955). Some conservative politicians and their supporters and fundamentalist religious leaders promote this traditional interpretation of "the family" as essential to the stability of society.

Conflict Perspective.   Conflict theorists remind us that, in most societies, differences exist between men and women in the areas of physical, economic, and political power. A colleague of Karl Marx, Friedrich Engels (1902/1884), said that capitalism intensifies male domination because it creates more wealth, which in turn gives greater power to men as owners of property or primary wage earners. Evidence of male domination in contemporary society is reflected in economic and political-related inequities, and gender-related violence. This is discussed further in the section that follows.

Constructionist Perspective.   As noted previously, gender is socially constructed. Language and concepts of gender are intertwined. For example, not long ago the term *mankind* was used to refer to all members of the human race, leaving many women feeling excluded. The use of *inclusive language* is now encouraged in professional writing and public discourse. See, for example, the "guidelines to reduce bias in language" in the *Publication Manual* of the American Psychological Association (2009). Many formerly sexist terms have been replaced (e.g., the traffic caution sign "Men Working" now reads "People Working," and "postman" has been replaced by "mail carrier"). While some people consider this overzealous political correctness, language does shape our view of reality.

The social construction of appropriate gender roles has been in flux over the past 40 or 50 years in this country. Especially as more women have entered the paid workforce in large numbers, including leadership roles, assumptions about women's capabilities have changed dramatically. Also, a perception that only men were "family breadwinners" and women were working by choice (i.e., just for supplemental income) has changed.

American Society and the Experience of Inequity
Related to Gender

Although not a numerical minority, women are considered a minority in the sense that they exercise less power than men in American society. In the past, laws prevented women from voting, holding property, establishing credit in their own names, serving on juries, and entering certain professions, while other laws subjugated them to the control of their fathers and husbands. Whereas this is no longer the case and much progress has been made, there remain significant areas of gender inequality.

Gender-segregated, or *sex-typed work* refers to a pattern of employment wherein men and women are found in different occupations (Padavic & Reskin, 2002). Examples would be nurses, secretaries, and flight attendants (female-dominated) and physicians, business executives, and airplane pilots (male-dominated). These occupational choices reflect gendered expectations— that women will nurture and provide assistance and men will take charge and make decisions. In 2007, many of the occupations with the highest concentrations of women (e.g., nursing and child care) reflect this. Women were well-represented in several industry sectors, including education and health services, leisure and hospitality, and other services (U.S. Bureau of Labor Statistics, 2008). They were underrepresented in agriculture, mining, construction, manufacturing, and transportation (U.S. Bureau of Labor Statistics, 2008) (see Table 7.1).

Women typically hold lower status, lower-paying jobs than men with similar educational backgrounds. Cross-cultural and historical research has shown that the status given an occupation is higher when most jobs in it are filled by men and lower if those same jobs are filled by women. For example, a hundred years ago, most secretaries were men and the job had relatively high prestige. Now that 96.7 percent of all secretaries and administrative assistants are women (U.S. Bureau of Labor Statistics, 2008), the job is accorded lower esteem. In short, it is not the work that provides the prestige, but the gender with which the work is associated.

TABLE 7.1   *Concentration of Women in Different Occupations, 2007*

Occupation Title	*Percentage of Women*
Dental hygienist	99.2
Speech-language pathologist	98.0
Preschool and kindergarten teachers	97.3
Secretaries and administrative assistants	96.7
Child-care workers	94.6
Hair stylists and cosmetologists	92.9
Registered nurses	91.7
Social workers	82.0
Veterinarians	48.4
Post-secondary teachers (professors)	46.2
Lawyers	32.6
Physicians and surgeons	30.0
Dentists	28.2
Architects	24.7
Police and sheriffs patrol officers	13.7
Mechanical engineers	7.3
Firefighters	5.3
Logging workers	1.5
Masons (brick and stone layers)	1.2

Source: U.S. Bureau of Labor Statistics (2008, Report 1011). *Women in the labor force: A databook*, Table 11.

A majority of women in contemporary American society actually fill two roles, as paid and unpaid workers, and are easily exploited in both. Padavic & Reskin (2002) suggest that the burden of the second shift will probably preserve women's inequity at home and in the workplace for another generation. The *second shift* refers to the child care and housework responsibilities that women assume after returning home from their paid employment (Hochschild, 1989). Women still do more housework than men and they are more likely to perform time-consuming and routine household tasks such as cooking and housecleaning, whereas men's chores involve fixing things and yard work (Coltrane, 2000; Sayer, 2005).

Even when women hold the same positions as men and have comparable skills and training, they tend to earn less. In the United States in 2007, women who worked full time had median weekly earnings of $614; this amount represents 80 percent of men's median weekly earnings of $766 (U.S. Bureau of Labor Statistics, 2008). Earnings of Asian ($731) and white ($626) women were substantially higher than the earnings of their black ($533) and Latino ($473) counterparts (U.S. Bureau of Labor Statistics, 2008).Women in year-round, full-time executive, administrative, and managerial positions earn only 61 percent of what men are paid in the same positions (Wright, 2007).

According to the U.S. Equal Employment Opportunity Commission (2008), "unwelcome sexual advances, requests for sexual favors, and other verbal or physical conduct of a sexual nature constitute *sexual harassment* [italics added] when this conduct explicitly or implicitly affects an individual's employment, unreasonably interferes with an individual's work performance, or creates an intimidating, hostile, or offensive work environment." In 1986, the U.S. Supreme court declared that sexual harassment violates the federal law against sex discrimination as outlined in the 1964 Civil Rights Act. Women's groups applauded the Court's decision in identifying harassment as a source of discrimination.

Sexual harassment has come to be understood more recently as an abuse of power (by a person of either sex) to force unwanted attention on a subordinate. According to the U.S. Equal Employment Opportunity Commission, "sexual harassment can occur in a variety of circumstances, including but not limited to the following:

- The victim as well as the harasser may be a woman or a man. The victim does not have to be of the opposite sex.
- The harasser can be the victim's supervisor, an agent of the employer, a supervisor in another area, a co-worker, or a non-employee.
- The victim does not have to be the person harassed but could be anyone affected by the offensive conduct.
- Unlawful sexual harassment may occur without economic injury to or discharge of the victim.
- The harasser's conduct must be unwelcome" (U.S. Equal Employment Opportunity Commission, 2008).

Employment is not the only area where men exercise power over women. Sexual violence should be understood as a dimension of gender stratification; it is fundamentally about power, not sex (Herman, 2001). The violence perpetrated against women by their partners is a reflection of a sexist, patriarchal society that treats women as if they were property. Women are five to eight times more likely than men to become victims of domestic violence (ACLU, 2007). Approximately one-third of the women murdered in the United States each year are killed by an intimate partner (ACLU, 2007).

Marital rape is more common than one would think. Of women who seek help at domestic violence shelters, between one-third and one-half are victims of marital rape (Bergen, 1996). Until the late 1970s, most states did not consider spousal rape a crime (National Center for Victims of Crime, 2004). Currently, rape of a spouse is a crime in all 50 states and the District of Columbia. While spousal rape is now considered a crime, victims often have to overcome additional legal hurdles to prosecution not present for other victims of rape. These include time limits for reporting the offense and a requirement that force or threat of force be used by the offender (National Center for Victims of Crime 2004). Some victim advocates argue that the term *marital rape* needs to be expanded to include sexual assault by cohabiting partners. Partner abuse can also include psychological abuse, such as intimidation, threats, public humiliation, and intense criticism (Crawford & Unger, 2003).

Date rape/acquaintance rape is relatively common but underreported on most college campuses. About 3 percent of college women are sexually assaulted during a typical college year (South Carolina Coalition Against Domestic Violence and Sexual Assault, 2002).

Male power is also demonstrated in the pornography industry. *Pornography* is material that appears to endorse, condone, or encourage sexual abuse or degradation. Feminists suggest that the objectification and control of women's bodies portrayed in pornography contributes to violence against women, in part by reinforcing rape myths (e.g., that women secretly want to be raped). Pornography is not limited to adult bookstores; it is a big business that includes Internet sites easily accessible to children. Music videos, while not legally pornographic, commonly include content that is *misogynistic* (demeaning of females).

Men also experience issues of gender inequity. The gender roles that men labor under are much more constraining than those available for women. For example, a man is expected to be his family's "breadwinner"; being a "stay-at-home father" may bring social ostracism. Men are also expected to hide their feelings and, in comparison to women, to have a less nurturing relationship with children and friends. Perhaps the most noteworthy inequity is the societal expectation that males, but not females, go into combat when needed.

Gender Around the World

Female Genital Mutilation. Female genital mutilation, also called *female genital cutting*, refers to "all procedures involving partial or total removal of the external female genitalia or other injury to the female genital organs for non-medical reasons" (World Health Organization, 2008). According to the World Health Organization (WHO), between 100 and 140 million girls and women are estimated to have undergone this procedure. An additional 3 million girls are estimated to be at risk (Yoder, Abderrahim, & Zhuzhuni, 2004). The practice is most prevalent in western, eastern, and northeastern regions of Africa, some countries in Asia and the Middle East, and among certain immigrant communities in America and Europe. The procedure is thought to inhibit sexual desire and ensure marital fidelity. Beside the intense pain, female genital mutilation is associated with infertility, infection, and even death (World Health Organization, 2008). The UN Committee on the Elimination of All Forms of Discrimination against Women, the UN Committee on the Rights of the Child, and the UN Human Rights Committee have been active in condemning the practice and recommending measures to combat it, including criminalization.

Literacy and Education. Illiteracy rates are high for women in many countries. More than 56 percent of the 104 million out-of-school children in the world are girls, and over two-thirds of the world's 860 million illiterates are women (UNESCO, 2004). More than half of the adult female population in 32 countries cannot read or write; 22 of these countries are in Africa ("Women of Our World," 2002). Other countries with high rates of female illiteracy include Pakistan, Afghanistan, and Laos. In some countries, such as parts of Afghanistan under Taliban rule, girls were not allowed to attend school. Because school fees are required in many countries and families have limited resources, they may decide to invest in their sons' educations rather than their daughters' (UNESCO, 2004). Girls are also more likely to be victims of sexual harassment and violence in schools, which leads to high drop-out rates (UNESCO, 2004).

Women in Positions of Political Leadership.   Within the last 60 years, a number of countries have had female heads-of-state. These include Liberia and Rwanda (in Africa), Indonesia, the Philippines, Bangladesh, India, Pakistan, and Sri Lanka (in the Asian subcontinent), Great Britain, Finland, France, Germany, Ireland, Latvia, Portugal, Poland, Switzerland, and Turkey (in Europe), Israel (in the Middle East), Canada (in North America), and Argentina, Bolivia, Chile, Ecuador, Guyana, Haiti, Nicaragua, and Panama (in South and Central America) (Macionis, 2007).

Gender-Segregated Work Around the World.   According to Anker (1998, p. 411), three-quarters of women are employed in just seven occupations: nurses, caregivers, secretaries/typists, bookkeepers and cashiers, sewers and tailors, and housekeepers, building caretakers and cleaners. These employment categories reflect stereotypes of women as patient caregivers, cleaners, and nimble-fingered/detail-oriented individuals (Padavic & Reskin, 2002, p. 71). Although segregation of jobs by gender is declining, cultural patterns continue to impede change toward an integrated workforce.

Sexual Orientation

Sexual orientation is defined as a person's preference of partners in emotional-sexual relationships: same sex, other sex, or both sexes. Homosexuality (attraction to members of the same sex) and heterosexuality (attraction to members of the other sex) are not mutually exclusive; sexual orientation lies on a continuum rather than being a dichotomy (either/or). This understanding of sexual orientation leads us to other categories of sexuality, which include bisexual and transgendered individuals. *Bisexuality* refers to sexual attraction to people of either sex. *Transgendered* refers to people who feel they are one sex, even though biologically they are the other (Gagné, Tewksbury, & McGaughey, 1997).

It has always been difficult to get accurate information on the number of people who are sexual minorities. One of the few researchers who made an effort was Alfred Kinsey (1948, 1953), who estimated that 4 percent of males and 2 percent of females are exclusively homosexual.

It should be noted that homosexual activity or experiences are not the same thing as homosexual identity. Many heterosexuals have had homosexual encounters. According to a 2002 nationwide survey (U.S. National Center for Health Statistics, 2005), 11.2 percent of women and 6.0 percent of men said that they had had same-sex sexual contact in their lifetime. In the same survey, 4.1 percent of both men and women identified themselves as either homosexual or bisexual. More than 14 percent of women reported "at least some attraction" to other women, while 7.8 percent of men said they were attracted to other men.

Many research studies have linked homosexuality to biological factors, such as brain structure, hormonal influences, and genetics (Bem, 2001; King, 2005). Other authors suggest that sexual orientation is a product of society (Foucault, 1990), both society and biology (Bailey & Dawood, 1998; Schwartz & Rutter, 1998), or simply a personal choice.

Sexual Orientation as Community and Culture

Generally gay men and lesbians find large urban centers to be more hospitable to sexual diversity than rural areas. In some large cities, there are identifiable gay neighborhoods such as the Castro district in San Francisco, but even some smaller cities such as Key West, Florida, Provincetown, Massachusetts, and Santa Fe, New Mexico, have substantial gay populations. As noted in Chapter 6, there are also gay and lesbian communities that are not geographically anchored (Cruikshank, 1992).

The creation of these gay and lesbian identificational communities resulted from both experiences of discrimination and a sense of commonality. Without a strong gay community, the gay liberation movement would not have come into existence; the existence of that movement, in turn, helped to expand gay communities (Cruikshank, 1992). Stigmatization and social rejection prompted a sense of solidarity in response to isolation from mainstream American society, but Queralt (1996) argues that there would be a gay community even without elements of oppression.

"Even if sexual minorities do not have a culture in the traditional sense, in the process of accepting a homosexual identity, they are socialized into a new set of norms and values" (Lukes & Land, 1990, p. 156). Not all gay men and lesbians belong to or participate in an identifiable culture related to their sexual orientation; nevertheless, there are elements of a common cultural experience that include pairing behavior; definitions of family; the time, place, and reason for celebrations; and religious services (Lukes & Land, 1990, p. 156). Cruikshank (1992) argues that, in its broadest terms, the essence of gay and lesbian cultures is self-determination. "To follow a different path openly and wholeheartedly rather than furtively, [lesbians and gay men] have created a culture in which homosexuality is the norm" (p. 139).

Understanding Social Stratification and Sexual Orientation

Functionalist Perspective.   Because functionalists assume a complementary set of roles for men and women, they do not see a legitimate place for gay men and lesbians in society; in fact, they perceive them as a threat to traditional family arrangements. This perspective tends to support the status quo and the view that a stable society is one wherein members share a common set of values, beliefs, and behavioral expectations. Thus there is an absence of widespread support for civil rights for gay men and lesbians. Although gay men and lesbians have advocated for themselves and experienced success in a variety of venues, they continue to be marginalized by society.

Conflict Perspective.   The existence of gay and lesbian lifestyles is considered by many to be a threat to the institution of marriage and the family. Sexual minorities are routinely oppressed in American society. Social conflict theorists believe that, in defense of their idea of "the family," conservatives are willing to sacrifice the individual rights of gay men and lesbians in order to preserve their own social standing.

An example of efforts to restrict the rights of gay men and lesbians can be found in the customary use of sodomy laws. Sodomy laws (making anal and oral sex illegal) were on the books in 13 states until struck down by a U.S. Supreme Court decision (*Lawrence v. Texas*) in June 2003. They were rarely enforced and when they were, they were mainly used to criminalize sexual activity between men. But sodomy laws also were cited in denying custody to gay and lesbian parents, in keeping gay or lesbian couples from adopting children, and in justifying employment discrimination because all gay men and lesbians were considered "potential felons" (Madden, 2003). Other landmark court cases in GLBTQ law include *Boy Scouts of America v. Dale, Cammermeyer v. Perry, Nabozny v. Podlesny*, and *Brandon v. Richardson County.*

Lambda Legal is the oldest national organization pursuing litigation, public education, and advocacy on behalf of equality and civil rights for lesbians, gay men, bisexuals, transgender people, and people with HIV. This organization helps individuals secure their rights by providing legal information about federal laws and the laws in their state (Lambda Legal, 2009).

Constructionist Perspective.   Just as gender is a social construction, so are sexual orientation and socially approved sexual relationships. A variety of sexual expressions have been found in almost all societies, but different cultures tend to privilege one orientation (usually heterosexism) over others. While in the United States homosexuality is often viewed as a deviant lifestyle, other countries and cultures are or have been more accepting of same-sex attraction (Gramick, 1983). In ancient Greece and Japan, male–male relationships were held in higher esteem than male–female relationships (Gramick, 1983; Greenberg, 1988). In Brazil, labeling of homosexuality depends upon whether the male takes an active penetrating role, in which case he would be considered heterosexual regardless of the sex of his partner (Cherlin, 2008). By calling homosexual behavior a "sin," and gay men and lesbians "sinners," religious conservatives impose a moral judgment that justifies and encourages discrimination against this vulnerable population.

American Society and the Experience of Inequity Related to Sexual Orientation

Homophobia is the unreasonable fear of homosexuals and homosexuality. *Heterosexism* is the view that heterosexuality is "normal" and that any other pattern of intimate interpersonal relationship is inherently abnormal or wrong. Unlike racism and sexism, heterosexism is widely tolerated in our society, legally supported under most circumstances, and even encouraged in some sectors. It was not until 1973 that homosexuality was eliminated as a mental disorder from the *Diagnostic and Statistical Manual of Mental Disorders* (DSM) of the American Psychiatric Association.

Gay men and lesbians experience a wide range of discriminatory practices, including lack of protection from discrimination on the job and inability to serve in the military without hiding one's identity (see Chapter 3). In addition, gay and lesbian couples are denied many legal benefits granted to married heterosexual couples, for example, access to Social Security benefits after a partner's death; joint parenting rights, such as access to children's school records; bereavement leave upon the death of a partner; right to shared property, child support, and alimony after a divorce; automatic inheritance of shared assets after a partner's death; ability to file joint tax returns; veteran's discounts based on a partner's armed forces status; and reduced rate memberships at health clubs, social clubs, and other organizations.

Gay men and lesbians may be accused of seeking "special" rights when in fact they simply want the same basic civil rights and liberties available to heterosexual citizens. The question of legal protection for gays under the Fourteenth Amendment has not been ruled on by the U.S. Supreme Court, and there is no federal law prohibiting discrimination in the workplace on the basis of sexual orientation. Nevertheless, 12 states, the District of Columbia, and several hundred municipalities and counties have legal protections in place for public and private employees (Human Rights Campaign [HRC], 2008d). In addition, 16 states and the District of Columbia provide domestic partner benefits for state employees (HRC, 2008d). Gay men and lesbians may face ridicule or social ostracism when they live with a partner and do so openly, express affection toward a partner in public, or talk about their weekends, vacations, or other social events without disguising the gender of their partner. National surveys have documented strong negative attitudes toward gays; 48 percent of Americans believe that homosexual relations between consenting adults is morally wrong (Lacayo, 1998) and 46 percent believe that homosexuality is a sin (Leland, 2000).

Homophobic prejudices may be particularly difficult for adolescents who are gay or lesbian. In a 1997 survey, 46 percent of gay, lesbian, and bisexual youth in one state's high schools reported they had attempted suicide in the previous year (Peyser & Lorch, 2000). A 17-year-old adolescent gay activist interviewed for a *Newsweek* story noted, "If you're in a society that tells you you are an abomination, right or wrong, it's what you believe" (Peyser & Lorch, 2000, p. 56). In middle schools, homophobia can be even more pronounced. In a 2005 survey, 64 percent of middle school students reported antigay bullying and name-calling as major problems in their schools, 18 percentage points higher than what was reported by high school students (Kilman, 2007). Increasing numbers of schools are establishing *Gay Straight Alliance* (GSA) organizations to help protect and promote the rights of sexual minority students; at the end of the 2005/2006 school year, there were over 3,000 GSAs in the United States (Kilman, 2007). Twelve states and the District of Columbia have laws that prohibit discrimination, harassment, and bullying of students based on sexual orientation (HRC, 2009d).

Of more serious concern than simple harassment is physical violence against gays. Now that the FBI identifies specific hate crimes, evidence of such criminal activity is widespread. In 2006, there were 1,195 attacks on gays, or 15.5 percent of all hate crimes (HRC, 2009a). There is concern that negative rhetoric from conservative religious and political leaders may encourage these crimes (Lacayo, 1998). As of August 2008, 31 states and the District of Columbia had laws that address hate or bias crimes based on sexual orientation (HRC, 2009a).

Most states prohibit marriage for same-sex couples. According to the Human Rights Campaign organization (2009c), as of September 1, 2009, 29 states had constitutional amendments restricting marriage to one man and one woman and an additional 11 states had laws to that effect. Only six states in the United States have same-sex marriage: Massachusetts, Connecticut, Iowa, Vermont, Maine, and New Hampshire (effective January 1, 2010), while one state (New York) and the District of Columbia recognize marriages by same-sex couples legally entered into in another state (HRC, 2009b). In 2006, about half (51 percent) of those Americans polled opposed legalizing gay marriage, but the numbers had declined from 63 percent two years earlier (Pew Research Center for the People and the Press, 2006). Five states (California, Nevada, New Jersey, Oregon, and Washington) and the District of Columbia give the equivalent of state-level spousal rights to same-sex couples; three states (Hawaii, Colorado, and Wisconsin) give some state-level spousal rights to same-sex couples (HRC, 2009b). Some critics note that same-sex couples still report legal problems and trouble obtaining benefits in those states that honor civil unions (Kelley, 2007). There are a large number of state legislatures and courts dealing with these issues on a continuing basis, so readers might want to check the Human Rights Campaign web site for the most current status.

The determination of adoption is made on a case-by-case basis and it is a judicial decision whether to grant adoption petitions. According to the Human Rights Campaign organization (2008a), in many states the status of parenting laws for GLBT people is unclear and the laws governing adoption vary widely. There are ten states and the District of Columbia where same-sex couples can jointly petition to adopt and two states where same-sex couples have successfully petitioned to adopt in some jurisdictions. Same-sex couples are prohibited from adopting in Florida, Mississippi, and Utah. Florida is the only state that explicitly prohibits all GLBT people from adopting. In Arkansas, there is a statutory ban on adoption and fostering by unmarried individuals cohabiting with a sexual partner.

Second-parent adoptions are when a person petitions to adopt the child of his or her partner. Nine states and the District of Columbia allow second-parent adoption by same-sex couples; another 15 states permit second-parent adoption in some jurisdictions (HRC, 2008b).

Gay Rights in a Global Perspective

Same-Sex Marriage in Other Countries.   The legal definition of marriage is in flux, particularly in the developed world, as governments re-examine what long seemed to be a well-established aspect of civil law. Beginning legal efforts on behalf of same-sex couples originated in 1989 when Denmark instituted "registered partnerships" that extended property and inheritance rights (Lozano-Bielat, Masci, & Ralston, 2009; Vestal, 2008). In December of 2000, the Netherlands became the first country to legalize same-sex marriage (Lozano-Bielat, Masci, & Ralston, 2009). As of November 2008, gay marriage was recognized by six countries: Belgium (2003), Canada (2005), Norway (2008), South Africa (2006), and Spain (2005) (Johnson, 2008). Israel recognizes common-law status for gay couples and legally recognizes same-sex marriages performed in other countries as full marriages (Lozano-Bielat, Masci, & Ralston, 2009). More than a dozen other nations in Europe, South America, and elsewhere have expanded the rights of same-sex couples by permitting legal statuses that grant them some legal rights without using the term *marriage*, such as civil unions, civil partnerships, or domestic partnerships (Johnson, 2008; Lozano-Bielat, Masci, & Ralston, 2009).

There are many areas in the world where the debate is not centered on the recognition of same-sex unions, but rather on the acceptability of homosexuality *per se*. According to a 2000 survey by the Pew Research Center's Global Attitudes Project, a majority of the peoples in Africa, Asia, and the Middle East do not view homosexuality as an acceptable way of life (Lozano-Bielat, Masci, & Ralston, 2009).

Gays in the Military in Other Countries.   Some ancient armies, such as those in Japan and Greece, not only did not repress homosexual expressions among warriors, but actually encouraged them. In the contemporary world, 24 nations, including Canada, Australia, Israel, Norway, and the Netherlands allow gays to serve openly (HRC, 2007; RAND, 2000). The Netherlands uses education as a means to ensure the smooth integration of gays, women, and racial minorities into the military; and in the Danish and Norwegian military, discrimination or harassment against gays are grounds for fines, expulsion, or possible imprisonment ("Gays in Arms," 1992).

The United States, Turkey, and Portugal are the only NATO nations that forbid gays to serve openly (HRC, 2007). The issue of gay men and lesbians serving openly in the military remains contentious in the United States.

Disability

In the past two decades, there has been a dramatic change in the way that people with disabilities are perceived. The view has changed from one based on charity to one based on human rights (Quinn & Degener, 2002).

According to the U.S. Census Bureau (2005), there are 49.7 million Americans with one or more physical or mental disabilities (excluding those living in institutions and under age five); nearly one in five citizens has a disability. Counties with high rates of disability are clustered in the coal-mining areas of Kentucky, West Virginia, and Virginia. Across the country, disabilities rates are highest for African Americans and American Indians and Alaska Natives. In 2000, a higher proportion of people with disabilities (17.6 percent) were poor than were people without disabilities (10.6 percent). About 46 percent (46) of persons with a disability were working full-time or part-time in 2005 (U.S. Census Bureau, Survey of Income and Program Participation, 2005). Even though they hold jobs, people with disabilities often have lower incomes and are less likely to have health insurance than working people without disabilities (Ohlemacher, 2006).

One example of a population with a disability whose involvement in society has changed dramatically in the past generation is people with Down Syndrome. At one time, parents were encouraged to institutionalize their Down Syndrome children. Now most are raised at home, graduate from high school, and find employment. They have benefited from early intervention programs and mainstreaming in school classrooms, as well as advances in medical care that address common problems, such as heart and gastrointestinal defects, eye problems, and thyroid issues (Wallis, 2006). Their average expected life span has increased from 25 in 1983 to 56 today (Wallis, 2006). This creates a different kind of risk. Because federal policy fails to provide a coherent network of community services and support, many families are the sole providers for their adult children. Recent data indicate that 715,000 people with cognitive impairments of all kinds were living with caregivers aged 60 or older (Bauer, 2008).

An entirely different kind of problem results from the development of prenatal screening tests that identify Down Syndrome very early in the gestational cycle. Many physicians, ignorant of the potential of Down Syndrome children, often encourage the mothers to choose abortion (Carmichael, 2008). According to studies, 90 percent of women whose fetuses test positive for Down Syndrome choose to abort (Carmichael, 2008). A bill, the "Prenatally and Postnatally Diagnosed Conditions Awareness Act," was passed by Congress in September, 2008. The law would require giving families who learn that their child may be born or is born with a disability facts about the condition and information on the many options and support services available on caring for children with disabilities (Datiles, 2008). The legislation also provides for the further development of peer-support groups and of a national clearinghouse on information for parents of disabled children. In addition, the bill creates a national registry of families who are willing to adopt children with pre- or postnatal diagnosed disabilities (Datiles, 2008).

The vast majority of individuals with disabilities were not born that way, but were injured in an accident or war, or suffer from the effects of an illness. The number of persons with disabilities is greater now than in previous decades because of advances in medical technology that keep at-risk infants and accident victims alive and allow people to live longer, even though they have more impairments as they age.

Another significant source of disabilities is the injuries incurred by troops serving in Iraq and Afghanistan. Veterans are returning with blindness (Zoroya, 2007), loss of limbs (Ellison, 2008), and traumatic brain injuries (Emery, 2007). In fact, traumatic brain injury (TBI) has been called the "signature wound" of the Iraq war. Lingering effects of TBI include headaches, sleep disorders, memory loss and information processing problems, sensory processing issues, sensitivity to light or noise, irritability, depression, anxiety, personality changes, aggression, and social inappropriateness (Okie, 2005; Zoroya, 2005).

While there are many definitions of disability, they essentially fall into two major categories: (1) those that locate disability as internal to the individual and (2) those that situate the problem in the interaction between the disabled person and the social environment.

The first category is the one that social workers are most likely to encounter in their dealings with other human service and health care professionals. According to the 1990 Americans with Disabilities Act (PL 101-336), disability means "with respect to an individual, a physical or mental impairment that substantially limits one or more of the major life activities of such individuals, a record of such an impairment, or being regarded as having such an impairment." With these definitions, professionals are looking for a cure, or at least a way to rehabilitate the individual. These professionals may expect the person with the disability to be compliant and passive.

The second category of definitions establishes disability not just as a personal problem but also as a challenge to society to change attitudes and remove barriers (Karger & Stoesz, 2010, p. 94). This latter view sees the person's inability to function as the result of a handicapped environment, and disability as an element of human diversity (Gilson & DePoy, 2002).

Disability as Community and Culture

All who consider themselves disabled are potential members of the disability community. According to Linton (1998),

> we (disabled people) are bound together, not by . . . (a) list of our collective symptoms but by the social and political circumstances that have forged us as a group. We have found one another and found the voice to express not despair at our fate but outrage at our social positioning (p. 4).

Linton (1998) goes on to describe "the cultural stuff of the disability community" as being

> the creative response to atypical experience, the adaptive maneuvers through a world configured for nondisabled persons. The material that binds us is the art of finding one another, of identifying and naming disability in a world reluctant to discuss it, and of unearthing historically and culturally significant material that relates to our experience (p. 3).

The construction of disability as a community and culture constitutes a range of understandings. One noteworthy position on this continuum is that of the Deaf community. People in the Deaf community perceive deafness not as a disability, but as a minority culture (Luey, Glass, & Elliott, 1995; Padden & Humphries, 1988). Perhaps because deaf children are routinely separated from their families to attend special residential schools for the deaf at an early age, they are more likely to develop a unique and/or bicultural orientation to the world than are people with other kinds of disabilities. Among communities of disabled persons, the Deaf community stands alone in having its own language, American Sign Language (ASL). ASL is usually dominant in residential schools; fluency in ASL has the effect of cementing the culture and creating a different worldview, particularly for those who grow up with it (Luey, Glass, & Elliott, 1995). According to the National Association of the Deaf (NAD, n.d.), deaf and hard of hearing people feel that the words "deaf" and "hard of hearing" are not negative in any way. Instead, they view "hearing-impaired" as negative, because the label focuses on what they cannot do.

Understanding Social Stratification and Disability

Functionalist Perspective.   The functionalist perspective uses a medical model to explain the role of disability in society. A medical model suggests that pathology resides within the individual. (This contrasts with the social work understanding of person-in-environment, wherein disability may be viewed as a lack of fit between the individual and his or her environment.) From a functionalist perspective, people with disabilities are restricted to the role of chronic patient. They are perceived as being unable to work, or at least unable to work as productively as the able-bodied.

Conflict Perspective.   Conflict theorists argue that people with disabilities belong to a minority group that is kept in a subservient position and exploited by the health care industry (Albrecht, 1992). People with disabilities are treated as second-class citizens. Categorizing them as "deserving poor" and giving them subsistence-level grants does little to bring them to full inclusion in society. Restrictions of opportunities for schooling, employment, and housing continue to limit their options.

A *caste system* is a form of social stratification in which one's status is lifelong and unchangeable. Szymanski and Trueba (1994) argue that

> the difficulties faced by persons with disabilities are not the result of functional impairments related to the disability, but rather are the result of a castification process embedded in societal institutions for rehabilitation and education that are enforced by well-meaning professionals (p. 12).

For example, federal policy related to disability benefits forces recipients to choose between a limited grant and Medicaid, versus accepting a job with an income that will threaten their eligibility for health care coverage. Vocational rehabilitation agencies, with pressures of high caseloads and limited resources, also keep persons with disabilities locked into their low status by referring them to sources of employment that are easily available, such as dishwashing and custodial work (Mackelprang & Salsgiver, 1999).

Constructionist Perspective.   The social construction of disability is a process that has for the most part marginalized people with disabilities. People with disabilities are sometimes perceived as dangerous, especially persons with mental retardation or mental illness, when there is a proposal to move them into a group home in a residential neighborhood. They are more often thought of as helpless, dependent, incompetent, and tragic figures, or even as "perpetual children" (Mackelprang & Salsgiver, 1999, p. 6). The response to this construction is a patronizing stance that may result in their exclusion from activities or places that are considered to be suitable only for adults, including those arenas where they could effectively advocate for themselves.

When not perceived as victims, people with severe disabilities are sometimes portrayed as heroes who miraculously overcome all obstacles to lead a "normal" life. Members of the disability community sometimes refer to such individuals as "supercrips" (people with severe disabilities who seem to excel and receive lots of media coverage) (Shapiro, 1993). This image is also misleading. Linton points out that persons with disabilities are

> not only the high-toned, wheel chair athletes seen in recent television ads, but the gangly, pudgy, lumpy, and bumpy of us, declaring that shame will no longer structure our wardrobe or our discourse. We are everywhere these days, wheeling and loping down the street, tapping our canes,

sucking on our breathing tubes, following our guide dogs, puffing and sipping on the mouth sticks that propel our motorized chairs. . . . Our symptoms, though sometimes painful, scary, unpleasant, or difficult to manage, are nevertheless part of the dailiness of life. They exist and have existed in all communities throughout time. What we rail against are the strategies used to deprive us of rights, opportunities, and the pursuit of pleasure. (Linton, 1998, pp. 3–4)

American Society and the Experience of Inequity Related to Disability

The issue of ascribed status is an important one for people with disabilities. Sociologists use the term *master status* to describe a perceived social status that dominates all the other statuses a person holds. Historically, occupation has been a master status for many men, and the most common master status for a woman was her role in the family as wife or mother. Being very rich or poor can be a master status, as well as being a member of a minority race or ethnicity in a society where discrimination is the rule. For many individuals, disability becomes a master status. For example, when individuals must use wheelchairs, their disability may override all other statuses they might enjoy, such as educational achievement or occupational success. The master status concept is often apparent in the media. Most television portrayals of people with disabilities highlight the disability; television and film directors are reluctant to insert an individual with a physical disability into a minor role where the disability is irrelevant to the story (Makas, 1993).

The built environment is probably the most potent symbol of exclusion of people with disabilities from society. Mark Johnson, a disabilities activist (quoted in Shapiro, 1993, p. 128) notes that whereas African Americans fought for the right to sit at the front of the bus, persons with disabilities have had to fight for the right to *get on the bus.*

The current prevalence of "handicapped" parking places and bathroom stalls may lead the casual observer to believe that most public places are easily accessible to persons with mobility problems. Nevertheless, many amenities are inadequate or poorly designed or limited in their applicability. For example, trendy brick pavers may cause people using walkers to trip; sometimes a freight elevator at the back of the building may be the only available means of ascent. Public address announcements in airports are barely intelligible to people with normal hearing, much less to those who are hard of hearing. Most signs and signals in our built environment are purely visual; Braille labeling is provided in elevators but rarely in other public areas. The lack of convenient and accessible public transportation is a major impediment for many persons with disabilities.

Organized political activity by people with disabilities and their families was rewarded in 1990 with the signing of the Americans with Disabilities Act (ADA). The ADA extends to disabled people civil rights similar to those made available on the basis of race and sex through the Civil Rights Act of 1964. Nevertheless, stigma and oppression are ongoing problems for people with disabilities. As long as disability is viewed as an individual affliction rather than as a deficit in the physical or social environment, people with disabilities will continue to be an oppressed minority. If one accepts the assumption that stigma is a major barrier to full citizenship for people with disabilities, then advocacy for civil rights, in addition to the provision of social services and income maintenance, is the appropriate response (Hahn, 1991).

Disability in a Global Context

In developed countries, the disabilities rights movement concerns itself with human rights to ensure full participation in society. Some people are concerned, however, that the greatest need for advocacy is in developing countries. In those nations, basic needs, such as accessibility, education, and employment are not being met.

According to the United Nations (Quinn & Degener, 2002), over 6 million people, or approximately 10 percent of the world's population live with a disability of one form or another. Over two-thirds of these live in developing countries and only 2 percent of disabled children in the developing world receive any education or rehabilitation.

Looking Ahead

The chapters in Part III addressed social structure and its impact on vulnerable populations. In Part IV, we discuss social settings as contexts for human behavior. Social justice issues will be a continuing theme.

Part IV

INTRODUCTION TO SOCIAL SETTINGS

Drawing upon an ecosystems perspective, in Part III we discussed various niches in the social environment (Germain & Gitterman, 1995).

> The physical and social settings of community, workplace, school, and so on constitute the *habitat* [of human beings]. . . . Physical settings such as dwellings, buildings, rural villages, and urban layouts must support the social settings of family life, interpersonal life, work life, spiritual life, and so on in ways that fit the lifestyles, age, gender, and cultural patterns of the residents. (Germain, 1991, p. 45)

Traditionally, social work texts have not paid much attention to aspects of the physical environment, but that is changing gradually with the awareness of how environmental issues affect individuals and communities. On the other hand, "It is the understanding of *the person as a social being* [italics in original] that constitutes the main area for the contribution of the social work profession" (Chess & Norlin, 1991, p. 26). Thus social systems and social settings (e.g., families, groups, organizations, communities, and so forth) have long been the focus of attention of social work curricula. These social systems are studied both as entities *per se* within a larger environment and as contexts for smaller systems.

In Chapter 8, we discuss communities as geopolitical systems, that is, physical and social entities and settings (in contrast to the identificational communities described in Chapters 6 and 7). We look at the reasons for the decline of central cities and the accompanying growth of suburbs and the implications for community well-being. In Chapter 9, we draw on the large body of literature on organizational theories and assess their applicability to human service agencies and to the workplace as a social setting. In Chapter 10, we discuss a special type of organization, residential institutions. We provide an overview of the history of institutional care in this country and discuss the impact of institutional settings on the people who live in them.

Oppression of vulnerable populations occurs not only in residential institutions, but in organizations and communities as well. The profession's commitment to social justice suggests that oppression should be an area of concern (Council on Social Work Education, 2008, p. 6; NASW, 2006).

In addition to being the contexts for understanding human behavior, communities, organizations, and institutions also are settings for social work practice. Knowledge of how these collectivities operate will contribute to your professional effectiveness.

Locational Communities

The profession of social work has its roots in community practice. Social workers in settlement houses adopted communities as the arena for their interventions. These early social workers worked to improve housing and neighborhood conditions, and to establish day-care centers, educational programs, recreational opportunities, and job training and referral services. Community context continues to be critical for certain vulnerable groups, particularly for those who cannot move about easily, such as children, older adults, people with physical disabilities, and often poor families. Knowledge of community is essential for good social work at any system level, and community practice reflects the profession's commitment to social and economic justice.

Defining Community

Even within social work, the term *community* is often used to mean different things. In Chapter 6, we introduced the concept of identificational communities; here we restrict the use of the term to mean locational or geopolitical communities. There are three essential elements of locational community: geographical area, social interaction, and common ties (Hillery, 1955). Locational community is where person and environment meet. Community residents interact with each other, share common interests, use many of the same resources, and access many of the same services. This interdependence among residents, and between residents and their community environment, is basic to the concerns of social work.

    Communities are also social systems. Unlike organizations, which we will discuss in the next chapter, the relationships in communities are not based on formal, contractual expectations, but rather on mutual benefits. Communities usually do not have formal goals, but goals can be identified by examining the common needs and problems of people who share the same geographical space.

Types of Communities

Types of communities are defined in relation to population size and/or location and/or function. A *metropolis*, for example, is a city of 50,000 or more people. A *suburb* is a residential urban area beyond the political boundaries of a city; historically, some of these were small towns in their own right, but they have become connected to a larger city through the development of interstate highways and suburban sprawl. Many suburbs, called *bedroom communities*, are primarily residential and their inhabitants commute elsewhere to work during the day. An *exurb* is a settlement outside of a city, and usually beyond its suburbs, that is often inhabited by well-to-do families. An *edge city* is a business center some distance from the downtown but close to the intersection of major highways: typically it is a mix of corporate office buildings, medical centers, shopping malls, fast-food franchises, hotels, and entertainment complexes. The occupancy of the exurbs and bedroom communities peaks at night, while the occupancy of the edge city peaks during the day. Another term is *megalopolis*, which refers to one or more cities and their surrounding suburbs whose boundaries have converged; an example is the Boston to Washington, DC, corridor.

Neighborhoods are important subsystems of cities. Fellin (1995, p. 77) defines *neighborhood* as a "geographical area which includes dwellings where people reside. . . . [Some also] contain nonresidential buildings such as schools, churches, stores, service buildings, police stations, fire stations, and offices." The boundaries of a neighborhood may be politically set, as with voting wards, school districts, or church parishes. Social factors may also be used in the definition of neighborhoods. For example, the *Social Work Dictionary* says neighborhood inhabitants "share certain characteristics, values, mutual interests, or styles of living" (Barker, 2003, p. 292). Often neighborhoods are occupied by people of the same racial or ethnic background or sexual orientation, similar social class, or by families who are in the same stage of the family life cycle. Examples of mutual interests or styles of living might be found in a "university neighborhood," an "Italian neighborhood," or a "singles neighborhood."

Slums, ghettos, and barrios are special types of neighborhood. These terms are often associated with high-poverty neighborhoods in large urban areas. *Slum* implies an area of extreme poverty, with deteriorated and abandoned structures. Although often used interchangeably with slum, the terms *ghetto* and *barrio* refer to neighborhoods with distinct racial or ethnic cultures that often are, but are not necessarily, poor. There are features of strong resident identification and positive social interaction within their boundaries, but few links with the larger community (Fellin, 1995, p. 88).

Issues and Trends in Communities

Cities and Suburbs

The number of large U.S. cities continues to grow. In 1990, the census recorded 199 cities with populations over 100,000; in 2000, there were 243 cities with populations of this size or greater (Wright, 2007). Most of the large cities in the United States can be classified as "postindustrial"— that is, their economies are dominated by "light" industry, information processing services, educational complexes, medical centers, convention and entertainment centers, and shopping malls

(Kendall, 2008). In 1950, nine of the ten largest cities were in the "snowbelt" (North) and in 2004, seven of the top ten were in the "sunbelt" (South) (Macionis, 2007).

Two significant trends of the last half-century that have implications for communities are the decline of central cities and the growth of suburbs. Several factors have contributed to these interrelated trends. These include a period of economic prosperity beginning at the end of World War II, increasing reliance on automobiles for transportation, government policies that penalize central cities and support suburbs, political fragmentation that prevents effective regional planning, and the loss of blue-collar jobs due to the relocation of industries. These factors are discussed in more detail next.

Between 1945 and 1960, per capita income in America increased by 35 percent (Coontz, 1992). This made it possible for working-class and middle-class people to purchase single-family homes. Eighty-five percent of the new homes of this period were built in the suburbs (Mason, 1982).

When workers bought automobiles, they no longer needed to live close to jobs or public transportation systems. Even though President Eisenhower's new interstate highway system was promoted to serve important military functions, the primary beneficiaries were suburbanites who used it for commuting back and forth to work (Jackson, 1985). Although in the past few years more communities are taking a critical look at the effects of outward growth, by and large suburbs were and continue to be designed and built around the needs of cars (Cieslewicz, 2001). That is unlikely to change as cars now outnumber licensed drivers in the United States and one in five new homes has a three-car garage (Naughton, 2003).

The government subsidizes suburban commuters by failing to collect in gasoline or other taxes the full cost of road construction and maintenance, patrol and rescue services, and environmental damage. Other subsidies come to the suburbs in municipal outlays for extensions of electric power, water, and sewage lines. Perhaps the greatest impact of government policy results from national tax and economic policies directly related to housing. In the 1950s, almost half of the housing built in the suburbs depended on federal financing (Coontz, 1992; Duany, Plater-Zyberk, & Speck, 2000). The federal government provided insurance to lenders, and mortgages to families through the G.I. Bill and Veterans Administration, the Federal Housing Authority (FHA), the Federal National Mortgage Association ("Fannie Mae"), and the Government National Mortgage Association ("Ginnie Mae"). In the post–World War II period, millions of Americans received mortgage loans with artificially low interest rates (2 to 3 percent) and down payments of as little as 5 to 10 percent (or even just a single dollar when borrowing from the Veterans Administration) (Lee, 1986).

National tax and economic policies continue to favor wealthy suburban dwellers. In 2005, home mortgage interest deductions cost the U.S. government more than $75 billion (Brunori, 2005), much more than the amount that it spent for low-income housing. Low-income taxpayers, especially those who are younger and live in urban areas, are less likely to own homes and thus less likely to itemize; therefore, they do not benefit from home mortgage interest deductions. Additionally, many low-income retirees tend to have less interest outstanding on home loans—that is, their home mortgages are paid off; this eliminates the tax benefit of the home mortgage interest deduction to them. Because high-income earners have more valuable homes, they make higher interest payments on their mortgages; the result was that 36 percent of home mortgage interest deductions were claimed by taxpayers with adjusted gross incomes over $100,000 in 2003 (Prante, 2006). Some critics of this policy call the various federal tax deductions "mansion subsidies" (Lazare, 2001). Urban advocates suggest that government subsidies that go to suburban homeowners might be more wisely spent in cities for mass transportation or infrastructure maintenance.

The *political fragmentation* of large metropolitan areas has resulted in lack of regional planning and support for central cities. Although many suburbanites rely on the nearby city for employment, entertainment, air travel hubs, specialized medical care, and various public services, they pay their local property taxes only to suburban governments. Because suburbanites are able to use the resources of the city without contributing to its maintenance costs, they have little motivation to assume any responsibility for solving city problems (Altshuler, Morrill, Wolman, & Mitchell, 1999; Schneider, 1992).

The last factor contributing to the decline of central cities is the decrease in real opportunity brought about by the loss of blue-collar jobs due to deindustrialization and the suburbanization of employment (Wilson, 1987). Heavy industries have moved out of cities to rural areas, or even other countries, where space and labor costs are lower. Light industries and service businesses have moved to edge cities where land is cheaper, and utility rates and property taxes are lower. Although many inner-city residents have been able to find jobs in service and retail sectors, their average annual earnings fell by 25 to 30 percent (Wilson, 1996).

The Minority Urban Experience

As discussed here, structural factors—particularly economic changes—affect all communities. In the "rust belt" of the upper Midwest, African Americans suffered most from the decline of central cities. A logical response to repressive conditions was the migration of middle- and working-class African Americans out of the inner city into areas with more favorable economic conditions. The result was that there was an increased concentration of the very poor in the central cities. Middle-class urban residents continue to leave cities and those who remain behind are at opposite ends of the income spectrum—either very rich or very poor. Wilson (1987, 1996) argued that the social life of poor inner-city neighborhoods declined because of the intensification of poverty and the accompanying isolation from mainstream institutions and role models.

While Wilson (1987, 1996) focused on the mass "out-migration" of middle-class blacks from inner-city Chicago, Latino communities have experienced only gradual out-migration of successful residents and at the same time welcomed vast waves of energetic and hopeful new immigrants. A result of this pattern was that well-established Latino families could be found living next door to new immigrants and relationships across social class were developed and maintained (Valdez, 1993; White, 1988). This meant that local institutions, such as churches, might have changed, but they were not abandoned. In the case of Central American immigrants in Los Angeles, new small businesses—stores, markets, restaurants, and street vendors—continually appear, contributing "to the bustling street life and ethnic identity of the neighborhood" (Chinchilla, Hamilton, & Loucky, 1993, p. 55).

Like inner-city African Americans, Latinos suffered from economic restructuring. Since most Latinos lived in areas other than large Midwestern cities, however, their experience of economic change was shaped according to location. Historically, Latino barrios in the Southwest were scattered throughout the metropolitan areas so social isolation was not as much of a problem. Latinos live in neighborhoods where houses are both closer to job opportunities and cheaper. One factor contributing to their affordability is the contribution of in-kind assistance. For example, in Albuquerque, not only do many Mexican American carpenters and laborers build their own homes, but they also help in the construction and repair of the homes of their friends and relatives (Gonzales, 1993). In addition, Latinos are unlikely to experience the level of housing discrimination that plagues African Americans (Fellin, 1995). Among Mexican immigrants, 46.4 percent own their own homes (Pew Hispanic Center, 2008b). This contributes to neighborhood stability and pride.

Obviously there is great diversity within ethnic groups. A combination of ethnic/racial identity and social class may affect housing arrangements and locations (Fellin, 1995). For example, Cubans are more likely to be found in suburbs and Puerto Ricans in central cities. Filipinos, Koreans, and Indians, because they are more likely to be of a higher social class than other Asian groups, are less likely to live in segregated inner-city areas and more likely to live in suburban neighborhoods. Southeast Asians, who arrived in this country as impoverished refugees, are likely to live in segregated areas. Many Native Americans reside in inner-city neighborhoods, although these neighborhoods usually include other ethnic minorities.

Like the Latino communities discussed above, urban Chinatown communities, particularly in San Francisco, Los Angeles, and New York, have been reinvigorated by an influx of new refugees who created new demands for food, goods, services, and entertainment (Gold, 1999; Portes & Rumbaut, 2006; Yung, 1999). Vietnamese and other Indochinese refugees have established enclaves adjacent to Chinatowns, or in new locations, notably in the California cities of Westminster, Long Beach, San Diego, Santa Ana, Garden Grove, and San Jose (Min, 1995b). Southeast Asian refugees developed a large number of voluntary associations that serve myriad functions and helped to build organized communities. The development and unification of Southeast Asian communities has been supported by an active media which produces newspapers, magazines, and radio and cable television programs (Gold, 1999, p. 518).

Another minority population that has had a relatively positive urban experience is the gay community. In the 1970s, many lesbians and gay men gravitated to specific neighborhoods in large cities that were known to be accepting. Among the most prominent of these geographically bounded areas are the West Village in New York City, the Castro District in San Francisco, the South End in Boston, the Dupont Circle area in Washington, D.C., Newtown in Chicago, and West Hollywood in Los Angeles (Garnets & D'Augelli, 1994). Research studies indicate that there is an association between sizeable gay communities and economically viable cities. Other cities across the country are now looking hard at the contribution gays bring. Some cities, for example, are trying to lure gay residents by offering domestic partner benefits to city employees.

Suburban Sprawl and New Urbanism

While there is a general understanding that central cities are often inhospitable environments (Helling, 2002; Lazare, 2001; Wilson, 1987, 1996), suburbs generally do not carry similar negative connotations. In fact, suburbanites are significantly more satisfied with their communities than are residents of cities, small towns, or rural areas, according to a recent national survey (Morin & Taylor, 2009). Nevertheless, some urban designers describe the character of modern American suburbs as "soulless subdivisions, residential 'communities' utterly lacking in communal life; strip shopping centers, 'big box' chain stores, and artificially festive malls set within barren seas of parking; antiseptic office parks, ghost towns after 6 p.m.; and mile upon mile of clogged collector roads" (Duany, Plater-Zyberk, & Speck, 2000, p. 5). Since each piece of suburbia serves exclusively one type of activity (e.g., residential, commercial, office, recreation, industrial), residents must spend much of their time getting from one place to another, usually driving alone in a private automobile because walking, bicycling, and public transportation are rarely options.

The result of continuous, unplanned outward growth (called *suburban sprawl*) is the abandonment of existing, more centrally located neighborhoods. Squires (2001) suggests that suburban sprawl detracts not only from connectedness to place but also from a sense of community. Schneider (1992) asserts that the major attraction of suburbs is privatization: backyard patios or decks instead of front porches, private cars instead of buses, video rentals instead of theaters, and privately owned malls instead of town squares. The increasing segregation and homogeneity of neighborhoods, too

FIGURE 8.1   *Critical Thinking About Community Life*

Interview your parents or grandparents about their childhood neighborhood. How many facilities (school[s], houses of worship, grocery stores, drugstore, barbershops/beauty salons, etc.) were located within walking distance of their home? What changes in community design have occurred over the past two generations?

much time devoted to commuting and too little time available for civic engagement, and the separation of home and work result in both physical and social fragmentation (Putnam, 2000).

In a relatively recent approach to urban planning, a small group of developers is applying what they've learned about the flaws of modern subdivisions and the relative benefits of traditional neighborhoods to build model communities such as Seaside and Celebration (in Florida), Laguna West (in California), Harbortown (in Tennessee), and Middleton Hills (in Wisconsin). Following the prescriptions of *new urbanism,* these towns offer streets laid out in a grid pattern, front porches instead of large lawns, small shops and offices within walking distance of homes—or even attached to homes— and many small shared green areas (Duany, Plater-Zyberk, & Speck, 2000; Penn, 1998; "Principles of Urbanism," n.d.). These efforts at a more logical construction of communities have not been widely copied. Overall, the trends of the last half-century clearly do not reflect a history of successful community development or maintenance. The major barriers to implementing new urbanism are the restrictive zoning codes (e.g., minimum lot size and restrictions on commercial use) currently in force in most municipalities and the ongoing investment in roads ("Principles of Urbanism," n.d.).

Rural Communities

At the time of the Revolution, nine in ten Americans were farmers; that number dropped to one in five in the 1930s and today stands at one in 150 (or one in 500 if one counts only full-time farmers (Grunwald, 2007)). Fifteen million acres of agricultural land have been developed for housing in the first five years of the twenty-first century, and an additional 25 million acres of ranchland in the Rocky Mountain West is at risk of being developed for housing by 2020 (Breslau, 2004).

The Bureau of the Census defines *rural* (also called "nonmetropolitan areas") as a county or group of counties without a large central city (i.e., a city having a population of at least 50,000). Three major characteristics of rural communities are small-scale, low-density settlement; distance from large urban centers; and a specialized, nondiverse, rural economy (Deavers, 1992). In contrast to urban communities, rural communities have less adequate public services, such as schools, fire protection, road maintenance, health care, and recreation and entertainment facilities (Copeland, 2008; Ginsberg, 1993; Queralt, 1996). Unemployment rates are also likely to be higher.

The most rural state in the country is Vermont, where more than 61.7 percent of residents live in rural areas; the most urban states are California and New Jersey, where less than 6 percent live in rural areas (Wright, 2007). Rural areas contain both the most ethnically homogenous and ethnically diverse communities in the United States, depending on the region of the country (Flora, Flora, & Houdek, 1992).

Historically, it was not unusual for rural communities to depend on industries related to natural resources (e.g., agriculture, forestry, fishing, mining) to sustain their economy. Although farming and mining still dominate the local economy of many rural counties, those areas are losing population. In some agricultural areas, family farms have been replaced by large-scale meat and poultry processors (Johnson, 1999). The contemporary economic base of many rural counties is dependent on government funding (payrolls) for military bases, prisons, and state universities (Flora, Flora, & Houdek, 1992; Huling, 2002). In the 1970s, lower wages in rural areas made it profitable for companies to move production facilities out of cities, but beginning in the 1980s the trend shifted to moving plants overseas, where labor was even cheaper. In rural areas, many shutdowns devastated company towns with long-established ties to a single manufacturer (Geller, 2003).

Most of the counties with the highest poverty rates in the United States are rural; and at 16 percent, rural poverty rates are higher than the national average of 13 percent (Henslin, 2008) Compared to urban Americans, the rural poor are less educated and employment opportunities available to them pay less than similar jobs in urban areas (Arsneault, 2006).

Although declining population has been a common problem in rural counties in the past, during the decade of the 1970s, more than 80 percent of rural counties gained population (Johnson, 1999). This trend slowed in the 1980s, but returned in the 1990s, when 71 percent of rural counties gained population. Sociologists call this trend a *rural rebound* (Henslin, 2008; Macionis, 2007). New arrivals in rural communities include blue-collar workers (who comprise 30 percent of the workforce in rural areas), disenchanted city dwellers, and many older adults. Wealthy retirees are attracted to the forested lake counties of Minnesota, Wisconsin, and Michigan, winter sports areas in California, Nevada, Wyoming, and Utah, coastal areas of California, South Carolina, and Florida, and the foothills of the Ozark Mountains in Arkansas and of the Appalachian Mountains in Virginia, Kentucky, North Carolina, and Tennessee (Johnson, 1999). When rich former city dwellers purchase or build vacation or retirement homes in rural areas, they drive up the cost of housing, but they may at the same time produce a demand for workers in construction, retail, service, and other local businesses, providing new employment opportunities.

Understanding Communities

Ecosystems Perspective

As noted in Chapter 1, the ecosystems perspective views person and environment as integrated, interdependent systems. Often concerns about *habitat* (meaning, in this case, the natural home of an organism) are expressed in discussions about the degradation of wetlands or rainforests and the loss of wildlife. To view community as habitat is a useful way to understand the individual in his or her environment. This perspective should lead social workers to consider the physical aspects of the environment such as crowding, noise levels, air pollution, sanitation, and access to transportation. Habitats are especially important for some populations. For example, both young children and older adults are more dependent on their local environments than other age-groups that have more independent mobility.

Mismatch theory is a hypothesis that explains high rates of depression and anxiety in modern life as the result of humans living in habitats quite different from those for which natural selection shaped their hominid ancestors (Wright, 1995). Not only is the physical setting of large building and paved streets different from the forests and savannahs of humans' ancestral Africa, but the resulting social environment is very different too. Primitive humans lived in small bands of related individuals who interacted almost continuously. In today's society, social isolation is a result of the physical structure of communities, particularly for stay-at-home suburban mothers. Even in cities, loneliness can occur in a crowd of strangers, where interactions tend to be economic rather than social.

The ecosystems perspective also encourages an examination of the fit between a community and its larger environment. Communities that are unable to obtain needed resources experience *entropy*, which means decline or breakdown. This occurs whenever a system uses up more energy than it takes in. Thus, when a city spends more on police and fire protection than it receives in taxes, the community experiences entropy. People who drive through central cities with boarded-up storefronts and garbage-filled streets have witnessed the results of the process of entropy.

Another ecological term that can be applied to communities is *succession.* In the natural environment, succession occurs when one species is displaced by another, such as when African killer bees drive out local populations of native honeybees. In the community, succession directs us to look at the process of neighborhood change when one population replaces another. One example is when one ethnic group is replaced by another, such as when Mexican Americans replaced the Lithuanians in the Marquette Park area of Chicago in the mid-1980s. Another example of succession is when a low-income population is replaced by young, upper-middle-class individuals through the process of gentrification. *Gentrification* is the renovation or replacement of older homes in desirable areas with upscale residences. Gentrification often results in the removal of poor and elderly residents for whom affordable replacement housing is scarce.

Functionalist Perspective

In Part II, we discussed social institutions and the functions that they perform in society. These functions are usually carried out on the local level. They include production, distribution, and consumption of goods and services; planning and decision making; law enforcement, public safety, and social control; education and socialization; provision of health care and social welfare; and information dissemination. Warren (1978, p. 9) defined community as "that combination of social units and systems that perform the major social functions having locality relevance." Thus communities provide the settings for the local components of major social institutions: businesses, local governments, schools, places of worship, clinics and hospitals, social service agencies, media outlets, and other organizations.

Communities are the interface between individuals or families, and social institutions. Healthy communities provide necessary supports and resources that enhance the functioning of smaller social systems. At an informal level and on a spontaneous basis, communities provide opportunities for social participation and mutual aid and support. An example would be the way that neighbors organize multifamily garage sales or share tasks like transporting children to and from after-school events. Another informal function of communities is provision of a base for political action.

Breakdown in the functioning of one subsystem in a community requires that another subsystem step in. For example, if there is not adequate planning for recreation, bored adolescents are more likely to get into trouble, requiring extra police patrols. Or, if the economic system falters and there are massive layoffs, local food banks may be called upon to fill the gap in the provision of nutrition basics.

Conflict Perspective

Conflict theorists argue that community life reflects the inequalities of wealth and power in American society. Community viability is influenced by investment decisions made by the political and economic elite who entertain little input from local residents. The societal oppression of poor people and people of color is readily apparent in American communities. This is seen most clearly in patterns of segregation and environmental injustice, topics which are discussed in depth under the section "How Communities Deter Well-Being" later in this chapter.

Rational/Social Exchange Perspective

An important premise of the rationalist perspective is that individuals act in their own self-interest. "Rational" does not mean that people get together to determine what would bring the greatest good to society as a whole, or even to large numbers of people in the community, but only to themselves and their immediate family.

This idea of self-interest is particularly evident in the pattern of automobile dependence in our society. Hart and Spivak (1993) explain that Americans do not seek alternatives to use of the private automobile because it is a "free good"; in other words, they pay only a fraction of the actual cost. If motorists were required to absorb the true expense of building roads, paving parking lots, cleaning up pollution, and providing emergency medical care for accident victims, the cost of gasoline would increase by four to ten dollars a gallon (Hart & Spivak, 1993; Holtzclaw, 1993; Korb, 1996). But because gas taxes are kept artificially low, others must shoulder the costs of suburban sprawl. As confirmed individualists, Americans prefer to go where they want, when they want, without taking into account the needs of others. Only when mass transit alternatives are readily available and the cost of driving and/or parking is prohibitive, will Americans give up traveling in their own private cars. New York, where the cost of parking is extravagant, is the only American city in which the majority of households don't own one or more automobiles (Seabrook, 2002).

Constructionist Perspective

A constructionist perspective would emphasize the different meanings that people give to the term *community*. Sociologist Ferdinand Tonnies (1963/1887) used the terms *gemeinschaft* and *gesellschaft* to describe the ways that people related to each other in their communities. *Gemeinschaft* is found in communities where residents share traditions, know each other well, and are eager to offer mutual support. *Gesellschaft* describes communities where relationships are impersonal and contractual. Tonnies believed that communities could exhibit both characteristics, but that usually one was predominant. Tonnies suggested that as society became more urban and industrialized, communities would exhibit more features of *gessellschaft* than *gemeinschaft*. Despite his predictions, many Americans would still describe their community experience as *gemeinschaft*, reflecting on their involvement in neighborhood associations, shared interests and responsibilities for local children, participation in holiday or ethnic celebrations, support for school or city sports teams, and socializing in local taverns and restaurants (Fellin, 1995; Oldenburg, 2001).

Preferred Perspectives

Descriptions of communities often focus on deficits, particularly in relation to communities of people of color. Despite obvious challenges in many poor and minority communities, the strengths perspective promotes the assumption that all communities have assets. There are many kinds of community assets: natural beauty, a pleasant climate, strategic location, thriving industries, skilled leaders, and strong social institutions. Distinct from these is the idea of social capital

(Bourdieu, 1986; Coleman, 1988; Putnam, 2000; Warren, Thompson, & Saegert, 2001). In this text, *social capital* is defined as

> the set of resources that inhere in relationships of trust and cooperation between people. . . . Social capital is a collective asset, a feature of communities, rather than the property of an individual. As such, individuals both contribute to it and use it, but they cannot own it. (Warren, Thompson, & Saegert, 2001, p. 1)

Stolle and Rochon (2001, pp. 145–146) include in their list of "indicators" of social capital such factors as participation and engagement in "politics generally and in the community specifically," generalized trust that fosters "norms of reciprocity" within the community, trust toward public officials and institutions, individual willingness "to do one's share in collective endeavors," and optimism about the future in relation to social and political relationships.

One type of social capital is bonding within communities. Strong community institutions, such as schools, places of worship, parent/teacher groups, fraternal organizations, and small business associations are essential for creating an environment where social capital can develop (Warren, Thompson, & Saegert, 2001).

Historically and currently, immigrants and refugees, and ethnic enclaves (see Chapter 6) have been a constructive force in many cities. These areas of concentrated entrepreneurship rely on three conditions: the presence of a number of immigrants with substantial business expertise acquired in their homeland, access to a small amount of capital, and labor (Portes & Rumbaut, 2006, pp. 28–29). Typically the labor requirement is found in family members initially and later in more recent immigrants. In addition to the economic vitality of immigrant-serving businesses, traditional social controls are revived, networks are strengthened, and old community institutions are changed or new community institutions emerge to meet the needs of new residents (Gold, 1999; Moore & Pinderhughes, 1993; Padilla, 1993; Wysocki, 1991). Mutual aid linked to strong extended family networks is a characteristic of many immigrant groups.

In poor communities, social capital is a critically important factor for survival when other forms of capital (e.g., financial capital) are missing. The use of social capital is often the only factor that allows community residents to cope. Poor communities are more likely to have religious institutions whose missions may include more than just the spiritual life of its members. African Americans develop and maintain some of the strongest forms of social capital, stemming from a tradition of high rates of church membership and participation (Lincoln & Mamiya, 1990). Even the much-maligned public housing projects at one time provided a positive home and close-knit community for many inner-city African American residents. In describing her experiences growing up in the Ida B. Wells Homes in Chicago in the 1950s, newspaper columnist Leanita McClain spoke of

> lives as full of personal cheer as anyone else—birthday parties, graduation celebrations, block club parties . . . [T]here were dance classes and sewing classes and charm classes, when we weren't roller skating or bicycling. There was a corner soda shop, Doc's, that made the best malts in our limited world. People raised money to pay the rent by selling baked goods or chicken dinners. Every Sunday there was a parade of scrubbed Sunday school children. . . . And there were fathers who were fathers to those without them, and plenty of working people, factory workers and domestics whose rush hour began long before dawn. (1986, pp. 141–142)

Nevertheless, even high levels of social capital cannot withstand the overwhelming negative forces found in oppressive economic and political systems. Wuthnow notes that a significant share of the decline in social capital in the United States over the past two decades has occurred among marginalized groups:

> [P]eople need to feel entitled in order to take part in the political process, and they need to feel that their participation will make a difference. Part of the decline is also due to the fact that people need other resources in order to create social capital, not the least of which are adequate incomes, suffi- cient safety to venture out of their homes, and such amenities as child care and transportation. (2002, p. 101)

The Impact of Communities on Individuals and Families

How Communities Deter Well-Being

Negative Impacts on Childhood.   In his studies of concentrated poverty, Jargowsky (1997) noted that where one lives clearly affects how one grows up. Some groups of people in particular are affected by neighborhood deficits: these categories include people living in extreme poverty, older adults, and children. They are trapped in the sense that they cannot move and many do not even leave the neighborhood regularly because they lack access to transportation or are too frightened to go out.

When they enter school, children encounter the world beyond their family and home. Schools that are prepared to deliver sound educational services to children and their families are critical in communities that are economically deprived (Garbarino, 1992). Unfortunately, it is the poorest communities that are most likely to have schools that are only marginally able to meet the needs of students (Kozol, 1991).

Growing children also need safe areas for play. A recent study found that inner-city chil- dren who lived in neighborhoods with parks gained about 13 percent less weight over a two-year period than children who lived with less greenspace (Gupta, 2008). Heavily trafficked streets, alleys strewn with litter and used drug paraphernalia, playgrounds with broken equipment, and dark stairwells and hallways limit children's access to healthy physical activity. Heavy auto traffic also produces high levels of ozone. Children are thought to be particularly at risk from the effects of ozone; this might account for increasing asthma rates among children, which doubled between 1980 and 1995 (Spake, 2005).

Childhood safety is also threatened by community violence. A 13-year-old describes his life on the South Side of Chicago:

> If you act like a little kid in this neighborhood, you're not gonna last too long. 'Cause if you play childish games in the ghetto, you're gonna find a childish bullet in your childish brain. If you live in the ghetto, when you're ten you know everything you're not supposed to know. When I was ten I knew where drugs came from. I knew about every different kind of gun. I knew about sex. I was a kid in my age but my mind had the reality of a grown-up, 'cause I seen these things every day! (Jones & Newman, 2000, p. 116)

Researchers have confirmed that the experience of this child is not uncommon. A third of inner- city children have witnessed a homicide by the time they reach age 15 (Bell, 1991).

This child's perspective demonstrates how blighted neighborhoods present not only physical threats, but psychological ones as well. As cognitive powers develop and children are able to make social comparisons, they become aware of the discrepancies between their home neighborhood and more affluent ones. Kozol records how a 15-year-old Harlem resident views her environment:

> "It's not like being in jail," she says, "It's more like being 'hidden.' It's as if you have been put in a garage where, if they don't have room for something but aren't sure if they should throw it out, they put it there where they don't need to think of it again." (1995, pp. 38–39)

Another community factor that detracts from the well-being of children is the lack of social density. *Social density* measures "the degree to which an environment contains a diversity of roles for children to learn from and for parents to draw upon. . . . " (Garbarino, Galambos, Plantz, & Kostelny, 1992, p. 208). Poor neighborhoods that lack such diversity impoverish the experiences of the children living there. Children are enriched when they can observe different occupational, kinship, and acquaintance roles. A neighborhood made up exclusively of mother-headed families, with no adult male role models and no consistent male disciplinary presence leaves boys to "learn about manhood on the streets, where the temptation is strong to demonstrate prowess through lawbreaking, violence, and fathering a child" (Schorr, 1989, p. 20). McClain (1986) speaks of a "poverty of the spirit" that differentiates such neighborhoods from "poverty of the pocket." Lack of social density is also apparent in new residential suburbs where children are likely to grow up surrounded by young families in similar middle-class circumstances. The only adult roles these children encounter in their neighborhoods are those of parents, joggers, dog walkers, and the ice cream vendor. They don't have regular interaction with shopkeepers, mechanics, retirees, or even extended family members.

Environmental Racism. *Environmental racism* is the term used to describe the consistent pattern whereby environmental hazards are located near poor people of color (Bullard, 1990; Hoff & Rogge, 1996; Wolcott & Milligan, 1992). Ethnic minority groups are disproportionately exposed to the dangers associated with environmental degradation (Bullard, 2004). For example, Hoff and Rogge (1996) noted that just three communities, all of them more than 78 percent minority, hold 40 percent of the landfill capacity of the entire country. Lipsitz (2002, pp. 67–68) summarizes a number of reports documenting the inequitable distribution of risks; among them, in Houston, Texas, African Americans make up 25 percent of the population but 75 percent of the municipal garbage incinerators and 100 percent of the city-owned garbage dumps are located in black neighborhoods; penalties for violating federal environmental laws regulating air, water, and waste pollution were 46 percent lower in minority communities than in white communities; and across the nation, 60 percent of African Americans and Latinos live in communities with uncontrolled toxic waste sites. The short- and long-term effects of exposure to toxic elements in the environment remain unclear (Rogge, 1993). Nevertheless, for young people, local environmental hazards have been associated with high rates of stunted growth and lead poisoning, and residents of all ages are susceptible to asthma, various types of cancer, and other serious illnesses (Lipsitz, 2002).

Interventions also may differ depending on the race of those affected. An article published in the *Washington Post* (Duke, 2007) chronicled the story of one African American family living in rural Tennessee whose well-water was contaminated by trichloroethylene [TCE], a carcinogen, leaking from a nearby county landfill. Records indicate that when state environmental and water officials became concerned about potential TCE leaks, they hastily tested the wells of nearby white families but waited nine years to test the well of the African American family. Ten of their relatives, who live near each other and the landfill, were diagnosed with various kinds of cancer.

Conflict theory suggests that it is more difficult for marginalized populations to keep their communities free of environmental degradation. Poor communities without other choices may accept environmentally hazardous industries and/or commercial waste operations in their neighborhoods in order to create jobs in the local economy (Beasley, 1990; Bullard & Wright, 1986; Monk & Fretwell, 2008). The relationship between poverty and environmental threats is clear

> in polluted inner city neighborhoods where children of color suffer from high rates of asthma; in crop lands where poor migrant workers carry agricultural pesticides home to their families on their work clothes; in low-income Louisiana parishes along the industrial "Cancer Alley" stretch of the Mississippi; and in the unsanitary, crowded, hastily and poorly constructed *maquiladoras* that house Mexican plant workers along the United States-Mexico border. (National Association of Social Workers, 2000, pp. 103–104)

The pattern exists on the international level as well. The imbalance of power among nations is reflected in the movement of toxic chemicals from industrialized to developing countries (Rogge & Darkwa, 1996). Between 60 and 80 percent of electronic waste (e.g., cell phones and computers parts) is shipped overseas, mostly to China, India, and Pakistan where poor laborers, wearing no protective gear, "scratch for precious metals in pools of toxic muck" (Royte, 2005, p. 84). Waste is dumped into fields and streams where hazardous chemicals accumulate in the soil and water and contribute to high rates of birth defects, infant mortality, blood diseases, and severe respiratory problems.

In the United States, violations of indigenous peoples provide the most graphic and poignant illustrations of environmental racism (Hoffe & Rogge, 1996, p. 45). For example, the Goshute reservation in Utah is surrounded by a magnesium plant on the north, a stockpile of chemical weapons on the east, an Army testing ground for exposure to nerve gas on the south, and a bombing range and hazardous waste incinerator on the west (Wolfson, 2000). In order to secure donations for a cultural center and desperately needed jobs, the tribal chairman agreed to let eight power companies from California, New York, Minnesota, Wisconsin, Michigan, Georgia, Pennsylvania, Florida, and Alabama use a part of the reservation as a nuclear waste dump. Corporations and even the federal government "systematically target Native American reservations when looking for locations for hazardous waste incinerators, solid waste landfills, and nuclear waste storage facilities" (LaDuke, 1993; Lipsitz, 2002, p. 68).

Segregation by Class.   In America, a limited number of financial institutions and developers finance and construct most suburban housing and large city projects. Given the dynamics of the capitalist system, their motivation rests not in benefiting the community, but in making a profit. Developers are seldom called upon to think about, much less pay for, the impact of their development on surrounding areas in terms of traffic congestion, pollution, excessive demands on infrastructure (schools, utilities, water and sewers), or destruction of existing neighborhoods. Typically, it is people of color and the lower social classes who pay disproportionately for these developments even though they derive little direct benefit from them (Feagan & Parker, 1990).

Prior to the 1960s, although many neighborhoods were segregated by race and ethnicity, most were integrated by socioeconomic class, both in large cities and small towns (Fellin, 1995). Historically in America, gulfs between classes were not reflected in physical distances; even in cities with terrible slums, the middle class lived with or very near the poor (Coontz, 1988). As whites and middle-class blacks and other minorities moved to the suburbs, center cities became more homogenous by race and class, and poverty and deprivation become increasingly more concentrated (Jargowsky, 2002; Powell, 2002; Wilson, 1987). Between 1970 and 1990, the number of poor persons living in high-poverty neighborhoods almost doubled (Jargowsky, 1997). (*High-poverty neighborhoods* are defined as census tracts with poverty rates of 40 percent or higher.) This trend was reversed during the prosperity of the1990s; however, it is likely that the recent economic downturn will signal a return to the previous pattern (Jargowsky, 2003). The most debilitating effect of the concentrated poverty of those left behind in the central cities is not lack of lawns and shopping malls, but denial of access to educational and employment opportunities. Unemployment and underemployment rates for African American teenagers in central cities runs about 90 percent, well above the 25 percent jobless rate for the nation during the Great Depression (Schaefer, 2008). At the opposite end of the continuum, census data also confirm that between 1970 and 2000, there was a 32 percent increase in the residential separation of high-income Americans (those in the top income quintile) from all other Americans (Taylor & Morin, 2008).

Seldom are developers interested in building affordable or low-income housing in new suburbs. Instead, they concentrate on upscale, high-profit neighborhoods. Adding insult to injury, many of the most exclusive new neighborhoods are literally walled off from the rest of the community. Duany, Plater-Zyberk, and Speck (2000) note that it is not the walls *per se*, however, that threaten social unity, but the homogeneity and exclusivity of the people living behind them. The residents of these private, gated communities are uniform in terms of both race and class. They have little regular contact with people at the lower end of the socioeconomic ladder—with the exception of the cleaning ladies and yardmen who show up to do the tasks that wealthy residents prefer to hire out.

Suburbs are rarely zoned for multifamily dwellings or other forms of affordable housing. Codes that restrict the building of houses in a new development that do not meet minimum cost or square footage requirements are used to separate even the very rich from the very, very rich. For the first time in our history,

> we are now experiencing ruthless segregation by minute gradations of income . . . To prove this point, one need only to attempt to build a $200,000 house on an empty lot in the $350,000 cluster; the homeowners' association will immediately sue. . . . The real estate business caters to this elitism so relentlessly that even some mobile home parks are marketed in this way. (Duany, Plater-Zyberk, & Speck, 2000, pp. 43–44)

Wealthy and powerful community residents use building codes and zoning ordinances not only to insulate themselves from their poorer neighbors, but also to exclude people with disabilities. Persons with mental illness or retardation, for example, who are able to live in a group home in the community are often shut out of upscale neighborhoods by property holders who assert "I think it's great a to have half-way houses for people like that, just not here!" Such N.I.M.B.Y. ["not in my backyard"] attitudes often result in needed facilities being clustered in older transitional neighborhoods bordering on retail or industrial areas where public transportation is available, houses are relatively large, and political power is small.

While suburban areas focus on segregation by class, center cities struggle with a lack of affordable and structurally sound housing. During the 1950s and 1960s, while the Federal Housing Authority (FHA) provided subsidies for suburban housing, the federal government built large, high-rise housing projects in major cities. Because tenant selection procedures were done without resident input, urban renewal projects had the effect of destroying important social networks that had existed in the poor neighborhoods that were razed, and instead promoted anonymity and social isolation (Goering, Kamely, & Richardson, 1997). Ninety percent of the low-income housing units removed during the urban renewal programs were never replaced (Lipsitz, 2002, p. 65). Even the construction of interstate highways was detrimental to those living in the central city. Overpasses destroyed or devalued urban neighborhoods and limited access roads were used as physical barriers between neighborhoods, separating different racial and ethnic communities. For example, the Dan Ryan Expressway in Chicago established a barrier between African American neighborhoods to the east and white ethnic neighborhoods to the west. Many stable racial minority communities were destroyed; more than 60 percent of those displaced by urban renewal projects were people of color (Jackson, 1985; Zarembka, 1990).

Segregation by Race and Ethnicity.   The most pervasive forms of residential segregation, by far, are by race and ethnicity (Taylor & Morin, 2008). Although housing segregation by class is a new and growing concern, segregation by race has a long history in this country. It was and is fostered by different mechanisms. As southern blacks migrated to northern industrial centers, and especially after desegregation laws made it harder to avoid contact with African Americans, whites moved to outlying areas. (This pattern is called *white flight*.) Although it might appear at first that patterns of residential segregation can be attributed solely to the personal choices of individual white homeowners, Powell (2002) explains how the government was significantly involved in the segregation of people of color into less desirable neighborhoods. Beginning in the 1920s and extending through the post–World War II period, government housing authorities instituted policies that were specifically designed to discriminate against minorities in mortgage loans and insurance. These government agencies assessed neighborhoods in which people of color lived in the lowest value category, without consideration of the actual worth of the housing stock. On FHA maps, these neighborhoods were marked in red ink. The term *redlining* thus came to refer to the practice of identifying minority neighborhoods to be excluded from consideration for granting mortgage funding. While federal programs denied home ownership to minorities, the same policies encouraged investment in white-only suburbs. A third mechanism of racial discrimination against minority individuals is mortgage lending. As discussed in Chapter 6, more than half of African Americans and almost half of Latinos pay a higher-than-typical interest rate for home mortgages compared to whites (less than 20 percent) (Aversa, 2006). A final mechanism is *steering*. This occurs when real-estate agents take people of color to see houses in some neighborhoods and direct white people to others (Feagan & Sikes, 1994).

The most racially segregated cities for African Americans in America are found in the North: Detroit, Milwaukee, New York, Newark, Chicago, Cleveland, Buffalo, and Cincinnati (Taylor & Morin, 2008). For Latinos, the most racially segregated cities in the United States are Providence (Rhode Island), New York, Newark (New Jersey), Hartford (Connecticutt), Los Angeles, Chicago, Philadelphia, Milwaukee (Wisconsin), and Boston (Taylor & Morin, 2008).

Regardless of the actual patterns of segregation in the country, the Pew Research Center (Taylor & Morin, 2008) reports that 65 percent of Americans say they prefer to reside in a racially mixed community, while 20 percent say they would prefer to live in a community made up only of members of their own race. Blacks (83 percent) are more likely than whites (60 percent) to say they prefer a diverse community and younger adults are more likely to prefer diverse communities than are older adults. People in the Midwest demonstrate the least support for racially diverse communities, but even among Midwesterners, diversity is preferred by a margin of more than two to one.

How Communities Promote Well-Being

Communities promote well-being at three levels: formal service organizations, small businesses that meet a service need, and families and individuals acting as neighbors. Various formal local organizations provide services to community residents. These include neighborhood centers, Boys and Girls Clubs, schools, places of worship, VFW halls, and lodges. Some of the services and settings that are offered include day-care centers and preschools, recreation opportunities for children and older adults, disaster shelters, food pantries, health services (e.g., flu shots, blood pressure screening), and space for organizations ranging from Scouts to Alcoholics Anonymous and Weight Watchers. Such activities are not limited to white, middle-class communities. Solomon (1976, p. 220) reported that, contrary to common perceptions, voluntary associations "abound" in black communities. These include church-related organizations; lodges; veterans groups; political clubs; professional, business and service groups; sports and athletic clubs; civil rights or social action groups; and social clubs. In Latino communities, Catholic churches and Protestant evangelical churches may provide a range of social services (Chinchilla, Hamilton, & Loucky, 1993; Moore & Vigil, 1993). Concrete services might include help finding an apartment or getting food and furniture; providing literacy training and English-as-a-second-language classes; assistance in locating jobs; and counseling and legal assistance regarding immigration, and filling out forms for permanent resident visas. Services might also include advocacy on behalf of neighborhood residents for a supermarket chain to improve the quality of its products, for an insurance company to lower exorbitant rates, for politicians to improve transportation services, or for a corporate office park to provide jobs.

Particularly in minority communities, small businesses may fulfill both commercial and social service roles. For example, African American barbershops and beauty parlors are not only a forum for the exchange of ideas (McCormick, 1998), but also sources of information on how to prevent death from breast and prostrate cancer (Halebar, 2002). Studies of Latino/a-owned businesses have documented their provision of social services (Delgado, 1998). They also provide financial services (e.g., check-cashing, loans)—assistance made necessary by the absence of banks and automated teller machines in many Latino neighborhoods (Levitt, 1995). Latina business owners report that they have both an obligation and a God-given gift to be of help to their communities (Delgado, 1998; Lazzari, Ford, & Haughey, 1996). Many small businesses (e.g., bookstores, theaters, and restaurants) in lesbian and gay neighborhoods foster a powerful psychological sense of community and encourage information exchanges among different social networks (Garnets & D'Augelli, 1994). During the 1980s, urban gay communities in New York, San Francisco, and Los Angeles responded to the challenge of the HIV/AIDS crisis by constructing entire caring systems (Garnets & D'Augelli, 1994).

In addition to formal helping organizations and local businesses, families and individuals in communities also offer services to each other. These may involve a network of neighbors, such as those in Neighborhood Watch Associations or babysitting exchange groups. On an individual level, neighbors take in mail while others go on vacation, share tools, help look for lost pets, swap plant cuttings, mow yards or shovel walks for neighbors who are elderly or sick, and provide food when there is a death in the family. "Neighboring" also can include "watching out" for each other, such as checking on older adults when the weather is extreme. These forms of mutual aid improve the quality of residents' lives.

Social Workers and Communities

The lives of the most vulnerable populations are inextricably linked to the condition of the communities within which they reside. Because communities both promote and deter the well-being of clients, social workers who are engaged in direct practice with individuals and families view the community as both a resource for clients and as a possible source of client problems.

The client system for other social workers is the community *per se*. These macro social workers engage in community planning and development, working in partnership with community members and groups to create a more positive social environment (Brueggemann, 2006). Macro social work practitioners should be prepared to view the community as possessing assets and solutions to problems, and to see partnership with community members and groups as a way to create a more positive social environment

In small or rural communities, social workers are more likely to have a broad range of responsibilities and engage in practice at several systems levels. They may use their generalist skills not only as direct service workers, but also as administrators, organizers, planners, and consultants (Ginsberg, 2001).

Looking Ahead

In the next chapter, we examine the role of organizations in communities and society. We also examine the influence of organizations on the lives of those who work there or receive services.

Chapter 9

Organizations

A large part of our daily lives, and the lives of our clients, occurs within the context of organizations: day-care centers, schools, and businesses. Social work students also must be concerned with organizations as providers of social services and as employers of social workers. Organizations act in ways that affect not only individuals and families, but also other organizations, communities, and even entire societies. Some sociologists argue that large organizations are the key phenomenon of our time (see Perrow, 1991).

Defining Organizations

A *formal organization* is a social system that is deliberately established for the purpose of achieving specific goals. Most organizations have both official goals and operative goals (Perrow, 1961). *Official goals* are goals the organization acknowledges in its charter, mission statement, annual reports, and other public documents. *Operative goals*, on the other hand, reflect what the organization actually does from day to day, regardless of what the official goals are. These may or may not reflect similar purposes. For example, some for-profit psychiatric facilities may advertise their organizational mission as helping people suffering from mental illnesses, while their operative goal is to admit patients who have good insurance coverage.

Goals in organizations change over time. There are two types of changes: goal displacement and goal succession (Etzioni, 1964). "*Goal displacement* often occurs when the means to a goal becomes the goal itself" (Holland & Petchers, 1987, p. 208). An example of this would be in a health care setting when filling out charts takes priority over patient care. The process, rather than successful consumer outcomes, then becomes the organization's product.

When an agency's mission is achieved, it doesn't go out of business. Instead it shifts its attention to new goals. *Goal succession* involves the replacement of an accomplished goal with a new one. A classic and often-cited example is the March of Dimes, which began as an organization dedicated to raising money to fund research to eradicate polio. The disease ceased to be a major health problem when an effective vaccine was developed and the March of Dimes turned to raising money to combat birth defects instead.

Pfeffer (1997) suggests that defining organizations in terms of goal pursuit is problematic in that many employees either do not know the organization's goals or do not support them (p. 7). On the other hand, he notes that there is one goal that appears to be common to all organizations. Whether acknowledged or not, the goal is its own survival. Organizations are more likely than other social systems to hold this goal of self-perpetuation (Pfeffer, 1997, p. 9). An example is the Interstate Commerce Commission, a federal agency that survived for almost 15 years after virtually all of its functions were removed (Sanger, 1996).

Types of Organizations

For social work purposes, organizations can be divided into three basic types: (1) public/government, (2) private nonprofit/voluntary, and (3) private for-profit. Examples of public/government organizations include public universities, welfare offices, and police departments. Examples of private nonprofit/voluntary organizations are United Way agencies, the NAACP, and privately funded foundations such as the Children's Defense Fund. Many social workers and their clients are employed by or otherwise affected by public and private/nonprofit organizations. Some for-profit organizations are owned by individuals or families; others are owned by stockholders who are paid dividends based on the profits the company earns. Examples of well-known private for-profit organizations are General Motors, Time-Warner, Wendy's, and Target. Today, large numbers of health provider organizations (e.g., hospitals, nursing homes, psychiatric in-patient units) are part of large, for-profit corporations. Many nonprofit organizations have chosen to pursue for-profit activities, blurring the distinction between them and the for-profits. Both of these trends have led to concerns about who will serve the most needy (Salamon, 1993).

Issues and Trends in Organizations

Technology

Technology, and especially "commuting electronically," has made working at home a possibility for many people. Tasks that once required an office setting can now be done at home if the worker has a fax machine, computer, and access to the Internet.

Some people who work at home, however, may miss the opportunities to socialize that face-to-face contact with coworkers offers. The potential for, or reality of, friendships in the work setting is clearly an important factor in the decision to be committed to a particular job. Another problem for those who work outside of the home as well as those who are paid for work they do at home is that the line between work and homelife is becoming more permeable. Even more so than the telephone, computer-mediated communication strengthens the expectation that workers will be available 24 hours a day, seven days a week. People have to use additional technology at home, such as answering machines, to shield themselves from work-related interruptions.

Accountability

Another trend is that human service agencies, like other organizations, are being asked to be accountable to their stakeholders, stockholders, and funding sources. Rather than just reporting activities or outputs (volume of work accomplished—such as how many clients were seen), they must measure and report on program outcomes (United Way of America, 1996). *Outcomes* are the actual benefits or changes experienced by individuals or client populations during or after participating in program activities; these might include new knowledge, increased skills, changed attitudes, modified behaviors, and improved conditions or altered statuses (United Way of America, 1996, pp. 2–3).

Criticism of Affirmative Action

Title IV of the Civil Rights Act of 1964 prohibits discrimination. *Affirmative action* goes beyond nondiscrimination to encourage special efforts to reach out to particular groups. It evolved over time from executive orders and court decisions. In practice, it is the explicit and intentional consideration of a person's group identity (race, ethnicity, gender) as a criterion in making selection decisions among candidates who are qualified on other criteria, members of underrepresented groups are selected in preference to those from overrepresented groups. Thus affirmative action addresses two goals: equal opportunity to redress the results of past discrimination and promotion of diversity within the organization.

There are three common misconceptions about affirmative action that contribute to its negative image: that it requires the use of rigid quotas, that it results in the selection of unqualified individuals, and that it is essentially "reverse discrimination." Although broad goals and timetables may be used anywhere, specific quotas apply only in cases where a court has found evidence of past discrimination within an organization. Affirmative action requires that gender and/or race or ethnic background be counted only in reviewing the files of *qualified* candidates; those who don't meet minimum requirements need not be considered, regardless of their group identity. Lastly, if the use of affirmative action "is viewed in the context of overall employment opportunity and the history of opportunity (both within the organization and within the society), then characterizing it as reverse discrimination seems inaccurate" (Cox, 1993, p. 249). In the opinion of many, American society has yet to establish the "level playing field" that would make affirmative action programs obsolete.

Nevertheless, critics of affirmative action argue that it promotes diversity at a special cost to some (white males) who cannot logically be held responsible for patterns of past discrimination. But many of those who protest most vocally are themselves the beneficiaries of another kind of insidious advantage—the *legacy privilege* that is accorded the relatives and friends of the rich, powerful, and well-connected (Kinsley, 2003).

Some have noted that a privileged woman who attends an Ivy League university may receive the benefit of affirmative action, while a poor, white male from Appalachia will not (Karger & Stoesz, 2010). Another ongoing debate about affirmative action is whether individuals from economically disadvantaged backgrounds should receive special consideration, regardless of race or gender. On the other hand, even the children of middle-class blacks may face unique challenges if they are members of the first generation to attend college or to apply for a white-collar job (Robinson, 2007).

Corporate Crime

Since the 1980s, corporate crime has emerged as topic of concern with the general public. Corporate crime is sometimes confused with white-collar crime. *White-collar crimes* are those committed by high status individuals within the context of their occupation (Sutherland, 1940). *Corporate crime* usually refers to organizational crime and includes offenses such as tax evasion, antitrust violations, food and drug violations, polluting the environment, knowingly selling faulty or dangerous products, bribery, fraud, and obstruction of justice, where the purpose is to increase profits at the expense of consumers, competitors, and the general public (Center for Corporate Policy, 2005b). The FBI reported an increase of 100 percent between 2003 and 2005 in the number of cases of corporate fraud investigated (U.S. Department of Justice, 2005).

Reiman (2007, p. 66) states that price-fixing, monopolistic practices, and consumer deception cost the public more money than all of the property crimes in the FBI index combined. Generally, reports of corporate crime do not appear on the evening news and those who commit it are not brought before criminal courts. Instead, these perpetrators appear before regulatory agencies that have no power to imprison (Henslin, 2001). It is unlikely that these crimes will be significantly punished and if they are punished, the price will be so small that it is considered part of the normal cost of doing business. For example, serious violations of the Occupational Safety and Health Administration Act (OSHA) carry an average fine of about $900, and often corporations can take tax deductions for that amount, meaning that taxpayers are picking up the tab (Center for Corporate Policy, 2005a). Since 1972, when OSHA was created, over 200,000 workplace deaths have been reported; of these, just 151 cases have been referred to the U.S. Justice Department and federal prosecutors decided not to act on more than half of these referrals (Barstow & Bergman, 2003).

The last time a major American corporation was faced with homicide charges was in 1978. According to the *Corporate Crime Reporter* ("Homicide charges should be brought against Blackwater," 2007) Indiana state prosecutors charged that the Ford Motor Company engaged in criminally reckless conduct in the design of the gas tank in the Pinto model after three teenage girls were burned to death when their car was rear-ended. A jury found Ford not guilty.

In late 2008, many Americans were shocked to learn that a favorite food was contaminated with salmonella. The Peanut Corporation of America processed and shipped batches of peanut products while allegedly knowing that they were contaminated with the bacteria. The Centers for Disease Control and Prevention (2009) tied 654 illnesses to the salmonella outbreak, and it is believed to have caused nine deaths. More than 2,000 products were recalled that contained peanuts, peanut butter, or peanut paste from the company (Martin, 2009). Other worrisome developments in recent years included children's toys with unsafe lead content and contaminated toothpaste and pet food, imported from China (Ang, 2007; Kerley, 2007).

Understanding Organizations

Throughout most of human history, most people lived and worked within small groups of relatives, friends, and neighbors. Only a few categories of organizations existed prior to industrialization; these included armies and religious orders, and in some societies, government bureaucracies created to collect taxes and build large structures, such as temples and fortifications. With industrialization, formal organizations became common and they are now a central feature of contemporary society.

Ecosystems Perspective

The environmental context in which an organization exists is critically important to the organization's ability to survive. Scientists who study *organizational ecology* (using what is called the *population-ecology model*) have applied Darwinian principles to organizational analysis (see Aldrich, 1979 and Hannan & Freeman, 1977). The population-ecology model emphasizes resource scarcity and competition.

As Darwin and other evolutionists pointed out, the evolution of natural species occurs through change in individuals. Population ecologists argue, on the other hand, that evolutionary dynamics must be studied at the level of the population. Thus analysis moves from explaining how individual organizations adapt to their environment to understanding how different "species" (types of organizations) or whole industries rise and fall (Morgan, 1986, p. 67).

In a series of studies, population ecologists Hannan and Carroll (1992) found a common pattern across many kinds of organizations. The first appearance of a new type of organization (such as life insurance companies or beer breweries) is followed by a gradual and then dramatic increase in numbers. Just as natural environments can support only so many individual organisms, the business environment can support only so many organizations of the same type. The organizations must compete with each other and only those that are most "fit" survive. Eventually the density falls to a level that can be supported by the environment and there is relative stability in numbers. Within these numbers, however, individual organizations come and go as some are better able to adapt to changing environmental resources and demands.

From an ecosystems perspective, it is important for an organization to establish a good fit between itself and its environment. Important aspects of the environment include economic and political trends, population patterns and the available workforce, and other organizations (Macionis, 2007, p. 178). Local demographics, for example, will determine the available workforce and the market for an organization's products or services.

Human service agencies depend on outside sources of funding; those that receive income from a variety of sources are in a better position to make independent decisions regarding their future. Human service organizations also compete for clients. They have learned from the business world how to market themselves, both through public relations efforts and through making their services more appealing and "user-friendly"—offering evening and weekend appointments, for example.

Rapid changes in society mean that organizations must remain flexible. For example, an agency that has received government funding in an era of relative prosperity must be ready to seek alternative revenue sources when there are budget cutbacks. An agency that has provided counseling to a middle-class clientele may find that as lower-income people move into the surrounding neighborhood, client demands change from psychotherapy to concrete services, such as provision of day care or a food pantry.

Functionalist Perspective

For functionalists, members of organizations come together to cooperate in achieving a common goal efficiently (Kendall, 2008). Their focus is on technical competence and task completion rather than in fostering positive ongoing personal relationships. Whereas a family might be able to operate a small restaurant, retail store, or repair shop, economy of scale and the need for uniformity and technical competence often favors large organizations.

Organizations are functional for society in that they epitomize productive efficiency. Large corporations are an important source of employment for people around the world. They tend to pay employees better than smaller firms and they usually have more formalized and objective hiring procedures, thus equalizing individual opportunities.

A number of systems terms can be explained in the context of organizations. All social systems perform a variety of functions; these categories of functions occur in families, groups, and communities, as well as in organizations. *Goal-directed functions* are those activities that directly address the purpose of the organization. Examples in a human service organization might include counseling clients or licensing foster homes. *Integrative functions* are those activities that are directed at maintaining peace and harmony among members of the system; in a human service organization, this might mean holding regular staff meetings. *Maintenance functions* are those activities that meet the needs of the organization; these might include staff training or strategic planning. (Effective organizations attend to their own needs as well as consumer needs.) The *adaptation function* refers to those activities involved in responding to changes in the environment; in an organization, these might include developing new services to accommodate changing client demographics.

As organizations grow and change, they become more complex and the units within them become more *specialized*. In other words, there is a division of labor. For example, in a small agency, the director might handle staff recruitment and hiring, public relations, fund-raising, and budget preparation. A large agency not only has more personnel, but each person is likely to have a more specialized role. In fact, there may be whole departments with special functions, such as personnel or accounting. Small isolated human service agencies are more likely to need generalist practitioners, while large, multifunction agencies are more able to hire practitioners with expertise in one or two areas.

Conflict Perspective

In the view of conflict theorists, the history of organizations is a history of asymmetrical power relations that result in the majority working to support the interests of the few. Whether the organization has as its goal the building of pyramids, the establishment of trade routes, the conquest of neighboring states, or the manufacturing of personal computers, the "pursuit of the goals of the few through the work and labor of the many continues. Organization, in this view, is best understood as a process of domination" (Morgan, 1986, p. 275).

Individuals' interests may be abused not only by the forces of societal oppression, but also by the normal functioning of impersonal organizations (Scott, 1981). The many ways in which workers in organizations may suffer is detailed later in the section on how organizations deter well-being.

Sources of power in organizations include (among others) formal authority, control of scarce resources, control of information, and interpersonal alliances (Morgan, 1986, p. 159). Formal authority is related to one's position. There is also power associated with the resources that an individual or unit can bring and whether those resources are available through other means. Thus, a social worker who sees sliding-scale clients may have less power in a counseling agency than a psychiatrist who sees third-party-pay clients. The effectiveness of a strike by unionized workers (and hence their relative power) depends on the availability of other workers ("scabs") who might be hired to fill their positions. Some individuals can favor their own interests by withholding information or slowing its dissemination. Through various kinds of interlocking networks, some people in organizations are able to access mentors and other friends in high places. Politically astute workers build and cultivate informal alliances and coalitions, trading current support for the potential of future assistance in a ritual of mutually beneficial exchange.

Robert Michels (1949/1911) suggested that eventually all formal organizations, as they get bigger, replace the goals of meeting the needs of their customers or clients and the needs of the organization with serving the interests of a small number of individuals who have gained power within the organization. This theory is called the *iron law of oligarchy.* Although Michels studied political parties and labor unions, an excellent recent business example that supports his hypothesis would be the 2002 corporate scandals, in which top executives made themselves rich through unethical practices while their companies suffered, investors lost millions of dollars, and employees lost their pension funds and/or their jobs.

Rational/Social Exchange Perspective

The rational/social exchange perspective in organizations emphasizes efficiency. Programs are evaluated on the basis of the ratio of costs to benefits (Holland, 1995). If costs outweigh benefits, managers will look for ways to reduce costs or even cut programs. The rationalist perspective is also used to explain the relationship between management and employees. Using this perspective, managers act on the assumption that employees will put their own interests before those of the company (Hodge, Anthony, & Gailes, 1996). *Equity theory* suggests that if employees think they invest more in their work than they get back in wages and benefits, they will act to reduce the imbalance, perhaps by working less or taking company resources for personal use (Adams, 1963). An example would be using company computers and work-time for personal purposes, a practice known as *cyberslacking* (Henslin, 2008). Examples include downloading music, browsing online catalogues, and twittering. Organizations respond by setting up systems to monitor employees' time and use of resources.

Controlling employee behavior through close supervision of workers is one of several themes of *scientific management theory*, whose focus is maximum productivity (Taylor, 1911). Frederick Taylor was particularly interested in increasing the efficiency of factory workers. One way he did this was to conduct "time and motion" studies to determine the most efficient way of designing each job or task.

In common usage, bureaucracy has come to be associated with inefficiency and "red tape," particularly in public administration. Max Weber (1978/1922), however, originally assigned the term *bureaucracy* to organizations that employ strictly rational methods to maximize efficiency. In addition to a *hierarchy of authority* that ensures that each worker is closely supervised, Weber listed several other characteristics of an ideal bureaucracy: specialization, rules and regulations, written communications and records, qualification-based employment, and impersonality. *Specialization* means that each employee is responsible for a specific and limited number of tasks. Formal (usually written) and standardized *rules and regulations* guide the day-to-day operation of the organization. *Written communication* (e.g., memos) and records are used to track what is said and done. *Qualification-based employment* means that people are hired and retained based on their ability to perform the functions of their job, rather than any personal relationships or other factors not directly related to job performance. *Impersonality* means treating everyone the same, regardless of any special circumstances that fall outside of procedural guidelines.

Bounded rationality is a term coined by March and Simon (1958) to describe the limits on logical decision making in organizations imposed by incomplete information and the inability (due to limited resources, including time) to identify and explore all of the possible alternatives available. The result is an outcome called *satisficing* (March & Simon, 1958), or settling for a satisfactory solution rather than seeking an ideal one. An example would be sending only supervisors to receive training in a new clinical technique rather than sending frontline social workers. Another quasi-rational approach to decision making in organizations is *incrementalism* (Hickson, 1987), or making shifts in small steps to avoid conflict and limit irreversible commitment to a major change. In a school, this might mean using temporary portable classrooms rather than building a permanent addition.

Organizational rationality in the early twenty-first century represents a continuation of the scientific management approaches of Frederick Taylor. According to Ritzer (2000), the methods used by McDonald's restaurants have become the current model of rationality. *McDonaldization* is "the process by which the principles of the fast-food industry are coming to dominate more and more sectors of American society as well as the rest of the world" (Ritzer, 2000, p. 1). Organizations everywhere of every type (e.g., beauty parlors, hospitals and clinics, retail stores, universities, travel agencies, and car maintenance shops) are adopting the principles of McDonaldization: efficiency, calculability, predictability, and increased control though automation. For example, customers may experience *efficiency* as getting an entire breakfast by simply going through the McDonald's drive-thru and ordering an Egg McMuffin. Efficiency is also enhanced by having restaurant customers themselves place their orders, pick up their food, refill their drinks, and bus their tables. Ritzer explains *calculability* as an emphasis on the quantitative aspects of products (e.g., the Quarter Pounder) and the time it takes to deliver them ("ready in three minutes or it's free"). *Predictability* is the result of a highly rational approach that prescribes every ingredient and every step of the process. Predictability ensures that a Big Mac purchased in Los Angeles next year will be identical to one purchased in New York last year. At McDonald's, employees are trained to do a limited number of tasks in precisely the way they are told to do them. Managers make sure the workers follow the prescribed routine. But because human beings are not always predictable or controllable, the restaurant replaces them with machines, such as drink dispensers that shut off automatically when the cup is full or French fry machines that lift the basket out of the oil when the fries are crisp.

Constructionist Perspective

The constructionist perspective is implicit in the study of organizational culture. *Organizational culture* is "the constellation of values, beliefs, assumptions and expectations" that shape the behavior of members of an organization (Holland, 1995, p. 1789). "Shared meaning, shared understanding, and shared sense making" are different ways of describing organizational culture (Morgan, 1986, p. 128). Organizational cultures reflect larger, national cultures as well as regional cultures in a country as large and diverse as the United States. An American automobile manufacturing plant would have different expectations than a plant in Germany, and one in Michigan may have a different culture than one in Alabama or South Carolina.

Within a given workplace, organizational culture is the product of a stable social unit with a significant shared history—that means there may be several [sub]cultures operating, including a managerial culture, various occupationally-based cultures, and group cultures based on locational proximity (Schein, 1985). For example, in a hospital one might encounter nursing, social work, and accounting subcultures, as well as subcultures related to the intensive care unit, the emergency room, the pediatric wing, and outpatient services. In analyzing an organization's culture, we acknowledge the process of reality construction. Like other types of culture, organizational culture operates largely outside of the conscious awareness of group members.

If an organization has only a weak culture, employees with different perspectives, norms, and values are freer to act on their individual inclinations. In a human service agency, a weak culture can result in inconsistencies in the provision of client services. When norms and values are clearly laid out and enforced, an organization is said to possess a strong culture. In such organizations, the culture provides a behavioral standard to which everyone subscribes. Organizations with strong cultures may also have more informal penalties for nonconformity. For example, in an agency that has a cultural norm that prescribes that workers remain in the building at lunchtime so that they can be available for clients, a new worker who goes out to eat may be greeted by sarcastic comments from peers when he or she returns.

Edgar Schein (1985, p. 2) suggests "the only thing of real importance that [organizational] leaders do is to create and manage culture and that the unique talent of leaders is their ability to work with culture." Among the ways the leaders can reinforce organizational culture are through what they pay attention to, measure, and control; reactions to critical incidents; criteria for the allocation of rewards and status; criteria for recruitment, selection, promotion, and "excommunication" of employees; and deliberate role modeling, teaching, and coaching (Schein, 1985, pp. 224–225). For example, a manager who values group process can support that kind of organizational culture not only by creating many different committees and advisory groups, but also by attending their meetings.

The physical design of an organization also reflects its cultural values. The number, location, size and furnishings of private offices; the presence of conference rooms and break rooms; and the ambience of waiting areas (including the provision of comfortable seating, current magazines, a television, fish tank, or toys) speak volumes about the organization's regard for employees and clients. For example, "welfare clients in a drab, unattractive waiting room, sitting on hard benches, are being given an unequivocal message of their inferior status in the welfare system, if not in society" (Seabury, 1971, pp. 47–48).

In addition to organizational culture, the constructionist perspective also frames theories about management styles and employee motivation. Three names often associated with these topics are Douglas McGregor, Frederick Herzberg, and Elton Mayo.

Noting the importance of subjective assumptions, McGregor (1960) identified two management styles that he labeled "Theory X" and "Theory Y." Theory X managers view workers as motivated only by rewards or by threats of punishment; these managers respond by providing much structure and close supervision. Theory Y managers view employees as wanting to grow and develop, and being motivated by internal rewards; they respond by giving their workers new challenges and responsibilities.

Theory Y is consistent with Herzberg's classic theory of employee motivation. Herzberg (1986/1968) identified *hygiene factors*—such as pay, benefits, status, job security, and working conditions—that keep employees from being dissatisfied but do not motivate them. Truly *motivating factors* include opportunities for challenge, responsibility, advancement, recognition, or achievement.

Mayo conducted research at the Hawthorne Plant of the Western Electric Company between 1927 and 1932 (Homans, 1986/1941). Although his goal was to investigate the effects of physical conditions such as lighting, humidity, equipment, and worker fatigue on performance, he discovered that productivity increased regardless of changes in the physical environment or working hours. He concluded that psychological and social factors were as important as other work conditions. The attention given the workers in the experiment and their interpretation of this attention was a crucial factor in their increased productivity. This reaction has been dubbed the *Hawthorne effect*. The implication of this finding is that workers should be invited to participate in decisions that affect their work. In this and other experiments, Mayo also found that informal work group norms have a significant effect on worker output; production rates above or below the informal norms resulted in social pressure to conform. This emphasis on understanding and using psychological and social variables is part of the *human relations model* of organizational administration (Mayo, 1933). Interest in the human relations model led to further research on small groups and the development or refinement of concepts such as group norms, roles, leadership, and decision making. An understanding of organizational life is often dependent on an appreciation of the small groups that function within organizations.

Preferred Perspective

Among the alternatives to traditional, bureaucratic organizations are *consensus organizations* (Iannello, 1992). In consensus organizations, rules are kept to a minimum and decisions are reached by mutual agreement. Often leadership positions are rotated and there is no special financial reward for leaders. Authority rests with the members rather than with a select few individuals at the top of the organization. Examples of consensus organizations, especially popular in the 1970s, include alternative schools, free medical clinics, legal collectives, food cooperatives, communes, and, most common, craft cooperatives (Morgen, 1994). Consensus is most easily achieved in organizations that have a homogenous workforce and a strong, shared ideology and culture.

Collectives are consensus organizations that are owned and managed by the members. They tend to be quite small (averaging 6.5 member-employees) and to operate in special niches of the economy that exempt them from competing directly with conventional companies (Rothschild & Russell, 1986; Rothschild & Whitt, 1986). While workers are generally more satisfied and invest greater energy into collectives, stress and burnout may result (Rothschild & Russell, 1986). Rothschild and Whitt suggest that collectivist organizations represent a "countertrend" to the increasing concentration in both economic and government institutions of power and control in fewer and fewer units. They say that what collectivist organizations all have in common is the "simple, but profound, desire for self-initiated, self-paced, self-controlled work . . . [and] the desire for meaningful group life" (1986, p. 183).

Evidence indicates that without small size, nonbureaucratic forms of organization are difficult to establish and maintain (Rothschild & Russell, 1986). Nevertheless, in an attempt to reap some of the benefits of nonhierarchical organizations, some corporations have made efforts to broaden worker participation in decision making. For example, they may encourage the development of work teams and other intermediate bodies that promise to help decentralize their structures and empower workers.

An alternative to more traditional management styles is one often manifested by female managers (although not all women use it and some men do) (Cox, 1993). One characteristic of this style is a manner of communication that values sharing and willingness to ask questions in order to gain a fuller understanding of the situation (Helgesen, 1990; Tannen, 1994). This is in contrast to a "male" style of communication that is task focused and concerned about how asking questions will affect the questioner's image (Tannen, 1994). A second characteristic of women's management style is their relationship with subordinates. Women are less hierarchical and tend to offer greater autonomy to their subordinates (Helgesen, 1990; Rosener, 1990). This more egalitarian style of management is often misunderstood as a weakness (Tannen, 1994). It is likely that these differences in style are the result of the cultural socialization of females that leads them to recognize the

> value of supporting and nurturing others, of protecting long-term . . . relationships, of seeking solutions in which everyone wins, and wherever possible, of forging a mutuality of interests. As a result of women's intensive socialization for their likely role in the family, they have often been taught to be responsive to others' needs, to seek mutually acceptable and equitable solutions, to support others, and to share information. (Rothschild & Davies, 1994, p. 588)

The literature suggests that the full participation of members of different backgrounds in an organization promotes creativity, flexibility, and problem solving (Cox, 1993). Lack of diversity and the resulting omission of minority points of view may encourage *groupthink,* a tendency to suppress dissent, often in an effort to promote consensus (Janis, 1972; Miranda, 1994). Groupthink can result in errors in decision making and such errors lead to poor outcomes. According to Janis (1982), some factors that contribute to groupthink include groups composed of persons of similar backgrounds and ideologies, a high level of group cohesiveness, and group members who have weak ties with or awareness of external groups. An example of groupthink in an organization is the sex abuse scandal in the Catholic Church that was exposed in 2002. Primarily celibate older white men made decisions to protect the organization at the expense of vulnerable children. Critics of the Church have argued that if a more diverse group shared leadership roles, the abusive practices would not have been tolerated.

On the other hand, if diversity is not well managed, communication problems may increase and morale may suffer. Given the changing demographics of the workforce, workplace diversity is inevitable in most sectors. Social workers need to draw upon their values and skills to help make workplace diversity a positive feature of organizational life.

The Impact of Organizations on Individuals and Families

How Organizations Deter Well-Being

Labor history and literature suggest that organizational settings are sources of oppression and health hazards for many people. This section documents the ongoing negative effects of organizations on today's workforce.

Discrimination.   When a particular category of people (such as affluent white males) dominates the hierarchy of most organizations, the result is barriers against people in other categories, such as women and people of color. Even though discrimination based on race and sex has been against the law for some time, there still exist many examples of unfair treatment, as evidenced in the limited number of women and minorities in high-level positions, restricted access to authority even when they are in managerial jobs, and lower salaries for women and people of color when compared to white males with similar credentials and experience (Andersen & Taylor, 2007; Padavic & Reskin, 2002).

The nature of racial discrimination in organizations has changed. Although there are still instances of overt discrimination (Padavic & Reskin, 2002), usually the oppression of racial minorities is not so apparent. Today, blatant racism may affect profitability, so "companies must promote diversity—or at least pretend to" (Henslin, 2008, p. 192). The presence of people of color in the organization satisfies equal opportunity requirements and affirmative action goals. Sometimes people of color are hired or promoted in mostly white organizations to be used as *tokens*, or high-profile representatives of their race. Tokenism results in *surplus visibility* (Patai, 1991), or focused attention on the token individual whose achievements or mistakes are then viewed as a reflection on his or her whole race. The presence of a small handful of minorities also enhances *contrast effects*, or an exaggeration of the differences between groups and of the similarities within groups. Even if they are a significant part of a company's workforce, people of color are routinely channeled to support positions or departments where they are limited to dealing with other people of color who are customers or employees: their job assignments are comprised of affirmative action, community relations, and minority affairs (Collins, 1989, 1993; Cose, 1993; Padavic & Reskin, 2002). Despite important-sounding titles, these positions are unlikely to prepare the employee for advancement to more powerful positions in the organization.

Sometimes lateral moves to areas from which executives are promoted are blocked; the resulting barriers are called *glass walls* (Schaefer, 2008). Scholars have identified certain factors that account for the concentration of people of color in entry level or peripheral positions. Bernheide (1992) called this phenomenon the *sticky floor*. These factors include lack of mentors and role models, exclusion from informal communication networks, limited access to training, and early "tracking" into less challenging assignments (Cose, 1993; Feagin, 1991; Irons & Moore, 1985; Kanter, 1993/1977; Simon & Akabas, 1993).

Many of the same factors are cited to explain why women appear to perform more poorly than men in organizations. Surplus visibility, contrast effects, negative stereotypes, exclusion from informal networks, lack of mentors, limited training opportunities, and in addition, ill-fitting clothing or equipment designed for male bodies, inadequate bathroom facilities, and a climate of sexual harassment make some work environments more hostile for women (Simon & Akabas, 1993). Because women continue to carry major responsibilities for meeting family needs, they may be forced to take jobs that have short or flexible hours so that they can accommodate the schedules of their husbands and children. *Mommy track* is the term used to describe work affording flexible and/or shorter hours. The Pregnancy Discrimination Act of 1978 requires that employers treat pregnant workers the same as other employees with temporary medical disabilities and also forbids employers from discriminating against pregnant women by forcing them to take pregnancy leave (Lovell, O'Neill, & Olsen, 2007). The Family and Medical Leave Act of 1993 protects the job security of women who need to take time off work to care for a newborn, adopted or foster child, or other dependent family member with a serious health condition, but it does not require that the employer provide paid leave. Only 8 percent of workers in the United States receive paid family leave and only one quarter of the most family-friendly companies provide nine or more weeks of paid maternity leave (Lovell, O'Neill, & Olsen, 2007). The United States falls way behind other industrialized countries in mandating provisions for family leave (Cherlin, 2008). Women who take extended breaks from employment to deal with family needs may be penalized by missing opportunities for promotion or simply to gain seniority.

Women's advancement in corporate leadership continues to stagnate, with virtually no growth seen in women's share of top positions in recent years. In 2008, women constituted 15.7 percent of corporate officers in the largest 500 firms according to Catalyst, a New York-based women's advocacy group that collects the data annually ("Catalyst census," 2008).

The *glass ceiling* is the label given to the mostly invisible barrier that keeps women from being promoted to the highest levels of an organization. In contrast, men who are employed in traditionally female occupations, such as social work, nursing, and elementary education encounter not a glass ceiling, but a *glass escalator* that provides an express ride to the top. Compared to their female coworkers, they are promoted to higher level positions, given more desirable work assignments, and paid higher salaries (Williams, 1995). Another threat to women's career success, the *glass cliff*, was recently documented. In a study of 100 companies, the researchers found that "their [women's] leadership appointments are made in problematic organizational circumstances and hence are more precarious" (Ryan & Haslam, 2005, p. 87). In other words, they were appointed to senior positions only after a downturn in the company's fortunes had already occurred, leaving them standing on the edge of a glass cliff where they can easily be scapegoated if things continue to get worse.

Workplace Hazards and Other Forms of Exploitation of Employees.   Social work students may have learned about the 1911 Triangle Shirt Waist factory fire in New York that created the impetus for federal involvement in setting and enforcing worker safety standards. In spite of government regulations that should protect them, according to the U.S. Bureau of Labor Statistics, between 2002 and 2006 approximately 5,700 workers died from occupational injuries each year and during that same time frame, over 4 million workers sustained workplace injuries and illnesses each year (AFL-CIO, 2007). Parenti notes that this "is mostly due to inadequate safety standards and lax enforcement of codes" (1995, p. 109). Eighty years after the Triangle Shirt Waist factory fire, a fire at the Imperial chicken plant in Hamlet, North Carolina, killed 25 people and injured 49. Emergency exits had been chained shut. Company executives had ordered the doors locked "to keep employees from going outside for coffee breaks, or stealing chickens" (Wright, Cullen, & Blankenship, 1995). Most of those killed were African American women.

Meatpackers and poultry workers perform the most dangerous and physically demanding labor in the country; these workers are likely to suffer cuts, amputations, skin disease, permanent arm and shoulder damage, and even death (Compa & Fellner, 2005). OSHA does not have specific standards that allow it to cite employers for hazards relating to line speed and repetitive stress injuries. The workers in this industry are increasingly immigrants from Mexico and Central America. Companies are able to exploit them due to their limited English skills and uncertain legal status, and to block their attempts to unionize (Compa & Fellner, 2005).

In addition to occupations that have obvious dangers, such as law enforcement, or mining, workplace settings that expose workers to various hazardous materials include pest control and paper, chemical, drug, and paint industries, as well as beauty shops and drycleaners (Draper, 1993; Glausiusz, 2008).

Perhaps less alarming but more commonplace are the chronic physical and mental illnesses that result from psychological pressures in the workplace. These include cardiovascular diseases (high blood pressure, heart attacks, strokes), anxiety, and depression (Ironson, 1992). Moody (cited in Ehrenreich, 2001, p. 35) argues that there is a new system of " 'management by stress' in which workers in a variety of industries are being squeezed to extract maximum productivity to the detriment of their health." McNeely (1992, p. 235) reports that the satisfaction of female human service workers was affected much more than that of their male coworkers by perceptions of excessive on-the-job pressure and of job performance expectations—perhaps because they were at the same time experiencing work-family conflict.

A term used to describe one type of reaction to job stress is *burnout*. Burnout has been defined as "psychological withdrawal from work in response to excessive stress or dissatisfaction" (Cherniss, 1980, p. 16). Craig (1999) notes that individuals in the helping professions—social workers, police officers, nurses, therapists, teachers, and others who often work in tension-filled situations—are especially at risk. She says that those "who suffer job burnout are idealistic, highly motivated, extremely competent workers who finally realize they cannot make the difference they once thought they could" (pp. 336–337). An example of symptoms of burnout in a human service agency might involve a social worker who does the bare minimum in terms of job requirements, complains of psychosomatic illnesses, and is frequently absent as she or he "counts down" the months to retirement. Craig suggests that to avoid burnout, workers should be realistic in their goals, not take work troubles home with them, and develop interests outside of their jobs. Smaller caseloads, better pay, and other improvements in working conditions also would help alleviate burnout in human service workers.

In addition to threats to life and health, employees at the bottom of the organization are also subjected to exploitation in other forms. For example, companies can avoid paying overtime by labeling certain low-level employees "managers" who then become "exempt" from wage and hour regulations (and thus ineligible for overtime pay), or by hiring people for less than full-time schedules, or as contract workers, so that the company doesn't don't have to provide benefits such as health insurance or paid time off.

Worker Responses.   Although workplace conditions and family-related policies may be addressed by government or company directives, any hope for change has to take into account the unequal status of employee and employer; overall, working people have limited power to change the workplace to better accommodate their needs (Draper, 1993; Piotrkowski & Hughes, 1993). This is especially true for people from lower socioeconomic classes who have limited finances and limited alternatives. Employees are not passive victims of their work environments, however. Workers may respond to problematic situations by resistance, slowdowns, or strikes, and collective bargaining. Labor unions have contributed significantly to the 40-hour workweek standard, health and retirement benefits, and workplace safety, and union workers typically earn higher wages than do nonunion workers in comparable jobs. In the past 40 years, the *proportion* of unionized workers in the United States has declined, although the *number* of unionized workers has increased largely as a result of the growth of public employee unions (Kendall, 2008, p. 443).

Effects on Consumers.   In addition to the ways organizations obstruct the well-being of their employees, they may use their considerable power to inhibit the well-being of others who come into contact with them. An example that many people encounter is *red tape*, or a bureaucratic preoccupation with rules and procedures that get in the way of meeting the needs of customers and clients. Other frustrations occur when a company or agency puts its own needs ahead of those of consumers. Nearly everyone has experienced the frustration of dealing with an organization's ineffective phone answering system that was purportedly designed to "serve you better" but instead only replaces direct telephone contact with the organization's staff with a series of irrelevant tape-recorded messages.

On a more significant level, some organizations have chosen to put profits before the health and safety needs of consumers. One example is the ongoing promotion of cigarettes which contributes to the illness and deaths of many consumers despite a 1997 court ruling that regulated the sale of tobacco. This industry targets adolescents, women in their early twenties, blue-collar men,

FIGURE 9.1   *Critical Thinking About Bureaucracy*

One of the authors' brother supplied the following story, which serves to illustrate the workings of a large bureaucracy:

> Our friend's wedding invitation was returned to her. When she checked with us we confirmed that she had our address correct ("E456S4722 Lake View Lane"). Someone at the post office had circled the S and written 5 above it. Ours is the only house on Lake View Lane. Why do they need a nine-digit number to deliver the mail? Where else on Lake View Lane did they think it might go?

Often bureaucracies work smoothly and deliver products and services efficiently. An example would be the processing of millions of Social Security checks every month. At other times, some bureaucracies are plagued by inefficiency and "red tape" as in the example presented above. Can you think of an example of when a bureaucratic agency worked well for you? Can you think of an example of when a bureaucratic agency didn't work well?

African Americans and Latinos, and people in undeveloped countries. Reynolds Tobacco [RJR] has even developed candy- and fruit-flavored cigarettes aimed at the 12-to 13-year-old market, aware that 90 percent of adult smokers become addicted as kids (Califano & Sullivan, 2006).

How Organizations Promote Well-Being

Even traditional organizations can contribute to the well-being of employees through a variety of measures. In addition to the obvious advantages of salaries, benefits, and job satisfaction, these may include flextime and on-site day care to help with family responsibilities, employee assistance organizations (EAPs) to help with personal problems, on-site gyms to keep employees healthy, and employee stock ownership plans.

Every October *Working Mothers* magazine identifies the "ten best places to work" based on support for employees and their families. Some of the more unusual benefits noted were on-site auto maintenance for employees, take-home dinners, on-site hairstyling, and a gradual "phase back" program to reintegrate new moms and dads into the workplace after taking family leave. While these companies are notable, the reality is that they represent but a small portion of American employers.

Private corporations have led the way in promoting equal treatment of gay men and lesbians. According to the Human Rights Campaign (HRC), as of March 1, 2006, 49 percent of Fortune 500 companies offered domestic partner health benefits, up from just 25 percent in 2000 (Luther, 2006). There are no explicit federal or state laws requiring benefit plans for same-sex couples. As of March 1, 2006, the HRC Foundation was aware of 216 large employers that extended Family Medical Leave Act benefits to include leave on behalf of a same-sex partner. The HRC Foundation has tracked 129 not-for-profit institutions that provide same-sex partner health benefits, including AARP, the American Medical Association, the Brookings Institution, Pew Charitable Trusts and the World Bank Group.

Many corporations also make substantial contributions to charities and foundations. It should be understood, however, that this generosity allows these corporations to place their resources with nonprofits that benefit their employees and their communities at the same time that they enhance their public image and save on taxes (Odendahl, 1990).

Organizations as Providers of Social Services and as Employers of Social workers

Social workers are employed in a variety of organizations. In many, social workers are directly involved in meeting the primary goals of the organization. Examples would include agencies that provide child protection services, mental health or family counseling, and battered women's shelters. In others, called *host organizations*, social workers provide ancillary services. Examples of host organizations are schools, hospitals, and prisons. It is not uncommon for social workers in host settings to be called upon to work with clients' families, and to locate and arrange for services or funding from other agencies. These social workers also may be called upon to present, explain, and defend social work values and to advocate for clients. In addition to providing social services *per se*, many social workers in various organizations supervise support staff, paraprofessionals, and volunteers.

Social service agencies and host organizations are subject to the same economic trends as other companies. In difficult economic times, staff are likely to be asked to do more with less, to live with threats of being "downsized," or to focus services on clients who can pay full fees themselves or have adequate insurance coverage. These situations present barriers to optimal services as well as ethical dilemmas.

Looking Ahead

In Chapter 10, we address a special kind of organization, residential institutions. These are not the social institutions we discussed in Part II, but rather the settings and facilities that house individuals who pose a threat to society or have very special needs that cannot be met in the community.

Chapter 10
Residential Institutions

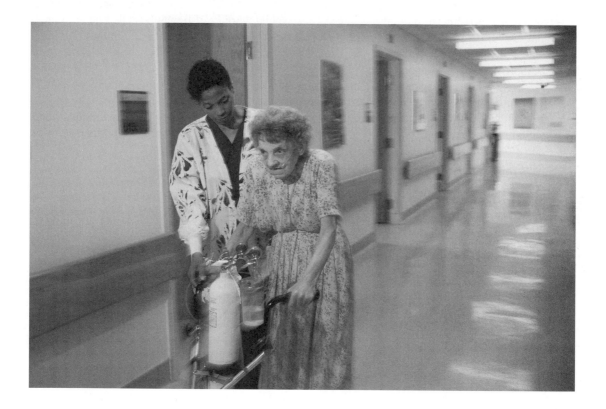

The role of institutions in America has changed dramatically in the past two centuries. For example, "jails and prisons have increasingly become America's social agency of first resort for coping with the deepening problems of a society in perennial crisis" (Currie, 1998, p. 34). Many social workers are (or will be) employed in large group care settings (Ginsberg, 2001).

Defining Institutions

Institutions are organizational settings where residents exercise little or no choice about their participation, have virtually no input into how they are treated, and cannot leave without being officially released or discharged. Moore and Starkes (1992) identified three kinds of institutional settings: those that are medically oriented, those that are residential and service oriented, and those that are custodial and/or correctional. "All provide some mix of custody and treatment," they note, and the total milieu is considered to be part of the service delivery process. This total milieu idea was emphasized in a book about residential child-care centers, *The Other 23 Hours* (Trieschman, Whittaker, & Brentro, 1969), which pointed out that what happens in the hours outside of the therapy session may have more of an impact than what happens in it, and that the cook or the groundskeeper, not to mention the recreation therapist and the child-care staff, may play as important a role in the youths' treatment as their therapists.

Erving Goffman (1961) perceived the defining characteristic of an institution to be the inability of residents to leave at will. Wolf Wolfensberger (1972), on the other hand, believed that it was the features of *deindividuation* that make institutions different from other organizations and residences. These features include numbers of residents distinctly larger than might be found in a large family, a high level of regimentation, a physical or social environment that aims at a low common denominator, and a place in which all or most of the transactions of daily life are carried out under one roof or on one "campus" (Wolfensberger, 1972, pp. 28–29). For example, a traditional children's residential treatment center might have dozens or even hundreds of residents; it certainly would not be mistaken for a typical single family home even if it were located in a residential neighborhood. Residents all eat breakfast at 7 a.m. and dinner at 5:30 p.m. whether they are hungry or not; there are craft activities on Wednesday evenings and videos on Fridays; group therapy is offered on Tuesdays and Thursdays. If the neediest resident can't manage an outing to the mall, then no one can go to the mall. Most residents sleep, eat, socialize, attend classes, study, play, exercise, watch TV, and receive counseling on the same campus, if not in the same buildings, day after day.

At a less coercive level on the continuum are institutional settings where people live for extended periods of time, but are not so isolated from society. These include assisted living centers, halfway houses, group homes, and other *community-based facilities*. Residents living in these facilities often participate in the same activities, at the same locations, as other community members. For example, children living in a community-based group home are likely to attend a public school and swim at the local Y. At the other end of the continuum are *total institutions* (Goffman, 1961), those organizations that isolate residents (sometimes called *inmates* in these settings) from the rest of society and put them under the control of the officials who run the institution. Usually total institutions attempt to resocialize the residents to become more compliant and accepting of institutional and societal norms. Rewards (or more commonly punishments) are used to encourage conformity. The success of total institutions in rehabilitating and preparing their clients for reintegration into society has been strongly and widely challenged.

A Brief History of Institutions

In the mid-nineteenth century, there appeared a well-intentioned effort to provide a new kind of help for at least some at-risk populations. Originally conceived as sanctuaries, *asylums* were established in the countryside with the intention of resocializing and rehabilitating inmates (including not only prisoners, but also people with mental illness, mental retardation, and dependent children) in a wholesome environment far from the chaos, temptations, and exploitations of the city (Rothman, 1971). Physical separation of the asylum from the community was consistently practiced.

At the turn of the century, what began as efforts toward reform had been transformed into a system of custodial and/or punitive care. By the 1950s, public attention was brought to bear on the deplorable conditions that existed in asylums. Exposés such as Goffman's *Asylums* (1961) pointed out the deleterious effects of institutions on the lives of inmates who were given minimal custodial care without treatment (a process called *warehousing*). At the same time, the growing costs of institutional care, advances in pharmacology, and changes in public assistance policies supported a drive for deinstitutionalization. The term *deinstitutionalization* refers to preventing inappropriate admissions to institutions and developing appropriate alternatives in the community.

The civil rights movement in this country provided fertile ground for legal action on behalf of institutionalized persons. Reflecting the "due process clause" of the Fourteenth Amendment to the Constitution, several court cases that were heard during the 1970s and early 1980s, augmented by federal and state statutes, public licensing, and private accreditation standards, affirmed the basic rights of institutionalized people (see Figure 10.1).

Unfortunately, the implementation of desinstitutionalization policies often resulted in the precipitous discharge of residents without concurrent development of family support and community resources (DiNitto & Cummins, 2007). Thus, many patients with chronic mental illnesses became homeless "street people," while others ended up in places smaller but no less "institutional"

FIGURE 10.1   *The Rights of Institutionalized People**

❑ to be housed in the least restrictive setting;
❑ to receive minimally adequate, reasonable, appropriate, and humane treatment, rehabilitation, or training in the least restrictive manner (e.g., without the unnecessary or excessive use of physical restraints or isolation);
❑ to receive adequate medical care, or care that generally meets a "community standard";
❑ to refuse treatment;
❑ to refuse to participate in involuntary or uncompensated work for nontherapeutic reasons;
❑ to be assured of confidentiality of records and privacy in treatment;
❑ to have personal property (within reason) and to wear their own clothes;
❑ to live without supervision in the community if they pose no threat to themselves or others.

*Although prisoners must be treated humanely, many of these rights do not apply to them. On the other hand, unnecessary restraints and excessive use of seclusion in prisons also have been ruled unconstitutional.
Sources: The Pew Center on the States (2008); Saltzman, & Proch (1990).

than their previous setting, or worse yet, in local jails. This pattern of moving from one institution to another is called *transinstitutionalization* (Segal, 2008).

Issues and Trends in Institutions

Privatization

A recent trend in institutional care is the privatization of facilities. Large private, for-profit corporations have developed nursing homes, psychiatric treatment centers, and especially prisons (Karger & Stoesz, 2010). The trend toward privatization in prisons was presented in more detail in Chapter 3.

"Revolving Door" Care

The term *revolving door* refers to a pattern of institutional care that involves repeated admissions and discharges. This has been particularly problematic in the case of people with chronic mental illnesses. Although the push for deinstitutionalization has prevented unnecessary, long-term custodial care, it also has encouraged premature discharges and repeated readmissions (Segal, 2008). In general, patterns of mental health admission to institutions now are periodic, temporary, frequent, and short term (Moore & Starkes, 1992, p. 173). The term can also be applied to other institutionalized populations. More than half of released offenders return to prison within three years, either after being convicted of a new offense or for probation violations (Pew Center on the States, 2008). (The percentage of convicts who are re-arrested is called the *recidivism rate.*)

Moore and Starkes (1992, p. 173) also note that concern now seems to have turned away from the location of care to issues of continuity-of-care. The *continuity-of-care* perspective views institutionalization as only one aspect of treatment and assumes that professionals will develop and implement a plan for working with significant others in the clients' lives and for appropriate aftercare and follow-up after discharge.

Other trends in institutional care in America vary by population. Some of these patterns have been well publicized, while others are less well known. They are discussed next.

Offenders

There has been extensive press coverage of the explosion in the prison population in this country, thanks in part to data collected by the nonprofit watchdog group, The Sentencing Project (www.sentencingproject.org). The United States is the world's leader in incarceration with 2.1 million people currently in the nation's prisons or jails—a 500 percent increase over the past 30 years. These trends have resulted in prison overcrowding and state governments being overwhelmed by the burden of funding a rapidly expanding penal system, despite increasing evidence that large-scale incarceration is not the most effective means of achieving public safety (The Sentencing Project, 2009). The Sentencing Project (2008) reported that one in four jail inmates in 2002 was in jail for a drug offense, compared to one in ten in 1983; drug offenders constituted 20 percent of state prison inmates and 55 percent of federal prison inmates in 2001.

The exploding inmate population just referenced necessitated a boom in federal and state prison construction. Much of the prison boom has been concentrated in small towns and rural areas that have seen their economic base erode as factories close down or relocate. A PBS documentary, *Prison Town, USA* (Galloway & Kutchins, 2007), reported that 350 rural counties saw prisons open between 1980 and 2001. The possibilities of employment and a boost for local businesses were often part of the campaign to bring prisons to such localities.

The promised benefits, however, were not always realized. The jobs that new prisons brought were often filled by outsiders. Many local workers were not qualified for some positions, such as corrections officer, and those positions were filled by people living outside of the community. Some jobs for which locals were qualified, both inside and outside the prison walls, were performed instead by prison labor (Huling, 2002). Often secondary benefits, such as contracts with local businesses to provide goods or services to the prison were lost as prison management chose to renegotiate contracts or outsource aspects of the work. A 2003 study of prisons sited in rural communities found that there was no overall effect on local employment, per capita income, or consumer spending, three leading indicators of economic vitality (Galloway & Kutchins, 2007). Other problems include the many incidents of racism that have been documented in prisons in rural areas where correctional officers are predominantly white and prisoners are predominantly people of color (Huling, 2002).

Although prison overcrowding is an ongoing concern, *jails* currently represent one of the most problematic aspects of institutional care. Jails serve a "catch-all function," holding individuals pending arraignment or trial, convicted offenders serving short-term sentences, convicted offenders awaiting transfer to prison, probation and parole violators, vagrants, drunks, people who are mentally ill and/or homeless, and increasingly, juveniles. In addition to being overcrowded, many jails are old and unsanitary, and inadequately staffed (Territo, Halsted, & Bromley, 2004). Problems result from the limited and unstable nature of local taxes, a general lack of public support for jail reform, rapid rates of inmate turnover that makes it difficult to develop and coordinate programs, and the immense diversity of risks and needs found among inmates (Bohm & Haley, 2007). Jails are the "revolving door" of the justice system (Siegel, 2010).

Older Adults

Older adults who were confined to public mental hospitals were the principle beneficiaries of policies of deinstitutionalization, but in the last decade there has been a steady growth in the institutionalization of older adults (Segal, 2008, p. 710). According to 2004 data reported by the National Center for Health Statistics (2004), at any one time, about 3.6 percent of the population over 65, and 13.9

percent of those over 85, can be found in a nursing home. Current estimates suggest that 35 percent of Americans aged 65 in 2005 will spend some time in a nursing home during their lifetime; 18 percent will reside in a nursing home for at least one year and 5 percent for at least five years (Houser, 2007).

In both 1985 and 1997, the main reasons for admission were cognitive impairment, incontinence (difficulty controlling bowel or bladder functions), and other types of functional decline, although cardiovascular diseases were the most common malady (Sahyoun, Pratt, Lentzner, Dey, & Robinson, 2001). The most common categories of primary diagnoses reported in 2004 included mental disorders, Alzheimer's, and diseases of the circulatory system (National Center for Health Statistics, 2009, Table 33). While the number of residents has remained constant, the number of nursing homes has dropped from 19,100 in 1985 to 16,100 in 2004 (Houser, 2007), suggesting that facilities are either larger or more crowded.

According to a study ordered by Congress (Fleck, 2002), more than 90 percent of the nation's nursing homes are inadequately staffed, putting residents at risk for bedsores, blood-borne infections, dehydration, malnutrition, and pneumonia. A *Consumer Reports* study ("Nursing homes," 2006) found that not-for-profit facilities employ more staff and do a better job in providing good care. The same analysis showed that independently run homes do a better of providing care than do chains. The nursing home industry blames low rates of reimbursement under federal Medicaid and Medicare programs. Critics counter that government rates more than doubled between 1992 and 1998, and nursing homes chose to use the money to boost profits or to finance takeovers rather than to increase staffing (Fleck, 2002, p. 16).

The *Consumer Reports* investigation ("Nursing homes," 2006) found that state officials responsible for overseeing nursing home care have often failed to correct problems. The most usual remedy for violations of standards in nursing home care is a "plan of correction." In this situation, the nursing homes acknowledged the problem and promised to address it within a specified period. Often the problem is corrected, but soon resurfaces, a phenomenon regulators call *yo-yo compliance*, and fines tend to be "absurdly" low ("Nursing homes," 2006).

People with Mental Illness

After deinstitutionalization led to the closing of most wards in state mental hospitals without the adequate development of community-based alternatives, care of the mentally ill population shifted to detention centers, jails, and prisons. About two-thirds of jail inmates report having a mental health problem; more than 100,000 people in jail today suffer from psychosis and more than 400,000 have some form of mental disorder (James & Glaze, 2006). In any given year, about half of the people who die while in jail committed suicide (Cole & Smith, 2007). Most mentally ill offenders are arrested for minor offenses such as trespassing, vagrancy, urinating in public, or shoplifting at the corner convenience store. Many of them also have substance abuse problems, but cannot get into drug- and alcohol-treatment programs because of their mental illnesses. Due to budget cuts and lack of space in state mental health hospitals, some mentally ill individuals may remain in jail for up to two years— even with court intervention—before being admitted to a more appropriate facility (Bell, 2002).

People with Developmental Disabilities

Before deinstitutionalization, many people with developmental disabilities (e.g., mental retardation) lived in the same institutions as people with mental illnesses. The former population, however, has been more successful in obtaining political support and financial resources due to stronger lobbies and a public perception of worthiness (Segal, 2008). Contemporary practice emphasizes habilitation and rehabilitation training, and consumer-driven, highly individualized supports (Freedman, 1995). Most people with disabilities live with their families or reside in community-based facilities, including intermediate-care facilities, foster homes, group homes, boarding homes, and supervised apartments (Segal, 2008).

Children and Youth

The number of children living in institutions reached a low in 1960 and then more than doubled in the 1980s and 1990s, leveling off in 2000 at 144,981 (Segal, 2008). Over that time period, the names and/or purposes of the facilities have changed. "Facilities went from being organizations [children homes] focused on the normalized growth and development of their children to being residual repositories [residential treatment centers] of the failures of foster family care" (Segal, 2008, p. 15). Some of these treatment centers, particularly unlicensed, unregulated private facilities, are associated with reports of exploitation and mistreatment of children (U.S. General Accounting Office, 2007).

A study conducted by the American Bar Association found that thousands of children were placed by their parents in privately run, unregulated residential facilities (Behar, Friedman, Pinto, Katz-Leavy, & Jones, 2007). Seductive advertisements, particularly on the Internet, aim their messages at parents who are struggling to find help for their problematic children. Many of these programs do not require a professional assessment prior to admission. Many programs severely limit parental contact.

Because there are gaps in local services, or because parents cannot afford treatment, some families resort to other service systems. In 2003, the U.S. General Accounting Office (GAO) reported that the parents of thousands of children sought alternate out-of-home living arrangements by inappropriately placing their children in public child welfare or juvenile justice facilities in order to obtain mental health services (U.S. General Accounting Office, 2003). No formal or comprehensive federal or state tracking system exists to collect data on this issue.

Understanding Institutions

Ecosystems Perspective

Because they cannot voluntarily leave, institutional residents are more affected by the physical characteristics of their environment than people who can come and go at will. Historically, most institutions were immense buildings with high ceilings, long corridors, and large sleeping wards. The recognition of the importance of architectural design in promoting healthier social functioning created an impetus for new institutional facilities. In psychiatric hospitals, there was a shift from large wards to smaller rooms and more home-like, personalized spaces. Research suggests that violence in prisons would be reduced if facilities had carpeted floors, conventional upholstered furniture, and rooms with outside windows (Wener, Frazier, & Farbstein, 1985). Similarly, more home-like designs, privacy and personal control in settings for persons with profound retardation would decrease social withdrawal and dependency (Friedman, 1976). An example of another innovation in institutional design is the use of enclosed outdoor patio pathways that allow patients with dementia to "go for walks" without getting lost or wandering away from the facility.

Unfortunately, for many residents in institutions, negative reactions to the setting are viewed as examples of individual pathology rather than as normal responses to a hostile environment (see, for example, Rosenhan, 1973). An example is the common reaction by residential group care facilities to children who "act out" upon returning from a weekend "home visit"; the staff decide to limit family contact rather than to explore aspects of the facility or program that make it a negative place to live (Bush, 1980; Milham, Bullock, Hosie, & Haak, 1986).

The general concept of person-environment fit was discussed in Chapter 1. Lawton (1982) and others (see Cavanaugh & Blanchard-Fields, 2002; Lawton & Nahemow, 1973; Murray, 1938) have suggested that one way of examining the person-environment fit is to look at the individual's level of *competence* (his or her capacity to function across several dimensions) and *environmental press* (the demands of the environment). If competence and press are in balance, there is *adaptation*. If there are too many demands and too little competence, the result is maladaptive behavior and negative affect. And if there are too few demands and excess competence, the result is still maladaptive behavior and negative affect. This latter condition is applicable to many institutional settings where there is little in the daily routine that might offer a challenge or opportunity for growth to residents. For example, many nursing home staff members assume a lower level of functioning for residents than they are capable of and make decisions for them, causing residents to appear to be even more dependent than they are (Baltes, 1994; Wahl, 1991; Zarit, Dolan, & Leitsch, 1999). When researchers introduced decision-making options for residents, they not only demonstrated higher activity levels and greater well-being, but also lower mortality rates (Langer & Rodin, 1976; Rodin & Langer, 1977; Schulz & Hanusa, 1979).

Functionalist Perspective

Functionalists recognize several societal benefits of institutions. Some inmates are in institutions because they represent an immediate threat to society. In removing "deviants" from the community and punishing them, institutions help to reinforce a greater commitment on the part of the conforming majority to conventional norms and behaviors (Henslin, 2008).

A latent function of institutions is providing employment. An example would be a new prison built in a rural area that lacks other kinds of industries. Functionalists would hold that the employment opportunities and economic growth that result are a positive contribution to the well-being of an area that extends beyond the manifest functions of the institution itself. Studies have shown, however, that the actual outcomes are less encouraging (see Chapter 8).

Rational/Social Exchange Perspective

Institutions are a special type of organization, called *coercive organizations* by many sociologists because, for the most part, residents are there against their will. As organizations, institutions are designed using a bureaucratic model (see Chapter 9). That means that they have a hierarchical structure, a complex division of labor, and many rules and regulations that apply to staff as well as residents. One of the major complaints that are made about many nursing homes, for example, is that their programs serve to meet the needs of the institution rather than the needs of residents. Regimented scheduling is valued by such facilities despite arguments by gerontologists that such routines are detrimental to residents' well-being (Langer & Rodin, 1976).

On an individual level, the rationalist perspective underlies the deterrence theory of imprisonment (see Chapter 3). *Deterrence theory* suggests that the punishment of one person serves as an example to others who will make a rational choice based on their observation that crime does not pay (Macionis, 2007).

On a societal level, a cost-benefit analysis of institutional care suggests that really not much rational thought has gone into planning. The same amount of money invested in preventive programs and community-based care would improve the lives not only of those who might be placed in institutions but others as well.

Conflict Perspective

From a conflict perspective, institutions satisfy the need to remove from society those who are unable to comply with the demands of the capitalist system (Henslin, 2008). These would include those who are too old or too young to work, those who are chronically ill, and/or those who are a danger to themselves or others. Spitzer (1980) stated it more strongly, saying that institutions are an instrument of social control, used to warehouse the surplus labor population that fails to contribute to capital accumulation.

In institutions, differences in power are everywhere. For residents, freedom of movement is restricted, contact with staff and outsiders is limited, and personal privacy is minimal. Although they are monitored almost continuously, residents have so little power that they may be treated as if they are invisible. Rosenhan (1973, p. 256), for example, reported incidents of ward attendants abusing mental patients in front of other patients, and of a nurse who "unbuttoned her uniform to adjust her brassiere in the presence of an entire ward of viewing men" as if they weren't there. Although in the past few decades laws and regulations have been put in place to protect the basic rights of many institutionalized adults, the reality is that they are still among the most oppressed of our society's citizens.

Given the current social climate, the mistreatment of inmates in American prisons and jails is often ignored or even condoned. There is a general attitude that convicted and incarcerated felons have forfeited their rights to be treated as human beings (Stringfellow, 1990/1991); thus the potential for human rights abuses at both large "supermax" facilities (Pupovac, 2008) and at smaller, overcrowded facilities is great.

Constructionist Perspective

According to labeling theory, labels such as *patient* or *criminal* may result in institutional residents accepting and internalizing the attributes of those roles (Goffman, 1961). The impact of labeling is not limited to the label recipient but extends to those with whom she or he interacts. For example, once a person is labeled a psychiatric patient, staff may interpret even normal behaviors as symptoms of mental illness (Rosenhan, 1973).

Preferred Perspectives

Along with deinstitutionalization came a movement for institutional reform called *normalization*. In simple terms, *normalization* means making available to institutionalized people living arrangements that closely resemble those enjoyed by other citizens (Nirje, 1976; Wolfensberger, 1972). This approach suggests that facilities should be small (i.e., designed for no more than six to eight residents). They should resemble valued homes in the community—there should be no signs in front (or on the program vehicle) that identify the residents inside as different from other citizens. Facilities should be integrated into the community so residents can walk to, or have available public transportation to the library, shopping centers, movie theaters, bowling alleys, and so forth. Residents should work and/or receive services away from the facility. There should be a continuum of options available, but residents should not have to move simply because their needs change; instead, services should be adapted so that residents can experience a sense of permanence and security in their living arrangement.

A more recent effort to reform institutions is called the *Eden Alternative*™. This approach was a response to the sterile, pathology-based, treatment-orientation of nursing homes that results in loneliness, helplessness, and boredom. Eden Alternative™ founder William Thomas enumerates three fundamental principles of this new kind of care: acknowledging each resident's capacity for growth, focusing on the needs of the residents rather the needs of the institution, and emphasizing quality long-term nurturing care while providing short-term treatment as needed (Thomas, 1994). This new philosophy of care involves

> aesthetically transforming the physical environment of facilities with the addition of pets, plants, and children, creating a 'human habitat'; placing maximum possible decision-making authority in the hands of residents and those who care for them; de-emphasizing program activities by encouraging resident involvement in the 'human habitat'; and de-emphasizing the use of prescription drugs. (see Long-term Care Paradise, 1999)

Kalb and Jaurez (2005) describe how, in the next phase, called the *Green House*™ *Project*, Eden principles are implemented in community-located houses designed for six to eight residents who require skilled nursing care.

In contrast to the usual hierarchical, bureaucratic, department-based organizational design of most nursing homes, in the Eden Alternative™ facilities, staff members form multidisciplinary work-teams that assume responsibility for an area and make their own schedules and work assignments. Thus, a cooperative work environment is cultivated and staff feel empowered.

The Impact of Institutions on Individuals and Families

How Institutions Deter Well-Being

Erving Goffman was a well-known early critic of psychiatric hospitals and other "total institutions," such as prisons and concentration camps. In his groundbreaking ethnographic work, *Asylums: Essays on the Social Situation of Mental Patients and Other Inmates*, Goffman argued that institutionalization was a traumatic and "mortifying" experience brought on by isolation, invasion of privacy, regimentation, and labeling (1961, pp. 13–14). Deegan (1993) echoes this sentiment in describing psychiatric hospitalization as the "radically dehumanizing and devaluing transformation from being a person to being an illness" (p. 7).

Most people dread living in an institutional setting because of the expected loss of freedom and privacy. The powerlessness and deindividuation associated with most institutions leads members of many vulnerable populations, such as the aged and those with chronic physical or

FIGURE 10.2   *Critical Thinking About Nursing Home Environments*

Research studies suggest that the Eden Alternative™ may not make a significant difference in improving nursing home residents' survival, infection rate, or cognitive functioning. A more important question might be whether residents experience a better quality of life—which is more difficult to measure. What would you use as indicators of quality of life in an institutional setting?

Sources: Fitzsimmons S. (2002). *Alternative therapies. American Journal of Alzheimer's Disease and Other Dementias, 17*, 200; Coleman, M. T., Looney, S., O'Brien, J., Ziegler, C., Pastorino, C. A., & Turner, C. (2002). The Eden alternative: Findings after 1 year of implementation. *The Journals of Gerontology: Biological Sciences & Medical Sciences, 57*, M422–M427.

mental illnesses, to choose marginally adequate living arrangements in the community or even homelessness over inpatient status.

The regimentation of most institutions results in residents becoming institutionalized. *Institutionalization* is a syndrome characterized by apathy, withdrawal, submissiveness, and a reluctance to leave the institutional setting (Johnson & Rhodes, 2007). In other words, residents are resocialized to become compliant and dependent. In learning to adapt to the institutional environment, they lose the skills and attitudes—such as self-care and independent decision making, assertiveness, and self-confidence—they need to reenter and function successfully in the outside community. Wirt (1999) suggests "the restrictive environment of institutional settings coupled with oppressive staff [are] capable of producing institutionalism in almost any person regardless of diagnosis, predispositions, or personality" (p. 260). Prolonged confinement in isolation in prisons can even provoke symptoms usually associated with psychosis or other severe disorders, such as panic attacks (Human Rights Watch, 1999).

In some institutional settings, particularly those designed for offenders, a *deviant subculture* develops and imposes its values and patterns on the residents, regardless of what goes on in the rest of the institution (Polsky, 1962; Sykes, 1958). Sometimes called the *convict code, inmate subculture, inmate social code* or *deprivation model* in corrections settings, this theory suggests that an environment of shared deprivation gives inmates a basis for solidarity (Siegel, 2010). The subculture represents a functional, collective adaptation of inmates to their environment. Norms of the convict code include not informing the staff about the illicit activities of other prisoners, skill in "conning" and manipulation of staff, and an ability to show strength, courage, and toughness. Criminologists say that there probably no longer exists one overriding inmate subculture, but rather several subcultures that are divided along racial and ethnic lines (Cole & Smith, 2007; Siegel, 2010).

One might ask whether the funds used for institutional care might be put to better use in prevention or community-based services. "The money spent on prisons is money taken from the parts of the public sector that educate, train, socialize, treat, nurture and house the population—particularly the children of the poor" (Currie, 1998, p. 35).

How Institutions Promote Well-being

For small numbers of individuals, institutional placement is the most appropriate alternative both for them and for the rest of society. Some people are clearly a danger to themselves and/or others and need a protective, structured environment. Institutions do have a place in a modern, democratic society. Problems occur when they are overcrowded, underfunded and understaffed, poorly designed, and used by default rather than by plan.

Institutions in Other Countries

In other countries, institutions are still used for purposes that are no longer common in the United States. For example, couples who adopt from abroad may pick up their babies in orphanages in Russia, Romania, China, or Guatemala. Most of these facilities are clean and well run.

Nevertheless, there are investigations that document deplorable conditions in institutions in some places. Recently, for example, Mental Disabilities Rights International, a U.S.-based human rights group, issued a report on the abuse of mentally disabled patients housed in Serbia's psychiatric hospitals (Stojanovic, 2007). There children with disabilities were left tethered to cribs for days. The report attributed abuse and neglect largely to problems of under-staffing and underfunding in a country recovering from a series of civil wars in the 1990s. The same group has documented abuses in institutions in Romania, Hungary, Russia, Turkey, Mexico, Peru, Uruguay, and Argentina.

Social Work in Institutions

Ginsberg (2001) summarizes the many tasks that social workers perform in institutional settings. In hospitals, they work on discharge planning and help patients arrange for financial support. They not only provide social services in long-term care facilities for older adults, but also provide consultation around licensing issues. In prisons, they may be called upon to provide individual counseling and group therapy sessions and to help inmates stay in contact with their families.

Because most clients in institutional settings are involuntary, social workers have a special ethical responsibility to them. Often "it is social workers who must inform those who have been insti-tutionalized or who face institutionalization of their rights or interpret their rights for them. Many times only social workers are available to act as advocates for those who are institutionalized, insur-ing that their rights are recognized and respected" (Saltzman & Proch, 1990, p. 360). In a corrections context in particular, and in other institutional settings as well, social workers must be prepared to advocate "for safe, humane, and equitable treatment of all individuals" (NASW, 2000, p. 57).

CONCLUSION

In this book we have explored the ways in which large systems both promote and deter the well-being of individuals and families. We have suggested that using different perspectives provides conceptual frameworks that are useful in understanding social institutions, social structure, and social settings. It is clear that large systems influence the lives and affect the daily experiences of individuals and families. Given the events of the first decade of this century, it is difficult to predict how these systems may change over the next few years. For example, as this book goes to press, the ramifications of the recent economic crisis are still unfolding and the national debate over health care reform continues.

More so than many other professionals, social workers embrace the idea that people cannot be understood separate from the social environments in which they live. This person-in-environment approach is dependent upon up-to-date information about local, state, national, and global trends. As you complete your formal education, we encourage you to continue to become more knowledgeable about emerging societal trends and changing environmental contexts in order to provide informed and appropriate interventions at all levels of practice, and to promote social and economic justice.

This text could lead students to be pessimistic about the immense power associated with the larger social environment and the potential of social workers to achieve positive change. The reality is that individuals, in connection with other like-minded souls, have the capacity within them to make change occur. When we say we are powerless, we give power away. When we believe we can make a difference, the strengths perspective is realized within ourselves, our colleagues, and those whom we seek to support. As Margaret Mead said, "Never doubt that a small group of thoughtful, committed individuals can change the world: indeed it is the only thing that ever has."

REFERENCES

Abramovitz, M. (2001). Everyone is still on welfare: The role of redistribution in social policy. *Social Work, 46*, 297–308.

Abramowitz, A., & Bishop, B. (2007, March 1). The myth of the middle. *Washington Post*, p. A17.

Adams, J. S. (1963). Toward an understanding of inequity. *Journal of Abnormal and Social Psychology, 67*, 422–436.

Adler, J. (2009, February 16). Why there won't be a revolution. *Newsweek*, pp. 32–34.

AFL-CIO (2007). *Fact and stats.* Retrieved March 7, 2009 from http://www.aflcio.org/issues/safety

Ahmad, M. (2002). Home insecurities: Racial violence the day after September 11. *Social Text, 20* (3 72), 101–115.

Albrecht, G. L. (1992). *The disability business: Rehabilitation in America.* Newbury Park, CA: Thousand Oaks.

Aldrich, H. (1979). *Organizations and environments.* Englewood Cliffs, NJ: Prentice-Hall.

Alter, J. (2006, September 15). Packaging patriotism. *Newsweek*, pp. 52–54.

Alter, J. (2008, August 31). Why the 2008 election is bringing power to the people. *Parade*, pp. 4–5.

Altman, A., Barovick, H., Cruz, G., Fetini, A., Pickert, K., Romero, et al. (2009, April 6). An end to the death penalty. *Time*, p. 15.

Altshuler, A., Morrill, W., Wolman, H., & Mitchell, F. (Eds.). (1999). *Governance and opportunity in metropolitan America.* Washington, DC: National Academic Press.

Amer, M., & Manning, J. E. (2008, December 31). Membership of the 111th Congress: A profile. *Congressional Research Service.* Retrieved March 21, 2009 from http://www.crs.gov

America's wars: U.S. casualties and veterans. (February 8, 2008). *Info please.* Retrieved February 8, 2008 from http://www.infoplease.com/ipa/A0004615.html

American Academy of Child and Adolescent Psychiatry. (2002, November). *Children and TV violence* (Issue Brief No. 13). Retrieved January 24, 2009 from http: //www.aacap.org/cs/root/facts_for_Families/children_and tv_violence

American Academy of Child and Adolescent Psychiatry. (2004, July). *The influence of music and music videos* (Issue Brief No. 40). Retrieved January 24, 2009 from http://www.aacap.org/cs/root/facts_for_families/the_influence_of_music_and_music_videos

American Civil Liberties Union (ACLU). (2001). *Fact sheet on domestic violence.* Retrieved December 6, 2008 from http://www.aclu.org/Womensrights/

American Civil Liberties Union (ACLU). (2007, March 1). *Domestic violence: Protective orders and the role of police enforcement.* Retrieved February 22, 2009 from http://www.aclu.org/womensrights/violence/28743 pub2007 0301.html

American Psychiatric Association. (2000). *Diagnostic and statistical manual of mental disorders (DSM-IV-TR).* Arlington, VA: American Psychiatric Publishing, Inc.

American Psychological Association. (2005, August 19). *Review of research shows that playing violent video games can heighten aggression* [Review of the presentation *violence in video games: A review of the empirical research*]. Retrieved January 24, 2009 from http://www.apa.org/releases/violentvideo

American Psychological Association. (2007). *Psychological needs of military personnel and their families are increasing.* Retrieved December 16, 2008 from apa.org

American Psychological Association. (2008). *Violence on television: What can children learn? What can parents do?* Retrieved January 24, 2009 from http://www.apa.org/pi/vio&tv.html

Amy, D. J. (2005). *What is proportional representation and why do we need this reform?* Retrieved September 19, 2008 from http://www.mtholyoke.edu/acad/polit/damy/BeginningReading/whatispr.htm

Andersen, M. L., & Taylor H. F. (2007). *Sociology: The essentials* (4th ed.). Belmont, CA: Thomson.

Anderson, D. R., Huston, A. C., Schmitt, K. L., Linebarger, D. L., & Wright, J. C. (2001). Early childhood television viewing and adolescent behavior. *Monographs of the Society for Research in Child Development, 66* (1), serial number 264.

Anderson, G. F., Hussey, P. S., Frogner, B. K., & Waters, H. R. (2005). Health spending in the United States and the rest of the industrialized world: Examining the impact of waiting lists and litigation reveals no significant effects on the U.S. health spending differential [Electronic version]. *Health Affairs, 24* (4), 903–914.

Anderson, G. F., Reinhardt, U. E., Hussey, P. S., & Pertosyan, V. (2003). It's the prices, stupid: Why the United States is so different from other countries. *Health Affairs, 22* (3), pp. 89–105.

Anderson, R. E., Carter, I., & Lowe, G. R. (1999). *Human behavior in the social environment: A social systems approach* (5th ed.). Hawthorne, NY: Aldine de Gruyter.

Ang, A. (2007). China bans toxic syrup in toothpaste. *ABC news.* Retrieved October 19, 2007 from http://www.abcnews.go.com

Anker, R. (1998). *Gender and jobs: Sex segregation of occupations in the world.* Geneva: International Labor Organization.

Anti-Defamation League. (2007). *ADL survey: Anti-Semitism in America remains constant; 15 percent of Americans hold 'strong' Anti-Semitic beliefs.* Retrieved

February 21, 2009 from http://www.adl.org/PresRele/ASUS_12/5159_12.htm

Appelbaum, B., & Mellnik, T. (2005, September 4). Black homebuyers far more likely to pay high interest. *The State* [Columbia, SC], p. G5.

Arab American Institute. (2009). *Arab Americans.* Retrieved February 14, 2009 from http://www.aaiusa.org/arab-americans/22/demographics

Arsneault, S. (2006). Implementing welfare reform in rural and urban communities: Why place matters. *American Review of Public Administration, 36,* 173–188.

Assistant Secretary for Planning and Evaluation. (2005). *Overview of the uninsured in the United States: An analysis of the 2005 Current Population Survey.* U.S. Department of Health and Human Services. Retrieved December 30, 2008 from http://aspe.hhs.gov

Aubrey, J. S., & Harrison, K. (2004). The gender-role content of children's favorite television programs and its links to their gender-related perceptions. *Media Psychology, 6,* 111–146.

Austin, E. W., Chen, Y., Pinkleton, B. E., & Johnson, J. Q. (2006, March 3). Benefits and costs of Channel One in a middle school setting and the role of media-literacy training. *Pediatrics, 117.* Retrieved September 28, 2008 from http://www. pediatricsOrg/cgi/content/full/117/e423

Aversa, J. (2006, September 9). Loan study finds inequality. *The State* [Columbia, SC], p. B9.

Baca Zinn, M., Wells, M., & Wells, B. (2000). Diversity within Latino families: New lessons for family social science. In D. H. Demo, K. R. Allen, & M. A. Fine (Eds.), *Handbook of family diversity* (pp. 252–273). New York: Oxford University Press.

Bagdikian, B. H. (2004). *The new media monopoly* (2nd ed.). Boston: Beacon Press.

Bailey, M. J., & Dawood, K. (1998). Behavioral genetics, sexual orientation, and the family. In C. J. Patterson, & A. R. D. Augelli (Eds.), *Lesbian, gay, and bisexual identities in families Psychological perspectives* (pp. 3–18). New York: Oxford University Press.

Bakan, J. (2004). *The corporation: The pathological pursuit of profit and power.* New York: Free Press.

Baker, R. (1997, September/October). The squeeze. *The Columbia Journalism Review,* pp. 30–36.

Baltes, M. M. (1994). Aging well and institutional living: A paradox? In R. P. Abeles, H. C. Gift, & M. G. Ory (Eds.), *Aging and quality of life* (pp. 185–201). New York: Springer.

Banks, J. A. (1997). Arab Americans: Concepts and materials. In J. A. Banks (Ed.), *Teaching strategies for ethnic studies* (6th ed., pp. 489–510). Boston: Allyn & Bacon.

Barber, B. R. (2007). *Consumer: How markets corrupt children, infantilize adults, and swallow citizens whole.* New York: W. W. Norton Company.

Barker, R. L. (2003). *The social work dictionary* (5th ed.). Washington, DC. NASW Press.

Barner, M. B. (1999). Sex-role stereotyping in FCC-mandated children's educational television. *Journal of Broadcasting & Electronic Media, 43,* 551–564.

Barnett, W. S. (1995, Winter). Long-term effects of early childhood programs on cognitive and school outcomes. *The Future of Children, 5,* 25–50.

Barry, P. (2002, June). Drug profits vs. research. *AARP Bulletin,* pp. 8–9, 10.

Barstow, D., & Bergman, L. (2003, January 10). Death on the job, slaps on the wrist. *Wall Street Journal.* Retrieved February 17, 2003 from http://wsj.net/

Bartlett, D. L., & Steele, J. B. (2002, December 16). Indian casinos: Wheel of misfortune. *Time,* pp. 44–58.

Bauer, P. (2008, August 17). A movie, a word and my family's battle. *Washington Post.* Retrieved August 16, 2008 from http://www.washingtonpost.com/wp-dyn/content/article/2008/08/14

Beasley, B., & Collins Standley, T. (2002). Shirts vs. skins: Clothing as an indicator of gender role stereotyping in video games. *Mass Media Communication & Society, 5,* 279–293.

Beasley, C., Jr. (1990). Of pollution and poverty, part 3: Deadly threat on native lands. *Buzzworm, 2* (5), 39–45.

Beeghley, L. (2008). *The structure of social stratification in the United States* (5th ed.). Boston: Allyn & Bacon.

Begley, S. (1995, February 13). Three is not enough: Surprising new lessons from the controversial science of race. *Newsweek,* pp. 67–69.

Begley, S. (2008, March). The myth of "Best in the World." *Newsweek,* p. 47.

Behar, L., Friedman, R., Pinto, A., Katz-Leavy, J., & Jones, J. G. (2007). Protecting youth placed in unlicensed, unregulated residential "treatment" facilities. *Family Court Review, 45,* 399–413.

Bell, C. (1991). Traumatic stress and children in danger. *Journal of Health Care for the Poor and Underserved, 2,* 175–188.

Bell, N. M. (2002, October 31). Mentally ill inmate will move to hospital. *The State* [Columbia, SC], p. B3.

Bellah, R. N. (1967). Civil religion. *Daedalus, 96,* 1–21.

Bergen, R. K. (1996). *Wife rape: Understanding the response of survivors and service providers.* Newbury Park, CA: Sage.

Best, J. (1989) Extending the constructionist perspective: A conclusion and introduction. In J. Best (Ed.), *Images of issues typifying contemporary social problems* (pp. 243–252). New York: Aldine de Gruyter.

Billingsley, C. A. (1992). *Climbing Jacob's ladder: The enduring legacy of African-American families.* New York: Simon & Schuster.

Bishop, B. (2008). *The big sort: Why the clustering of like-minded America is tearing us apart.* Boston: Houghton Mifflin.

Bohm, R. M., & Haley, K. N. (2007). *Introduction to criminal justice* (5th ed.). New York: Glencoe/McGraw-Hill.

Bok, D. (2003). *Universities in the market place: The commercialization of higher education.* Princeton, NJ: Princeton University Press.

Bollinger, L. C. (2003, January 27). Diversity is essential. *Newsweek*, p. 32.

Bonacich, E. (1972). A theory of ethic antagonism: The split labor market. *The American Sociological Review, 37*, 547–549.

Borlik, A. K. (1998). *Military commemorates 50 years of racial integration.* American Forces Press Service. Retrieved December 16, 2008 from http://www.defenselink

Bourdieu, P. (1986). The forms of capital. In J. Richardson (Ed.), *Handbook of theory and research for the sociology of education* (pp. 241–258). New York: Greenwood Press.

Brady Campaign Fact Sheets. Retrieved November 8, 2008 from www.brady.campaign.org/facts/factsheets

Brant, M. (2006, April 24). No child left behind. *Newsweek*, pp. 32–33.

Breslau, K. (2004, October 18). Working to save the west. *Newsweek*, pp. 56–57.

Brewer, D. J., Gates, S. M., & Goldman, C. A. (2002). *In pursuit of prestige: Strategy and competition in U.S. higher education.* New Brunswick: Transaction Publishers.

Bridges, G. S., & Steen, S. (1998). Racial disparities in official assessments of juvenile offenders: Attributional stereotypes as mediating mechanisms. *American Sociological Review, 63*, 554–570.

Brill, A. (2005, March 12). Will love drive out fear, hatred? *The State* [Columbia, SC], p. A9.

Brink, S. (2005, March 28). Health & medicine. *U.S. News & World Report*, pp. 57–58.

Brinson, C. S. (2003, December 6). Public colleges' future grows more uncertain as state funding slides. *The State* [Columbia, SC], p. A7.

Brody, D. (1980). *Workers in industrial America: Essays on the twentieth-century struggle.* New York: Oxford University Press.

Brown, P. L. (2002, July 27). Sex-charged TV steams up airwaves. *Herald-Leader* [Lexington, KY], p. A3.

Brueggemann, W. G. (2006). *The practice of macro social work* (3rd ed.). Belmont, CA: Thomson Brooks/Cole.

Brunori, D. (2005, October 23). Bush's tax panel has a crazy idea. Let's go for it. *Washington Post.* Retrieved October 24, 2005 from http://www.washingtonpost.com

Bullard, R. D. (1990). *Dumping in Dixie: Race, class, and environmental quality.* Boulder, CO: Westview Press.

Bullard, R. D. (2004). Environmental racism. In J. H. Skolnick & E. Currie (Eds.), *Crisis in American institutions* (pp. 237–244). Boston: Pearson.

Bullard, R. D., & Wright, B. H. (1986). The politics of pollution: Implications for the black community. *Phylon, 68* (1), 71–78.

Burbules, N. C. (2000). Universities in transition: The promise and the challenge of new technologies. *Teachers College Record, 102*, 271–294.

Burrell, B. (1996). *A woman's place is in the house: Campaigning for Congress in the feminist era.* Ann Arbor: University of Michigan.

Bush, M. (1980). Institutions for dependent and neglected children: Therapeutic option or choice of last resort? *American Journal of Orthopsychiatry, 50*, 239–255.

Calder, L. G. (1999). *Financing the American Dream: A cultural history of consumer credit.* Princeton, NJ: Princeton University Press.

Califano, J. A., & Sullivan, L. W. (2006, June 29). The flavor of marketing to kids. *Washington Post.* Retrieved June 29, 2006 from http://www.washington.com

Campbell, A. C. (2004). The invisible welfare state: Establishing the phenomenon of twentieth century veteran's benefits. *Journal of Political and Military Sociology, 32*, 249–267.

Campo-Flores, A. (2005, March 21). The battle for Latino souls: Pentecostal churches are using savvy marketing to attract traditionally Catholic Hispanics. A holy struggle in Chicago. *Chicago Tribune*, p. B1.

Canadian Holistic Medical Association. (2008). *What is holistic medicine?* Retrieved November 30, 2008 from http://www.holisticmed.com/whatis.html

Carmichael, M. (2003, May 12). Help from far away. *Newsweek*, p. E16.

Carmichael, M. (2008, December 15). New era, new worry. *Newsweek*, p. 60.

Carothers, S. C. (1990). Catching sense: Learning from our mothers to be black and female. In F. Ginsberg, & A. Lowenhaupt Tsing (Eds.), *Uncertain terms: Negotiating gender in American culture* (pp. 232–247). Boston: Beacon Press.

Castex, G. M. (1994). Providing services to Hispanic/Latino populations: Profiles in diversity. *Social Work, 39*, 288–297.

Catalyst 2008 census of the Fortune 500 reveals women gained little ground advancing to business leadership positions. (2008). *Catalyst.* Retrieved March 7, 2009 from http://www.catalyst.org

Cavanaugh, J. C., & Blanchard-Fields, F. (2002). *Adult development and aging* (4th ed.). Belmont, CA: Wadsworth/Thompson.

Center for American Women and Politics. (2009). *Women in elective office 2009.* Retrieved April 5, 2009 from cawp\informationservices\Factsheets\Fact2009\

Center for Corporate Policy. (2005a). *Corporate crime and abuse: Cracking down on corporate crime.* Retrieved March 4, 2009 from http://www.corporatepolicy.org/issues/crime.htm

Center for Corporate Policy. (2005b). *Corporate crime and abuse: Tracking the problem.* Retrieved March 4, 2009 from http://www.corporatepolicy.org/issues/crimedata.htm

Center for Disease Control. (2006, September 1). Youth exposure to alcohol advertising on radio. *Morbidity & Mortality Weekly Report, 55* (34), 937–940.

Center for Disease Control and Prevention. (2003). *Women, injection drug use, and the criminal justice system.* Retrieved June 30, 2003 from http://www.thebody.com/cdc/women_idu.html

Center for Responsive Politics. (2008). *PAC dollars to incumbents, challengers, and open seat candidates.* Retrieved September 19, 2008 from http://www.opensecrets.org/bigpicture/pac2cands

Center for Responsive Politics. (2009a). *Top industries.* Retrieved April 11, 2009 from http://www.opensecrets.org/lobby/top

Center for Responsive Politics. (2009b). *Top spenders.* Retrieved April 11, 2009 from http://www.opensecrets.org/lobby/top

Center sues to remove monument. (2002, April). *SPLC [Southern Poverty Law Center] Report, 32* (1), p. 4.

Chambliss, W. J. (2007/1973). The saints and the roughnecks. In J. M. Henslin (Ed.), *Down-to-earth sociology: Introductory readings* (14th ed.). New York: The Free Press.

Cherlin, A. J. (2008). *Public and private families: An introduction.* New York: McGraw-Hill.

Cherniss, C. (1980). *Staff burnout: Job stress in the human services.* Beverly Hills, CA: Sage.

Chesney-Lind, M. (2002). Imprisoning women: The unintended victims of mass imprisonment. In M. Mauer and M. Chesney-Lind (Eds.), *Invisible punishment: The Collateral consequences of mass imprisonment* (pp. 79–94). New York: The New Press.

Chess, W. A., & Norlin, J. M. (1991). *Human behavior and the social environment: A social systems model* (2nd ed.). Boston: Allyn & Bacon.

Chinchilla, N., Hamilton, N., & Loucky, J. (1993). Central Americans in Los Angeles: An immigrant community in transition. In J. Moore, & R. Pinderhughes (Eds.), *In the barrios: Latinos and the underclass debate* (pp. 51–78). New York: Russell Sage Foundation.

Churchill, W. (1994). *Indians are us? Culture and genocide in Native North America.* Monroe, ME: Common Courage.

Cieslewicz, D. J. (2001). The environmental impacts of sprawl. In G. D. Squires (Ed.), *Urban sprawl: Causes, consequences & policy responses* (pp. 23–38). Washington, DC: The Urban Institute.

Close, E. (2000, September 18). What's white anyway? *Newsweek*, pp. 64–65.

Cloward, R. A., & Ohlin, L. E. (1960). *Delinquency and opportunity: A theory of delinquent gangs.* New York: Free Press.

Cohen, L. (2003). *A consumers' republic: The politics of mass consumption in postwar America.* New York: Alfred A. Knopf.

Cole, G. F., & Smith, C. E. (2007). *The American system of criminal justice* (11th ed.). Belmont, CA: Thomson Wadsworth.

Coleman, J. S. (1988). Social capital in the creation of human capital. *American Journal of Sociology, 94* (supplement), S95–S120.

Collins, R. (1979). *The credentialed society: An historical sociology of education and stratification.* New York: Academic Press.

Collins, S. (1989). The marginalization of black executives. *Social Problems, 36,* 317–331.

Collins, S. (1993). Blacks on the bubble: The vulnerability of black executives in white corporations. *Sociological Quarterly, 34,* 429–448.

Coltrane, S. (2000). Research on household labor: Modeling and measuring the social embeddedness of routine family work. *Journal of Marriage and the Family, 62,* 1208–1233.

Common Cause. (2000, November 14). *98 percent of house incumbents win reelection in 2000.* Retrieved January 13, 2001 from http://www.commoncause.org/publications/nov00

Compa, L., & Fellner, J. (2005, August 3). Meatpacking's human toll. *Washington Post.* Retrieved August 3, 2005 from http://www.washingtonpost.com

Connolly, C. (2008, December 4). Obama policymakers turn to campaign tools. *Washington Post.* Retrieved December 11, 2008 from http://www.washingtonpost.com/

Coontz, S. (1988). *The social origins of private life: A history of American families 1600–1900.* New York: Verso.

Coontz, S. (1992). *The way we never were: American families and the nostalgia trap: The myth of the traditional family.* New York: Basic Books.

Cooperman, A. (2005, October 20). Bush's faith plan faces judgment: Court assesses mission to give federal funds to religious charities. *Washington Post.* Retrieved October 20, 2005 from http://www.washingtonpost.com

Copeland, L. (2008, June 17). South's rural towns shrink as economic troubles grow. *USA Today*, pp. A1–A2.

Cose, E. (1993). *The rage of a privileged class.* New York: HarperCollins.

Cosgrove, L., Krimsky, S., & Vijayaraghavan, M. (2006). Financial ties between DSM-IV panel members and the pharmaceutical industry [Electronic version]. *Psychotherapy and Psychosomatics, 75,* 154–160.

Council on Social Work Education. (2008). *Educational policy and accreditation standards.* Alexandria, VA: Council on Social Work Education.

Cox, T. H. (1993). *Cultural diversity in organizations: Theory, research, and practice.* San Francisco: Berrett-Koehler.

Craig, G. J. (1999). *Human development* (8th ed.). Upper Saddle River, NJ: Prentice Hall.

Croteau, D., & Hoynes, W. (2003). *Media society: Industries, images, and audiences* (3rd ed.).Thousand Oaks, CA: Pine Forge Press.

Crumbo, C. (2003, May 25). Military attracts blue-collar recruits. *The State* [Columbia, SC], pp. A1, A10.

Cruikshank, M. (1992). *The gay and lesbian liberation movement.* New York: Routledge.

Curran, J. (1992). Mass media and democracy. In J. Curran, & M. Gurevitch (Eds.), *Mass media and society* (pp. 82–117). London: Edward Arnold.

Currie, E. (1998). *Crime and punishment in America.* New York: Metropolitan Books.

Dale, J. G., Andreatta, S., & Freeman, E. (2001). Language and the migrant worker experience in rural North Carolina Communities. In A. D. Murphy, C. Blanchard, & J. A. Hill (Eds.), *Latino workers in the contemporary south* (pp. 93–104). Athens, GA: University of Georgia Press.

Datiles, J. M. (2008, September 26). *Fighting against eugenic abortions: Federal legislation protecting Down Syndrome babies passes Senate and House.* Retrieved March 1, 2009 from http://blog.aul.org/2008/09/26/

Davis, K., & Moore, W. (1945). Some principles of stratification. *The American Sociological Review, 10*, 242–249.

Davis, N. J., & Robinson, R. V. (1996). Are the rumors of war exaggerated? Religious orthodoxy and moral progressivism in America. *American Journal of Sociology, 102,* 756–785.

Day, P. J. (2009). *A new history of social welfare* (6th ed.) Boston: Allyn & Bacon.

Death Penalty Information Center. (2009). *Facts about the death penalty.* Retrieved August 28, 2009 from http://www.deathpenaltyinfo.org/

Deavers, K. (1992). What is rural? *Policies Studies Journal, 20,* 183–189.

Deegan, P. E. (1993). Recovering our sense of value after being labeled mentally ill. *Journal of Psychosocial Nursing, 15*, 3–19.

Delgado, M. (1998). Latina-owned businesses: Community resources for the prevention field. *Journal of Primary Prevention, 18*, 447–460.

Delpit, L. (1995). *Other people's children: Cultural conflict in the classroom.* New York: New Press.

Devine, P. G. (1995). Prejudice and out-group perception. In A. Tesser (Ed.), *Advanced social psychology.* New York: McGraw Hill.

DiNitto, D. M., & Cummins, L. K. (2007). *Social welfare: Politics and public policy (Research navigator Edition, with themes of the times for social welfare policy)* (6th ed.). Boston: Allyn & Bacon.

Dionne, E. J., Jr. (2007, March 16). Christians who won't toe the line. *Washington Post.* Retrieved March 16, 2007 from http://www.washingtonpost.com

Dionne, E. J., Jr. (2008, August 19). The new evangelical politics. *Washington Post.* Retrieved August 19, 2008 from http://www.washingtonpost.com

Draper, E. (1993). Fetal exclusion policies and gendered constructions of suitable work. *Social Problems, 40*, 90–107.

Duany, A., Plater-Zyberk, E., & Speck, J. (2000). *Suburban nation: The rise of sprawl and the decline of the American dream.* New York: North Point Press.

Duke, L. (2007, March 20). A well of pain. *Washington Post.* Retrieved March 20, 2007 from http://www.washingtonpost.com

Durkeim, E. (1965/1912). *The elementary forms of the religious life.* New York: Free Press.

Dye, T. R. (1998). *Understanding public policy* (9th ed.). Upper Saddle River, NJ: Prentice Hall.

Dyer, J. (2000). *The perpetual prisoner machine: How America profits from crime.* Boulder, CO: Westview Press.

Economic Policy Institute. (2002). *Pulling apart: A state by state analysis of income trends.* Retrieved August 25, 2003 from http://www/epi.org

Ehrenreich, B. (2001). *Nickel and dimed: On (not) getting by in America.* New York: Metropolitan Books.

Ellison, J. (2008, December 15). A new grip on life. *Newsweek*, p. 64.

Emery, E. (2007, April 16). TBI: Hidden wounds plague Iraq War veterans. *The Denver Post.* Retrieved April 16, 2007 from http://www.veteransforcommonsense.org/articleid/7406

Engels, F. (1902/1884). *The origin of the family.* Chicago: Charles H. Kerr.

Engstrom, J. D. (2001). Industry and immigration in Dalton, Georgia. In A. D. Murphy, C. Blanchard, & J. A. Hill (Eds.), *Latino workers in the contemporary South* (pp. 44–56). Athens, GA: University of Georgia Press.

Ephron, D. (2007, November 26). A learning disability. *Newsweek*, pp. 40–41.

Epstein, H. (2003, October 12). Enough to make you sick? *The New York Times.* Retrieved October 12, 2003 from www.nytimes.com/2003/10/12/magazine/12HEALTH.html

Escott, P. D., & Goldfield, D. R. (1991). *The South for new southerners.* Chapel Hill: University of North Carolina Press.

Etzioni, A. (1964). *Modern organizations.* Englewood cliffs, NJ: Prentice Hall.

Ewalt, P., & Mokuau, N. (1996). Self-determination from a Pacific perspective. In P. L. Ewalt, M. Freeman, S. A. Kirk, & D. L. Poole (Eds.), *Multicultural issues in social work* (pp. 255–268). Washington, DC: NASW Press.

Falicov, C. J. (1998). *Latino families in therapy: A guide to multicultural practice.* New York: The Guilford Press.

Feagan, J. R., & Parker, R. (1990). *Building American cities: The urban real estate game* (2nd ed.). Englewood Cliffs, NJ: Prentice-Hall.

Feagan, J. R., & Sikes, M. P. (1994). *Living with racism: The black middle class experience.* Boston: Beacon.

Feagin, J. R. (1991). The continuing significance of race: Antiblack discrimination in public places. *American Sociological Review, 56*, 101–116.

Feagin J. R., & Feagin, C. B. (1999). *Racial and ethnic relations* (6th ed.). Englewood Cliffs, NJ: Prentice-Hall.

Federal Election Commission. (2008). *FEC records slight increase in the number of PACs.* Retrieved

September 19, 2008 from http://www.fec.gov/press/press2008/20080117paccount.shtml

Federal minimum wage hike affects relatively few workers. (2008, July 27). *The State* [Columbia, SC], p. A18.

Fellin, P. (1995). *The community and the social worker* (2nd ed.). Itasca, IL: F. E. Peacock.

Fineman, H., & Lipper, T. (2003, January 27). Spinning race. *Newsweek*, pp. 26–29.

Finnigan, T. (2007, March 7). *All about pork: The abuse of earmarks and the needed reforms. Citizens against Government Waste*. Retrieved April 11, 2009 from http://www.cagw.org/site/PageServer?pagename=reports_earmarks

Fixico, D. L. (2002). The reservation conflict continues. In T. O'Neill (Ed.), *The Indian reservation system* (pp. 113–125). San Diego, CA: Greenhaven Press.

Fletcher, M. A. (2008, January 21). Highly skilled and out of work. *Washington Post*. Retrieved January 21, 2008 from http://www.washingtonpost.com

Flora, J. L., Flora, C. B., & Houdek, E. (1992). *Rural communities: Legacy and change* (Study guide). Boulder, CO: Westview Press.

Foley, M. W., McCarthy, J. D., & Chaves, M. (2001). Social capital, religious institutions, and poor communities. In S. Saegert, J. P. Thompson, & M. R. Warren (Eds.), *Social capital and poor communities* (pp. 215–245). New York: Russell Sage Foundation.

Fontes, L. A. (2005). *Child abuse and culture: Working with diverse families*. New York: Guilford Press.

Foucault, M. (1990). *The history of sexuality: An introduction* (R. Hurley, Trans.). New York: Vintage.

Fouhy, B. (2008, November 10). Obama team works for "wired" presidency. *The State* [Columbia, SC], p. A4.

Fouts, G., & Burggraf, K. (1999). Television situation comedies: Female body image and verbal reinforcements. *Sex Roles, 40,* 473–481.

Fox, J. (2007, December 10). The end of spend. *Time*, pp. 56–57.

Fox, J. (2008, April 14). Holding back the flood. *Time*, p. 44.

Fox, J. A. (2008). Fueling a contagion of campus bloodshed. *Chronicle of Higher Education, 54*, A36.

Freedman, M. (2009, February 16). Big government is back – big time. *Newsweek*, pp. 24–28.

Freedman, R. I. (1995). Developmental disabilities: Direct practice. In R. L. Edwards et al. (Eds.), *Encyclopedia of Social Work* (19th ed., Vol. 1, pp. 721–729). Washington, DC: NASW Press.

Freking, K. (2008). Children's food ad tab: $1.6 billion. *The State* [Columbia, SC], pp. A9–A10.

French, R. (2009, March 22). Church striking at stained-glass ceiling. *The State* [Columbia, SC], p. B6.

Friedman, A. (1976, September). On politics and design. *Contract*, pp. 6, 10, 12.

Friedman, T. L. (2002, May 14). Satellites, Internet spread hate, not understanding. *The State* [Columbia, SC], p. A9.

Friedrich, L. K., & Stein, A. H. (1975). Prosocial television and young children: The effects of verbal labeling and role playing on learning and behavior. *Child Development, 46,* 27–38.

Fry, R. (2007, June 6). *How far behind in math and reading are English language learners?* Pew Hispanic Center, Retrieved September 26, 2007 from http://pewhispanic.org/reports.

Fuller-Thomson, E., & Minkler, M. (2000). African American grandparents raising grandchildren: A national profile of demographic and health characteristics. *Health & Social Work, 25,* 109–118.

Gagné, P., Tewksbury, R., & McGaughey, D. (1997). Coming out and crossing over: Identity formation and proclamation in a transgender community. *Gender and Society, 11,* 478–508.

Gagnon, M., & Lexchin, J. (2008, January). The cost of pushing pills: A new estimate of pharmaceutical promotion expenditures in the United States [Electronic version]. *PLoS Medicine, 5* (1), pp. 29–33.

Gallimore, R., Boggs, J. W., & Jordan, C. (1974). *Culture, behavior and education: A study of Hawaiian-Americans*. Beverley Hills, CA: Sage Publications.

Galloway, K., & Kutchins, P. (2007). *Prison town, USA*. Public Broadcasting System. Retrieved August 27, 2007 from http://www.pbs.org/pov/pov2007/prisontown/for.html

Gamboa, S. (2008, May 1). S.C.'s Hispanic growth leads all states. *The State* [Columbia, SC], p. A3.

Garbarino, J. (1992). *Children and families in the social environment* (2nd ed.). New York: Aldine de Gruyter.

Garbarino, J., Galambos, N. L., Plantz, M. C., & Kostelny, K. (1992). The territory of childhood. In J. Garbarino (Ed.), *Children and families in the social environment* (2nd ed.). New York: Aldine de Gruyter.

Garnets, L. D., & D'Augelli, A. R. (1994). Empowering lesbian and gay communities: A call for collaboration with community psychology. *American Journal of Community, 22*, 447–470.

Garnett, R. W. (2008, January 28). When Catholicism was the target. *USA Today*, p. 9A.

Gays in arms: Can gays in the military work? In countries around the world, they already do. (1992). The Free Library. Retrieved February 26, 2009 from http://www.thefreelibrary.com

Geis, G. (1999). Is incarceration an appropriate sanction for the nonviolent white-collar offender? Yes. In C. B. Fields (Ed.), *Controversial issues in corrections* (pp. 152–158). Boston: Allyn & Bacon.

Geller, A. (2003, August 10). Rural South reels as plants move out, ship jobs abroad. *The State* [Columbia, SC], pp. F1, F4.

George, J. (2007, December 31). Candidates come marching in with religion. *Chicago Tribune*, pp. 1, 8.

Gerbner, G., Gross, L., Morgan, M., & Signorielli, N. (1982). Charting the mainstream: Television's contributions to political orientations. *Journal of Communication, 32*, 100–127.

Gerbner, G., Gross, L., Morgan, M., & Signorielli, N. (1994). Growing up with television: The cultivation perspective. In J. Bryant and D. Zillmann (Eds.), *Media effects: Advances in theory and research* (pp. 17–41). Hillsdale, NJ: Lawrence Erlbaum.

Gerencher, K. (2005, July 14). Americans pay more for care than anyone. *The State* [Columbia, SC], pp. A1, A5.

Germain, C. B. (1991). *Human behavior in the social environment: An ecological view.* New York: Columbia University Press.

Germain, C., & Gitterman, A. (1995). Ecological perspective. In R. L. Edwards et al. (Eds.), *Encyclopedia of Social Work* (19th ed., Vol. I, pp. 816–824). Washington, DC: NASW Press.

Gibbs, N. (2008, October 13). Real patriots don't spend. *Time*, p. 96.

Gillborn, D. (1992). Citizenship, "race," and the hidden curriculum. *International Studies in the Sociology of Education, 2*, 57–73.

Gilson, S. F., & DePoy, E. (2002). Theoretical approaches to disability content in social work education. *Journal of Social Work Education, 37*, 153–165.

Ginsberg, L. H. (1993). *Social work in rural communities* (2nd ed.). Alexandria, VA: Council on Social Work Education.

Ginsberg, L. H. (2001). *Careers in social work* (2nd ed.). Boston: Allyn & Bacon.

Gitlin, T. (2001). *Media unlimited: How the torrent of images sounds overwhelms our lives.* New York: Metropolitan Books.

Glausiusz, J. (2008, Winter). Dying for a manicure? *On Earth,* p. 16.

Goering, J., Kamely, A., & Richardson, T. (1997). Recent research on racial segregation and poverty concentration in public housing in the United States. *The Urban Affairs Review, 32*, 723–745.

Goffman, E. (1961). *Asylums: Essays on the social situation of mental patients and other inmates.* Chicago: Aldine.

Goffman, E. (1963). *Stigma: Notes on the management of spoiled identity.* Englewood Cliffs, NJ: Prentice Hall.

Goffman, E. (1974). *Frame analysis: An essay on the organization of experience.* Boston: Northeastern University Press.

Gold, S. J. (1999). Southeast Asians. In E. R. Barkan (Ed.), *A nation of peoples: America's multicultural heritage* (pp. 505–519). Westport, CT: Greenwood Press.

Golding, P., & Murdock, G. (1992). Culture, communications, and political economy. In J. Curran and M. Gurevitch (Eds.), *Mass media and society* (pp. 15–32). London: Edward Arnold.

Goldscheider, F. K., & Bures, R. (2003). The racial crossover in family complexity in the United States. *Demography, 40*, 569–587.

Gonzales, P. B. (1993). Historical poverty, restructuring effects, and integrative ties: Mexican American neighborhoods in a peripheral sunbelt economy. In J. Moore and R. Pinderhughes (Eds.), *In the barrios: Latinos and the underclass debate* (pp. 149–171). New York: Russell Sage Foundation.

Goodman, P. S. (2008, July 20). Too big to fail? *The New York Times.* Retrieved April 5, 2009 from http://www.nytimes.com

Goodstein, L. (2007, February 25). Gay issue might tear churches apart: Episcopalians may face banishment if they keep accepting homosexuals. *The State* [Columbia, SC], p. A9.

Gordon, D. M. (1973). Capitalism, class and crime in America. *Crime and Delinquency, 19*, 163–186.

Gould, E. (2003). *The university in a corporate culture.* New Haven, CT: Yale University Press.

Goulden, J. C. (1971). *The money givers.* New York: Random House.

Gramick, J. (1983). Homophobia: A new challenge. *Social Work, 28,* 137–141.

Green, C. R., Ndao-Brumblay, S. K., West, B., & Washington, T. (2005). Differences in prescription opioid analgesic availability: Comparing minority and white pharmacies across Michigan. *The Journal of Pain, 6* (10), 689–699.

Greenberg, D. F. (1988). *The construction of homosexuality.* Chicago: University of Chicago Press.

Greene, R. R. (1999). Ecological perspectives: An eclectic theoretical framework for social work practice. In R. R. Greene (Ed.), *Human behavior theory and social work practice* (2nd ed., pp. 259–300). New York: Aldine de Gruyter.

Greenstein, R. (2007, September 18). Misreading the poverty data. *Washington Post.* Retrieved September 19, 2007 from http://www.washingtonpost.com

Gross, D. (2009, March 9). Reigning in bubbles so they won't pop. *Newsweek,* pp. 44–46.

Grunwald, M. (2007, November 12). Down on the farm. *Time*, pp. 26–36.

Grusky, D. B. (1994). The contours of social stratification. In D. B. Grusky (Ed.), *Social stratification: Class, race, and gender in sociological perspective* (pp. 3–35). Boulder, CO: Westview Press.

Guerard, E. B. (2002). GAO: Tax credits help neediest students least. *Education Daily, 35* (117). Retrieved November 25, 2003 from Expanded Academic database.

Gupta, S. (2008, December 8). Slender in the grass. *Time*, p. 60.

Gutierrez, D. G. (1999). Mexicans. In E. R. Barkan (Ed.), *A nation of peoples: A sourcebook on America's multicultural heritage* (pp. 373–390). Westport, CT: Greenwood Press.

Hahn, H. (1991). Alternate views of empowerment: Social services and civil rights (Editorial). *The Journal of Rehabilitation, 57* (4), 17–20.

Hajela, D. (2007, December 13). Some families in the US rejoice after changes to rules for crack-cocaine sentences. *The State* [Columbia, SC]. Retrieved December 14, 2007 from http://www.thestate.com/nation-extra/v-print/story/256707.html

Halebar, J. (2002, September 9). Beauty shops offer breast cancer information. *The State* [Columbia, SC], p. B5.

Haneef, S. (1993). *What everyone should know about Islam and Muslims.* Chicago: Kazi Publications.

Haney, C. (2005). *Death by design: Capital punishment as social psychological system.* New York: Oxford University Press.

Hannan, M. T., & Carroll, G. R. (1992). *Dynamics of organizational populations: Density, legitimation, and competition.* New York: Oxford University press.

Hart, S., & Spivak, A. (1993) *The elephant in the bedroom: Automobile dependence and denial; impacts on the economy and environment.* Pasadena, CA: New Paradigm Books.

Hartman, T. (2002). *Unequal protection: The rise of corporate dominance and the theft of human rights.* New York: St. Martin's Press.

Hate Websites Active in 2008. (2009, Spring). *Intelligence Report*, pp. 59–65.

Hearn, G. (1979). General systems theory in social work. In F. J. Turner (Ed.), *Social work treatment* (pp. 333–359). New York: Free Press.

Heath, S. B. (1982). Questioning at home and at school: A comparative study, doing the ethnography of schooling. In G. Spindler (Ed), *Educational anthropology in action.* New York: Holt, Rinehart, Winston.

Heilbroner, R. (1993). *21st century capitalism.* New York: W. W. Norton & Company.

Heinlein, G., & Cain, C. (2008, May 2). Prison costs on agenda: Experts to discuss reforms to help state handle corrections spending. *Detroit News.* Retrieved May 8, 2008 from http://www.detnews.com

Helgesen, S. (1990). *The female advantage: Women's ways of leadership.* New York: Doubleday.

Helling, A. (2002). Transportation, land use, and the impacts of sprawl on poor children and families. In G. D. Squires (Ed.), *Urban sprawl: Causes, consequences & policy responses* (pp. 119–139). Washington, DC: The Urban Institute.

Helminiak, D. A. (1994). *What the Bible really says about homosexuality.* San Francisco: Alamo Square Press.

Hendren, J. (2005, February 25). Bill would end ban on gays in military. *Los Angeles Times*, p. A8.

Henslin, J. M. (2001). *Sociology: A down-to-earth approach.* Boston: Allyn & Bacon.

Henslin, J. M. (2008). *Sociology: A down-to-earth approach* (9th ed.). Boston: Allyn & Bacon.

Herbert, B. (2006, June 20). Possible change on the killing floor. *The State* [Columbia, SC], p. A9.

Here! Gay television on demand. Here TV. Retrieved January 24, 2009 from http://www.heretv.com/AAboutPage.php

Herman, D. (2001). The rape culture. In J. J. Macionis, & N. V. Benokraitis (Eds.), *Seeing ourselves: Classic, contemporary, and cross-cultural readings in sociology* (5th ed.). Upper Saddle River, NJ: Prentice-Hall.

Hernandez, R., & Chen, D. W. (2008, October 19). Companies donate to lawmakers' pet charities. *The State* [Columbia, SC], p. A14.

Herring, R. D. (1999). *Counseling with Native American Indians and Alaska natives: Strategies for helping professionals.* Thousand Oaks, CA: Sage.

Hersch, J. (2006, April 14). *Skin color and wages among new U.S. immigrants.* Cambridge, MA: Society of Labor Economists.

Hertz, T. (2006, April 26). Understanding mobility in America. *American Progress.* Retrieved April 15, 2009 from http://www.americanprogress.org/issues/2006/04/

Herzberg, F. (1986/1968). One more time: How do you motivate employees? In M. T. Matteson, & J. M. Ivancevich (Eds.), *Management classics* (3rd ed., pp. 282–297). Plano, TX: Business Publications, Inc.

Herzog, J. R. (2008). *Secondary trauma in family members of combat veterans.* Unpublished dissertation, University of South Carolina.

Hickson, D. J. (1987). Decision-making at the top of organizations. *Annual Review of Sociology, 131*, 165–192.

Hill, J., & Cheadle, R. (1996). *The Bible tells me so: Uses and abuses of holy scripture.* New York: Anchor/Doubleday.

Hill, R. B. (1999). *The strengths of African American families: Twenty-five years later.* Lanham, MD: University Press of America.

Hillery, G. (1955). Definitions of community: Areas of agreement. *Rural Sociology, 20*, 111–123.

Himmelstein, D. U., Warren, E., Thorne, D., & Woolhandler, S. (2005, February 2). Illness and injury as contributors to bankruptcy. *Health Affairs* (Web Exclusive). DOI: 10.1377/hlthaff.w5.63

Hine, T. (2002). *I want that! How we all became shoppers [a cultural history].* New York: HarperCollins.

Ho, M. K. (1987). Family therapy with Asian/Americans. In M. K. Ho (Ed.), *Family therapy with ethnic minorities* (pp. 24–38). Beverly Hills, CA: Sage.

Hochschild, A. (1989). *The second shift: Working parents and the revolution at home.* New York: Viking.

Hodge, B. J., Anthony, W. P., & Gailes, L. M. (1996). *Organization theory: A strategic approach* (5th ed.). Upper Saddle River, NJ: Prentice Hall.

Hodson, R., & Sullivan, T. A. (1990). *The social organization of work.* Belmont, CA: Wadsworth.

Hoff, M. D., & Rogge, M. E. (1996). Everything that rises must converge: Developing a social work response to environmental injustice. *Journal of Progressive Human Services, 7*, 41–57.

Holland, T. P., & Petchers, M. K. (1987). Organizations: Context for social service delivery. In A. Minahan et al.

(Eds.), *Encyclopedia of Social Work* (18th ed., Vol. 2, pp. 204–215). Silver Spring, MD: National Association of Social Workers.

Holland, T. P. (1995). Organizations: Context for social service delivery. In R. L. Edwards et al. (Eds.), *Encyclopedia of Social Work* (19th ed., Vol. 2, pp. 1787–1794). Washington, DC: NASW Press.

Holtzclaw, J. (1993, Winter). America's autos on welfare: A summary of studies. *Transportopia Bulletin*, p. 11.

Homans, G. C. (1986/1941). The Western electric researches. In M. T. Matteson, & J. M. Ivancevich (Eds.), *Management classics* (3rd ed. pp. 35–43). Plano, TX: Business Publications, Inc. (Originally published in *Fatigue of Workers* by George C. Homans, Reinhold, 1941, pp. 56–65).

Homicide charges should be brought against Blackwater (2007, October 18). *Corporate Crime Reporter.* Retrieved October 19, 2007 from http://www. corporatecrimereporter.com/blackwater

Houser, A. N. (2007). *Nursing homes.* American Association of Retired Persons. Retrieved April 25, 2008 from http://www.aarp.org/research/longtermcare/nursing homes/

Huling, T. (2002). Building a prison economy in rural America. In M. Mauer and M. Chesney-Lind (Eds.), *Invisible punishment: The collateral consequences of mass imprisonment* (pp. 197–213). New York: The New Press.

Human Rights Campaign. (2007). *The U.S. military: Where it's illegal for gay people to be honest.* Retrieved February 26, 2009 from http://www.hrc.org/

Human Rights Campaign. (2008a). *Parenting laws: Joint adoption.* Retrieved February 26, 2009 from http://www.hrc.org/

Human Rights Campaign. (2008b). *Parenting laws: Second parent adoption.* Retrieved February 26, 2009 from http://www.hrc.org/

Human Rights Campaign. (2008c). *State hate crimes laws.* Retrieved August 6, 2008 from http://www.hrc.org/

Human Rights Campaign. (2008d). *Statewide employment laws & policies.* Retrieved February 26, 2009 from http://www.hrc.org/state_laws

Human Rights Campaign. (2009a). *About hate crimes.* Retrieved February 26, 2009 from http://www.hrc.org/issues/hate_crimes/

Human Rights Campaign. (2009b). *Marriage equality & other relationship recognition laws.* Retrieved September 2, 2009 from http://www.hrc.org/documents/Relationship_Recognition_Laws_Map.pdf

Human Rights Watch. (1999). *Red Onion State Prison: Super-maximum security confinement in Virginia.* Retrieved August 2, 2005 from http:/hrw.org/legacy/reports/1999/redonion

Human Rights Watch, & ACLU. (2008). *A violent education: corporal punishment of children in US public schools.*

Retrieved April 25, 2009 from http://www.hrw.org/en/reports/2008/08/19/violent-education

Hunter, J. D. (1991). *Culture wars: The struggle to define America.* New York: Basic Books.

Hutson, J. (1998). *"A Wall of Separation:" FBI helps restore Jefferson's obliterated draft.* The Library of Congress. Retrieved December 22, 2008 from http://www.loc.gov

Iannello, K. (1992). *Decisions without hierarchy: Feminist interventions in organization theory and practice.* New York: Rutledge.

Inequality and health care. (2006, December 14). *Washington Post.* Retrieved December 13, 2006 from http://www.washingtonpost.com

Irons, E. D., & Moore, G. W. (1985). *Black managers: The case of the banking industry.* New York: Praeger.

Ironson, G. (1992). Work, job stress, and health. In S. Zedeck (Ed.), *Work, families, and organizations* (pp. 33–69). San Francisco: Jossey-Bass.

Isaacs, J. B. (2007a, November). *Economic mobility of black and white families.* Brookings Institution Economic Mobility Project. Retrieved November 14, 2007 from http://www.brookings.edu/papers/2007/11-blackwhite_isaacs.aspx?

Isaacs, J. B. (2007b, November). *Economic mobility of families across generations.* Brookings Institution Economic Mobility Project. Retrieved November 14, 2007 from http://www.brookings.edu/papers/2007/11-generations_isaacs.aspx?

Isaacs, J. B. (2007c, November). *Economic mobility of men and women.* Brookings Institution Economic Mobility Project. Retrieved November 14, 2007 from http://www.brookings.edu/papers/2007/11-menwomen_isaacs.aspx?

Isaacson, W. (2009, February 16). How to save your newspaper. *Time*, pp. 31–33.

Isikoff, M., & Reno, J. (2007, October 29). How do you fund a war, but not the casualties? *Newsweek*, p. 10.

Jackson, D. (2007, June 2). With children, sound crowds out sense. *The State* [Columbia, SC], p. A9.

Jackson, J. (2003, July 27). Old South holds back new South's potential. *The State* [Columbia, SC], p. D3.

Jackson, K. (1985). *Crabgrass frontier: The suburbanization of the United States.* New York: Oxford University Press.

Jacobson, M. F., & Mazur, L. A. (1995). *Marketing madness: A survival guide for consumer society.* Boulder, CO: Westview Press.

James, D., & Glaze, L. (2006). *Mental health problems of prison and jail inmates.* Washington, DC: Bureau of Justice Statistics.

Jargowsky, P. A. (1997). *Poverty and place: Ghettos, barrios and the American city.* New York: Russell Sage Foundation.

Jargowsky, P. A. (2002). Sprawl, concentration of poverty, and urban inequality. In G. D. Squires (Ed.), *Urban sprawl: Causes, consequences & policy responses* (pp. 39–72). Washington, DC: The Urban Institute.

Jargowsky, P. A. (2003, May). *Stunning progress, hidden problems: The dramatic decline of concentrated poverty in the 1990s.* Retrieved May 28, 2003 from http://www.brookings.edu/es/urban/publications/jargowskypoverty.htm

Jennings, J., & Rentner, D. S. (2006, October). Ten big effects of the No Child Left Behind Act on public schools. Phi Delta Kappan, pp. 110–113.

Johnson, K. M. (1999). The rural rebound. *Reports on America, 1* (3), 1–21.

Johnson, M. M., & Rhodes, R. (2007). Institutionalization: A theory of human behavior and the social environment. *Advances in Social Work, 8* (1), 219–236.

Johnson, R. (2008, November 5). Where is gay marriage legal? *Gay Life.* Retrieved February 26, 2009 from http://gaylife.about.com/od/samesexmarriage/a/legalgaymarriage

Johnson, S. (2009). The quiet coup. *The Atlantic.* Retrieved April 5, 2009 from http://www.theatlantic.com/

Jones, L., & Newman, L. (2000). Our America: Life and death on the south side of Chicago. In D. N. Sattler, G. P. Kramer, V. Shabatay, & D. A. Bernstein (Eds.), *Lifespan development in context: Voices and perspectives* (pp. 116–121). Boston: Houghton Mifflin.

Jones, S. J. (2006). *Sunday morning apartheid: A diversity study of the Sunday morning talk shows.* Retrieved January 24, 2009 from http://www.nul.org/publications/policyinstitute/Apartheid_report.pdf

Joseph, N., & Stone, B. (2005, April 25). Diagnosis: Internet phobia. *Newsweek*, p. 74.

Joyce, C. A. (2008). *The world almanac and book of facts.* New York: Reader's Digest.

Kaiser Family Foundation. (2005). *Sex on TV.* Retrieved December 15, 2008 from http://www.kff.org

Kaiser Family Foundation. (2007). *New study finds that food in the top product seen advertised by children.* Retrieved December 15, 2008 from http://www.kff.org.entmedia

Kalb, C., & Juarez, V. (2005, August 1). Small is beautiful. *Newsweek*, pp. 46–57.

Kanter, R. M. (1993/1977). *Men and women of the corporation.* New York: Basic Books.

Kantrowitz, B. (2004, August 30). Education: Not head of the class. *Newsweek*, p. 9.

Kaplan, M. S., Huguet, N., McFarland, B., & Newsom, J. T. (2007). Suicide among male veterans: A perspective population-based study. *Journal of Epidemiol Community Health, 61* (7), 619–624.

Karger, H. J., & Stoesz, D. (2010). *American social welfare policy: A pluralist approach* (6th ed.). Boston: Allyn & Bacon.

Kehoe, A. B. (1999). American Indians. In E. R. Barkan (Ed.), *A nation of peoples: A sourcebook on American's multicultural heritage* (pp. 48–74). Westport, CT: Greenwood Press.

Kelly, N. (2008). The voice on the other end of the phone. [Electronic edition]. *Health Affairs, 27* (6), 1701–1706.

Kelley, T. (2007, October 28). Same-sex couples say civil unions fall short. *San Francisco Chronicle*, p. A13.

Kendall, D. (2008). *Sociology in our times* (7th ed.). Belmont, CA: Wadsworth.

Kerley, D. (2007, May 23). US to China on pet food: The marker will be the enforcer! *ABC news.* Retrieved October 19, 2007 from http://www.abcnews.go.com

Kershaw, S. (2005, April 5). Crisis of Indian children intensifies as families fail. *The New York Times*, p. A13.

Kerwin, A. M. (1992, June 13). Behind the waltzing. *Editor and Publisher*, p. 18.

Kilbourne, J. (1999). *Deadly persuasion: Why women and girls must fight the addictive power of advertising.* New York: The Free Press.

Kilman, C. (2007, Spring). This is why we need a GSA. *Teaching Tolerance*, pp. 30–37.

Kim, K. C. (1999). Koreans. In E. R. Barkan (Ed.), *A nation of peoples: America's multicultural heritage* (pp. 354–371). Westport, CT: Greenwood Press.

Kincheloe, J., Steinberg, S., Rodriguez, N., & Chennault, R. (Eds.). (1998). *White reign: Deploying whiteness in America.* New York: St. Martin's Press.

King, B. M. (2005). *Human sexuality today* (5th ed.). Upper Saddle River, NJ: Prentice Hall.

Kinsey, A. C. (1948). *Sexual behavior in the human male.* Philadelphia, PA: W.B. Saunders.

Kinsey, A. C. (1953). *Sexual behavior in the human female.* Philadelphia, PA: W.B. Saunders.

Kinsley, M. (2003, January 27). How affirmative action helped George W. *Time Magazine*, p. 70.

Kinsley, M. (2006, March 31). *The twilight of objectivity.* Retrieved March 31, 2006 from Washingtonpost.com

Kirwan, W. E. (2006, August 14). Security through education. *Washington Post.* Retrieved August 14, 2006 from http://www.washingtonpost.com/

Knell, G. E. (2006, May 1). The view from Sesame Street. *Washington Post.* Retrieved May 1, 2006 from http://www.washingtonpost.com

Kohn, M. L. (1977). *Class and conformity: A study in values* (2nd ed.). Homewood, IL: Dorsey Press.

Korb, L. J. (1996, September 18). Holding the bag in the gulf. *The New York Times*, p. A21.

Korten, D. C. (1995). *When corporations rule the world.* West Hartford, CT: Kumarian Press.

Korten, D. C. (1999). *The Post-corporate world: Life after capitalism.* San Francisco: Berrett-Koehler.

Korten, D. C. (2006). *The Great Turning: From empire to earth community.* San Francisco: Berrett-Koehler.

Kozol, J. (1991). *Savage inequalities: Children in America's schools.* New York: Crown.

Kozol, J. (1995). *Amazing grace: The lives of children and the conscience of a nation.* New York: Crown.

Kozol, J. (2005). *The shame of the nation: The restoration of apartheid schooling in America.* New York: Crown Publishers.

Krugman, P. (2005, April 20). On health care, America spends a lot, gets little. *New York Times.*

Kundanis, R. (2003). *Children, teens, families, and mass media: The millennial generation.* Mahwah, NJ: Lawrence Erlbaum Associates.

La Brack, B. (1999). South Asians. In E. R. Barkan (Ed.), *A nation of peoples: America's multicultural heritage* (pp. 482–503). Westport, CT: Greenwood Press.

Lacayo, R. (1998, October 26). The new gay struggle. *Time,* pp. 32–36.

LaDuke, W. (1993). A society based on conquest cannot be sustained: Native peoples and the environmental crisis. In R. Hofrichter (Ed.), *Toxic struggles: The theory and practice on environmental justice* (pp. 98–106). Philadelphia, PA: New Society Publishers.

LaFayette, J. (1998, August 10). News study: Violence still dominates. *Electronic Media,* pp. 22, 24.

LaFromboise, T. D., & Graff Low, K. (1998). American Indian children and adolescents. In J. T. Gibbs, & L. N. Huang (Eds.), *Children of color: Psychological interventions with culturally diverse youths* (pp. 112–142). San Francisco: Jossey-Bass.

LaLonde, R. (2007, October 17). Helping workers where it hurts. *Washington Post.* Retrieved October 17, 2007 from http://www.washingtonpost.com.

Lambda Legal. (2009). *Our work.* Retrieved February 26, 2009 from http://www.lambdalegal.org/our-work

Langer, E. J., & Rodin, J. (1976). The effects of choice and enhanced personal responsibility for the aged: A field experiment in an institutional setting. *Journal of Personality and Social Psychology, 34,* 191–198.

Lareau, A. (2002). Invisible inequality: Social class and child rearing in black and white families. *American Sociological Review, 67,* 747–776.

Lareau, A. (2003). *Unequal childhoods: Class, race, and family life.* Berkeley, CA: University of California Press.

Larson, J. (1996, February). Temps are here to stay. *American Demographics,* pp. 27–31.

Lauzen, M. M., & Dozier, D. M. (2005). Recognition and respect revisited: Portrayals of age and gender in prime-time television. *Mass Communications & Society, 8,* 241–256.

Lawless, J. L., & Fox, R. L. (2005). *It takes a candidate: Why women don't run for office.* New York: Cambridge University Press.

Lawton, M. P. (1982). Competence, environmental press, and the adaptation of old people. In M. P. Lawton, P. G. Windley, & T. O. Byerts (Eds.), *Aging and the environment: Theoretical approaches* (pp. 33–59). New York: Springer.

Lawton, M. P., & Nahemow, L. (1973). Ecology of the aging process. In C. Eisdorfer, & M. P. Lawton (Eds.), *The psychology of adult development and aging* (pp. 619–674). Washington, DC: American Psychological Association.

Lazar, B. A. (1994). Under the influence: An analysis of children's television regulation. *Social Work, 39,* 67–74.

Lazare, D. (2001). *America's undeclared war: What's killing our cities and how we can stop it.* New York: Harcourt.

Lazzari, M., Ford, H., & Haughey, K. J. (1996). Making a difference: Women of action in the community. *Social Work, 41,* 197–205.

Lee, D. (1986). Government policy and the distortions in family housing. In J. Peden, & F. Glahe (Eds.), *The American family and the state* (p. 312). San Francisco: Pacific Research Institute for Public Policy.

Lee, J. (2001). *The empowerment approach to social work practice: Building the beloved community.* New York: Columbia University Press.

Leighninger, R. D. (1978). Systems theory. *Journal of Sociology and Social Work, 5,* 446–480.

Leland, J. (2000, March 20). Shades of gay. *Newsweek,* pp. 46–49.

Lester, P. M. (Ed.) (1996). *Images that injure: Pictorial stereotypes in the media.* Westport, CT: Praeger.

Levitt, P. (1995). A todos les llamo primo (I call everyone cousin): The social basis for Latino small businesses. In M. Halter (Ed.), *New migrants in the marketplace: Boston's ethnic entrepreneurs* (pp. 120–140). Boston: University of Massachusetts.

Lewis, K. R. (2008, January 27). Consumption wasn't always pillar of economy. *The State* [Columbia, SC], p. D2.

Lewis, M. (1996, July 21). God is in the packaging. *The New York Times Magazine,* pp. 14–16.

Lewis, O. (1966, October). The culture of poverty. *Scientific American, 215,* 19–25.

Lewis, R. G. (1995). American Indians. In R. L. Edwards et al. (Eds.), *Encyclopedia of Social Work* (19th ed., Vol. 1, pp. 216–225). Washington, DC: NASW Press.

Lincoln, C. E., & Mamiya, L. H. (1990). *The Black church in the African American experience.* Durham, NC: Duke University Press.

Linn, S. (2005). *Consuming kids: Protecting our children from the onslaught of marketing and advertising.* New York: Anchor Books.

Linton, S. (1998). *Claiming disability: Knowledge and identity.* New York: New York University Press.

Lippa, R. A. (2002). *Gender, nature, and nurture.* Mahwah, NJ: Lawrence Erlbaum.

Lipset, S. M. (1996). *American exceptionalism: A double-edged sword.* New York: W. W. Norton Company.

Lipset, S. M., & Raab, E. (1995). *Jews and the new American scene.* Cambridge, MA: Harvard University Press.

Li-Vollmer, M. (2002). Race representation in child-targeted television commercials. *Mass Communications & Society, 5* (2), 207–228.

Lockheed Martin. (2008). *About us.* Retrieved December 10, 2008 from http://www.lockheedmartin.com/aboutus

Long-term care paradise (1999, September). *Executive Solutions for Healthcare Management*, pp. 13–16.

Lovell, D., O'Neill, E., & Olsen, S. (2007). Maternity leave in the United States: Paid parental leave is still not standard, even among the best US employers. Institute for Women's Policy Research.

Lowry, D. T., & Shidler, J. A. (1993). Prime time TV portrayals of sex, (safe sex) and AIDS: A longitudinal analysis. *Journalism Quarterly, 70*, 628–637.

Lozano-Bielat, H., Masci, D., & Ralston, M. (2009, January 22). *Same-sex marriage redefining marriage around the world.* Pew Forum. Retrieved March 1, 2009 from http://pewforum.org

Luey, H. S., Glass, L., & Elliott, H. (1995). Hard-of-hearing or deaf: Issue of ears, language, culture, and identity. *Social Work, 40*, 177–182.

Lukes, C. A., & Land, H. (1990). Biculturality and homosexuality. *Social Work, 35*, 155–161.

Lundquist, J. H. (2004, December). When race makes no difference: Marriage and the military. *Social Forces, 83* (2), 731–757.

Luther, S. (2006, March). *Domestic partner benefits: Employer trends and benefits equivalency for the GLBT family.* Human Rights Campaign Foundation. Retrieved April 15, 2006 from http://www.hrc.org/workplace

Maciel, D. R., & Herrera-Sobek, M. (1998). Introduction. In D. R. Maciel, & M. Herrera-Sobek (Eds.), *Culture across borders: Mexican immigration and popular culture* (pp. 3–26). Tuscon: The University of Arizona Press.

Macionis, J. J. (2007). *Sociology* (11th ed.) Upper Saddle River, NJ: Prentice Hall.

Mackelprang, R. W., & Salsgiver, R. O. (1999). *Disability: A diversity model approach in human service practice.* Pacific Grove, CA: Brooks/Cole.

Madden, E. (2003, June 28). Ruling makes gays, at last, equal citizens. *The State* [Columbia, SC], p. A13.

Madoff's Victims. (2009). *Wall Street Journal.* Retrieved February 7, 2009 from http://s.wsj.net/public/resources/documents/st_madoff_victims_

Makas, E. (1993). Changing channels: The portrayal of people with disabilities on television. In G. L. Berry, & J. K. Asamen (Eds.), *Children & television: Images in a changing sociocultural world.* Newbury Park, CA: Sage.

Mander, J. (1991). *In the absence of the sacred.* San Francisco: Sierra Club Books.

Manning, R. D. (2000). *Credit card nation: The consequences of America's addiction to credit.* New York: Basic Books.

March, J., & Simon, H. (1958). *Organizations.* New York: Wiley.

Martin, A. (2009, February 14). Peanut corporation of American to liquidate. *The New York Times.* Retrieved March 7, 2009 from http://www. nytimes.com

Martino, S. C., Collins, R. L., Elliott, M. N., Strachman, A., Kanouse, D. E., & Berry, S. H. (2006). Exposure to degrading versus nondegrading music lyrics and sexual behavior among youth. *Pediatrics, 118* (2), 430–441.

Maruschak, L. M. (2008). *Medical problems of prisoners.* Retrieved November 11, 2008 from Bureau of Justice Statistics http://www.ojp.usdoj.gov/bjs/

Mason, J. (1982). *History of housing in the U.S.* Houston: Gulf.

Massey, D. S., Charles, C. Z., Lundy, G. F., & Fischer, M. (2003). *The source of the river: The social origins of freshmen at America's selective colleges and universities.* Princeton, NJ: Princeton University Press.

Masters, B. A. (2006, May 26). White-collar crime's new milestone. *Washington Post.* Retrieved May 26, 2006 from http://www.washingtonpost.com/

Masterson, P. (1993, January 11). Many editors report advertiser pressure. *Advertising Age*, p. 22.

Mastro, D. E., & Behm-Morawitz, E. (2005). Latino representation on primetime television. *Journalism & Mass Communication Quarterly, 82*, 110–131.

Mastro, D. E., & Greenberg, B. S. (2000). The portrayal of racial minorities on prime time television. *Journal of Broadcasting & Electronic Media, 44*, 690–703.

Mauss, A. L. (1975). *Social problems of social movements.* Philadelphia, PA: Lippencott.

Mayhew, M. (2003, December 14). Levi's zipping up last U.S. plant next month. *The State* [Columbia, SC], p. F3.

Mayo, E. (1933). *The human problems of industrial civilization.* New York: McMillan.

McCarus, E. (Ed.). (1994). *The development of Arab-American identity.* Ann Arbor: University of Michigan Press.

McChesney, R. W. (2000). *Rich media, poor democracy: Communication politics in dubious times.* New York: The New Press.

McClain, L. (1986). More of a home to me now . . . In C. Page (Ed.), *A foot in each world: Essays and articles by Leanita McClain* (pp. 140–143). Evanston, IL: Northwestern University Press.

McClam, E. (2008, January 19). Next wave of homeless vets emerges. *USA Today.* Retrieved January 28, 2008 from http://usatoday

McCormick, J. (1998, August 20). A gathering of men: African-Americans come to barbershops for haircuts, camaraderie. *The State* [Columbia, SC], pp. D1, D6.

McDermott, M., & Samson, F. L. (2005). White racial and ethnic identity in the United States. *Annual Review of Sociology, 31*, 245–261.

McGeary, J. (1997, February 24). Echoes of the Holocaust. *Time*, pp. 36–40.

McGregor, D. (1960). *The human side of enterprise.* New York: McGraw Hill.

McGuire, M. B. (1997). *Religion: The social context* (4th ed.). Belmont, CA: Wadsworth.

McIntosh, P. (2001). White privilege and male privilege: A personal account of coming to see correspondences through work in Women's Studies. In M. Anderson, & P. H. Collins (Eds.), *Race, class, and gender: An anthology* (pp. 95–105). Belmont, CA: Wadsworth Publishing.

McNeely, R. L. (1992). Job satisfaction in the public social services: Perspectives on structure, situational factors, gender, and ethnicity. In Y. Hasenfeld (Ed.), *Human services as complex organizations* (pp. 224–255). Newbury Park, CA: Sage.

Meacham, J. (2009, January 26). Who we are now. *Newsweek*, pp. 37–42.

Media Matters for America. (2007). *Sunday shutout: The lack of gender & ethnic diversity on the Sunday morning talk shows.* Retrieved January 24, 2009 from http://mediamatters.org/items/printable/200705140001

Merton, R. K. (1949). *Social theory and social structure.* Glencoe, IL: Free Press.

Meyerson, H. (2007, March 21). God and his gays. *Washington Post.* Retrieved March 21, 2007 from http://www.washingtonpost.com

Michels, R. (1949/1911). *Political parties.* Glencoe, IL: Free Press.

Milbank, D. (2008). Auto execs fly corporate jets to D.C., tin cups in hand. *Washington Post.* Retrieved November 21, 2008 from http://www.washingtonpoost.com

Milham, S., Bullock, R., Hosie, K., & Haak, M. (1986). *Lost in care: The problems of maintaining links between children in care and their families.* Brookfield, VT: Gower.

Miller, L. (2008, February 25). In defense of secularism. *Newsweek*, p. 15.

Min, P. G. (1990). Ethnicity: Concepts, theories and trends. In P. G. Min, & R. Kim (Eds.), *Struggle for ethnic identity: Narratives by Asian American professionals* (pp. 16–46). Walnut Creek, CA: Altamira.

Min, P. G. (1995a). An overview of Asian Americans. In P. G. Min (Ed.), *Asian Americans: Contemporary trends and issues* (pp. 10–37). Thousand Oaks, CA: Sage.

Min, P. G. (1995b). Major issues relating to Asian American experiences. In P. G. Min (Ed.), *Asian Americans: Contemporary trends and issues* (pp. 38–57). Thousand Oaks, CA: Sage.

Mirowsky, J., & Ross, C. E. (1989). *Social causes of psychological distress.* New York: Aldine de Gruyter.

Mishel, L., Bernstein, J., & Shierholz, H. (2009). *The state of working America 2008/2009.* Washington DC: Economic Policy Institute.

Mishori, R. (2008, December 21). How spirituality keeps you well. *Parade*, p. 14.

Mogelonsky, M. (1995, August). Asian-Indian Americans. *American Demographics, 17*, 32–39.

Mokuau, N., & Tauili'ili, P. (1992). Families with native Hawaiian and Pacific Island roots. In E. W. Lynch, & M. J. Hanson (Eds.), *Developing cross-cultural competence* (pp. 301–318). Baltimore: Paul H. Brookes.

Monk, J., & Fretwell, S. (2008, November 17). We are the pay toilet of the nation. *The State* [Columbia, SC], pp. A1, A6–A7.

Moore, E. E., & Starkes, A. J. (1992). The group-in-institution as the unit of attention: Recapturing and refining a social work tradition. *Social Work with Groups, 15*, 171–192.

Moore, J., & Pinderhughes, R. (Eds.). (1993). *In the barrios: Latinos and the underclass debate.* New York: Russell Sage Foundation.

Moore, J., & Vigil, J. D. (1993). Barrios in transition. In J. Moore and R. Pinderhughes (Eds.), *In the barrios: Latinos and the underclass debate* (pp. 27–49). New York: Russell Sage Foundation.

Moore, R. K. (2004, May 19). Cost should be a factor in prison sentences. *Los Angeles Times.* Retrieved May 8, 2008 from http://www.geocities.com/three_strikes

Morgan, G. (1986). *Images of organization.* Beverly Hills, CA: Sage.

Morgan, R. (2004). Ashcroft vs.Washington: Fighting words for a secular America. *Ms,* pp. 47–49.

Morgen, S. (1994). Personalizing personnel decisions in feminist organizational theory and practice. *Human Relations, 47*, 665–684.

Morin, R. (2006, October 18). Immigrants and the whiter-shade-of-pale bonus. *Washington Post.* Retrieved February 2, 2007 from http://www.washingtonpost.com

Morin, R., & Taylor, P. (2009, February 26). *Suburbs not most popular, but suburbanites most content.* Pew Center. Retrieved March 15, 2009 from http://Pewsocialtrends.org/pubs/727/content-in-american-suburbs

Morris, R. (1986). *Rethinking social welfare: Why care for the stranger?* New York: Longman.

Morris, R. (2003, October 7). For USC, the show must go on. *The State* [Columbia, SC], pp. C1, C4.

Moskos, C. C. (2000). Toward a postmodern military: The United States as a paradigm. In C. C. Moskos, J. A. Williams, & D. R. Segal (Eds.), *The postmodern military armed forces after the cold war* (pp. 14–31). New York: Oxford University Press.

Moskos, C. C., & Butler, J. (1996). *All that we can be: Black leadership and racial integration in the Army.* New York: Basic Books.

Moskos, C. C., Williams, J. A., & Segal, D. R. (Eds.). (2000). *The postmodern military armed forces after the cold war.* New York: Oxford University Press.

Mumola, C. J. (2000, August). *Incarcerated parents and their children.* U.S. Department of Justice, Office of Justice Programs. Retrieved March 17, 2003 from http://www.ojp.usdojgov/bjs/

Murray, H. A. (1938). *Exploration in personality.* New York: Oxford University Press.

Murray, S., & Most, M. (2008, November 10). Under Obama, web would be the way. *Washington Post.* Retrieved from http://www.washingtonpost.com/

Muscati, S. A. (2002). Arab/Muslim "otherness": The role of racial constructions in the Gulf War and the continuing crisis in Iraq. *Journal of Muslim Minority Affairs, 22,* 131–148.

Mutter, A. (2008, March 29). Newspaper revenue crisis mounts. *Reflections of a newsosaur.* Retrieved December 12, 2008 from http://newsosaur.blogspot.com/2008/03/

Myers, D. G. (1999). *Social psychology* (6th ed.). Boston: McGraw-Hill.

Myrdal, G. (1944). *An American dilemma: The Negro problem and modern democracy.* New York: Harper.

National Alliance on Mental Illness. (2007). *Mental illness facts and numbers.* Retrieved November 8, 2008 from http://www.nami.org

National Alliance on Mental Illness. (2008a, October 3). *Victory on parity.* Retrieved January 1, 2009 from http://www.nami.org

National Alliance on Mental Illness. (2008b). *What is mental illness?: Mental illness facts.* Retrieved November 8, 2008 from http://www.nami.org.

National Association of Social Workers. (2000). Environmental policy. In *Social work speaks: National Association of Social Workers policy statements 2000–2003* (pp. 101–108). Washington, DC: Author.

National Association of Social Workers. (2002). *NASW priorities on faith-based human services initiatives.* Retrieved March 30, 2006 from http://www.socialworkers.org/advocacy/positions/faith.asp

National Association of Social Workers. (2006). Social work speaks: National Associations of Social Workers policy statements, 2006–2009. Washington, DC: NASW Press.

National Association of the Deaf. (n.d.). *What is wrong with the use of these terms: "Deaf-mute," "deaf and dumb," or "hearing-impaired"?* Retrieved March 1, 2009 from http://www.nad.org/issues/american-sign-language/community-and-culture-faq

National Center for Education Statistics. (2006). *Computer and internet use by students in 2003.* Retrieved November 3, 2008 from http://nces.ed.gov

National Center for Education Statistics. (2007). *Digest of education statistics.* Retrieved September 27, 2008 from http://nces.ed.gov

National Center for Education Statistics. (2008). *Special analysis 2008: Community colleges.* Retrieved September 27, 2008 from http://nces.ed.gov

National Center for Health Statistics. (2004). *Current resident tables – estimates.* Retrieved March 21, 2009 from http://www.cdc.gov/nchs/

National Center for Health Statistics. (2007). *Health, United States, 2007.* Retrieved March 21, 2009 from http://www.cdc.gov/nchs/

National Center for Policy Analysis. (1995). *Bringing down costs through privatization.* Dallas, TX: Author.

National Center for Victims of Crime. (2004). *Spousal rape laws: 20 years later.* Retrieved February 22, 2009 from http://www.ncvc.org

National Coalition for the Homeless. (2008). *How many people experience homelessness?* Retrieved February 1, 2009 from http://www.nationalhomeless.org/publications/facts/

National Geographic Society. (2008). *First-of-its-kind 14-country study ranks consumers according to environmental behavior.* Retrieved May 5, 2008 from http://press.nationalgeographic.com

National Public Radio. (2007). *Democrats to push Medicaid for children.* Retrieved June 1, 2007 from NPR.org.

National Public Radio. (2009). *Former "Post" editor details the "rules of the game."* Retrieved January 20, 2009 from http://nl.newsbank.com

Naughton, K. (2003, December 1). Three for the road: For today's family, two cars just aren't enough. *Newsweek,* p. 49.

Nelson, J. A. (1996). The invisible cultural group: Images of disability. In P. M. Lester (Ed.), *Images that injure: Pictorial stereotypes in the media* (pp. 119–125). Westport, CT: Praeger.

New project seeks justice for vulnerable children. (2007, Winter). *SPLC* [Southern Poverty Law Center] *Report*, pp. 1, 5.

Nielsen Media Research. (2006, December 19). *Nielsen study shows DVD players surpass VCRs.* Retrieved January 11, 2009 from http://www.nielsenmedia.com/

Nirje, B. (1976). The normalization principle. In R. B. Kugel, & A. Sheerer (Eds.), *Changing patterns in residential services for the mentally retarded* (pp. 179–195). Washington, DC: President's Committee on Mental Retardation.

Nishi, S. M. (1995). Japanese Americans. In P. G. Min (Ed.), *Asian Americans: Contemporary trends and issues* (pp. 95–133). Thousand Oaks, CA: Sage.

Nonprofit Voter Engagement Network. (2008). *Voter turnout 2008.* Retrieved April 19, 2009 from http://www.nonprofitvote.org/voterturnout2008

NORC. (2003). *General Social Surveys, 1972–2002: Cumulative Codebook.* Chicago: National Opinion Research Center.

Nursing homes: Business as usual. (2006). *Consumer Reports.* Retrieved August 8, 2006 from http://www.consumerreports.org

Oakes, J. (1985). *Keeping track: How high schools structure inequality.* New Haven, CT: Yale University Press.

Office of National Drug Control Policy. (1998). *The national drug control strategy, 1998.* Washington, DC: Author.

Ogunwole, S. U. (2006, February). *We the people: American Indians and Alaska Natives in the United States.* U.S. Census Bureau. Retrieved February 17, 2007 from http://www.census.gov/prod/2006pubs/censr-28.pdf

Ohlemacher, S. (2006, May 12). Most disabled people have jobs in U.S. *The State* [Columbia, SC], p. A12.

Okie, S. (2005, May 19). Traumatic brain injury in the war zone. *The New England Journal of Medicine, 352* (20), 2043–2047.

Oldenburg, R. (Ed.). (2001). *Celebrating the third place: Inspiring stories about the "great good places" at the heart of our communities.* New York: Harlowe & Company.

Oliver, M., & Shapiro, T. M. (1995). *Black wealth/white wealth: A new perspective on racial inequality.* New York: Routledge.

Orfield, G. (2009). *Reviving the goal of an integrated society: A 21st century challenge.* Los Angeles, CA: The Civil Rights Project/Proyecto Derechos Civiles at UCLA.

Ostrander, S. A. (1980). Upper class women: The feminine side of privilege. *Qualitative Sociology, 3,* 23–44.

Overholt, W. H. (2006, December 21). Globalization's unequal discontents. *Washington Post.* Retrieved December 21, 2006 from http://www.washingtonpost.com

Overview of homelessness. (2007, August 29). Retrieved January 28, 2008 from United States Department of Veterans Affairs http://www1.va.gov/homeless/page.cfm?pg=1

Packer, G. (2006, November 13). The megacity. *The New Yorker,* pp.60–74.

Pacyga, D. A. (1999). Poles. In E. R. Barkan (Ed.), *A nation of peoples: A sourcebook on America's multicultural heritage* (pp. 428–445). Westport, CT: Greenwood Press.

Padavic, I., & Reskin, B. (2002). *Women and men at work* (2nd ed.). Thousand Oaks, CA: Pine Forge Press.

Padden, C. L., & Humphries, T. (1988). *Deaf in America: Voices from a culture.* Cambridge, MA: Harvard University Press.

Padilla, F. M. (1993). The quest for community: Puerto Ricans in Chicago. In J. Moore, & R. Pinderhughes (Eds.), *In the barrios: Latinos and the underclass debate* (pp. 129–148). New York: Russell Sage Foundation.

Page, B. I., & Jacobs, L. R. (2009). *Class war? What Americans really think about economic inequality.* Chicago: The University of Chicago Press.

Palmer, L. D. (2003, September/October). Original intent? How corporations became "people." *Spirituality & Health,* p. 53.

Parenti, M. (1995). *Democracy for the few* (6th ed.). New York: St. Martin's Press.

Parfit, M. (1994, June). Powwows. *National Geographic,* pp. 85–113.

Park, A. (2008, December 1). America's health checkup. *Time,* pp. 41–48.

Parker, K. (2006, January 2). Lord of the blogs. *The State* [Columbia, SC], p. A9.

Parsons, T., & Bales, R. F. (Eds.). (1955). *Family, socialization and interaction process.* New York: Free Press.

Patai, D. (1991). Minority status and the stigma of "surplus visibility." *Chronicle of Higher Education, 38* (10), A52.

Payne, M. (1997). *Modern social work theory* (2nd ed.). Chicago: Lyceum.

PBS Kids. (2004). *Teletubbies 10.* Retrieved January 31, 2009 from http://pbskids.org/parentsteachers/progsummary.html

Penn, M. (1998, Winter). Taming the suburban wasteland. *In Wisconsin, 99* (6), 28–35.

Perrow, C. (1961). The analysis of goals in complex organizations. *American Sociological Review, 26,* 856–866.

Perrow, C. (1991). A society of organizations. *Theory and Society, 20,* 725–762.

Perse, E. M. (2001). *Media effects and society.* Mahwah, NJ: Lawrence Erlbaum Associates.

Peterson, R. D. (1991). *Political economy and American capitalism.* Boston: Kluwer Academic Publishers.

Pew Center on the States. (2008). *One in 100: Behind bars in America 2008.* Retrieved October 24, 2008 from http://www.pewcenteronthestates.org/report

Pew Forum on Religion and Public Life. (2008). *U.S. religious landscape survey: Summary of key findings.* Retrieved March 21, 2008 from http://religions.pewforum.org/reports

Pew Global Attitudes Project. (2002). *Among wealthy nations: U.S. stands alone in its embrace of religion.* Retrieved March 28, 2007 from http://people-press.org/reports/

Pew Hispanic Center. (2007, April 25). *Changing faiths: Latinos and the transformation of American religion.* Retrieved April 25, 2007 from http://pewhispanic.org/report

Pew Hispanic Center. (2008a, October 23). *Latinos account for half of the U.S. population growth since 2000.* Retrieved February 21, 2009 from http://pewhispanic.org/reports/

Pew Hispanic Center. (2008b, January 23). *Statistical portrait of Hispanics in the United States, 2006.* Retrieved February 15, 2009 from http://pewhispanic.org/factsheet

Pew Internet & American Life Project. (2008). *The future of the Internet III.* Retrieved January 31, 2009 from http://www.pewinternet.org/

Pew Internet & American Life Project. (2009). *Generations online in 2009.* Retrieved January 31, 2009 from http://www.pewinternet.org

Pew Research Center for the People and the Press. (2006, March 22). *Less opposition to gay marriage, adoption and military service.* Retrieved March 28, 2007 from http://www.people-press.org/reports/

Pew Research Center for the People and the Press. (2008, August 17). *Key news audiences now blend online and traditional sources: Audience segments in a changing news environment.* Retrieved September 22, 2008 from http://people-press.org/report/444/news-media

Peyser, M., & Lorch, D. (2000, March 20). High school controversial. *Newsweek,* pp. 55–56.

Pfeffer, J. (1997). *New directions for organization theory.* New York: Oxford University Press.

Phillips, M. (2007, September 10). Separation anxieties. *Newsweek,* p. 15.

Phillips, N. (2008, June 6). S.C. first in on-job deaths of Hispanics. *The State* [Columbia, SC], p. A1.

Philpott, T. (2005). *Rise in survival rate.* Military.com. Retrieved February 8, 2008 from http://www.military.com/forums/0,15240,80183,00.htm

Piotrkowski, C. S., & Hughes, D. (1993). Dual-earner families in context. In F. Walsh (Ed.), *Normal family processes* (2nd ed., pp. 185–207). New York: Guilford Press.

Piven, F. F., & Cloward, R. A. (1997). Low income people and the political process. In F. F. Piven & R. A. Cloward (Eds.), *The breaking of the American social compact* (pp. 271–295). New York: The New Press.

Pletcher, M. J., Kertesz, S. G., Kohn, M. A., & Gonzales, R. (2008, January 2). Trends in opioid prescribing by race/ethnicity for patients seeking care in U.S. emergency departments [Electronic version]. *JAMA, 229* (1), 70–78.

Polsky, H. W. (1962). *Cottage six: The social system of delinquent boys in residential treatment.* New York: Russell Sage Foundation.

Poniewozik, J. (2008, May 5). What's wrong with this picture? With talk of Katie Couric leaving CBS, politics is more diverse than the anchor desk. *Time*, p. 19.

Pope, E. (2003, November). Second-class care. *AARP Bulletin*, pp. 6, 7–8.

Portes, A., & Rumbaut, R. G. (2006). *Immigrant America* (3rd ed.). Berkeley, CA: University of California Press.

Postman, N., & Powers, S. (1992). *How to watch TV news.* New York: Penguin.

Powell, J. (2002). Sprawl, fragmentation, and the persistence of racial inequality: Limiting civil rights by fragmenting space. In G. D. Squires (Ed.), *Urban sprawl: Causes, consequences & policy responses* (pp. 73–118). Washington, DC: The Urban Institute.

Powers, R. (n.d.). *What the recruiter never told you.* About.com (part 5 & 6). Retrieved December 6, 2008 from http://usmilitary.about.com/cs/joiningup/a/recruiter5.htm

Prante, G. (2006). *Who benefits from the home mortgage interest deduction?* Tax Foundation. Retrieved March 28, 2009 from http://www.taxfoundation .org/research/printer/1341.html

Priest, D., & Hull, A. (2007). Soldiers face neglect, frustration, at army's top medical facility. *Washington Post.* Retrieved February 19, 2007 from http://www.washingtonpost.com

Prigmore, C. S., & Atherton, C. R. (1986). *Social welfare policy: Analysis and formulation.* Lexington, MA: Heath.

Principles of urbanism (n.d.). *New Urbanism.* Retrieved January 15, 2009 from http://www.newurbanism.org

Private warriors: Interview with Peter Singer. Retrieved July 30, 2005 from PBS.org/WGBH/pages/frontline

Public Papers of the Presidents of the United States, Dwight D. Eisenhower, 1960–1961. Retrieved November 11, 2008 from http://www.gpoaccess.gov/pubpapers/index.html

Pupovac, J. (2008, March 24). *Torture in our own backyards: The fight against supermax prisons.* AlternNet. Retrieved March 24, 2008 from http://www.alternet.org/module/

Putnam, R. D. (2000). *Bowling alone: The collapse and revival of American community.* New York: Simon & Schuster.

Queralt, M. (1996). *The social environment and human behavior: A diversity perspective.* Boston: Allyn & Bacon.

Quinn, G., & Degener, T. (2002). *Human rights and disability: The current use and future potential of United Nations human rights instruments in the context of disability.* New York: United Nations Publications.

Quinn, J. B. (2003, June 23). Tough course in tuition aid. *Newsweek*, p. 51.

Radzilowski, T. C., & Radzilowski, J. (1999). East Europeans. In E. R. Barkan (Ed.), *A nation of peoples: A sourcebook on America's multicultural heritage* (pp. 174–199). Westport, CT: Greenwood Press.

Raines, J. P., & Leathers, C. G. (2003). *The economic institution of higher education: Economic theories of university behavior.* Northampton, MA: Edward Elgar.

RAND (2000). *Research brief: Changing the policy toward homosexuals in the U.S. military.* Retrieved November 5, 2006 from http://www.rand.org/pubs/research_briefs

RAND Corporation. (2004). *Does watching sex on television influence teens' sexual activity?* Retrieved January 1, 2005 from http://www.rand.org/

Rasmussen, B. B., Klinenberg, E., Nexica, I.J., & Wray, M. (Eds.). (2001). *The making and unmaking of whiteness.* Durham, NC: Duke University Press.

Raspberry, W. (1999, September 26). Duty bound to pray for the heathen. *The State* [Columbia, SC], p. A6.

Rawe, J. (2007, November 19). Congress's bad drug habit. *Time*, p. 60.

Reiman, J. (2007). *The rich get richer and the poor get prison: Ideology, class, and criminal justice* (8th ed.). Boston: Allyn & Bacon.

Reinhardt, U. E., Hussey, P. S., & Anderson, G. F. (2004). U.S. health care spending in an international context: Why is U.S. spending so high, and can we afford it [Electronic version] *Health Affairs, 23* (3), 10–25.

Retsinas, N. P. (2002, June/July). The housing divide. *Habitat World*, pp. 8 – 9.

Rey, L. D. (1997). Religion as invisible culture: Knowing about and knowing with. *Journal of Family Social Work, 2*, 159–177.

Reynolds, J. R., & Ross, C. E. (1998). Social stratification and health: Education's benefit beyond economic status and social origins. *Social Problems, 45*, 221–245.

Rideout, V., Hamel, E., & Kaiser Family Foundation. (2006). *The media family: Electronic media in the lives of infants, toddlers, preschoolers, and their parents.* Kaiser Family Foundation. Retrieved January 31, 2009 from http://www.kff.org/entmedia/

Ritzer, G. (1999). *Enchanting a disenchanted world: Revolutionizing the means of consumption.* Thousand Oaks, CA: Pine Forge Press.

Ritzer, G. (2000). *Macdonaldization of society.* Thousand Oaks, CA: Pine Forge Press.

Ritzer, G. (2001). *Explorations in the sociology of consumption: Fast food, credit cards and casinos.* Thousand Oaks, CA: Sage.

Robbins, S. P., Chatterjee, P., & Canda, E. R. (1998). *Contemporary human behavior theory: A critical perspective for social work.* Boston: Allyn & Bacon.

Roberts, K. A. (1995). *Religion in sociological perspective.* Belmont, CA: Wadsworth.

Roberts, R., & Inskeep, S. (2007, May 7). Democrats to push Medicaid for children. *Morning Edition.* NPR. Retrieved May 8, 2007 from http://www.npr.org

Robinson, E. (2007, May 15). Obama opens debate on affirmative action. *The San Francisco Chronicle.* Retrieved March 4, 2009 from http://sfgate.com/cgi-bin/article.cgi

Rodberg, L., & McCanne, D. (2007, July 13). *Upgrading to national health insurance (Medicare 2.0).* Physicians for a National Health Program. Retrieved February 7, 2009 from http://www.pnhp.org/news/2007/ july/_health_insurance_fo.php

Rodin, J., & Langer, E. J. (1977). Longterm effects of a control-relevant intervention with the institutionalized aged. *Journal of Personality and Social Psychology, 35,* 897–902.

Rodu, B., & Cole, P. (2007, January 26). Here's to your health: Americans are posting gains in the most vital statistic of all. *Washington Post.* Retrieved January 26, 2007 from http://www.washingtonpost.com/wp-dyn/content/article

Roediger, D. R. (2002). *Colored white: Transcending the racial past.* Berkeley, CA: University of California Press.

Roesler, S. M. (2005). Women's human rights abuses in the name of religion. In A. Barnes (Ed.), *The Handbook of Women, Psychology and the Law* (pp. 280–292). San Francisco: Jossey-Bass.

Rogge, M. (1993). Social work, disenfranchised communities, and the natural environment. *Journal of Social Work Education, 29,* 111–120.

Rogge, M. E., & Darkwa, O. K. (1996). Poverty and the environment: An international perspective for social work. *International Social Work, 39,* 395–405.

Romano, L. (2006, November 9). Hill demographic goes slightly more female. *Washington Post.* Retrieved November 9, 2006 from http://www.washingtonpost.com

Rose, J. D. (1982). *Outbreaks.* New York: Free Press.

Rosenblatt, R. (2001, December 17). God is not on my side. Or yours. *Time,* p. 92.

Rosener, J. B. (1990). The ways women lead. *Harvard Business Review, 68,* 119–125.

Rosenhan, D. L. (1973). On being sane in insane places. *Science, 179,* 250–258.

Rosenthal, R., & Jacobson, L. (1968). *Pygmalian in the classroom: Teacher expectations and pupils' intellectual development.* New York: Holt, Reinhart and Winston.

Rothman, D. J. (1971). *The discovery of the asylum.* Boston: Little, Brown.

Rothschild, J., & Davies, C. (1994). Organizations through the lens of gender. *Human Relations, 47,* 583–590.

Rothschild, J., & Russell, R. (1986). Alternatives to bureaucracy: Democratic participation in the economy. *Annual Review of Sociology, 12,* 307–328.

Rothschild, J., & Whitt, J. A. (1986). *The cooperative workplace: Potentials and dilemmas of organizational democracy and participation.* New York: Cambridge University Press.

Royte, E. (2005, August). E-gad! *Smithsonian,* pp. 82–87.

Rubin, L. B. (1976). *Worlds of pain: Life in the working-class family.* New York: Basic Books.

Rust, M., & Yoder, C. (2007, May 20). From Lucy to Sanjaya: Broadcast TV isn't dead, but an explosion of media choices means it will never be the same. *Chicago Tribune,* p. 6.

Ryan, E. L., & Hoerrner, K. L. (2004). Let your conscience be your guide: Smoking and drinking in Disney's animated classics. *Mass Communications & Society, 7,* 261–278.

Ryan, M. K., & Haslam, S. A. (2005). The glass cliff: Evidence that women are over-represented in precarious leadership positions. *British Journal of Management, 16,* 81–90.

Ryan, W. (1976). *Blaming the victim.* New York: Vintage.

Sabol, W. J. et al (2007). *Prisoners in 2006.* In Bureau of Justice Statistics Bulletin (BJS publication No. NCJ 291416). Washington, DC: U.S. Department of Justice, Office of Justice Programs.

Sahyoun, N. R., Pratt, L. A., Lentzner, H., Dey, A., & Robinson, K. N. (2001). The changing profile of nursing home residents: 1985–1997. *Aging Trends*; No. 4. Hyattsville, MD: National Center for Health Statistics.

Saleebey, D. (2002). *The strengths perspective in social work practice.* Boston: Allyn & Bacon.

Saltzman, A., & Proch, K. (1990). The rights of institutionalized adults. In A. Salzman, & K. Proch (Eds.), *Law in social work practice* (pp. 359–373). Chicago: Nelson-Hall.

Samhan, H. H. (1999). Not quite white: Race classification and the Arab-American experience. In M. S. Suleiman (Ed.), *Arabs in America: Building a new future* (pp. 209–226). Philadelphia, PA: Temple University Press.

Samuelson, R. J. (2008, September 17). Wall Street's unraveling. *Washington Post.* Retrieved September 19, 2009 from http://www.washingtonpost.com

Samuelson, R. J. (2009, March 16). The shadow of depression. *Washington Post.* Retrieved March 16, 2009 from http://www.washingtonpost.com

Sanchez, M. (2006, October 20). Poverty is relative. *Washington Post.* Retrieved October 20, 2006 from http://www.washingtonpost.com

Sanger, D. E. (1996, January 1). A U.S. agency, once power-ful, is dead at 108. *The New York Times*, pp. 1, 9.

Saporito, B. (2007, November 12). Restoring Wal-Mart. *Time*, pp. 45–52.

Satullo, C. (2008, November 2). Any way you work it, a big shift for insurance. *The Philadelphia Inquirer*, p. A3.

Sayer, L. C. (2005). Gender, time, and inequality: Trends in women's and men's paid work, unpaid work and free time. *Social Forces, 84*, 285–303.

Schaefer, R. T. (2008). *Racial and ethnic groups* (11th ed.). Upper Saddle River, NJ: Prentice Hall.

Scharrer, E., Kim, D., Lin, K. M., & Liu, X. (2006). Working hard or hardly working? Gender, humor, and the per-formance of domestic chores in television commercials. *Mass Communication & Society, 9*, 215–238.

Schein, E. H. (1991/1985). *Organizational culture and lead-ership.* San Francisco: Jossey-Bass.

Schlosser, E. (1998, December.) The prison-industrial com-plex. *The Atlantic Monthly*, p. 54.

Schneider, W. (1992, July). The suburban century begins. *The Atlantic Monthly*, pp. 33–44.

Schorr, L. B. (1989). *Within our reach: Breaking the cycle of disadvantage.* New York: Anchor Books.

Schulz, R., & Hanusa, B. H. (1979). Environmental influ-ences on the effectiveness of control- and competence-enhancing interventions. In L. C. Permuter, & R. A. Monty (Eds.), *Choice and perceived control* (pp. 315–337). Hillsdale, NJ: Erlbaum.

Schutz, A. (1967). *The phenomenology of the social world* (G. Walsh, & F. Lennert, Trans.). Evanston, IL: North-western University Press.

Schwartz, D. (1996). Women as mothers. In P. M. Lester (Ed.), *Images that injure: Pictorial stereotypes in the media* (pp. 75–80). Westport, CT: Praeger.

Scott, W. R. (1981). *Organizations: Rational, natural, and open systems.* Englewood Cliffs, NJ: Prentice-Hall.

Screen Actors Guild. (2001). *Casting data report.* Retrieved November 5, 2001 from www.sag.org/diversity/castingdata.html

Seabrook, J. (2002, September 2). The slow lane: Can anyone solve the problem of traffic? *The New Yorker*, pp. 120–129.

Seabury, B. A. (1971). Arrangement of physical space in social work settings. *Social Work, 16*, 43–49.

Seastrom, M., Chapman, C., & Stillwell, R., (2006). *The aver-aged freshman graduation rate for public high schools from the common core of data: School years 2002–03 and 2003–04.* (NCES 2006–606). Washington, DC: U.S. Department of Education, National Center for Education Statistics.

Secrest, D. K. (1999). "Three strikes and you're out" legisla-tion: A cheap and effective crime control initiative? No. In C. B. Fields (Ed.), *Controversial issues in corrections* (pp. 129–135). Boston: Allyn & Bacon.

Segal, S. P. (2008). Deinstitutionalization. In R. L. Edwards et al. (Eds.), *Encyclopedia of Social Work* (20th ed., Vol. 2, pp. 10–20). Washington, DC: NASW Press.

Selzer, M. (1972). *"Kike"—Anti-Semitism in America.* New York: Meridian.

Sennett, R., & Cobb, J. (1973). *The hidden injuries of class.* New York: Vintage Books.

Sensi-Isolani, P. A. (1999). Italians. In E. R. Barkan (Ed.), *A nation of peoples: A sourcebook on America's multicul-tural heritage* (pp. 294–310). Westport, CT: Greenwood Press.

Sentencing Project. (2008). *Facts about prisons and prisoners.* Retrieved October 15, 2008 from http://www.sentencingproject.org

Sentencing Project. (2009). *Incarceration.* Retrieved March 21, 2009 from http://www.sentencingproject.org/IssueAreaHome.aspx?IssueID=2

Sewell, H. (2009). *Working with Ethnicity, Race and Culture in Mental Health: A Handbook for Practitioners.* Philadelphia, PA: Jessica Kingsley Publishers.

Shapiro, E. S. (1999). Jews. In E. R. Barkan (Ed.), *A nation of peoples: America's multicultural heritage* (pp. 330–353). Westport, CT: Greenwood Press.

Shapiro, J. P. (1993). *No pity: People with disabilities forging a new civil rights movement.* New York: Times/Random House.

Shichor, D. (1999). Has the privatization concept been suc-cessful? No. In C. B. Fields (Ed.), *Controversial issues in corrections* (pp. 113–120). Boston: Allyn & Bacon.

Siegel, L. J. (2010). *Introduction to criminal justice.* Belmont, CA: Wadsworth.

Signorielli, N. (1993). Television, the portrayal of women, and children's attitudes. In G. L. Berry, & J. K. Asamen (Eds.), *Children and television: Images in a changing sociocultu-ral world* (pp. 229–242). Newbury Park, CA: Sage.

Signorielli, N. (2001). Television's gender role images and con-tribution to stereotyping: Past, present, future. In D. G. Singer, & J. L. Singer (Eds.), *Handbook of children and the media* (pp. 341–358). Thousand Oaks, CA: Sage.

Signorielli, N. (2004). Aging on television: Message relating to gender, race, and occupation in primetime. *Journal of Broadcasting & Electronic Media, 48*, 279–301.

Signorielli, N., & Lears, M. (1992). Television and children's conception of nutrition: Unhealthy messages. *Health Communication, 4*, 245–257.

Simon, B. L., & Akabas, S. H. (1993). Women workers in high-risk public service: Tokens under stress. In P. A. Kurzman, & S. H. Akabas (Eds.), *Work and well-being: The occupa-tional social work advantage* (pp. 297–315).Washington, DC: NASW Press.

Simpson, V. L. (2008, May 31). Female priests face new hur-dle: Vatican to excommunicate women taking part in ordinations. *The State* [Columbia, SC], p. B3.

Skipp, C., & Ephron, D. (2006, October 23). Trouble at home. *Newsweek*, pp. 48–49.

Slivinski, S. (2007, May 14). *The corporate welfare state: How the federal government subsidizes U.S. businesses.* Retrieved April 11, 2009 from Cato Institute. http://www.cato.org/pub_display.php?pub_id=8230

Smith, A. (1937/1776). *An inquiry into nature and causes of the wealth of nations.* New York: Modern Library.

Smith, S. C. (1986). *The Macmillan dictionary of anthropology.* New York: Macmillan.

Snipp, C. M. (1999). The first Americans. In N. R. Yetman (Ed.), *Majority and minority: The dynamics of race and ethnicity in American life* (6th ed., pp. 131–143). Boston: Allyn & Bacon.

Solomon, B. (1987). Empowerment: Social work in oppressed communities. *Journal of Social Work Practice, 2,* 79–91.

Solomon, B. B. (1976). *Black empowerment: Social work in oppressed communities.* New York: Columbia University Press.

South Carolina Coalition Against Domestic Violence and Sexual Assault. (2002). *Date rape on college campuses.* Retrieved July 3, 2002 from http://wwww.scadvasa.org

Southern, D. (1987). *Gunnar Myrdal and black-white relations.* Baton Rouge: Louisiana State University.

Southwest Indian Foundation. (2009). *Mission.* Retrieved February 14, 2009 from http://www.southwestindian.com/service/mission.cfm

Spake, A. (2005, June 20). What could local zoning codes have to do with obesity and asthma? Maybe lots. *U.S. News and World Report*, pp. 54–55.

Spitzer, S. (1980). Toward a Marxian theory of deviance. In D. H. Kelly (Ed.), *Criminal behavior: Readings in criminology* (pp. 175–191). New York: St. Martin's Press.

Squires, G. D. (2001). Urban sprawl and the uneven development of metropolitan American. In G. D. Squires (Ed.), *Urban sprawl: Causes, consequences & policy responses* (pp. 1–22). Washington, DC: The Urban Institute.

Stack, C. (1997/1974). *All our kin.* New York: Basic Books.

Stange, M. Z. (2006, September 12). The "Daily Show" generation. *USA Today*, p. 15A.

Staples, B. (1998, October 4). The push to broaden God's market share. *The New York Times*, p. 14.

Steffensmeier, D., & Allan, E. (2000). Looking for patterns: Gender, age, and crime. In J. F. Sheley (Ed.), *Criminology: A contemporary handbook* (3rd ed.) (pp. 85–128). Belmont, CA: Wadsworth.

Stiglitz, J. E., & Bilmes, L. J. (2008, April). The Bush administration: The $3 trillion war. *Vanity fair.* Retrieved March 3, 2008 from http://www.vanityfair.com/politics/features.2008/04/

Stobbe, M. (2008, January 16). Americans fruitful, multiplying. *The State* [Columbia, SC], p. A8.

Stockard, J. (2000). *Sociology: Discovering society* (2nd ed.). Belmont, CA: Wadsworth/Thomson Learning.

Stoesen, L. (2005, April). Under-18 death penalty struck down. *NASW News*, p. 1.

Stojanovic, D. (2007, November 14). *MSNBC. Report: Disabled kids abused in Serbia.* Retrieved November 15, 2007 from http://www.msnbc.com/

Stolle, D., & Rochon, T. R. (2001). Are all associations alike? Member diversity, associational type, and the creation of social capital. In B. Edwards, M. W. Foley, & M. Diani (Eds.), *Beyond Tocqueville: Civil society and the social capital debate in comparative perspective* (pp. 143–156). Hanover, NH: University Press of New England.

Stringfellow, F. X. (1991, Spring/1990, Autumn). Society's rejection of the incarcerated. *Journal of Prisoners on Prisons, 3* (1–2).

Sudarkasa, N. (1997). African American families and family values. In H. P. McAdoo (Ed.), *Black families* (3rd ed., pp. 9–40). Thousand Oaks, CA: Sage.

Suleiman, M. S. (1999). Introduction: The Arab immigrant experience. In M. S. Suleiman (Ed.), *Arabs in America: Building a new future* (pp. 1–21). Philadelphia, PA: Temple University Press.

Survey finds many have religious ties. (2006, September 13). *The State* [Columbia, SC], p. A4.

Suskind, R. (2004, October 17). Without a doubt. *The New York Times.* Retrieved October 26, 2004 from http://www.nytimes.com

Sutherland, E. H. (1940). White collar criminality. *American Sociological Review, 5,* 1–12.

Svestka, S. S. (1996). Headstart and early Headstart programs: What we have learned over the last 30 years about preschool, families, and communities. *International Journal of Early Childhood, 28,* 59–62.

Swanson, C.B. (2008). *Cities in crisis: A special analytic report on high school graduation.* Editorial Projects in Education Research Center. Retrieved August 14, 2008 from http://www.edweek.org/rc/articles/2008/04/01/cities_in_crisis.html

Sweis, L., & Guay, A. (2007). Foreign-trained dentists licensed in the United States. Exploring their origins. *Journal of the American Dental Association, 138,* 219–224.

Swers, M. L. (2002). *The difference women make.* Chicago: University of Chicago.

Sykes, G. M. (1958). *The society of captives.* Princeton NJ: Princeton University Press.

Szymanski, E. M., & Trueba, H. T. (1994). Castification of people with disabilities: Potential disempowering aspects of classification in disabilities services. *The Journal of Rehabilitation, 60* (3), 12–21.

Takaki, R. (1993). *A different mirror: A history of multicultural America.* Boston: Little, Brown.

Tamura, E. H. (1999). Japanese. In E. R. Barken (Ed.), *A nation of peoples: A sourcebook on America's multicultural heritage* (pp. 311–329). Westport, CT: Greenwood Press.

Tanielian, T., & Jaycox, L. H. (2008). *Invisible wounds of war: Psychological and cognitive injuries, their consequences, and services to assist recovery* [Electronic version]. Center for Military Health Policy Research. Retrieved December 11, 2008 from http://www.rand.org/multi/military/veterans

Tannen, D. (1994). *Talking from 9 to 5: How women and men's conversational styles affect who gets heard, who gets credit, and what gets done at work.* New York: Morrow.

Tanner, L. (2007, August 17). Study: Golden arches beckons preschoolers. *The State* [Columbia, SC], p. B7.

Taylor, F. W. (1911). *Scientific management.* New York: Harper.

Taylor, P., & Morin, R. (2008, December 2). *Americans say they like diverse communities: Election, census trends suggest otherwise.* The Pew Center. Retrieved March 29, 2009 from http://pewsocialtrends.org/pubs

Telhami, S. (2002, Winter). Arab and Muslim America: A snapshot. *Brookings Review, 20,* 14–15.

Television Information Office. (1985). *A broadcasting primer with notes on the new technologies.* New York: Author.

Territo, L., Halsted, J. B., & Bromley, M. L. (2004). *Crime and justice in America: A human perspective.* Upper Saddle River, NJ: Pearson.

Texeira, E. (2005, August 19). Minority definition debated. *The State* [Columbia, SC], p. A4.

Thio, A. (1998). *Sociology* (5th ed.). New York: Longman.

Thio, A. (2000). *Sociology: A brief introduction* (4th ed.) Boston: Allyn & Bacon.

Thomas, W. H. (1994). *The Eden alternative: Nature, hope, and nursing homes.* Sherburne, NY: The Eden Alternative Foundation.

Thompson, B. W. (1994). *A hunger so wide and so deep: American women speak out on eating problems.* Minneapolis, MN: University of Minnesota Press.

Tobias, S. (1989, September). Tracked to fail. *Psychology Today,* pp. 54–58.

Tomsho, R. (2006, October 25). As tuition soars, federal aid to college students falls. *The Wall Street Journal,* p. B1.

Tonnies, F. (1963/1887). *Community and society.* New York: Harper & Row.

Torres, S. (1999). Has the privatization concept been successful? Yes. In C. B. Fields (Ed.), *Controversial issues in corrections* (pp. 105–112). Boston: Allyn & Bacon.

Trieschman, A., Whittaker, J. K., & Brentro, L. K. (1969). *The Other 23 Hours: Child care work in a therapeutic milieu.* Chicago: Aldine.

Tropman, J. E. (1989). *American values and social welfare: Cultural contradictions in the welfare state.* Englewood Cliffs, NJ: Prentice Hall.

Turow, J. (1992). A mass communication perspective on entertainment. In J. Curran, & M. Gurevitch (Eds.), *Mass media and society* (pp. 160–177). London: Edward Arnold.

Turow, J. (1997). *Breaking up America: Advertisers and the new media world.* Chicago, IL: University of Chicago Press.

Tyre, P. (2004, September 27). Combination therapy. *Newsweek,* pp. 66–67.

Uchitelle, L. (2003, October 5). U.S. companies "offshoring" jobs. *The State* [Columbia, SC], p. A14.

Uchitelle, L. (2006). *The disposable American: Layoffs and their consequences.* New York: Knopf.

Underwood, A., & Adler, J. (2005, April 25). When cultures clash. *Newsweek,* pp. 68–72.

Underwood, D. (1993). *When MBAs rule the newsroom.* New York: Columbia University Press.

UNESCO (2004). *EFA global monitoring report 2003/4.* Retrieved February 22, 2009 from http://www.unesco.org/en/education/efareport/reports/20034-gender

United Jewish Communities. (2001). *National Jewish Population Survey, 2000–2001.* New York: United Jewish Community.

U.S. Bureau of Labor Statistics. (2008). *Women in the labor force: A databook* (Table 11). Retrieved January 21, 2009 from http://www.bls.gov/cps/wlf-databook2008.htm

U.S. Bureau of Labor Statistics. (2009). *Union members summary.* Retrieved April 5, 2009 from http://data.bls.gov

U.S. Census Bureau. (2000). *Statistical abstracts of the United States: 2000.* Washington, DC: Author.

U.S. Census Bureau. (2007). *Selected characteristics of people at specified levels of poverty in the past 12 months.* Retrieved April 25, 2008 from http://www.factfinder.census.gov/

U.S. Committee for Refugees and Immigrants. (2008). *2008 world refugee survey.* Retrieved January 15, 2009 from http://www.refugees.org/

U.S. Courts. (2008, December 15). *Bankruptcy filings over one million for fiscal year 2008.* Retrieved April 5, 2009 from http://www.uscourts.gov

U.S. Department of Agriculture. (2008). *Food and nutrition service.* Retrieved October 19, 2008 from Program Data Web site: http://www.fns.usda.gov/pd/slmain.htm

U.S. Department of Agriculture. (2008). *National school lunch program: Total participation.* Retrieved December 16, 2008 from http://www.fns.usda.gov/

U.S. Department of Commerce, Economics and Statistics Administration. (2005). *Computer and internet use in the United States: 2003.* Retrieved January 28, 2006 from http://www.census.gov/population/www/socdemo/computer.html

U.S. Department of Health and Human Services. (2005). *Head start.* Retrieved December 1, 2008 from http://www.hhs.gov/headstart/

U.S. Department of Health and Human Services. (2006, December). *National Healthcare Disparities Report, 2006* [Electronic version]. Retrieved January 14, 2007 from http://www.ahrq.gov/qual/nhdr06/nhdr06.htm

U.S. Department of Justice. (2005). *Financial crimes report to the public.* Retrieved March 4, 2009 from http://www.fbi.gov/publications/financial/fcs_report

U.S. Equal Employment Opportunity Commission. (2008). *Sexual harassment.* Retrieved February 22, 2009 from http://www.eeoc.gov/types/sexual_harassment.html

U.S. General Accounting Office. (2003). *Child welfare and juvenile justice.* Washington, DC: GAO-03-397.

U.S. General Accounting Office. (2007). *Residential treatment programs.* Washington, DC: GAO-08-146T.

U.S. Government Accountability Office. (2007). *Preliminary observations on efforts to improve health care and disability evaluations for returning service members,* GAO publication No. GAO-07-1256T.

Valdez, A. (1993). Persistent poverty, crime, and drugs: U.S.-Mexican border region. In J. Moore, & R. Pinderhughes (Eds.), *In the barrios: Latinos and the underclass debate* (pp. 173–220). New York: Russell Sage Foundation.

Van Den Bergh, N. (1995). Feminist social work practice. In N. Van Den Bergh (Ed.), *Feminist practice in the 21st century* (pp. xi–xxxix). Washington, DC: NASW Press.

Van Wormer, K. (2001). *Counseling female offenders and victims: A strengths-restorative approach.* New York: Springer.

Vanneman, R., & Cannon, L. W. (1987). *The American perception of class.* Philadelphia, PA: Temple University Press.

Verba, S., Schlozman, K. L., & Brady, H. (1995). *Voice and equality: Civic voluntarism in American politics.* Cambridge, MA: Harvard University Press.

Vestal, C. (2008, March). *Gay marriage decisions in California, Connecticut.* Stateline.org. Retrieved March 1, 2009 from http://www.stateline.org

Von Bertalanffy, L. (1968). *General systems theory: Foundations, development, applications.* New York: George Braziller.

Von Drehle, D. (2009, March 9). House of cards. *Time,* p. 22.

Vyse, S. (2008). *Going broke: Why Americans can't hold on to their money.* Oxford: Oxford University Press.

Wahl, H. (1991). Dependence in the elderly from an interactional point of view: Verbal and observational data. *Adult Residential Care Journal, 5,* 113–129.

Walbridge, L. S. (1999). Middle Easterners and North Africans. In E. R. Barkan (Ed.), *A nation of peoples: A sourcebook on America's multicultural heritage* (pp. 391–410). Westport, CT: Greenwood Press.

Waldinger, R. (2007, October 25). *Between here and there: How attached are Latino immigrants to their native country?* Pew Hispanic Center. Retrieved February 15, 2009 from http://www. pewhispanic.org/reports/

Waldman, A. (2003, May 12). Some customer service jobs migrating to India. *The State* [Columbia, SC], p. A6.

Walker, J. E. K. (1999). African Americans. In E. R. Barkan (Ed.), *A nation of peoples: America's multicultural heritage* (pp. 19–47). Westport, CT: Greenwood Press.

Wallechinsky, D. (2007, January 14). Is America still no. 1? *Parade,* pp. 4–5.

Wallis, C. (2006, July 24). A very special wedding. *Time,* pp. 44, 45.

Wallis, C., & Steptoe, S. (2007, June 4). How to fix No Child Left Behind. *Time,* pp. 34–39.

Walt, V. (2008, September 29). Death in birth. *Time,* pp. 48–52.

Walzer, M. (1983). *Spheres of justice.* New York: Basic Books.

Wang, T. (2008, November 10). *Voting in 2008: Lessons learned.* Common Cause. Retrieved April 14, 2009 from http://www.commoncause.org

Warren, M. R., Thompson, J. P., & Saegert, S. (2001). The role of social capital in combating poverty. In S. Saegert, J. P. Thompson, & M. R. Warren (Eds.), *Social capital and poor communities* (pp. 1–28). New York: Russell Sage Foundation.

Warren, R. L. (1978). *The community in America* (3rd ed.). Chicago: Rand McNally.

Webb, J. (2009, March 29). Why we must fix our prisons. *Parade,* pp. 4–5.

Webb, N. B. 2001. *Culturally diverse parent-child and family relationships.* New York: Columbia University Press.

Weber, M. (1978/1922). *Economy and society.* Berkeley, CA: University of California Press.

Wener, R., Frazier, W., & Farbstein, J. (1985). Three generations of evaluation and design of correctional facilities. *Environment and Behavior, 17,* 71–95.

Werner, B. (2007, June 21). FTC settles board of dentistry case: Dispute reached back to 2001. *The State* [Columbia, SC], p. B.1.

Whalen, J., & Flacks, R. (1989). *Beyond the barricades: The sixties generation grows up.* Philadelphia, PA: Temple University Press.

White, M. J. (1988). *The segregation in residential assimilation of immigrants.* Washington, DC: The Urban Institute.

Wiener, R. (2006, January 2). Guess who's still left behind? *Washington Post.* Retrieved January 3, 2006 from http://www.washingtonpost.com/

Will, G. F. (2004, March 15). Paradoxes of public piety. *Newsweek,* p. 64.

Williams, C. (1995). *Still a man's world: Men who do women's work.* Berkeley, CA: University of California press.

Williams, R. (1957). *American society: A sociological interpretation* (2nd ed.). New York: Alfred Knopf.

Wilson, K. L., & Orum, A. M. (1976). Mobilizing people for collective political action. *The Journal of Political and Military Sociology, 4,* 187–202.

Wilson, T. C. (1996). Compliments will get you nowhere: Benign stereotypes, prejudice and anti-Semitism. *Sociological Quarterly, 37,* 465–479.

Wilson, W. J. (1978). *The declining significance of race: Black and changing American institutions.* Chicago: University of Chicago Press.

Wilson, W. J. (1987). *The truly disadvantaged: The inner city, the underclass, and public policy.* Chicago: University of Chicago Press.

Wilson, W. J. (1996). *When work disappears: The world of the new urban poor.* New York: Alfred A. Knopf.

Winthrop, R. H. (1991). *Dictionary of concepts in cultural anthropology*. New York: Greenwood.

Wirt, G. L. (1999). Causes of institutionalism: Patient and staff perspectives. *Issues in Mental Health Nursing, 20*, 259–274.

Wolcott, R. M., & Milligan, R. (1992). Findings and recommendations of EPA's Environmental Equity Workgroup. *EPA Journal, 18*, 21–22.

Wolfe, A. (1998, June 14). Religion, with a grain of salt. *The New York Times*, p. 15.

Wolfensberger, W. (1972). *The principle of normalization in human services*. Toronto: National Institute on Mental Retardation.

Wolfson, H. (2000, December 3). Tiny Indian tribe agrees to turn reservation into nuclear waste dump. *The State* [Columbia, SC], p. A4.

Women in the army. (2008). *U.S. army*. Retrieved December 9, 2008 from http://www.army.mil/women/

Women of our world. (2002). Washington, DC: Population Reference Bureau.

World Health Organization. (2002, October 30). *Years of healthy life can be increased 5-10 years*. Retrieved January 1, 2009 from http://www.who.int/mediacentre/news/

World Health Organization. (2008). *Eliminating female genital mutilation*. Retrieved November 8, 2008 from http://www.un.org/womenwatch/

Wright, J. P., Cullen, F. T., & Blankenship, M. B. (1995). The social construction of corporate violence: Media coverage of the Imperial Food Products fire. *Crime & Delinquency, 41* (1), 23–24.

Wright, J. W. (Ed.). (2007). *The New York Times almanac*. New York: Penguin Books.

Wright, R. (1995, August 28). The evolution of despair. *Time*, pp. 50–54, 56–57.

Wu, F. H. (2002). *Yellow: Race in American beyond black and white*. New York: Basic Books.

Wuthnow, R. (2002). United States: Bridging the privileged and the marginalized? In R. D. Putnam (Ed.), *Democracies in flux: The evolution of social capital in contemporary society* (pp. 59–102). New York: Oxford University Press.

Wysocki, B., Jr. (1991, January 15). Influx of Asians brings prosperity to Flushing, a place for newcomers. *The Wall Street Journal*, pp. A1, A8.

Yabroff, J. (2008, January 19). *Birth, the American way*. Retrieved January 26, 2009 from Newsweek.com

Yip, P. (2007, November 25). Another day older and deeper in debt. *The State* [Columbia, SC], pp. D1, D4.

Yoder, P. S., Abderrahim, N., & Zhuzhuni, A. (2004). *Female genital cutting in the demographic and health surveys: A critical and comparative analysis*. Calverton, MD: Macro International Inc.

Yung, J. (1999). Chinese. In E. R. Barkan (Ed.), *A nation of peoples: America's multicultural heritage* (pp. 119–137). Westport, CT: Greenwood Press.

Zald, M. N., & McCarthy, J. D. (1987). *Social movements in an organizational society*. New Brunswick, NJ: Transaction.

Zarembka, A. (1990). *The urban housing crisis: Social, economic, and legal issues and proposals*. Westport, CT: Greenwood.

Zarit, S. H., Dolan, M. M., & Leitsch, S. A. (1999). Interventions in nursing homes and other alternative living settings. In I. H. Nordhus, G. R. VandenBos, S. Berg, & P. Fromhold (Eds.), *Clinical Geropsychology* (pp. 329–343). Washington, DC: American Psychological Association.

Zemsky, R., Wegner, G. R., & Massy, W. F. (2005). *Remaking the American University: Market-smart and mission-centered*. New Brunswick, NJ: Rutgers University Press.

Zernike, K. (2006, February 12). Violent crime rising sharply in some cities. *The New York Times*, Retrieved March 30, 2008 from http://www.nytimes.com/2006/02/12/national/12homicide.html

Zoroya, G. (2005, March 3). Key Iraq wound: Brain trauma. *USA Today*. Retrieved March 1, 2009 from http://www.usatoday.com/news/nation/2005-03-03-brain-trauma-lede_x.htm

Zoroya, G. (2007, November 13). Blinded by war: Injuries send troops into darkness. *USA Today*. Retrieved February 8, 2008 from http://www.usatoday.com/news/military/2007-11-3-eyeinjuries_N.htm

INDEX

Note: The notation f, n, t, refer to figure, end-note number and table cited in the text respectively.